The History of Civilization
Edited by C. K. OGDEN, M.A.

Minoans, Philistines, and Greeks

The History of Civilization

Edited by C. K. OGDEN, M.A.

Introduction and Pre-History

The Early Empires and Greece

Rome and Beyond the Roman Empire

Middle Ages to Modern Times

Historical Ethnology

Subject Histories

* An asterisk indicates that the volume does not form part of the French collection "L'Évolution de l'Humanité".

A full list of the SERIES will be found at the end of this volume.

9

PLATE 1

THE WATER-FLOWER

Vase from Melos ; Late Minoan I

Minoans, Philistines, and Greeks

B.C. 1400–900

By

A. R. BURN

Sometime Scholar of Christ Church, Oxford

LONDON
KEGAN PAUL, TRENCH, TRUBNER & CO., LTD.
NEW YORK: ALFRED A. KNOPF
1930

PRINTED IN GREAT BRITAIN BY HEADLEY BROTHERS,
18, DEVONSHIRE STREET, E.C.2 ; AND ASHFORD, KENT.

PATRI OPTIMO
CVM PIETATE ET DESIDERIO
HOC OPVS DEDICAT AVCTOR

CONTENTS

CONTENTS

LIST OF ILLUSTRATIONS

*The Author and the Publishers desire to express their thanks to the Authors
and the Publishers of the above-named books for permission to reproduce
the illustrations which have been incorporated in this book.*

FOREWORD

*T*HE aim of this book is to produce a historical narrative of the fortunes of the Aegean peoples, including invaders of and fugitives from the Aegean area, from the end of the fifteenth to the end of the tenth century before Christ. The task will be a difficult one, but is not, in the writer's opinion, impossible. Certainly the attempt is worth making ; for in all human history there is no period, no subject, either of greater interest or of more profound importance.

This was the age which saw the gradual decline and fall of the brilliant Aegean culture, the first advanced civilization to arise in what are now called European lands ; and in these years the stage was set on which was to be played out the heroic tragedy of Greece. From the lands adjacent to the Aegean went out, during this age, those migrant peoples among whom the best known are the Philistines, destined profoundly to modify the history perhaps of Phœnicia, certainly of Judœa ; and hence, too, somewhat later in time, went forth the Etruscans, part of whose history is the early history of Rome. Rome—Hellas—Judaism ; so wide is the historic importance of the Age of the Sea-Raids in the Aegean World.

Nor is this age less interesting than momentous. The records of Egypt alone, whose history interacts with that of the Aegean throughout the greater part of our period, are full of memorable figures : Akhenaton the royal revolutionary and mystic, and Horemheb the restorer ; the gasconading trooper Rameses II, and his greater namesake, the Third, who broke the onslaught of the Sea-People ; Subbiluliuma, King of the Hittites ; the personal character of each one of these men had its effect upon the fortunes of men born beyond what Egypt called the Great Green sea. We shall meet too with others who, if of less importance, are of still *greater human interest—conspicuous among them the pathetically comic figure of Wen-Amon the ambassador. But these names do not stir the blood like some others that we shall have occasion to mention. It seems almost more than any historian has a right to expect, that among his most important, if obscurest, sources should be both the Hebrew books of the Judges and of Samuel and the Greek epics of Troy and of Odysseus. Yet so it is here. Ours is the period within which the bearers of a score of names, for ever famous in heroic story, lived and died : Sisera and Barak ; Saul, Jonathan, David ; Minôs the Sea-King ; Jason, Bellerophon, Agamemnon, Helen of Troy.*

Much has been written round so attractive a theme in modern times, but the difficulty of the subject seems so far to have deterred writers from attempting a narrative. This is not unnatural. Our entire subject bristles with unsolved problems. Who was Minôs? Who were the Achaioi ? Are they the same as the 'K'w'sh' (Akhaiwasha ?) of Egyptian history ? Who were the Pelasgoi? Who were the Dorians ? And who—if anybody—was Homer ?

This being so, most of the work that has been produced on our subject has naturally taken the form of critical essays, discussing this or that portion of Greek or Hebrew tradition, this or that group of archæological phenomena. It was indeed necessary for an authoritative publication like the Cambridge Ancient History to eschew any attempt at a narrative of this age and to keep to the critical style throughout ; for any narrative must at several points run the risk of being wrong, and an authoritative work, whose dicta are likely to be widely accepted, must not run the risk of being widely misleading.

On the other hand, much is lost by not attempting to tell of so thrilling a period in narrative form ; and so a young writer, with no reputation to imperil, may surely venture, after clearing the ground by discussions of the principal moot points, to make that attempt.

It is hoped that the narrative given in the main body of the book (Part II) may not be without interest to the general reader, without special archæological knowledge ; while some suggestions made in the critical sections (Part I), and applied to the Narrative, may be worth the attention of students of the period. It is in its criticism and handling of certain points arising out of the Greek legendary material that the book makes its only claim to originality. At other points I have attempted only to co-ordinate and combine into a history the conclusions reached by critics and archæologists. It may, it is true, be objected that the attempt is premature, and that further evidence should be awaited, for example, from the Hittite tablets now in course of publication. To this it may be replied that if we are to wait until the archæological evidence is as complete as it can humanly be made, we shall be waiting for another generation at least ; also that it is unlikely that any more progress will now be made towards a definitive solution of some aspects of the " Homeric Question ". Further, on some of the most important of these questions, a century of active and often acrimonious discussion has materially narrowed the gulf between the opposing views. In discussion, it tends to be the doubtful points that receive notice ; but actually those points are at least as important on which an agreement is not out of reach.

On the spelling of Greek names herein, it is perhaps desirable to say a few words.

The ancient Romans spelt Greek names phonetically, and, in spite of a few corruptions like " Hercules " or " Ulysses ", on the whole rendered the original sounds as accurately as could be expected in the defective Etruscan version of the alphabet that it is our misfortune to have inherited from them. English scholars have as a rule adopted the unfortunate course, not of imitating the Greek spelling, but of reproducing the Roman, though we pronounce it entirely differently. Consequently we neither boldly naturalize into our own language every foreign name, as is the French practice, nor yet imitate the Greek with fair accuracy, as do the Germans.

If our current renderings of the often beautiful Greek names were either euphonious or accurate, one might be disposed to overlook deficiencies in other directions ; but since the inaccuracy of such current barbarisms as "Mycenæ", "Meleager", "Lacedæmon" is only equalled by their ugliness, not even the high authority of the Hellenic Society appears to constitute a sufficient reason for adopting them. We no longer speak of "Jupiter", "Ulysses", and so forth when translating Homer; and the scholars of a few years ago were surely right in discarding such equally bad forms as "Hecuba" and "Cimon".

The practice here adopted has therefore been, when an English form of a name exists, to use it: Athens, Helen, Jason, etc. A few Latinisms that have become practically English words are also retained: Apollo, Cyprus, Cyclades, etc.; also, in the text only, and not without regret, the ugly form "Thucydides". In other cases the Greek names have been transliterated as well as is possible with an alphabet containing only six vowels. The circumflex, ^, has been employed in many names to distinguish η, ω, from ϵ, ο. It is omitted however in well-known names, wherever the quantities are as a rule correctly rendered; e.g., Theseus, Herakles. The sign ˘ has occasionally been used to mark a short vowel, if very liable to mispronunciation; elsewhere unmarked vowels are as a rule short, except in the invariably long terminations—ēs, -ōn, -ōr, in men's names, and -ē in those of women and places. Absolute consistency has not been attempted; the line has to be drawn somewhere, but there is no need to make matters worse by drawing it straight.

My heavy debt to many modern as well as ancient writers is, I hope, sufficiently acknowledged in the references appended to the text. These are numerous, but in handling a controversial subject it has seemed best to quote "chapter and verse" for most of the statements made. I must, however, especially render thanks to Mr. R. H. Dundas for a valuable revision of my proofs; to Mr. E. S. Kendall for valuable help with the Index; and also, for the stimulus of his teaching and writings, and for much kindly criticism and encouragement, to Professor J. L. Myres, the frequency and depth of my disagreements with whom are probably the best measure of the debt that I owe him.

The following abbreviations have been used in references to some of the better-known authorities, or those most frequently cited :

Ap. Rhod.	=	Apollônios Rhodios.
Apollod.	=	Apollodôros.
B.S.A.	=	*Annual of the British School at Athens.*
B.S.J.	=	*Bulletin of the British School at Jerusalem.*
C.A.H.	=	*Cambridge Ancient History.*
C.I.G.	=	*Corpus Inscriptionum Græcarum.*
C.I.S.	=	*Corpus Inscriptionum Semiticarum.*
D.H.	=	Dionysios of Halikarnassos.
D.S.	=	Diodôros of Sicily.
Evans, *P.M.*	=	*Palace of Minôs.*
F.H.G.	=	*Fragmenta Historicorum Græcorum,* ed. Müller.
Hdt.	=	Herodotos.
Hesiod, *W.D.*	=	*Works and Days.*
H.H.	=	*Homeric Hymns.*
J.H.S.	=	*Journal of Hellenic Studies.*
J.R.A.I.	=	*Journal of the Royal Anthropological Institute.*
N.D.	=	Nikolaos of Damascus.
Od.	=	*Odyssey.*
O.P.	=	*Oxyrhynchus Papyri,* ed. Grenfell and Hunt.
Paus.	=	Pausanias.
Plut., *Mor.*	=	Plutarch, *Moralia.*
Σ	=	Scholiast.
Servius, *ad Aen.*	=	*Commentary on the Aeneid.*
Str.	=	Strabo.
Thk.	=	Thukydides.

Other abbreviations, where used, have been such as to explain themselves.

B.C.	EUROPEAN MAINLAND ; THE BLACK SEA ; THE TROAD	GREEK MAINLAND
3500	? " Aryan " language being spoken in S. Russia.	Beginning of Bronze A
2500	? " Aryan " language (parent of Greek, etc.) being spoken in the " linguistic continuum " of the Balkan Peninsula?	c. 1900. Invasion fr north, introducing G Minyan pottery (primitive Greek speech
1850	Sack of Second City of Troy.	
	(c. 1680 ? Stonehenge built.)	
1600	" Climatic optimum " of post-glacial time ; peat-bogs, glaciers, Central European Lakes, at a minimum. (Early Bronze Age in Britain.)	Minoan colonization Argolis and Boiotia. Mykênai powerful un the " Shaft-Grav dynasty.
		c. 1550. Important ext sion of Minoan influen settlements at Pylos, e
1500	Sixth City of Troy (= Homeric Ilios) built and fortified. Rise of Dardanian power.	? Domed tombs of M ênai built.
1400	Bronze leaf-shaped sword gradually evolved in Hungary.	
	Geometric meander-pattern in use for pottery-painting in Macedonia (Buboshta).	Widespread influence Mycenæan (= mainl version of Minoan) ci zation.
1300	Sudden climatic break in Central Europe.	? " Heroes " from T saly found the Acha dynasties.
	1288 Dardanians among the Hittite mercenaries at Kadesh.	Leaf-shaped swords ap
	? Voyage of Argonauts to Kolchis. (No evidence as to date.)	? Raids from Thrace Central Greece. Thra kingdom in Phôkis (or later).
1200	? Phrygians cross from Thrace into Asia Minor and overthrow Hittite Empire.	? Pelops (refugee f Asia Minor) founds a k dom in Peloponnese.
		Atreus, son of Pelops, of Mykênai.
	Iron being mined in Hungary (Velem).	Achaians destroy } N Kadmeian Thebes.
1100	Troy sacked by Achaians.	Trojan War. ea
	Disturbances in Macedonia (destruction of villages at Vardaroftsa and Chauchitza). Central European pottery and brooches. Iron swords.	Renewed immigration from Thrace ; destruction of Trojan kingdom.
	Greek settlements in the Troad.	Return of the Heraklei sack of Mykênai, Tir etc. Dorian kingd founded.
1000		End of Aegean civili predominate everywhe
		c.950. Dorian Spar Temple of Artemis Or founded.
900	Etruscan settlements in Italy.	

CRETE AND THE AEGEAN	EGYPT, ASIA, AND THE LEVANT
st Early Minoan period. gyptian contact with Crete. 2200. Middle Minoan period. 1625. Catastrophic earth-uake. End of Middle Minoan aase.	Sumerian Civilization already old. First Dynasty in Egypt. c.2800. Sargon of Akkad reaches the Mediterranean. c.2200. Twelfth Dynasty in Egypt.
ate Minoan I.	1580. Eighteenth Dynasty; Hyksos expelled from Egypt.
"Great Palace Period."	Thothmes I conquers Syria.
etan supremacy in the yclades.	
"Baroque" art at Knôssos.	c.1479. Thothmes III reaches the Euphrates. Keftiu depicted in tomb of Rekh-ma-ra.
Minoan expedition to Sicily.	Rise of Hittite power; Subbiluliuma, c.1411.
1400. Sack of Knôssos.	Cyprus: Mycenæan civilization (? colonization from Greek mainland, introducing Arkadian dialect?). Growth of piracy in the Levant.
ate Minoan III (a). Minoan t becoming stylised. In-ence of Mainland upon ete.	c.1370. Akhnaton pharaoh. Fall of Egyptian power in Asia. "Shardana" mercenaries mentioned. 1350. Nineteenth dynasty; Horemheb pharaoh; treaty with Hittites. 1315. Seti I reconquers Palestine from Hittites.
Pelasgoi active by sea.	? Aegean mercenaries at Bethshan.
Achaians reach Crete.	1290. Rameses II renews Hittite war.
Greece and Crete.	1288. Battle of Kadesh. Both sides employ Aegean or West Asian mercenaries.
aracian sea-raids: Naxos, ast of Thessaly, Euboia ow or later).	c.1230. Attarsiyas of Akhhiyawa fights Hittites in Pamphylia, and raids Cyprus. Famine in Asia Minor. 1221. Sea-peoples allied with Libyans, but defeated by Pharaoh Merenptah. Leaf-shaped sword in Egypt.
ate-Minoan III (b).	c.1200. Fall of Hittite Empire; general migration by sea and land. Rameses III saves Egypt. Philistines settle in Canaan. Cyprus devastated.
ægean art becoming puerile. ccelerated decline of civiliza-on. Last archæological evi-nce for contact with Egypt.	Quasi-Aegean civilization in Philistia; late Mycenæan pottery, etc. Iron weapons common. Philistine-Phœnician war; Philistines sack Sidon. c.1115. Voyage of Wen-Amen.
rrhenians (?) on Lemnos.	? Sisera's "oppression" of Israel; Battle of the Kishon. Period of Cypriote "thalassocracy", followed by rise of sea-power of Phœnician cities. Philistines subdue Israel. c.1025. Saul, King of Israel; Philistine Wars. Battle of Gilboa.
lonization of Ionia by refu-es from Greece. ocal Geometric art-styles	David captures Jerusalem, and renews Philistine war. Battle of Baal-perazim. Decline of Philistine power.
	c.950. Empire of Solomon. Hiram, King of Tyre. Prosperity of Tyre and Sidon; trade and colonization in Spain and Africa. Traces of Aegean civilization survive among the Greeks of Cyprus.
ic poetry in Ionia: Homer.	

PART ONE

CRITICAL

"ἡ μὲν γὰρ τῶν ἀναγραφομένων ἀρχαιότης, δυσευρετὸς οὖσα, πολλὴν ἀπορίαν παρέχεται τοῖς γράφουσιν"—*Diodôros of Sicily*, IV, 1.

"Though ye have lien among the Pots, yet shall ye be as the Wings of a Dove."—*Psalm* lxviii, 13.

PART ONE

CHAPTER I

Methods and Materials

I. Archæology and the Legends

THE material at our disposal falls under three heads. We have, first, references to the Mediterranean peoples in the extant official documents of the Egyptian and Hittite Empires ; second, the actual remains left to us by the Aegean peoples of the Late Bronze and Early Iron Ages ; and third, Greek and Hebrew with the fragments of Phœnician and Lydian tradition and story.

Of these the second must needs form the foundation of our narrative. Contemporary references to the Aegean peoples by Hittites and Egyptians are valuable, but all too few. Moreover they are often either difficult to interpret, or only too easy—that is to say capable of more interpretations than one. For instance, the thirteenth century sea-raider, references to whose activities have recently been found in the Hittite tablets and whose name in the Hittite script is rendered as T-r-s-y-s, is vocalized by his discoverer, Dr. Forrer, as " Attarissiyas " and identified with Atresas, an uncontracted form of the name of Atreus, father of King Agamemnon. Professor Sayce however pours scorn on this identification, which he believes to be " phonetically impossible ", and prefers to write the word Tarsiyas and identify the owner of the name with the hero Perseus or Pterseus. Both scholars seem to be at one only in this, that both seem certain that this troubler of the coasts of Asia must be identical with some Greek hero famous in heroic story.

Even more uncertain must be conclusions based on the Greek legends. These are certainly numerous and suggestive enough, but the possibilities of difference in interpreting them are endless. Also they may have suffered change through generations of mainly oral transmission and through " editing " by poets concerned not with history but with artistic effect. To what extent they can be used as historical material we shall have to consider in the following pages ; but we may safely state at once the principle that legend must be used merely to illustrate and supplement the record of archæology. Legend is subjective and our versions of the legends are the product of ages far removed from the events of which they purport to tell. Archæological data may at times admit of more than one interpretation—for instance it may be questionable whether a particular type of pottery was introduced into a certain area by way of trade or conquest ; but they remain objective and contemporary. " Every Minoan potsherd ", it has been said, " is an original document."

And, as is well-known, archæology even without the assistance of any tradition, can, like geology, tell a story of a kind. Fragments of pottery—so necessary, so easily broken, and so easily replaced—are especially useful. They can, better than any other type of relic, be arranged, according to the stratification of the site where they are found and the sequence of styles in shape or decoration, in a series that may be traceable over thousands of years. Contact between different lands can be traced by the appearance of foreign products, foreign artistic motifs, among the native remains ; migrations of peoples may leave their traces in the sudden appearance of burial customs new to a country and perhaps (not always) an entirely new art style. The sack of a city will be marked by fire-blackened walls and the ashes of charred beams. By such traces, archæologists are prepared to sketch in outline the history of Aegean culture from ages long before the earliest to which any literary evidence refers.

It is as enabling us to fill in the blanks within this bare outline that our other types of evidence are of value. The Egyptian and Hittite documents at least give us, here and there, a fact. Synchronisms with Egypt give us here and there a fixed date for some event in the Aegean ; the golden example being the date, very shortly after 1400, fixed by changes in the artistic style of objects of Aegean provenance found in Egypt, for the great catastrophe of the Sack of Knôssos. And the legends give us, now and then, those glimpses of men and women as they lived and spoke which archæology cannot give. We may not be certain of the amount of history contained in the legends ; but our uncertainty matters the less for this reason, that they are important first and foremost as telling us, not what happened on one given occasion, but the kind of thing that must have happened on more than one.

If however we can extract a few items of actual history from the legends, all the better ; and the attempt is worth making, for all the necessary uncertainty of the results. Our first and most difficult task must therefore be to con- sider the nature of the tradition which the Greek stories represent. To what extent can they be taken seriously by the would-be historian ? And in particular, can the genealogies of the Greek heroes be used as the framework of a scheme of chronology ?

And first of all, though we need not go over all the ground so well trodden by the feet of great authorities (the dust of whose highly controversial passing still in places obscures the air) it is necessary to state, briefly and somewhat dog- matically, the view hereinafter adopted of the "Homeric Question".

II. HOMER AND THE EPIC TRADITION

The Iliad and Odyssey, both the earliest and by far the most important of our legendary sources, were universally believed in Hellenic times to be the work of a single poet named Hŏmêros, " Homer ".

This name, " Hostage ", is an unusual one, but was by no means unknown in historic times among the northern sections of the Greek people.[1] It would probably be given, like several other Greek names, with reference to the father's condition at the time when a child was born (cf. among other names,

---

[1] E.g. in Aitolia (Collitz, *Dialektinschriften*, 2520) and Thessaly (*ib*. 2138 ; Dittenberger's *Sylloge* (3) 1059 I, 3).

Eurymedon, Karystonîkos[1]—who figures in an Athenian casualty list of about 440 B.C. and was clearly born in 472, the year of the Athenian conquest of Karystos—Têlemachos, Odysseus[2]). " Homer " is in short a real man's name, and not, as has occasionally been supposed, a mere title given to the " Fitter Together " of short lays into a long epic poem.

No Greek seems to have dreamed of doubting that the two great epics were in substance the work of a single hand, excepting the late but learned scholars of the school known as the Chôrizontes, who on stylistic grounds doubted the authenticity of the Odyssey ; and their view was never widely accepted.

On the other hand, there was an extraordinary dearth of knowledge of the personality of the great poet. Notoriously, no one knew even when he had lived, nor what was his native city—and that in a country where a man's home was normally mentioned with his name whenever reference was made to him. Many cities were anxious to claim him but none could make out a satisfactory case. To classical Athens, as to ourselves, nothing remained of Homer but two tremendous poems and a man's name.[3]

Mr. T. W. Allen, in his " Homer : the Origins and the Transmission ", by far the most learned of recent English studies of the Homeric question, has attempted to squeeze some information out of the soi-disant "Lives" of the poet which remain to us from the Hellenistic Age ; but what really does seem to emerge from his careful scrutiny is that, as far back as we can trace an interest in the Homeric question (and Mr. Allen shows that the lives preserve quotations from one or more poems probably not later than the seventh century B.C.), the same ignorance prevails. If the guild of poets in Chios, who called themselves " Children of Homer " and who still existed in the fifth century B.C., had really had, as Mr. Allen supposes, any authentic information to give about their ostensible ancestor, a deeply interested world would not have allowed it to be forgotten. As it is, the spuriousness of the details given in these deplorable documents—documents more

---

[1] Hicks and Hill, *Greek Historical Inscriptions*, 46, l. 27.
[2] See *Od.*, XIX, ll. 407-9.
[3] For the chaotic state of the question in early Christian times, after several centuries of learned guesswork, cf. Eusebios, *Preparation for the Gospel*, pp. 491-2, and authorities there quoted.

resembling mediæval Lives of the Saints than anything else Hellenic—is only to be paralleled by their extreme fatuity[1].

The poems, it is clear, were widely famous, while the personality of their author had been completely forgotten before the end of the sixth century B.C. By that date we find arrangenents being made by Peisistratos for their regular recitation at Athens,[2] Kynaithos of Chios introducing them at Dorian Syracuse,[3] Dorian poets of Troizen and Kyrene writing sequels to them[4]—to say nothing of Ionia, the original home of the Greek epic. Kyrene, in fact we are told, was one of the latest Greek states to receive the epics[5]; yet Eugammon of Kyrene was writing his sequel to the Odyssey before the middle of the sixth century. So Homer was already ancient then.

How much further back can we trace the existence of the poems ?

Back, it would appear, into the ninth century at least, for in the eighth century they were already famous enough for poets of Asia Minor to be writing " cyclic " poems which presuppose the existence of the Iliad. Arktinos of Miletos and Lesches of Mytilene, who " rounded off " the story by continuing it down to the fall of Troy, are placed before 700 B.C. by the late Greek chronologists ; and the " Cyprian Verses " which formed a prelude to the Iliad seem to have been earlier still—the name of their author, given variously as Hêgêsias or Stasînos of Cyprus, was in a fair way to be forgotten altogether.

Further, the existence and the great prestige of the Homeric poems, at least in the Asian cities of Hellas, is presupposed by Hesiod's *Works and Days*. Nothing could have led Hesiod, a Boiotian whose father had lived in Asia, to choose the epic style as the vehicle for his hints on farming except the conviction that the Homeric was *the* literary style par excellence. Tradition, too, which definitely asserts so little about Homer, seems to be clear on the fact that he was earlier than Hesiod.

But Hesiod's date has been computed on astronomical evidence.[6] Hesiod bids his farmer begin to cut over his vines

---

[1] They can be conveniently read in Wilamowitz' edition, published in Dr. Lietzmann's Kleine Texte series.

[2] According to a late tradition ; Paus. VII, 26, Cicero *de Or.*, III, 34, etc.

[3] Σ on Pindar, *Nemean Odes*, II, 1.

[4] See below, p. 15.

[5] Maximus of Tyre, XVII, 5.

[6] Allen, *op. cit.*, quoting Dr. A. A. Rambaut of the Radcliffe Observatory.

by the rising of Arcturus, sixty days after the winter solstice[1]. The sixty days may be taken as an exact number ; as Mr. Allen points out, epic Greek has no objection to numbers other than round ones, so that if Hesiod meant fifty-nine he would say it. At the present day Arcturus rises fifty-seven days after the solstice. The interval between the two events is decreasing ; and Hesiod's words apply to the eighth or even ninth century B.C.

We have traced the fame of Homer back to the ninth century, the date to which Herodotos tentatively assigned him[2]—a later date, the historian's words seem to imply, than that preferred by most of his contemporaries. Beyond this there is blackness ; the age was a pre-historic one which remembered only very striking events indeed, and the life of a poet contained no such events. Also, in that age of slow transmission of the works of a poet, his fame too would be slow to spread ; and by the time his name had become widely famous, all knowledge of Homer's life had passed into oblivion.

For further investigation we must depend solely upon the evidence furnished in the poems themselves.

One thing we can say at the outset. Homer, who belongs at latest to the ninth century, cannot at earliest have lived much before that period ; for his favourite unfavourable comparison of the men of his own day with the heroes of old shows that he lived some considerable number of generations after the events which he describes. But the Dorian Invasion which broke up the old Achaian " heroic " world was itself an event or series of events of the eleventh century (not earlier, as we shall see on a later page) ; and the Trojan War was, according to a strong tradition, one of the last achievements of the Achaian kings.

The next question, all-important for our present purpose, is " Whence did Homer get his information of these events which took place two or three hundred years before him ? And what sort of use did he make of his material ? "

We have no evidence except that furnished by the poems themselves, but to the first question at least Homer himself supplies a ready answer. Homer had, as material to work on,

[1] *Works and Days*, l. 564.
[2] II, 53.

a considerable mass of older poetry, and his narrative is based ultimately on the metrical sagas, so to speak, of the Trojan War which were composed by the court minstrels of Achaian kings within the lifetimes of the men who fought in it.   The Odyssey is full of allusions to this historical minstrelsy ; among other subjects, bards sing of a quarrel between Achilles and Odysseus in the camp before Ilios, of the tale of the Wooden Horse, and of the " dolorous home-coming " of the Achaians ; and Helen in the Iliad looks forward bitterly to the time when her faithlessness shall be " a matter for minstrels among men yet to be."[1]   Homer implies that many before him had handled the story of Odysseus, when he invokes his Muse with the words " of these matters, O Muse, daughter of Zeus, speak to me *also*."[2]

In what, then, did Homer's original contribution consist, and why is it that his name is remembered to the exclusion of those of all his predecessors ?

It is again Mr. Allen who suggests an answer.

There is extant a Latin translation (as well as a fragment of the Greek original) of what purports to be an independent non-Homeric account of the Siege of Troy by one Diktys of Crete.   As it stands, it is an obviously Hellenistic work, and after the manner of such works omits the divine interference, which later ages have always found so irritating in the Iliad, while introducing a strong romantic love-interest.   For the rest, it introduces nearly all the incidents of the Iliad, but in a quite different order, an order that, if adopted by Homer, would stultify his plot.   On the other hand—very significant —when covering the ground *not* touched by Homer, " Diktys " agrees very closely with the Cyclic poems, so far as we can judge from the epitome of their contents given us by the Neoplatonist Proklos.

The usual explanation of the differences between Homer and Diktys is the obvious one, that a late Greek writer re-arranged Homer arbitrarily.   But Mr. Allen points out that though later writers took considerable liberties with Homer they did not usually alter his facts.   They contented themselves with introducing heroes who do not figure in the Iliad, such as

---

[1] *Od.*, VIII, 73 ff., 499 ff., I, 325 ff., *Il.*, VI, 358.
[2] *Od.*, I, 10.

Têlephos, Palamêdes, Prôtesilaos. Also, if " Diktys " were re-arranging Homer, why should he respect the Cyclic Poems ?

It really looks as if Mr. Allen were right in his daring suggestion that Diktys derives, as he claims to do, from independent non-Homeric material. This sounds too good to be true, but is by no means impossible, especially since "Diktys " hails from Crete. Crete, like Sparta and Kyrene, was a part of Greece which, we are told, was slow to take up the Homeric poems—and in which consequently some of the old lays, which the fame of Homer elsewhere caused to be forgotten, may have survived long enough to be copied. As late as the fourth century B.C. the Cretan in Plato's *Laws* assures us that his countrymen " took little notice of foreign poems "—and it is especially Homer (as the context shows) that he has in mind.

Homer's original contribution was therefore probably the great idea of a long epic on the grand scale, with a plot ; not a mere lay, nor yet a loosely knit string of lays such as every clever bard doubtless had at his fingers' ends, ready to pick out any item at short notice. How much of the work of his predecessors—work that he had perhaps inherited—he incorporated verbatim in his great new poem on the Wrath of Achilles, we cannot tell ; probably a good deal. There was no point in throwing away good work, except in so far as his own must needs supersede it ; and to incorporate one's predecessors wholesale is the regular procedure—as Professor Murray charmingly explains[1]—of the owner of a " Traditional Book ".

This theory seems to account as satisfactorily as any for the notorious difficulties raised by critics of the Iliad. On the one hand it is clear that that great poem has an internal unity ; on the other hand, it is equally clear that that unity is very imperfect. The parts of the work are in many respects greater than the whole ; and the writers of some parts clearly did not anticipate the existence of some other parts. In the account of Achilles' reconciliation with Agamemnon, for instance, it is at least surprising that no allusion at all is made to the fact that, forty-eight hours earlier, the aggrieved hero refused with scorn exactly the restitution that he is now receiving. True, it is the death of Patroklos in the meantime that accounts

[1] *Rise of the Greek Epic*, Lecture IV.

for Achilles' change of attitude ; but we should expect at least a remark explaining this fact. Again, the catalogue of the Achaian ships is obviously a list of the fleet as it assembled at Aulis, and not of the contingents as they fell in before action in the tenth year of the siege. Yet again, immediately after Zeus has very impressively sworn to Thetis that the Achaians shall be defeated in the absence of Achilles, and has sent a " deceitful dream " to lure Agamemnon into giving battle, to his ruin, it is clearly inartistic and inappropriate that the Achaians should promptly go out and win a victory ; and especially that, in a story whose hero is Achilles, Diomêdes should not only make almost equally great havoc of the Trojan array, but should even outdo Achilles' most sensational feats by attacking and wounding a god and a goddess. But it is needless to multiply instances, or to thresh out anew in full a question often discussed already. It must, however, surely be clear to all that our Iliad as it stands was not composed straight through from start to finish, by one and the same poet.[1]

But there is no difficulty, in our theory, in supposing that Homer, having planned his epic, and desiring to incorporate in it all that was best worth having of the Tale of Troy, accepted the disadvantages of his plan and put in, say, the poem of the Valour of Diomedes for the excellent reason that it was much too good to leave out. After all, he was not a dramatist, and an epic needs no such close-knit unity. Also he was, probably, as later guesses made him, a travelling rhapsode (this would account for the absence of any tradition as to his home) and may have had the fewer qualms about impairing the unity of his poem for the fact that it was certainly destined to make its appearance, as a rule, piecemeal, one or two comparatively short recitations at a time.

How much of the poem is actually of Homer's own composition we can only guess ; but we can say with confidence

---

[1] Or so one might have imagined ; actually it is notoriously not so ; as " Unitarians " from Andrew Lang to Mr. J. T. Sheppard continue to main tain their extreme position with a dexterity and grace worthy of Mr. G. K. Chesterton. In face of so touching a faith one can only re-assert the contrary dogma—that the flaws in the construction of the Iliad are serious, and are not satisfactorily plastered over by Mr. Sheppard's special pleading. Not even these gentlemen's literary charm can reconcile me to the idea that Homer was a bungler ; which is what, if they proved anything, the " Unitarians " would have proved.

that the " Catalogue " and some of the battle-pieces (of which
Homer apparently had more at his disposal than he needed)
are a good deal older than the later parts of the poem.   The
Catalogue, both that of the Greek ships and that of the Trojan
Allies, has all the appearance of being a genuine document
dating from before the Dorian invasion and the Ionian
migration ; it does not flatter any of the states most famous
in the Greece of post-conquest days, and in short there
could be no motive for composing it unless, at the time
when it was composed, it really described an actual state
of affairs.

With the fighting the case is different ; the reason for
supposing different parts of the poem to be of different dates
is the old difficulty, that an actual development in the art of
war seems to lie between some episodes of the Iliad and others.
On the whole, the fighting is consistent ; Andrew Lang has
laid for ever the ghost of the old stupid objection that troops
who advance and join battle in serried ranks ought not,
forsooth, to become scattered in the hurry of a swift flight and
pursuit.   The warriors are equipped, usually, with helmet,
shield, greaves, and corselet ; the shield being either round
and made of metal, or a large semi-cylinder of leather, "like a
tower ", covering the whole body.   But occasionally we come
across episodes in which the hero seems originally to have had
no corselet ; and here trouble arises.   It is highly probable
that some of the warriors who fought at Troy wore the recently
invented corselet and some did not ; just as some carried the
round shield that we see in Egyptian portrayals of the Sea-
Raiders who were attacking them about 1200 B.C., while others
had the huge leather shield familiar to us from the art of
Knôssos and Mykenai.   But Homer, living in an age when
corselets were universal, did not understand this.   Suspecting
that something was wrong, but not wishing to lose an exciting
episode, he brought the poem up to date by inserting this
item of equipment in several places.   Sometimes the expedient
is successful, but in one or two places the result is weird ; the
two best known instances are the Wounding of Menelaos in
Book IV, where Machaon is able to treat the wound apparently
without Menelaos taking his corselet off, and the passage twice
used, in Books III and VII, where Paris and Hektor are
represented as escaping death by dodging a spear that has

not only pierced the shield but has also "driven strongly through the richly-wrought corselet".

So much ink has been spilt from ingenious pen-nibs over the corselets of Homeric warriors that it is impossible to avoid spilling a little more, in the course of even the shortest exposition of a view of the Homeric question. Clearly these corselet-interpolations are simply expedients, like the lines added to the Catalogue of Ships to explain the absence from the field of heroes like Philoktêtes or Prôtesilaos, mentioned therein. Homer cannot have his heroes in one episode going into battle in a shield and a shirt when elsewhere they are properly "bronze-shirted" and "corseleted"; and so, rather than lose a whole episode, he puts in a line inserting the corselet, and makes the best of a bad job.

Lang objected that a poet with an eye to the proper military equipment of his heroes would never interpolate a line which, when scrutinized, makes nonsense of the passage. The objection however does not hold good. The answer is that the passage is not meant to be scrutinized; it is not even meant to be read. You are meant to hear it recited—*fast*—and though you may be momentarily puzzled as to how a man could dodge a spear-thrust through the breastplate, you will soon forget it as the narrative sweeps you along; in any case it would seem more glaringly wrong for a hero to be in the field with no breastplate at all, and the absurdity is mitigated by the fact that the clumsy early corselets were made almost bell-shaped at the waist to avoid galling the hips. A thrust through them certainly *might* miss the man inside (*cf.* Plate XII, e).

An amusing parallel to these armour-interpolations is afforded by C. E. Montague's novel "Right Off the Map", which was written in 1907, but only published twenty years later. The author, like Homer, added modernizing touches where it seemed desirable, so we have allusions to Lewis guns, the League of Nations, and the Greek campaigns of 1920-1 in Asia Minor (in the first draft, presumably, it was the Greco-Turkish War in Thessaly). But to insert modern aircraft in the account of the imaginary war with which the book deals would be altogether too big an affair; so we have not only the two armies approaching one another without aerial scouting, but actually a messenger escaping from a beleagured town and crossing scores of miles of occupied territory, by drifting in a home-made balloon—though the whole sky is presumably commanded by the victorious enemy's aircraft. This is a difficulty beside which the matter of Hektor's corselet is insignificant ; yet, not having come under the X-rays of the Higher Criticism, the point passed unnoticed by any of the " chorus of reviewers "—and that even in this post-war age !

In a word, the Iliad is not, every line of it, the work of one man, nor all of the same age.

One other point : it has been alleged to be impossible that a poet of Ionia in the early iron age could so successfully avoid anachronisms as Homer does. He would forget, we are told, and introduce Dorians and Ionians among the Achaians of his narrative. He would mention swords of iron, and not, as he does, keep them universally of bronze. Such anachronisms are perpetrated by the Attic tragedians, who make no attempt to avoid them ; surely then the earlier and more naïve poet would do so too ?

The answer is, bluntly, that it is not so. The geography remains that of the " pre-Conquest " world, just as that of old English " Beowulf " remains that of the days before the poet's ancestors left the shores of the Baltic. Primitive epic poetry does avoid anachronisms, as it were by instinct ; the old traditional epic phrases and " stock " accounts of sacrifices, burials, and the like would keep the poet aware that the world of his heroes was not that of to-day, and Homer had his old Catalogue-poem always before him to remind him of his geography. As to bronze, the introduction of iron was still recent enough for Hesiod to preserve the memory of a time when there was none, when all gear was of bronze ; and the perpetual mention of bronze swords and spears in all the old traditional parts of the poem were quite enough to keep Homer reminded that there were few iron weapons on the plains of Troy.

Much later in his life, when his fiery youth had given place to a mellow and gently humorous middle age, Homer composed the Odyssey, utilizing older material just as he had done for the Iliad ; but he profited by his experience, and the Odyssey as an artistic whole is a far more successful affair than the earlier poem. Once again, masses of material are used which are not strictly germane to the story of Odysseus ; but this time, with

great skill, all is worked in and made subordinate to the main
plot.   This time the poet never lets us feel that the action of
the main plot is being held up while he tells us of the adventurous voyage of Menelaos or the homecoming and murder of
Agamemnon ;   and he draws for us his famous and charming
pictures of peace and home life—as a foil to the adventures—
in which he shows as sure a touch as ever he had when he
portrayed the tender and passionate nature of Achilles, the
heroism of Hektor as he plays out his losing game, or the
pathetic figure of Andromache.   For the adventures of
Odysseus he used traditional material, such as the old tale
(found in the folk-lore of other European countries) of the
Blinding of the Giant ;   while some of the adventures which he
makes his hero undergo in the western seas beyond Ithaka
really belong to the story of the Cruise of the Argo in the Black
Sea.   In this connection Homer's geographical knowledge,
which was strictly limited, fails him altogether and he transfers
the Kimmĕrioi from the Crimea apparently into the utmost
west.   There is also one serious anachronism in the Odyssey,
which caused much heartburning to Andrew Lang with his
theory that there must be no internal inconsistencies at all in
the poems—where Homer allows his bronze-age heroes to
quote an iron-age proverb :   " Iron doth of itself draw a
man on ".   But, these details apart, the Odyssey is noteworthy for the fact that the whole is constructed with not
less skill than the parts are composed ;   and there can be no
higher praise.

To recapitulate : the theory as to the transmission to us of
the Tale of Troy, hereinafter assumed, is as follows.
The Achaian princes, who dominated Greece in the century
immediately preceding the coming of the Dorians and the
exodus of refugees to Ionia, delighted, like other Aryan-speaking
barbarians at the same stage of development, in hearing " the
famed deeds of heroes " chanted by bards to the accompani-
ment of the lyre.   The great pan-Achaian achievement of the
Taking of Troy was, naturally, a favourite subject in the
generation immediately before the catastrophe, for it was
recent, and " men always prefer the latest song ".[1]   After the
debacle of the Achaian kingdoms, the settlers in Aiolis and

[1] *Od.*, I, 350-2.

Ionia continued to re-tell the old stories ; but as republics gradually supplanted the old monarchies, so the bard with his lyre, the frequenter and celebrator of kings' houses, gave place to the rhapsode who recited, staff in hand, to the people at the corner of a street or market-place.

The pre-conquest stories continued to be favourites ; just so our own ancestors continued to sing of a pagan Beowulf dwelling by the Baltic, long after they had settled in Britain and adopted Christianity. Indeed, to the settlers in Ionia " the latest thing " ceased to be the favourite theme for their metrical sagas. Their own poor deeds, since the great disaster overwhelmed Achaia, seemed unworthy of narration, except for a few episodes in the conquest of their new homes, which were apparently remembered. Hence the " close of the canon " of Greek heroic legend, after the generation of Têlemachos and Orestes, and the dark age which divides the period depicted in the Odyssey from the earliest events mentioned by Herodotos.

Probably in the ninth century there arose a poet of genius, the wandering rhapsode Homer, who worked up a great and rather intractable mass of material, partly his own work, partly traditional, into the two brilliant Homeric Poems. The splendour of these thrilled the Greek world wherever they were heard, and in the course of a few generations, even with the slow methods of transmission then in vogue, they became famous in all parts of the Aegean. The old metrical sagas on which they were based were forgotten, except in a few districts such as the self-contained world of Dorian Crete where the Homeric poems were late in making their appearance.

Homer gave a new stimulus to the poetic art, and by the eighth century poets were already writing supplementary epics designed to round off his " Tale of Ilios " into a complete whole. Writing was a laborious business in those days, and a consider- able strain was thrown even upon the best-practised memory ; and none of these " Cyclic " poems approached those of Homer either in scale or quality—so Proklos tells us, remarking that one reads the cyclic poems, if at all, " rather for their subject matter than on their merits ". The Kypria, the " Cyprian verses " doubtfully attributed to a certain Stasînos, described in eleven books the origin and the earlier years of the war ;

then came the Iliad, twenty-four books dealing in the main with a single episode ; and then three short chronicle-epics, devoid, like the Kypria, of internal unity,[1] aggregating eleven books, and bringing the story down to the fall of the city, after the failure of the Trojans' last desperate efforts to find an ally who should drive the assailants into the sea. These were the Aithiopis, "the Story of the Dark Man", by Arktînos of Miletos; the Little Iliad of Lesches of Mytilene; and the Sack of Ilios, by Arktînos.

Rather later, other poets " rounded off " the Odyssey also. Agias or Hâgias of Troizên, the first Cyclic poet of Greece proper, described the homeward voyages of the heroes other than Odysseus in what must have been a unity-less and rather futile epic, though it was only five books long. As a matter of fact Homer had already cunningly contrived to tell the world all it could wish to know about the homecomings of the other chieftains, in the stories of their experiences told by Nestor and Menelaos to the son of Odysseus, and by the ghost of Agamemnon to Odysseus himself.[2] Lastly the short Story of Têlegonos, in two books, by the sixth-century poet Eugammon of Kyrene, filled in the last possible gap in the story by telling of the last days of Odysseus.

The " rounders-off " of the Iliad evidently, if Mr. Allen is right in his view of " Diktys ", took a much less free hand in recasting their material than Homer did. On the other hand they betray their later date by manifesting a much wider knowledge of geography than he possessed.

Meanwhile other poets too were attempting to deal in Homeric style with legends which Homer had left untouched. Eumêlos of Corinth handled the Argonaut myth, and Peisandros of Kameiros made a continuous narrative out of the tales of the Labours of Herakles, to name only two of the most important. Homer, naturally, knew these traditional stories

---

[1] Cf. Aristotle's well-known *obiter dictum* that Homer's genius is nowhere better shown than in the unity of his epics ; for in the *Iliad* and *Odyssey* one could find material for one or at most two dramas apiece, while the *Little Iliad* would provide at least eight plots for tragedies, and the *Kypria* even more. (*Poetics*, ch. 23.)

[2] Home-coming of Nestor, Diomedes, Idomeneus, Philoktêtes and the Myrmidons—*Od.*, III, 103-200. How Aias son of Oïleus was lost at sea, IV, 499-511. The adventures of Menelaos—III, 276-302, 311-12 ; IV, 351-592. The intrigues of Aigisthos, III, 255-75 ; his murder of Agamemnon, XI, 405-34; the revenge of Orestes, III, 303-10.

well[1], though he never has occasion for more than a passing allusion to them.

Only the scantiest fragments survive of any of these early post-Homeric epics, cyclic or otherwise ; and from the allusions to them by Greek prose writers it does not appear that their loss is very greatly to be deplored excepting on antiquarian grounds.

Lastly, standing quite apart from the Homeric and post-Homeric poems, come those of the Theban Cycle. They were very famous—a favourite quarry of material for the tragedians— and they were old enough for their authors' names to have been wholly forgotten. The general public ascribed them uncritically to Homer. It is not unlikely that they were older than the Iliad and represent the formless chronicle-poem of the pre-Homeric era. Their character is sufficiently indicated by the fact that the Thebaid covered, in some 7,000 lines, the whole story of the fall of the House of Oidipous, from Oidipous' cursing of his sons[2] to the destruction of the Argive invaders before the walls of Thebes and the death of the sons of Oidipous by each other's hand.

A sequel, the Epigonoi, of about equal length, told how Thebes was taken, in a second expedition, by the sons of the original Seven Chieftains. There was also a Story of Oidipous —presumably describing his life down to the discovery of his wife's and mother's identity. This story too is mentioned in the Odyssey (XI, 271-80).

The general practice among the Greeks was to ascribe nearly all their old epic literature—the whole of the Trojan and Theban cycles, together with various shorter pieces such as our so-called Homeric Hymns and preludes—to Homer. Kallînos, the early elegiac poet, for instance makes the Thebaid Homeric, and later non-technical writers follow the same course. Thucydides (III, 104) calls the Hymn to the Delian Apollo Homer's, and such writers as Pausanias and Diodôros quote the hymns in general as his, without discussion. Other writers are more

---

[1] "The famous Argo" mentioned, Od., XII, 1. 70. Euneôs king of Lêmnos, son of Jason and Hypsipyle, Il., VII, 468.

Herakles' subjection to Eurystheus, and labours, Il., VIII, 363 ; XV, 639-640, XIX, 95-124 ; the bringing up of the Hound of Hell, Od., XI, 617-626.

[2] Athenaios XI, p. 465, Σ on Sophokles, O.C. l. 1375. The length of the Thebaid and Epigonoi is given by the Contest of Homer and Hesiod, a work of the same character as the "lives" of Homer.

cautious ; Herodotos, notably, doubts the Homeric authorship of the Epigonoi and denies that of the Kypria, on internal evidence[1] ; Hellanikos denies that Homer wrote the Little Iliad. Finally in the Alexandrian literary critics we begin to hear other authors named for all but the oldest of the more famous cyclic poems.

III. LEGEND AND HISTORY

οἱ μὲν δὴ Ἑλλήνων λόγοι διάφοροι τὰ πλέονα καὶ οὐχ ἥκιστα ἐπὶ τοῖς γένεσίν εἰσι.—Pausanias, VIII, 53.2.

We may believe, then, that the Iliad and Odyssey are based on a continuous poetic tradition going back to the time of the Trojan War. Further, we may believe the same of many of the famous stories only known to us from later writers ; for these derived their information from early Ionian " logographers " or lyrists or epic and elegiac poets, and in any case ultimately from the same epic tradition which Homer used. And, as we have seen, the subjects of all the great cycles of legend—Thebes, Oidipous, the labours of Herakles, the Wild Boar of Kalydôn,[2] the Argo—were known to him ; and if they are as old as Homer, then it is much more likely than not that they date from before the Dorian conquest—from the Heroic Age itself, those " good old days " to which the stories popular in early Ionia almost exclusively referred.

So far so good. We have for example every reason to believe that there was a wild boar of abnormal size and ferocity, which terrorized the countryside of Kalydon one summer a generation or so before the Trojan War, and which was with difficulty killed after a great hunt, which fired the imagination of all who

[1] Hdt., II, 117, IV, 32. Incidentally the first of these two passages reveals a serious flaw in our evidence. Herodotos denies that the Kypria can be Homer's, because in that poem Paris reaches Troy only three days after setting sail from Greece with Helen, whereas Homer in the Iliad makes him visit Sidon before turning homewards. But in Proklos' alleged abstract of the Kypria, Paris does go to Sidon !
Accordingly some think that Proklos' copy of the *Kypria* was a forgery. This may be so, but it is uncertain. Equally well it may be that it only differed from Herodotos' copy through having been " edited " and having its gaps filled up by some scholar of Alexandria.
[2] *Il.*, IX, 533-49. For other references, see notes to last chapter.

2

took part in it. So too with such other matters as the two
wars between Argos and Thebes, or the cruise of the Argo.

But we must be careful. It is not only that one would
scruple to assert, even on Homer's authority, that Herakles
really led the three-headed watchdog of the gates of hell with
a collar round its multiple neck through the palace courts of
Tiryns. It is that, even apart from the introductions of the
supernatural, we have every reason to believe that the poets
took a very free hand in the use they made of their materials.
It was not history that they were composing, but historical
fiction ; and Homer, naturally, makes up fictitious characters
whenever his narrative seems likely to be the better for them.
Alkinoos and Nausikaa and their countrymen, with their names
invariably appropriate to a nation of sea-farers, are the most
obvious instance. The central figures of the Iliad story—
Priam, Paris, Helen, the sons of Atreus, Achilles—doubtless
really lived, whether or not their characters resembled those
that the great poet gives them ; but Andromache, who has no
part to play in the development of the story, and whose name
is Greek though she is a Trojan, is almost certainly the creation
of Homer's brain. Her and her husband's function in the poem
is simply to supply a foil to other characters—the sensitive,
self-centred, Greek chieftains, and more especially Paris and
Helen, the beautiful, attractive, worthless pair, for whose
selfishness Hektor and Andromache and their baby and
thousands of others have to suffer and die.

So too with incidents; we have seen Homer at work collecting
adventures for Odysseus even at the price of moving the
Kimmerian nation two thousand miles from their real habitat.

Moreover another factor began to operate soon after Homer's
time, if it was not already operative then ; the instinct of the
tidy Greek mind to clear up all the puzzles and to leave no
frayed edges hanging, and above all to know what relation
everybody was to everybody else, and everybody's genealogy
back to Adam. Even the worthless Thersîtes was supplied
with relations and affiliated so to speak to the royal house of
Aitolia, though he is the most obvious fiction in the Iliad—a
mere personified Impudence (" tharsos ") created by the poet
for use as an Aunt Sally. Arktînos took him up and gave him
a larger part to play in the Aithiopis than he had in the Iliad,[1]

---

[1] Proklos, Epitome : Apollodoros, *Library of Mythology*, I, 8, 6.

and Arktînos it probably was who supplied him with a father named Savage—Agrios—and made him into a cousin of Diomêdes. This sort of "manie cyclique" soon began to lead to the creation of eponymous ancestors for Greek tribes and founders for cities, many of the heroes' genealogies being ulitmately traced back to "Hellên and his sons ". Hellên, that palpably mythical creation of the racial consciousness of the people who were beginning to know themselves as Hellenes, apparently made his first appearance in the "Catalogue " poems ascribed to Hesiod.[1] Greeks of the time of Thucydides, including the great historian himself, firmly believed that they had really existed.[2] Even in Homer some evident eponyms are mentioned ; "fair-crowned Mykênê " for example, and Trôs and Dardanos at the beginning of his genealogy of the Trojan kings.[3]

In short, though the legends contain a core of historical truth, it is clearly also true that the poets considered themselves justified in drawing freely on their imaginations for the invention of details and of minor characters ; and these minor characters, if they caught the imagination, might " come alive ", be taken up by other poets, and find themselves ultimately enshrined in the mythology of the nation. Ancestors and connecting links between families, who had to be postulated, were also given names, and came to be believed in as real people by the poets' audiences. And characters and adventures out of one story were freely appropriated for use in another, as Homer takes up his savage tribes (out of the Argonaut traditions of the Black Sea) and his cannibal giant (out of ancient folk-lore) into the story of Odysseus. The story of the Blinding of the Giant belongs to the folk lore of Aryan nations as far afield as the Esthonians and Kelts. It also reappears, with several details that look like reminiscences of the Odyssey, among the tales of Sinbad the Sailor. A very popular hero such as Herakles naturally attracts to himself stories of every sort of adventure that could possibly befall a strong and resourceful child of Zeus, and is himself adopted into stories

[1] Σ on Apollonios of Rhodes, III, 1086, Σ on Pindar, *Pythian Odes*, IV, 263 (who quotes the passage). His " son " Aiolos—or at any rate " Aiolid " princes—is already known to Homer (*Il.*, VI, 154, *Od.*, XI, 537).
[2] Thk., I, 3.
[3] *Od.*, II, 120, *Il.*, XX, 215 ff.

with which he originally had nothing to do, such as that of the Golden Fleece.

In short, the ancient poets did not, like a modern novelist, invent their plot and characters en bloc ; but they did take practically every liberty short of that.

In this context a very important question indeed is to what extent the heroic genealogies can be taken seriously. For instance, if we can arrive at a date for the Trojan War, can we thence arrive at a date for King Minôs, whose grandson, according to Homer, fought in it ?

It seems to be commonly believed that we can.

After a period of undue scepticism, the age of the tendency, now happily dead and buried, to turn every heroic legend into a sun-myth, the pendulum of opinion seems to be swinging if anything too far the other way. Half a century's sensational discoveries of the remains of a civilization actually dating from the age to which the Greek legends refer, have prompted a reaction to the view, substantially that of the Hellenes themselves, that the hero-kings really did live and rule over the cities to which the legends assign them, towards the end of the bronze age.

Recently Professor Myres has even seriously proposed to make use of the heroic genealogies as the framework of a scheme of chronology.[1] He defends this daring attempt on the ground that vested interests would protect these genealogies from corruption. There can, he tells us, have been little if any pedigree-faking because in early Hellenic times the pedigrees were too widely known and were the patents of nobility of too many ancient families. All these would have been concerned to check and deride forgeries, and the great families kept their scutcheons clean. With the Greek interest in knowing just how everybody was related to everybody else,[2] one may compare the similar interest among the Norsemen in Iceland, who are always ready to hold up the narrative of a saga in order to hear the lineage of a character, and among whom trustworthy records of such matters were preserved for centuries by oral transmission alone.

---

[1] Cf. his lecture to the Hellenic Society, Nov. 5, 1928 (summary in *J.H.S.*, XLVIII, p. xx.).
[2] Cf. Homer's account of Peleus' interest in this study—πάντων 'Αργείων ρέων γενέην τε τοκόν τε.—*Il.*, VII, 128.

A would-be historian of the period could not but be anxious to accept Professor Myres' view if possible ; but there are various grounds for hesitation. It is easy to check serious pedigree-faking in a settled aristocratic society, such as, in spite of its turbulence, that of the Iceland of the Sagas. It is less easy in a period of disastrous wars and the breaking up of kingdoms, like that in which the Bronze-Age civilization of Greece went to its ruin. If the captain of a migrant war-band which has won itself a new home with the edge of the sword, announces himself or is hailed by his followers as a prince of the line of Herakles, who is to say him nay ? Not his trusty companions, for his glory is theirs also ; nor yet the cowed and conquered remnants of the old population. Very likely, in an age of disturbance he does not know who his grandfathers or at best great-grandfathers were. Presently his bard will, by the direct inspiration of the Muse, enshrine the conqueror's divine or heroic descent in a poem, along with the indubitably true story of his prowess, adding if need be (still by the Muse's inspiration) the names of one or two connecting links in the pedigree ; and the process is complete.

After all, the lineage of King George V can be convincingly traced back on one side to Adam, through various princes of Ireland and then through David of Israel, and on another, through Offa, king of Mercia, and the earlier Offa who is mentioned in *Beowulf*, to the god Odin.

Certainly there is nothing impossible in the claim of every Dorian ruling house in historic Hellas to descend from Herakles, of Athenian Eupatrids to descend from Aias or Nestor, or of Lesbian and other Aiolic nobles to descend from Agamemnon through Penthilos, son of Orestes ;[1] but it does seem unlikely that the ancient kingly families should not only one and all survive the collapse of the old order, but actually beget a much more numerous offspring just then than in the days of their pride. In such an age of disaster it is precisely the old kingly families that might be expected to be killed off. The colonization of Iceland, by chiefs who refused to submit to the novelty of a central government, is no parallel to the colonization of Ionia. The latter was the work of fugitives not from firm government but from a *dégringolade* of every stronghold of

---

[1] Cf. Alkaios. frag. 43 (Diehl), ll. 6, 7.

law and order in the Aegean.   A whole civilization foundered,
and though our traditions are probably ultimately derived,
through post-conquest epics, from pre-conquest metrical sagas,
it should not be forgotten that like the legends of King Arthur
they are tales of the beaten side.   No Greek hero—not even
Herakles—is quite so Keltically elusive as the prince of Britain ;
but still, the carrying of the stories across the sea by refugees
must have given opportunities for confusion ; for forgetting
in what chronological relation one story stood to another,
notably ; or for the placing of the same event in several
different localities, a phenomenon of which Greek mythology
offers several examples.   Much, too, must have been forgotten
altogether in the years of turmoil, and finally the residue that
was remembered—no more than a few of the more exciting
stories out of the full history and lore of the Achaian age—was,
it is quite clear from cases like that of Thersites, patched up
again into a fairly coherent whole by means of connections
freely *invented* by cyclic poets and the compilers, such as
Hesiod, of " catalogues " of heroes and heroines.

But, we are told, the genealogies are mutually consistent,
and that, too, in spite of the fact that their interrelations are
complicated ; and this would be hardly possible if they were
fabrications.

This statement requires careful examination.

It is true as a rule, we find, of the heroes of the Trojan cycle
of stories—that is to say, the heroes of the favourite tales.   But
almost everywhere else it is liable to break down disastrously.
For instance :

There was a hero of Megara whose name was Alkathoös.
He was not a native of the city, but coming to it from abroad
delivered the people by killing a terrible lion that had its den
in the fastnesses of Mount Kithairôn. (This exploit was
by others ascribed to Herakles—a good instance of the
" attraction " of one hero's adventures to the more famous
personality of another.)   In gratitude, King Megareus
(obviously a mere eponym) gave Alkathoös his daughter to
wife, and as the King's son had been slain while hunting the
lion, the newcomer presently succeeded to the throne.   One
of his achievements as king was the restoration of the walls
of the city, destroyed in the time of Nîsos, the father-in-law
and predecessor of Megareus, by Minôs, king of Crete.

Alkathoös' daughter married Telamon, lord of Salamis, and their son was Aias, who fought at Troy. Alkathoös himself, by the way, was a son of Pelops.[1]

We have thus the genealogy :

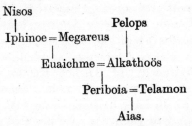

Nisos therefore appears to have lived four generations before the Trojan War.

But Minôs, son of Zeus, who attacked Nisos, is said to have lived only two generations before the war[2] ; and Theseus, Minôs' other antagonist, belongs only just to the generation before it. The legend that he was young enough to have carried off Helen early in her life, and fought her brothers the Dios Kouroi, is at least as early as the Cyclic poets.[3]

Even this is not the worst. Minôs was son of Zeus by Eurôpe, daughter of Phoinix.[4] But Eurôpe's brother was Kadmos, eponym of the Kadmeian Kings of Thebes, and he, according to the Theban genealogies, lived no less than *six* generations before the Trojan War. To get all the stories in, Minôs would have to be supposed to have reigned for some two hundred years, and the would-be systematizers of ancient times were constrained to cut the knot by inventing a second Minôs, abandoning Homer's genealogy, and saying that Minôs the son of Eurôpe was not the same as Minôs the grandfather of the Cretan leader at Troy ; " a gratuitous conjecture " as Grote remarked " which only adds one to the numerous artifices employed for imparting the semblance of history to the disparate matter of legend ".

---

[1] For the details, see Paus., I, 41. 4, 43. 4. Though not mentioned by Homer, the story is early ; it is alluded to as well known by the sixth-century Megarian poet Theognis (l. 774) ; also by Pindar, *Isthmians*, 7 (8), 67.

[2] *Il.*, XIII, 449-52.

[3] Σ on *Il.*, III, 242 ; Plutarch, *Theseus*, ch. 32, who quotes a fragment of an old epic.

[4] *Il.*, XIV, 321-2. The story was treated by the Hesiodic poets (Σ on *Il.*, XII, 292; *O.P.*, 1358. 1) but the earliest reference to Kadmos as Eurôpe's brother seems to be that in Hdt., II, 44, V, 57.

Or consider another legend known to Homer, that of Bellerophon. Bellerophon himself is said to be grandfather of Sarpêdon and Glaukos, the two Lykian chiefs at Troy[1]; but his contemporary Proitos, king of Tiryns and Argos, is actually great-great-great-great-grandfather of Sthenelos of Argos, who also fought at Troy.[2] Akrisios, brother of Proitos, occupies an intermediate position, being great-great-grandfather, on their mother's side, of Agamemnon and Menelaos.

The whole mythology of Thebes bristles with similar difficulties. It is embarrassingly rich. There are several cycles of legend which have nothing to do with one another; Pentheus, the enemy of Dionysos; Zêthos and Amphion, and their enemy Lykos; all these have to be fitted in somehow along with the house of Labdakos and Laïos, whose story has nothing to do with theirs, within the comparatively short space of the Heroic Age. The way in which it was done by the Greek antiquaries is a marvel of scholarly ingenuity.

Similar difficulties arise with regard to Herakles, who, it has been reckoned, would have had to live nearly three hundred years in order to come into contact with all the personages whom, in one or other of his adventures, he encounters.

In short the alleged consistency of the heroic legends with one another does not exist, and that in spite of the reconciling and systematizing labours of the later epic poets. The fact seems to be that to a people separated by a lapse of time and perhaps, like the Greeks, by a political catastrophe from a heroic age in the past, it is natural to think of " the time of the heroes " as one definite period, such as might be covered by a single lifetime; exactly as the countryman opined that " all them foreign parts is pretty close together ". The unsophisticated modern mind thinks of " Roman times ", for example, as a similarly short period; as did, for example, the very innocent little boy at a preparatory school who asked, when questions were invited after half an hour's struggle with Hannibal's crossing of the Alps, " Sir, what happens when he meets Cæsar ? " And so Greek heroic poetry has " telescoped" stories that probably should be scattered over a period of four or five centuries, ending about the time of the Trojan War,

---

[1] *Il.*, VI, 200 ff.

[2] The line of descent is: Proitos, Megapenthes, Anaxagoras, Alektor, Iphis, Euadne (wife of Kapaneus, who fell at Thebes), Sthenelos. For authorities and variations, see the Classical Dictionaries.

into a matter of six or seven—and most of them into two or three—human generations.

This is what we know to have happened under similar conditions in the heroic poetry of northern Europe, where we can speak with more certainty, because the names of some of the chief characters in the Epic also occur in the works of sober Roman chroniclers of the sixth century. King Eormenric whose historical prototype reigned north of the Black Sea in the third century of our era, Etzel (Attila, the Atli of the Norse version—fifth century) and Dietrich von Bern (Theodoric the Great—died 526) have all become attracted into the story of Siegfried-Sigurd and Kriemhild-Gudrun.

One may sum up in the words of Professor R. W. Chambers' commentary on the old English Catalogue-poem *Widsith* :

" It is an essential characteristic of heroic poetry that, while it preserves many historic names, it gives the story modified almost past recognition by generations of poetic tradition. Accurate chronology, too, is in the absence of written records impossible. All the great historic chieftains become contemporary ; their deeds are confused ; only their names, and sometimes their characters, remain."

IV.　FOLK-TRADITION

" What mean ye by these stones ? "
Joshua iv, 6 and 21.

We must also consider what attitude we ought to adopt towards the Greek traditions preserved otherwise than in epic poetry.

These traditions clearly were of some importance. Herodotos, who had a fine flair for historical evidence, is fond of referring to the stories attached to this or that famous monument or offering in a temple, or to the local traditions of this or that town. But are they likely to be useful to us in studying so remote a period as ours ?

The answer would seem to be the not very helpful one, " Sometimes ". It is very difficult to feel confident when using this kind of evidence, for it is extremely liable to all kinds of garbling. What appears to be " folk-memory " may prove to be merely myth—aetiological myth, explanatory of a custom or a religious ritual, being a common type.   Again, it may turn out to be based not on a genuine oral tradition but on a more or less corrupt reminiscence of epic or other literature ; there is a clear case of this in the Thessalian story that Paris was killed by Achilleus and Patroklos on the banks of the Spercheios river.[1]   It is more liable than the epic to become garbled, it tends even more strongly to " telescope " long processes into a single event, and it loves to group as many stories as possible around one famous name—as, for instance, " Cromwell " (Thomas or Oliver ?) is often credited by local tradition with all the damage done to the fabric of English cathedrals and churches by the " Protestant " vandalism of over a century.   Lastly, folk-memory preserves no chronology worth speaking of. " A long time ago ", or at best " before the Trojan War " is the best that it can do for us.

Yet with all its faults, popular tradition is not always to be despised, especially *local* tradition.   A people, whether in the historic or the prehistoric stage, will often have some tradition as to whence, or at any rate from what direction, their ancestors came into the land they now occupy.   They may even be able to tell us why they moved and who led the migration.   The traditions reported by Strabo and Pausanias about the Dorian conquest of Argolis and the Great Migration to Ionia are cases in point.[2]   It may be little more than a name attached to a place, a mound, or a shrine, but it may still be very useful ; for instance the Têmenion, down by the sea, the traditional site where Têmenos and his Dorians encamped for their operations against Argos ; or Solygeia, the mound where Alêtes and *his* Dorians encamped for their attack on Corinth ; or merely the name Minoa, attached to several places and harbours up and down the coasts of the Greek world.   A tradition that has a place or an object to crystallize around, so to speak, often shows great tenacity of life.

Ancient man knew this, and many of his barrows and rough stone monuments are intended definitely to act as the focus of traditions.   The early books of the Bible are full of allusions to the setting up of Standing Stones to mark the site of some

---

[1] Istros, quoted by Plutarch (*Theseus*, c. 34) who is much worried at such perversity in a reputable writer.
[2] Paus., II, 13. 1 ff. (north-east Peloponnese), VII, chaps. 2-5 (Ionia); Str., XIV, chap. III (Ionia).

notable event,[1] and Joshua's stone circle (?) where the people under him crossed the Jordan is definitely intended to prompt, in every generation, the question, "What mean ye by these stones ? "[2] Hektor in the Iliad looks to the burial-mounds of his foes to keep his fame alive, and the last injunction of the dying Beowulf is to the same effect :

" Bid the heroes raise at the sea-headland a gleaming mound after the burning. It shall tower high on Hronesness, a token to the people, so that the sea-farers hereafter may call it Beowulf's cairn, when from afar the ships drive over the dark sea."[3]

After all in the last resort every story must be criticized on its own merits. Mere eponyms of races or customs, like " Hellên and his son Amphiktyon " may naturally be neglected, as artificial creations—figures of myth. Significant names like Theseus, " Stablisher " (of law and government) are open to suspicion. But stories containing names that mean nothing, or are not Greek at all, like Minôs or Pelops, or names not specially appropriate to their bearers (Herakles, Menelaos) or stories that preserve a reference to old Aegean customs not shared by the Hellenes[4]—these deserve attention, as containing, perhaps, at least a core of genuine tradition.

v. WHO WAS MINÔS ?

ὅς βασιλεύτατος ἐγένετο θνητῶν βασιλήων
καὶ πλείστων ἤνασσε περικτιόνων ἀνθρώπων
Ζηνὸς ἔχων σκῆπτρον τῷ καὶ πολέων βασίλευε.
—Hesiod.

As Schliemann, when he made his sensational discoveries of the treasure of the Shaft Graves at Mykênai startled the world with the message that he had " found Agamemnon ", so it seemed to Sir Arthur Evans and his helpers, when the still more wonderful civilization of Knôssos came to light, that they had " found " the very palace and capital of Minôs the Sea-King, famed in story. Hence the name " Minoan " given by

[1] E.g. *Genesis* xxviii, 18 ; xxxi, 45 ff.
[2] *Joshua* iv, 1-9, 20-22.
[3] *Beow.*, XXXVIII, ad fin.
[4] Cf. pp. 96, n., 98, below.

Sir Arthur to the pre-Hellenic civilization of the whole South Aegean area.

We now believe that the Treasure of the Shaft Graves dates from centuries before the time of Homer's King of Men ; and doubts have also been suggested whether Minôs had anything to do with Minoan civilization.   Ridgeway, in a hard-hitting and characteristic paper, argued, some twenty years ago, before the British Academy,[1] that Minôs, if a historical character and an Achaian hero, as Homer presents him, was "the destroyer rather than the creator of the so-called Minoan Civilization ".   Granted the premises, the conclusion certainly follows.   But *was* Minôs an Achaian ?   Sir Arthur Evans, at any rate, remains unconvinced.   Most modern writers, however, tend to accept Ridgeway's view that Minôs was not a native Cretan but an intruding Greek from further north.[2]

This difference of opinion raises at once in an acute and typical form that whole question of critical method which we have just been discussing—the question of the proper use of the different kinds of evidence, the archæological and the traditional, on the history of a prehistoric or protohistoric age.

Ridgeway's case rests entirely upon the evidence of the genealogies.   According to the Iliad, Minôs was grandfather of Idomeneus, the Achaian lord of Crete, who fought at Troy. According to the most popular of several late Greek computations, based on genealogies, Troy was taken early in the twelfth century B.C.   Therefore, Minôs must have " flourished " about the middle of the thirteenth century, nearly one hundred and fifty years after the date which satisfactory archæological evidence, based on contacts with Egypt, fixes as that of the fall of the " Minoan " empire of Knôssos.

But we have just seen that the heroic genealogies are in part mutually contradictory and in part artificial constructions, containing names which like those of Trôs, Dardanos, and Mykêne in Homer are mere eponyms of tribes and places. It is also an indubitable fact that Eratosthenes' computation of the date of the Trojan War, which most recent writers, amazingly, treat with respect, is based on a wild over-estimate of the average length of a generation.[3]   The

---

[1] *Proceedings of the British Academy*, 1909.
[2] E.g. Hogarth in *The Twilight of History*, 1926 ; Wace, in *C.A.H.*, II.
[3] Chadwick, *The Heroic Age*, pp. 180 ff.   See below, pp. 52-5.

evidence for dating Minôs' reign about 1250 B.C. is therefore worthless.

On the other hand, the account of Minôs' character and exploits in the old stories is much more likely to preserve traditions of some value ; that character and those exploits suit much better the view that he was, as Sir Arthur Evans would have him, a native Cretan king, or the personification of a dynasty, belonging to the great age of Knôssian imperialism, the fifteenth century B.C. Above all things Minôs was remembered as lord of the seas ; and nothing about fifteenth century Knôssos is more striking than that it was as unfortified as London to-day. Clearly its defence was the " wooden wall " of an unrivalled navy. The heavily fortified settlements of other ages in the Aegean are a significant contrast. Minôs sent out expeditions which conquered or colonized widely in the South Aegean, and even as far afield as Sicily, leaving the place-name Minoa, like the Georgetowns and Victorias of modern times, to testify to his power in later days. But there is clear archæological evidence that Cretan influence was being widely felt abroad in the sixteenth and fifteenth centuries *and at no later date*. After 1400, Cretan civilization is influenced by, rather than influences, that of the mainland of Greece. Minôs was a great absolute monarch, a king even in the house of Hades, a brother of the law-giver Rhadamanthys the just, and moreover, unlike the Homeric heroes, a priest-king, who " knew God face to face " ; and this, too, suits what can be learned of the character of old Aegean kingship from the remains of the kings' palaces.[1] Minôs was patron of Daidalos, the eponymous hero of all " cunning artificers " ; and as such he should presumably belong to the age of the zenith of a civilization rather than its decline.

Such were the traditions of Minôs as remembered by those who admired him.

There was also among the Greeks a hostile tradition, pre-served on the mainland, by the Athenians, the only people on that coast in historic times who had been there since the Minoan age. This tradition sees the great king as an oppressor whose invincible fleets brought sorrow in their wake. But this version describes the same character, only from another point of view ; and it, too, agrees with the theory that Minôs was a

[1] Notably that at Mallia.

" Minoan " prince or dynasty of the age before 1400. Minôs, we are told, levied as part of the tribute he took from the states he terrorised, a tax in youths and maidens, to be torn by " Minôs' Bull "—to translate, instead of transliterating, the word Mino-tauros. At once we are reminded of the sport that fifteenth century Knôssos loved to watch, in which boy and girl athletes vaulted, or failed to vault, clear over the sharp horns of a charging bull, for the delectation of Cretan lords and ladies. Lastly, the very place where Minôs' Bull was kept, from whose tortuous and endless passages no captive had ever found his way back, is called in the stories the Labyrinth, a word which has no etymology in Greek, but whose meaning was brilliantly elucidated by Ronald Burrows.[1] There was a Karian word " Labrys ", meaning a double-headed axe, such as has been found as a sacred symbol in a hundred contexts in prehistoric Crete. Zeus of Labraunda, a sacred place in Karia was regularly represented in art as carrying the Labrys.[2] Now it is likely on several grounds that the Karians spoke a language of the same group as the pre-Hellenic tongue of Crete. And the termination -nth- occurs both in numerous Aegean place-names and in many Greek words which have no Aryan etymology and which are just such as an incoming race would be likely to learn from its predecessors, such as names of plants. " Labyrinth " is therefore not a Greek word, but Cretan and Karian, having originally meant the House of the Double Axe, the sacred symbol of the Cretan god to whom bulls were also sacred ; though to the Hellenes it came to mean an inextricable maze of passages, such as the House of the Double Axe actually was.

No, Minôs the sea-king, the law-giver, the friend of Zeus, was not an Achaian and was not grandfather of Idomeneus. The latter's pedigree in the Iliad is the flattering and artificial concoction of a poet.[3] Minôs' very name is of a native Mediterranean type, with the same termination as, for example

[1] *The Discoveries in Crete*, p. 117.
[2] Plutarch, *Moralia*, p. 302.
[3] It is perhaps worth noting that the genealogies, if accepted, prove far too much. Minôs' predecessor and " earthly father " Asterios is called son of Tektamos the son of Dôros the son of Hellên. (Diodoros, IV, 60.) So it appears that he was not even an Achaian, but a Dorian, a thesis which does not seem hitherto to have been properly exploited. There is still room here for an interesting paper by anyone who desires to be original.

Glôs,[1] Tamôs,[2] Tachôs,[3] Inarôs,[4] all names well known in historic times among the maritime folk of the Nile Delta, a race more Mediterranean than Nilotic ; and his character in the stories is that of a lord of Knôssos of the time before the disaster of 1400 B.C.

EXTANT REFERENCES TO THE MINÔS LEGEND.

The extant evidence on the personality of Minôs is as follows :

I. The Epic tradition :

Homer, *Iliad.*, XIII, 449-52, gives the pedigree, Zeus, Minôs, Deukalion, Idomeneus.

Il., XIV, 321-2, names Eurôpe, daughter of Phoinix, as mother, by Zeus, of Minôs and Rhadamanthys.

Il., XVIII, 591-2, mentions the dancing-floor " that Daidalos made in Knôssos for fair-tressed Ariadne ".

Odyssey, IV, 561 ff. mentions " the Êlysian plain, where brown-haired Rhadamanthys is."

Od., VII, 321-4, the connection between Rhadamanthys and the Phaiâkes, the heaven-favoured sailors.

Od., XI, 321-5. " Fair Ariadne, daughter of Minôs of the baleful counsels, whom Theseus once was bringing from Crete to the hill of holy Athens ; but he gat no joy of her, for Artemis slew her ere that, in sea-girt Dia, by the witness of Dionysos."

[This passage, which contains Homer's only undoubted mention of Theseus, contains also, in the adjective applied to Minôs, the only trace in Homer of the anti-Minoan tradition.]

Od., XI, 568-71. Minôs in Hades, a judge among the dead.

Od., XIX, 172-9. Populousness of Crete and mixture of races there ; Knôssos mentioned as " a great city, where Minôs ruled for nine seasons, the familiar friend of great Zeus ".

Hesiod, quoted by Plato, *Minôs*, p. 320 : " Minôs who was most royal of mortal kings, and ruled most widely among men round about, having the sceptre of Zeus ; therefore he ruled over many ".

II. Local traditions :

Bakchylides, I, 1. 7 : Keian tradition that Minôs visited the island with fifty ships ; story of how Theseus brought up again the ring which Minôs threw into the sea.

Herodotos, I, 171, 173 : Sarpêdon, brother and rival of Minôs, led a colony to Lykia ; Leleges of ancient Karia manned Minôs' fleets. Hdt., VII, 169-71 : Tradition of the "True-Cretans" of Praisos about a Cretan "Sicilian expedition" to Kamikos, to avenge Minôs who had died among the Sikanoi " by a violent death ".

Hdt., III, 122 and Thukydides, I, 4 : Minôs' sea-power, and rule over the Cyclades.

Traditions of Minoan rule at Paros, Apollodôros, II, 5. 9. 3 ; at Karpathos, Diodôros, V, 54 ; of the siege and capture of Nîsa (the older city of the Megarid), Pausanias, II, 34. 7, Apollod., III, 15. 8.

Miletos said to have been founded by a refugee-movement from Crete, connected with that of Sarpêdon : Apollod., III, 1. 2 ; Paus., VII, 2. 4 ; Strabo, XIV, p. 634, quoting Ephoros : Chios and Erythrai by Rhadamanthys, Diod., V, 84.

Evidence of the place-names " Minoa " and " Cretan Harbour " : Diod., V, 84.

[1] Polyainos, VII, 20 , Xenophon, Anabasis I, 4. 16, etc., with variant form Γλοῦς.

[2] Thk., VIII, 31, etc.

[3] Plutarch, *Agêsilaos*, 36-40, etc.

[4] Thk., I, 104, Str., XVII, 801, etc.

Athenian tragedy seems to have taken up and developed the local traditions hostile to Minôs ; cf. Sokrates' comment (Plato, *op. cit.* pp. 318-19) on a remark that Minôs was a tyrant. He calls this view 'Αττικὸν καὶ τραγικόν.

III. The Minotaur, as a bull-headed human-bodied monster slain by Theseus, first appears on Athenian vases, as early as the sixth century. A similar monster appears on a Cretan seal of Minoan date.

IV. Detailed accounts of Minôs' death at the hands of Kôkalos king of the Sikanoi, and of a sack of the palace of Knôssos by Theseus, are late (Diodôros, IV, 79, and Plutarch, *Theseus*, XIX, respectively) ; both stories however preserve allusions to old Aegean customs not in vogue in Hellenic times, and therefore are probably in some measure based on a genuine tradition of some sort. See Part II, chapter III, below.

CHAPTER II

NATIONS AND LANGUAGES

ἄλλη δ' ἄλλων γλῶσσα μεμιγμένη·ἐν μὲν Ἀχαιοί,
ἐν δ' Ἐτεόκρητες μεγαλήτορες, ἐν δὲ Κύδωνες
Δωριέες τε τριχάϊκες, δῖοί τε Πελασγόι.

—*Odyssey*, **XIX**, 175-7.

I. ARYANS AND ARCHÆOLOGISTS

THE great problem of early Aegean ethnology can be briefly
stated. Greek, like Latin and Sanskrit, like Persian,
like the Keltic and Teutonic tongues, is an " Aryan " language,
and the " Aryan cradle ", the land in which long ago must have
been spoken a language the common ancestor of all these
tongues, is best identified with the park-land border between
steppe and forest, north of the Black Sea.[1] But the commonest
Greek physical type in historic times, like that known to us
from Minoan art and from the skeletons of the race that created
it, is typically " Mediterranean "—a slender, active type,
black-haired, dark-eyed, artistic, not very warlike, of less
stature and less heavily boned than either the rugged Alpine
or the tall blonde Nordic types of central and northern Europe.

Hence the problem. In Greece as in other parts of the world,
how does an Aryan language come to be spoken by men whose

---

[1] So, e.g., Myres, *Dawn of History*, pp. 195 ff. ; Peake, *The Bronze Age and
the Celtic World*, pp. 132 ff.   Giles, in *Camb. Anc. History*, Vol. II, pp. 28 ff.
prefers the similar park- and grass-land of Hungary.   In either area the early
" Wiros," as Giles has christened them, could have lived the life suggested by
the small stock of words common to all or most Aryan languages ; a life
partly, but not wholly, nomadic and waggon-dwelling, with a little agriculture
(a word for a plough is widespread among the daughter-languages), familiar
with several of the northern deciduous forest trees, possessing little or no
metal, but having domesticated the horse, dog, cow, goat, sheep and pig.
The Russian area is to be preferred since the Wiros before their dispersion
seem to have had contacts with the earliest Mesopotamian civilization of
Sumer.   Hence they imported both a few objects such as axes, and the
Sumerian name for them—pilakku, cf. Gk. " pĕlĕkȳs," if this is indeed an
Aryan and not an Aegean word—and perhaps a few ideas : cf. our word
" star ", Gk. aster, Latin astrum or stella (a diminutive) with the goddess-name
Ishtar, for which a star was the ideogram in Babylonian writing.   Cf. V. G.
Childe, *The Aryans*, pp. 183-204.

physical type does *not* suggest that their ancestors are to be sought on the fringes of the northern steppe, but rather that they are true children of the aboriginal inhabitants, who held the land before Aryan speech had ever been heard there ? And more particularly, when and by whom was an Aryan language (i.e. Greek) first introduced ?

It might be expected that archæology would have discovered clear traces of the immigration from the north that must have accompanied so important an event ; but it is not so. It is true that among early remains of Dorian Sparta are found brooches of a very characteristic type that also occurs in central Europe.[1] It is true that among the latest pre-Dorian remains, which one would naturally associate with Homer's Achaioi, occur slashing swords of the " leaf-shaped " type, which was certainly developed in Hungary[2] ; and it is true that about the same time, in the Aegean, cremation, a rite long practised in Central Europe, was being adopted (but nowhere universally), instead of inhumation of the dead, that geometric ornament was replacing naturalistic painting on vases, and that the spread of the safety-pin or brooch shows that loose and simple garments, the tunic and plaid of Homer's heroes, had replaced the old closely fitting Minoan clothes which needed no such fastening. But in spite of all this, the archæologists assure us that there is no complete and abrupt break in the development of Aegean life. " The change is not a sudden one. . . . There is no abrupt cataclysm, for the Mycenæan civilization did not perish but gradually evolved into another."[3] Moreover, even the geometric art-style is in part a descendant of earlier Aegean styles, and in part an importation from no further away than Macedonia.[4]

Nor had the Greeks themselves any tradition of a migration from the far north. The Dorians are said to come no further than from the northern frontiers of Greece—" a Makednian

---

[1] Cf. British Museum, *Early Iron Age* guide, pp. 36-8, figs. 36, 37 (Hallstatt) with *British School at Athens, Annual*, XII, p. 321, XIII, pp. 112-3 ; Blinkenberg, *Fibules Grecques* (Copenhagen, 1926), pp. 254-5, 263-4. But the Spartan brooches do *not* date, apparently, from the earliest Dorian period—a very puzzling fact.

[2] Peake, *Bronze Age*, pp. 81-91.

[3] Wace, in *C.A.H.*, II, p. 466. Cf. Childe, *Aryans*, pp. 48-9, 55.

[4] British School's discoveries at Buboshta, 1927 ; *Times*, 19.7.27 ; *Journal of Hellenic Studies*, XLVII, pp. 243-4 ; W. A. Heurtley, in *British School Annual*, 1928.

tribe", Herodotos calls them[1]; while their predecessors, Achaians, Arkadians, and the rest, were definitely stated by the catalogue-poets to be autochthonous[2]—" aboriginal ".

Yet the evidence of the language shows that there must have been immigration at some time ; and the evidence of the Greek dialects shows that Greek was firmly rooted, even in the innermost centre of the Peloponnese, before the Dorians came. For the most archaic of those dialects, that spoken in Cyprus, was spoken also in Arkadia ; and Arkadia was in historic times a wholly inland district, cut off from the sea by Dorians and other later intruders. It is therefore clear that Dorians must have overrun parts, including the whole coast-land, of the formerly much larger area held by those Arkadian-speaking Greeks who colonized Cyprus.

We can at any rate say with safety two things ; first that Greek was introduced, not by an invasion that exterminated or expelled the earlier inhabitants—such an event would leave its mark on archæology—but, like Aryan languages in many other parts of the world, by comparatively gradual infiltration of folk from whom Aryan speech, probably the best vehicle of expression yet devised by man, was in course of time adopted by the natives. Secondly, the immigration of the people who first brought in Greek speech took place long enough before the heroic age for the bards, whose audiences, as Homer's Têlemachos reminds us, always wanted "the latest", to have ceased to be interested in it. Tales of the immigration were no longer being told ; and consequently Homer and his successors never heard of it.

Professor Childe has further narrowed the field of search by pointing out that both the earlier and the " conquest " dialects of Greek must have developed within a linguistic continuum ; an area, that is to say, between all parts of which there was sufficient coming and going to prevent the divergence of a common speech into different languages.[3] Such a continuum he finds in the Balkan area in the third millennium B.C., where

---

[1] Hdt., I. 56, VIII, 43.
[2] Cf., for instance, Hesiod, quoted by Σ on Pindar, *Nemeans*, III, l. 21. —Myrmidons created out of ants by Zeus in Aigina island. Yet these " Myrmidons and Hellenes and Achaioi" (*Iliad*, II, 684—the first appearance in history of the Hellenic name) under their fair-haired prince Achilles (*Il.*, I, 197) should be Nordic incomers if any Achaian was.
[3] *The Aryans*, p. 43.

a single pottery style is spread over a vast culture-province
from the lower Danube to Illyria and even upper Italy, already
developing into local styles in the south-west Balkan region
by 2000 B.C. His theory of the origin of the Greek dialects
identifies, tentatively, the proto-Hellenes with the makers of
the pottery conventionally called Grey Minyan ware. This
unmistakable fabric, unpainted, smooth, and " soapy " to
the touch, and " with a tendency to fantastic elaboration of the
handles ", makes its first appearance in Thessaly in or about
the twenty-fourth century ; at which time (the " Third
Thessalian " period of the archæologists) Thessaly becomes
part of the above-mentioned great Balkan culture-province.[1]

At some period early in the second millennium important
movements take place. The cultural continuity of the Balkan
region is broken ; and southwards the users of this grey ware
overrun central Greece, and penetrate into Attica and the
Peloponnese. These movements involved no extermination of
the earlier inhabitants ; their matt-painted pottery continues
in use in the succeeding period alongside the intrusive Grey
Ware.[2] Childe observes that whereas in central Greece the
Grey pottery is in common domestic use, in the Peloponnese it
is a luxury article, and deduces that while the northerners had
colonized extensively in central Greece, in the south they were
fewer in number and formed a conquering aristocracy. The
invaders were a warlike folk ; weapons are the chief objects
buried with them in their cist-graves, and trade, of which there
had been a good deal in Greece in the preceding period, seems
to have wilted under their rule.[3]

After this, Childe supposes the invaders to have Hellenized,
by degrees in the following centuries, the aboriginal Helladic
folk, thus giving rise in the Peloponnese to the Arkadian and
perhaps in Attica to the Ionian dialect ; while Aiolic Greek
will be the speech of the descendants of the Grey Ware people
in Thessaly and central Greece.[4]

Certainty is not at present obtainable on this question, but
the above theory does satisfy the various requirements of our

[1] The Aryans, pp. 58 ff.
[2] Childe, Dawn of European Civilisation, pp. 77-8.
[3] Ibid.
[4] Ionic, however, it is at least equally probable, may have diverged from
Aiolic only in the course of the Dark Age that followed the Dorian Invasion,
in the linguistic continuum of the group of states that revered the sanctuary
of Delos.

rather complicated mass of evidence. Especially it accounts for the salient fact that Arkadian was being spoken in Greece in time for Cyprus to be colonized by users of this dialect, before the Dorian invasion cut off Arkadia from the sea, and while the Minoan script was still in use ; for the Greeks of Cyprus, instead of adopting the Phœnician alphabet, continued to use a syllabary based on the Minoan far into the Hellenic period. Cyprus appears from the sudden flood of Mycenæan pottery, which deluges its market in the period following 1400 B.C., to have received its colonists from the mainland of Greece about that time ; which makes it almost certain that Arkadian Greek was the language of the Peloponnese in the "Mycenæan" Age. Greek seems to have continued to be spoken there throughout the sixteenth and fifteenth centuries in spite of the conquest of the Argolid, certainly by Cretan civilization, and probably by Cretan colonists ; though it was doubtless at this period that the Greeks adopted most of their list of pre-Aryan and presumably Minoan civilization-terms.

It remains to account for the Dorians and the Achaians ; for the latter—at least if one may judge from the Achaians of the north-Peloponnese in historic times—were first-cousins of the Dorians and like them spoke a "western-Greek" dialect of the "Conquest" group. They, too, are satisfactorily accounted for on Childe's theory; for the Grey Ware culture in Thessaly is continuous with the "proto-Dorian" of the British School's recent discoveries in Macedonia, and also with the immediately pre-Dorian—presumably Achaian—pottery of Leukas in the west of Greece.[1]

Professor Childe's view of the origin of "Minyan" pottery has come in for a certain amount of criticism ; the British School's excavations in Macedonia, in particular, show that this ware occurs on the coast but *not* further north, as it would if it were of northern Balkan origin[2] ; and Mr. Frankfort's careful study leads him to the conclusion that its distribution precludes the idea that it came either from the north or from overseas.[3] In short, Grey Minyan ware, properly so called, seems to be native to Greece. At first sight this objection to

[1] *Aryans*, p. 59.
[2] Cf. report on Heurtley's excavations in Chalkidike ; *J.H.S.*, XLVIII, pp. 185-6.
[3] *Studies in Early Pottery of the Near East*, II : *Europe, Asia and the Aegean and their Earliest Interrelations*, p. 140.

Childe's theory of the origin of the Greek language seems fatal, but on further thought it proves to be little more than a matter of terminology. Frankfort's own view of the matter—a view, indeed, already foreshadowed by Childe—is that "Minyan" arose in Phokis after a Danubian immigration; he speaks of the Danubian immigrants as having a highly-polished, dark, carboniferous ware characteristic of their southern region, and most plentiful in Phokis and Boiotia.[1]

In the last resort, it is not of vast moment to the philologist what terminology may be adopted by the experts in ceramics. What is of importance is that their studies do lend support to the idea that there was a northern migration into Greece, not indeed during or shortly before the Heroic Age, but in the earlier generations of the second millennium. There can be little doubt that it was this migration that introduced Aryan speech into Greece.

As to the arrival of Aryan speech in the Balkan and Danube lands from the "Aryan cradle" in south Russia, it seems most probable that it occurred rather before the middle of the third millennium. At this time we know, at least, that Thessaly was invaded by a folk from beyond the Balkan range who introduced the "megaron" type of house and a style of painted pottery, new to the country, but closely resembling the neolithic ware found at Schipenitz, Tripolje, and other sites in the Bukovina and the Ukraine.[2]

II. WHO WERE THE ACHAIOI ?

The view that roundly equates Homer's Achaioi with the creators of the Aegean civilization may be said to be obsolete; it was virtually destroyed by Ridgeway in his *Early Age of Greece*, published in 1901, though a recent writer has resurrected it,[3] ignoring rather than explaining the differences, pointed out by Ridgeway, between Achaian civilization as depicted by Homer and "Mycenæan" in its prime. But the equation "Achaian=Mycenæan" breaks down disastrously. To mention only a few of the differences, the Mycenæans inhumed

[1] *Op. cit.*, p. 42 ; cf. Childe, in *J.H.S.*, XXXV, pp. 196 ff.
[2] Burkitt, *Our Early Ancestors*, pp. 138-143.
[3] Allen, *Homer, the Origins*, etc., Chapter VI.

their dead; Homer's heroes invariably cremate. The Mycenæans used thrusting swords, broad-bladed near the hilt and tapering to a point, useless for a cutting; Homer's swordsmen almost invariably use the edge. The Homeric Achaian is as a rule armed in corselet and greaves, while the Mycenæan has no armour other than his helmet and enormous shield. But it might be claimed that these differences mark only the passage of time, not a difference of race, were it not that in the valley of the Spercheios, the home of Homer's " Hellenes and Achaioi " par excellence, not a single Mycenæan tomb or settlement has been discovered. (This, it must be confessed, is an argument *ex silentio*.)

The appearance of Ridgeway's book marked an epoch in the discussion of the Achaian question. He claimed, on the strength of the appearance in Homer's world of various apparently northern features (cremation, slashing swords, new fashions in clothing; also the Homeric " hall " with its central hearth—a type of house suitable to a cold country) that the Achaioi were a Central European tribe of Keltic affinities, who had invaded the Aegean world. Certainly Homer's men—both lords and commons—are great meat-eaters, like the Aryan lords of the great Indian poems, and conspicuously unlike the historic Greek, who lives sparely on bread, cheese, and vegetables, with fish as a luxury. Ridgeway even claimed that Homer describes the Achaians as fair-haired, an assertion which requires, to say the very least of it, drastic qualification.

There is so much obvious truth in Ridgeway's view that it is not surprising that it held the field for several years. Then, as it gradually became clear that the study of the pottery brought to light no sign of the passage of these Keltic invaders, and as it was pointed out that there was no Greek tradition of an Achaian coming, that Homer only describes a few of his heroes as " fair "—presumably to distinguish them from a dark majority ?—and that in any case *xanthos* only means " brown ", not yellow, a reaction set in. Bury, in his chapter on the Achaians in the *Cambridge Ancient History* says roundly,[1] " The truth seems to be that the north, from 1500 to 1200 B.C., exercised no great influence on the civilization of the Aegean." The megaron or hall type of house, it is pointed out, occurs within the Aegean area at Troy, as well as in the self-contained

[1] *C.A.H.*, II, p. 474.

Thessaly, far back into the third millennium, and, it is suggested, is perhaps an Asian rather than a Central European invention. Cremation it is true is well-known in Central Europe, but as it occurs, in the Aegean, first in the islands and on the coast of Karia, and only later on the mainland of Greece, it seems likely that it, too, came to the Aegean from Asia Minor. And of late Blinkenberg has expressed the opinion that even the safety-pin, with which the Homeric chieftain secured his plaid, is a native Aegean invention of late but true Mycenæan date.[1]

Professor Childe, like Bury, believes the Achaioi to be simply a tribe of north Greece, from the Spercheios region, and would account for any northern contacts that may appear in remains of the Achaian Age by the hypothesis merely of " a culture contact with the north and a tribal movement within the Balkans ".[2] In the same way he would account for the Dorians ; and in accordance with his valuable conception of the linguistic continuum he asserts strongly that if the speakers of the pre-conquest dialects were at a given time already settled in Greece, then the proto-Dorians were certainly not as far away as the Danube.[3]

To this last statement it seems possible to take exception. Once the Greek language was thoroughly established, there seems to be no impossibility in two different dialect groups remaining mutually intelligible even if the linguistic continuum is broken for a time ; and in fact the possibility is proved by the fate of Arkadian and Cypriote, which diverged from one another hardly at all in seven or eight centuries of complete separation.

But to return to the Achaioi ; there seem to the present writer to be, in spite of all, some considerations to be urged in favour of at any rate a modified version of Ridgeway's theory.

First, the arrival of the leaf-shaped slashing swords does not seem to be satisfactorily explained by a " culture contact " (=trade ?). Mr. H. J. E. Peake, who has made a special study of these weapons, traces their evolution, in the region of the Middle Danube, in a succession of types ; and *all* the

---

[1] *Fibules Grecques et Orientales*, p. 40.
[2] *Aryans*, p. 55.
[3] *Ibid.*, p. 43.

eleven specimens recorded in modern times from lands surrounding the Eastern Mediterranean—viz., one from Boiotia, four from Argolis, two from Crete, one from Cyprus and three from Egypt—belong to two successive types, D and E.[1] None of the earlier types, A, B, C, are represented.

If the Greeks acquired these swords through trade, they woke up to the desire for them very suddenly.

But in fact there is no reason why the Greeks should have wanted to buy these swords. They were already fairly well armed with the native Aegean spear, short bow, dagger, axe, and so-called rapier, the tapering thrusting sword, better described as an elongated dirk ; and one would expect them to continue to prefer the weapon and the sword-play with which they were familiar.

It seems much more natural to suppose that these swords were carried into the southland by one or more bands of warriors, leaving home during the thirteenth century to seek their fortunes abroad. To speculate a little, it may have been these newcomers who stimulated the Achaians of northern Greece into the activity—the unwonted activity—which they displayed during the following century. If Professor Childe is right in supposing that the Greek language originated in the huge Balkan culture-province of the third millennium, then it is not unlikely that warriors from the Danube could still in, say, the year 1300, understand the speech of Thessaly. Breton sailors can still make themselves understood in Cardiff, after a much longer separation.

The warriors who brought the leaf-shaped sword into Greece may, too, have been stragglers from the Phrygian horde which, crossing via Thrace into Asia, about 1200 B.C. virtually made an end of the Hittite empire in Asia Minor. It would be in keeping with this that big slashing swords are several times said by Homer to come from Thrace.[2] Asia Minor being almost a blank to the archæologist, we cannot tell for certain how the destroyers of the Hittite realm were armed, but such indications as we have favour the view that they carried the leaf-shaped sword of Peake's Type D. Such a sword—carefully cut, as though the sculptor were interested in it—is certainly worn by a warrior on a rude Hittite relief from Sinjerli in north Syria,

---

[1] Peake, *Bronze Age*, pp. 81-96, 96-7.
[2] *Il.*, XIII, 577, etc.

dating from the age following the great invasion.[1] In Syria the Iron Age had already begun at this date, but even if this warrior's sword is to be imagined as being of iron, it is certainly modelled on a Danubian leaf-shaped bronze-age original.

Such an "infiltration" of a few northern warriors would account for the appearance in Greece of central European weapons and ornaments, while it naturally would not leave a mark on the history of ceramics. Soldiers and gentlemen-adventurers toil not, neither do they make pots ; and as, in this case, they were moving into a land of more elegant luxury than their own, they were presumably quite content with what they found.

Secondly, the available evidence does seem to show, not indeed that a fair physical type was prevalent either among the Achaioi or at any time in early Greece, but that it existed and—which is significant—that fair colouring was felt to be characteristic of princes, aristocrats, and gods.

But to collect and consider this evidence, of which too often a mere selection is quoted in favour of some preconceived view, must be a task for a separate section.

III. THE EVIDENCE FOR FAIR TYPES AMONG THE ANCIENT GREEKS

The adjective " xanthos ", applied by Homer to several of his heroes, indubitably means "fair-haired". The word is also used of bay or chestnut horses, and of fried fish, and the verb corresponding to it is used of roast meat " browning ".[2] As applied to human hair, it may therefore be presumed to mean golden, or auburn, or light-brown ; in any case fair as compared to the ordinary black of the Mediterranean. It does *not* mean fair in the sense of pale yellow. The Greek language contains no adjective to describe hair of that colour, so that Diodôros (V, 32) has to describe that of the children on the Belgic coast as " white "—πόλιος—like the hair of old men.

The uses of the word in the Epic, however, do not help us much. A few heroes are called " fair ", perhaps, as we have

---

[1] Plate II (c.), p. 61.
[2] Aristophanes, *Acharnians*, l. 1047 ; Homer, *Il.*, XI, 680 ; Antiphanes, *Philothêbaios*, frag. quoted by Athenaios, XIV, p. 622 f.

said, by way of contrast to a dark majority ; Achilleus,[1] Menelaos[2] and Meleagros[3] in the Iliad ; Polyneikes in the Thebaid[4] ; Odysseus and Rhadamanthys in the Odyssey,[5] of whom the last at any rate—a brother of Minôs, and bearer of a name with -nth- in its termination—ought, *a priori*, to have been a good black-haired specimen of the Mediterranean Race. One is in fact left doubting whether the use of the word implies the existence of any tradition at all, or whether the poet merely used it as he felt inclined. There is no reason whatever in Homer to suppose that fair colouring was specially admired or considered aristocratic ; for among the gods themselves, not only Poseidon is black-haired,[6] as befits the lord of the (Mediterranean) sea, but also Zeus,[7] who ought to be " Aryan " and " Nordic " if anyone ought.

Nor do the later epic poets give support to any " Nordic " theory " about the Greek gods and heroes. In the Homeric Hymns, Ganymede is fair,[8] Hades black-haired[9]—naturally— and Dêmêtêr, equally naturally, has fair hair[10]—the colour of corn. In Hesiod, Ariadne is fair[11]—but she is not an Achaian but Cretan and daughter of Minôs. Dionysos again, coming from Thrace, might be expected to be " Nordic ", but he, too, is dark.[12]

It is in the lyric poets for the first time that we find a tendency to make most of the gods fair. In Bakchylides Hera[13] and Athene[14] are *xanthai*,while Apollo is "golden-tressed[15]; as is Kypris in a papyrus fragment ascribed at a venture to Ibykos.[16] Some lesser divine beings are dark-tressed, however; Thetis,[17] the spirit " Victory ",[18] the nymph Thêbe,[19] the Muses.[20] So also, among mortals, Helen[21] and Brisêïs[22] are fair, Theseus red-headed[23]—like Neoptolemos, son of Achilleus, as his nick-name Pyrrhos shows. (Red hair is said to be often a result of the crossing of dark and fair strains.) Others, however,

[1] *Il.*, I, 197.
[2] *Il.*, passim.
[3] *Il.*, II, 642.
[4] In Athenaios, XI, p. 465 e.
[5] *Od.*, IV, 564, XIII, 399, 431.
[6] *Od.*, IX, 536, etc.
[7] *Il.*, I, 528.
[8] *Aphrodite*, l. 202.
[9] *Dêmêtêr*, l. 347.
[10] *Ibid.*, 302.
[11] *Theogony*, l. 947.
[12] *Hymn to Dionysos*, l. 5.

[13] *Epinikia*, X, 51.
[14] *Ibid.*, V, 92.
[15] *Ibid.*, IV, 2.
[16] *O.P.*, XV, 1790, l. 9.
[17] Bakch., *Paian*, VI, 83.
[18] *Epinikia*, V, 33.
[19] *Ibid.*, IX, 54.
[20] Pindar, *Ol.*, VI, 91.
[21] *O.P.*, XV, 1790, l. 5.
[22] Bakch., *Epinikia*, XII, 136.
[23] *Id.*, *Paian*, XIII, 51.

are dark, like Marpêssa[1] and the daughters of Proitos[2] in Bakchylides. It was in the time of these poets, too, that the practice arose of making the images of the gods, whenever funds permitted, of gold and ivory—gold for the hair, and ivory for the skin. In painted marble statues, the hair is usually a reddish-brown, but this is merely an accident; a head in the National Museum at Athens has gold-leaf *over* the red pigment.

Bakchylides also uses the word " xanthos " of Aglaos, an Athenian athlete for whom he wrote a victory-ode[3] and of a chorus of Spartan girls[4]; these uses are really of more interest as showing that in the poet's own time some individuals at Athens were fair, and probably a good many at Sparta—though the chorus of which he speaks belongs to the heroic age, not to his own day. So also, turning to a sober historian, we are told that fair hair was common among the Thebans[5]—a people who, like the Spartans, had come in with the conquest.

At Athens, fair hair, though probably uncommon, was so far held in honour that young princes and princesses in tragedy wore yellow wigs,[6] and ladies, whose hair was not by nature of the coveted colour, frequently kept cosmetics—" xanthismata " —to remedy the defect.[7]

Even in Hellenistic times, a fragment from a historian[8] assures us that throughout the Greek area, in out of the way places " where the race was purest ", fair or moderately fair types might be found :

" Where the Hellenic race has been preserved in its purity, the men are big, broader than the average, straight, strongly-built, white-skinned, and fair, having moderately fair hair, soft and pleasantly wavy. The face is square, the lips thin, the nose straight."

Lastly, as we have spoken of the gold and ivory statues of Greek gods and goddesses, a note will be relevant on the

---

[1] *Id., Paian,* XIX, 5.
[2] *Id., Epinikia,* X, 83.
[3] *Ibid.,* IX, 16.
[4] *Id., Paian,* XIX, 2.
[5] Paris Fragment, ascribed to Dikaiarchos of Messene ; = Frag. 59 in Müller's *F.H.G.,* Vol. II.
[6] Cf., e.g., Euripides, *Elektra,* l. 515.
[7] Euripides, *Danae* ; Frag. 324 (Dindorf).
[8] Pŏlĕmon, quoted in the *Physiognŏmika* (B.32) of Adamantios (fifth century A.D.).

origin and antecedents of the Greek temple in which those statues were housed.

Notoriously, the Greek temple is the translation into marble of the Homeric chieftain's " hall " ; and it is a type of house that is not native to the Aegean, but comes from Asia Minor or from the north ; by far its earliest appearance on the Aegean coasts is in the twenty-third century B.C., in the Second City at Troy. In origin it is a strongly built rectangular log-hut, intended to defy a severe climate. Whether it was invented in central Europe or, as some have recently suggested, in Asia Minor, matters little ; the two areas were in touch in very early times, via Troy and the natural highway of the Danube.[1] But two highly significant developments of the type are known from Germany, as early as the later Stone Age.

The first of these—found also in Thessaly, at Dimini and Sesklo, in association with the new Second Thessalian type of pottery from the Ukraine[2]—consists in the prolongation of the two long walls of the rectangular house beyond the front end-wall, in which is the door. This is an obvious prototype both of the Homeric house with its great porch in front, and of the simple form of temple called the temple *in antis*.

Second, and still more interesting, is a slightly later development, also—like the former—from the Rhineland. It is a log-hut that has been constructed with enormous eaves, to keep the walls dry ; after which an outer row of posts has been added to support the weight of the widely overhanging roof.[3] In less rainy and much sunnier lands the same arrangement was found to provide a pleasantly shady verandah or covered walk. Little more than a copy in stone of this arrangement is the typical Greek " peristyle " temple with its surrounding marble colonnade.

That is the evidence. Clearly it does not prove all that some devotees of the " Nordic theory " would like us to suppose. It does prove, however, that in historic times there were types in Greece which were by no means " Mediterranean " ; that these types existed even among the Athenians, who claimed

---

[1] Childe, in *Antiquity*, I, pp. 79-91.
[2] Wace and Thompson, *Prehistoric Thessaly*.
[3] Burkitt, *Our Early Ancestors*, pp. 88-90.

to be aboriginal ; and that among the aristocrats of Thebes and Sparta, whose ancestors had " come in with the Conqueror " they were actually common. Also, the fair beauty was more admired than the brunette ; golden hair was attributed to young heroes and heroines on the Athenian stage, and sought after by ladies ; and the gods were represented as golden-haired, ivory-skinned princes and princesses dwelling in the " great halls " of the Homeric age.

On the other hand, it is most important to note that Homer does not share this feeling, or he would not make his Zeus " dark-browed " and *distinguish* some few of his heroes by calling them fair. Whatever classical Greece may have felt, the Heroic Age clearly had no feeling that fair colouring was in any way either racially or socially significant.

This makes it clear that there had been no conquest of a dark by a fair race, at any rate before the Dorian movement. There had only been the introduction of a non-Mediterranean strain into the population of the Aegean lands, through the migration of individuals and small bands of adventurers.

To which of the common European racial types a modern ethnologist would have assigned the fairer individuals in ancient Greece, we have not sufficient evidence to say. All we can be sure of is that they were not the real flaxen-haired Nords of the Baltic, or the Greek language would not have remained without an adjective to describe this kind of hair. The Danubian introducers of the leaf-shaped sword may have been long-headed and comparatively fair quasi-Nordic folk ; but the Dorian wearers of the double-spiralled spectacle-fibula of Illyria ought, if one may judge by the modern inhabitants of the land from which they seem to have come, to be of the intermediate square-headed " Alpine " type. The slightly idealised but detailed description of the " pure Hellenic " type, given by Polĕmon—broad, brown-haired and " square-faced "— sounds quite Swiss. It would also suit well enough some of the solid young Dorian athletes sculptured by Polykleitos of Argos.

The comparatively fair strains will have been enabled to survive in Greece by the mountainous nature of the country ; mountains, probably because of their cooling effect on the climate of the surrounding country, seem often to permit the survival, or perhaps even the development, of fairer types in what would otherwise be a torrid climate, demanding a deeply pigmented humanity.   One may instance the blue or grey-eyed and red or brown-bearded men found among pure native stocks in modern Morocco, Afghanistan and Kashmir, and in ancient times in Thrace and, if the ancient Egyptian painters may be trusted, both in Libya and in the south Syrian hills.

CHAPTER III

Chronology

THE golden age, not perhaps of Minoan art, but certainly of Cretan power and prosperity—the periods Late Minoan I and II of Sir Arthur Evans' scheme of arrangement—can be confidently stated to have lasted from about 1580 to about 1400 B.C., on the evidence of finds of Minoan pottery—and paintings of the men who brought it—in Egypt, and of Egyptian objects, such as scarabs and faïence ware, in Crete and the Argolid.

There follow two centuries, the centuries of the supremacy of Mykenai in the Aegean, during which an occasional flash of light is shed on politics in the Aegean by Hittite or Egyptian references to the activities of possibly Achaian sea-rovers and raiders along the Levantine coasts. These centuries cover the period from the Sack of Knôssos to the destruction of the Hittite empire by invaders from the north and the attack on Egypt by Levantine and Asiatic migrants, perhaps driven on by these invaders. During these centuries the pottery painting of the period Late Minoan III is gradually stiffening and becoming more conventional and less life-like, moving, in fact, away from the free Minoan in the direction of the wholly conventional Geometric style ; and the pottery of the Philistines, who settled in Canaan, with their Aegean civilization, after the failure of the attack on Egypt, shows us how far the process had gone by the beginning of the twelfth century.

Next comes an age in which art in the Aegean is becoming more and more crude, while cremation, the fibula, the leaf-shaped sword, in fact the whole complex of " Homeric " features, gradually make their appearance. Finally this Sub-Mycenæan age is ended by the destruction by fire, apparently within a short period of years, of nearly all the Mycenæan settlements of the mainland of Greece, after which a purely Geometric pottery characterizes the settlements that reoccupy the land.

This catastrophe can be confidently identified with the " Dorian Invasion " of Greek tradition ; but to date it is difficult, for the once flourishing Egyptian trade had withered away long since, leaving us without means of establishing more than a relative chronology based on the archæological record. We can describe tendencies in art in their proper chronological order, but we cannot put a date to an event.

In these circumstances we have to fall back on an attempt to compute a date for the final débacle from the evidence of certain Greek genealogies. These pedigrees dating from early Hellenic times are, of course, much more likely to be genuine than those given by epic poets to personages of the Heroic Age.

We have five apparently trustworthy Greek pedigrees claiming to go back to the Heroic Age, and, though we may feel compelled to doubt their claims in one case to descent from a god and in the other four from famous legendary heroes, the number of generations in each pedigree may give us a clue to the date at which settled life began again after the turmoil of the migrations.

The five genealogies are :

First, that of Hekataios of Miletos, who claimed, to the amusement of Herodotos, to be sixteenth in descent from a god.[1] Hekataios was alive in 500 B.C., so the fifteen generations, after which human ancestry ceased, take us back to 1000— perhaps the approximate date of the Ionian capture of Miletos from the Karians.

Second, that of the great Athenian family of the Philaïdai,[2] in which line Miltiades the victor of Marathon was believed to be fifteenth descendant of Aias, son of Telamôn, the hero of the Trojan War. Taking 500 B.C., again, as date of Miltiades' " floruit ", we get 966 as the rough date of Philaios, founder and eponym of the clan. This, it may be conjectured, may be the generation that marks the end of the troublous times, when Attica was invaded by the Dorians and crowded with refugees from lands less successfully defended.

Third, Pyrrhos the famous king of Epeiros, who " flourished " about 320, claimed to be nineteenth from Pyrrhos-Neoptolemos, the son of Achilles[3] ; whence it appears that in this

---

[1] Hdt., II, 143.
[2] Pherekydes (in Marcellinus, *Life of Thukydides*).
[3] Pausanias, I, xi, 1.

4

north-westerly region, too, the kings could trace their line uninterrupted back to the middle of the tenth century—i.e., there had probably been no great shifting of peoples since then.

Fourth is the genealogy of Arkesilaos IV, King of Kyrene, for whom Pindar wrote his famous Fourth Pythian ode, about the year 466, and who claimed to be twenty-third in descent from Euphêmos the Minyan,[1] a member, according to Pindar, of the crew of the Argo. But here care is needed ; the last seven generations are Kings of Kyrene, and royal generations, being reckoned from eldest son to eldest son, are usually shorter than the average. The average reign of the Kings of Sparta in the fifth and fourth centuries works out at just over twenty-five and a half and just over twenty-five years respectively in the two royal houses. Allowing the kings of Kyrene the same amount, we get 640 as the approximate date of Battos I, the founder of the city ; so Euphêmos, his sixteenth ancestor, " flourished " about 1173, or 1140 if Pindar counted inclusively as he probably did. If Euphêmos is a real person, this may mean that Dorian Thêra, the old home of the colonists of Kyrene, had been undisturbed since the twelfth century ; this is quite possible ; the Odyssey[2] speaks of Dorians in Crete and the Iliad[3] of Herakleids in Rhodes and the neighbouring islands long before they were established in the Peloponnese.

Fifth and last is the genealogy of the Kings of Sparta, in the two royal houses.[4] The evidence of the two pedigrees agrees closely. Kleomenes and Dêmarâtos, who were kings in 500 B.C.—about the time when Greek chronology becomes really accurate—were the seventeenth and sixteenth kings in their respective lines ; so that if the reigns of the earlier kings, like those of the fifth and fourth centuries, averaged about twenty-five years in length, the end of the tenth century is indicated as the date of the foundation of the Spartan community. This agrees very fairly with the Attic, the Milesian and the Epeirote genealogies, and also with the date computed by the excavators from the British School at Athens for the earliest Dorian remains found ; they suggested 950 B.C. as a date which would give reasonable time for the deposits to accumulate.

[1] Pindar, *loc. cit.*
[2] *Od.*, XIX, 177.
[3] *Il.*, II, 653-60, 676-80.
[4] Hdt., VII, 204, VIII, 131.

Lists of early Dorian kings of Argos, Corinth and Messene are also extant, but are unsatisfactory ; the Argive list is variously given by different authorities, the Corinthian is suspicious, containing several probably fictitious names, and the Messenian is disproportionately short. Chadwick[1] prefers to base no conclusions on the insecure foundation of their authority.

Four of the five genealogies, then, agree in leading us to suppose that in the tenth century Greece was beginning to recover from the fever of the Migrations.

Further back we cannot penetrate. It seems likely, however, from what is known of the tendencies of " folk-memory," that the Dorian Invasion was a more long-drawn affair even than suggested by the extant late Greek accounts of the traditions of it, and that the invaders were not as uniform a body as the legend of the three brothers drawing lots for Argos, Sparta and Messene would imply. How long the period of confusion lasted, before the stillness of exhaustion supervened, there is no means of knowing : perhaps a century, perhaps more or less. It is a reasonable conjecture, but no more than that, that it was between 1050 and the end of the century that Tiryns, "Mykênai rich in gold", and the Lakedaimon of Menelaos were given to the flames.[2]

As to the date of the Trojan War, the uncertainty is even greater ; but tradition may be right in implying that it was the last great achievement of the pre-Dorian Greek confederacy, and that it was in the time of King Tisamenos, grandson of Agamemnon, that ruin came. If so, the Trojan War will come not long before the beginning of the eleventh century.

That the War was a very late Achaian exploit is suggested also by an archæological consideration. Nothing is more characteristic of the world depicted by Homer than its funeral-rites ; that is to say, cremation, followed by the placing of the ashes in an urn (sometimes) and the heaping over them of a barrow.[3] But cremated barrow-burials of the Homeric type

---

[1] *Heroic Age*, pp. 181 ff.

[2] Cf. Casson, in *B.S.A.*, XVI ; also his *Macedonia, Thrace and Illyria*, p. 156 and note, quoting Blegen's *Korakou*.

[3] *Il.*, XXIII, ll. 110-253 (Patroklos), cf. *Od.*, XXIV, 60 ff. (Achilles) : also the obsequies of Hektor, *Il.*, XXIV, 784 ff., Eëtion, *Il.*, VI, 415 ff., and Elpênor, *Od.*, XII, 11-15. Speakers sometimes use phrases more appropriate to simple inhumation, however (*Il.*, IV, 174, XXIII, 91)—perhaps anachronistically ?

have only been found dating from the early but full Iron Age.[1] This discrepancy between the remains and Homer's descriptions is best accounted for on the supposition, probable in other respects, too, that Homer, following contemporary songs, describes a single moment, as it were, in the decline of Aegean culture, and a moment of which no burials happen to have come to light. Just as in Homer the big Mycenæan shield occurs along with the round targe and body-armour of the age of the sea-raids, so what is known to us as an Iron-Age funeral rite is found, in a generation in which iron, though well-known, is not yet commonly used.

The fact that the Homeric Age is a time of transition appears even in its geography, in the Catalogue, that curious document which almost certainly describes a genuine state of affairs, since it flatters no later Greek political aspirations and therefore is unlikely to have been invented. In this document, over practically the whole of central Greece the political map is that familiar in historic times ; Attica, Boiotia, Phôkis, Lokris, Aitolia, have all taken shape ; though in the Peloponnese there is still no hint of the great changes soon to take place. Thucydides, who like all his contemporaries thinks of the Great Migrations as a shorter and swifter process than they probably were, is thoroughly puzzled at the appearance in the Homeric Catalogue of what he knew to be a " conquest people "[2] ; finally realizing that the solution is that between Othrys and the Isthmus the infiltration of the new peoples was already taking place.

It cannot be too strongly emphasized that the traditional date of the Trojan War, 1194-84, adopted by Eratosthenes and more or less tentatively accepted in so many modern books, is absolutely worthless. A moment's examination of the Spartan genealogies, for which Eratosthenes had a great respect, shows that a greatly exaggerated estimate of the average length of a generation has been adopted ; an estimate apparently of forty years. Leônidas and Lâtychidas, kings in 480, are fifteenth from Eurysthenes and Prokles, the first of the two lines ; but the year of the conquest is given as 1104— allowing actually more than forty years per generation. The

[1] Childe's *Aryans*, p. 52.
[2] Thk., I, 12.

Trojan War, two generations earlier, is said to end in 1184. It is extraordinary that a great scientist should have been content with this estimate.[1]

There is in short no good evidence for fixing the date of the fall of Troy ; within wide limits, we must simply guess. We must choose, it is true, a period at which the war fits in with what we know of the history of the Hittites, for example; but the trouble is that it fits in almost anywhere ; it would go very well into the fourteenth or the thirteenth century, for instance. It is only archæology, and the belief that the war comes late in the Achaian period, that suggests a later date—somewhere round about 1100.

The attempt has been made to find confirmation for Eratosthenes' date, by identifying the battle of the assembled Phrygians against the Amazons, on the banks of the Sangarios, when King Priam was young,[2] with the battle by which in about 1200 B.C. the destroyers of the Hittite empire must have forced their way into the interior of the peninsula. But the attempt is foredoomed. There is much to be said for the identification in some contexts at least, of Homer's " Amazons " with the Hittites[3] ; but the passage in Iliad III certainly does not refer to a war of conquest by the Phrygians over the older races. Priam speaks of the time " when the Amazons *came* " ; and as he was not a modern politician laying the blame of aggression on the enemy, it is clear that the Phrygians and their allies were already firmly established on the plateau, and now engaged in a war of defence.

A reference to the fall of the Hittite empire does come, if anywhere in Greek story, in the account of how Pelops son of Tantalos, a Phrygian[4] or Paphlagonian[5] or Eneteian[6]—a member, that is, of some Asiatic race of which in historic times

---

[1] On this Prof. Myres comments : " The great scientist knew that Spartans did not marry till they were about forty, and so allowed more than the thirty year average." To account for the shorter reigns of the fifth-fourth century kings, he suggests that after the case of Anaxandridas in the sixth century, who kept the city waiting for some years in anxiety as to whether he was going to have a son at all, the kings may have married much earlier, whereas formerly they may have married late and so had longer reigns on the average. This may be true.

[2] *Il.*, III, 184 ff.

[3] See below, p. 129.

[4] Paus., II, 22. 4, V, 13. 4.

[5] Apoll. Rhod., II, 358, and Σ there and on l. 790.

[6] *Ibid.*

the very name had perished—was driven from his father's kingdom by Ilos the son of Trôs[1] : for the Fall of the Hittite power certainly was caused by an invasion of the central plateau of Asia Minor by tribes already established in the Troad. Pelops then takes refuge in Greece ; and if the genealogy Pelops—Atreus—Agamemnon is to be trusted, Agamemnon will have besieged Troy late in the twelfth century—which is the earliest date archæologically possible.

Eratosthenes' inflated estimate of the length of an average reign or generation has also, by the way, affected the late Greek chronologists' computations of dates early in the historic period. There are only two points at which the traditional chronology can be tested, but both tests give the same result.

First and most valuable of our opportunities for testing the traditional system is that offered by Assur-bani-pal's reference to the death of Gugu of Luddi, who is certainly the Gyges of Lydia, of Herodotos and other Greek historians.

Herodotos gives definite figures implying that Gyges fell in battle in 678 B.C. ; but the Assyrian records make it certain that it was really in 652 at the earliest, with a possible margin of error of eight years, or down to 644.

But this alteration of the date of Gyges necessitates the scaling-down of many other early Greek dates too ; that of Archilochos of Paros, in whose iambics Gyges is named ; and that of Kallînos of Ephesos, whose elegiacs were largely concerned with that inroad of Kimmerian barbarians in which Gyges perished ; and that of the colonization of Thasos, in which Archilochos took part ; and of the Milesians' occupation of Abydos on the Hellespont, which site Gyges ceded to them.

The other chronological test relies on less direct but scarcely less satisfactory evidence. Early Greek, like Minoan, painted vases can be dated by means of synchronisms with Egyptian and Asiatic remains, and Signor Orsi considers it proved that the earliest Greek pottery found among the remains of the Sicilian colonies dates from 700 B.C. at the earliest[2] ; not 735, as Thucydides would give us to expect.

Reckoning back from 500 B.C., the age of the earliest Greek prose-writers and so of the beginning of reliable chronology,

---

[1] D.S., IV, 76.
[2] *Notizie degli scavi*, 1895, pp. 109 ff.   Léon Homo (*Italie Primitive*, p. 79) and H. R. Hall (*Oldest Civilisation of Greece*, pp. 254-5) agree with him.

we find that a date, calculated by the Greeks as 178 years earlier, has to be reduced by at least twenty-six years, and a date, reckoned by them as 235 years earlier than the fixed point, by at least thirty-five years. In each case the reduction is one of about 15 per cent.—a minimum reduction be it noted —or very nearly that which would result from adopting the figure of thirty three and one-third years as the conventional average for a generation, in place of the over-estimate of forty years.

Herodotos, and doubtless other Greeks too, did at least in some cases reckon, as we do, three generations to a century, but it seems clear from their chronological errors that the forty-year estimate was used in computing many of the dates which they commonly accepted.

In short, it is almost certain that *all the dates before 500* B.C. *given by Greek historians should be reduced to* $\frac{33\frac{1}{3}}{40}$ *(=five-sixths) of their traditional distance from* 500 B.C. The date of the beginning of the Spartan monarchy has to be much more drastically scaled down, however, since in this case, for each forty years, we have to substitute not the third of a century of an average generation, but the quarter-century of an average reign.

As to the reckoning of Greek dates in terms of Olympiads, it is perhaps worth while to draw attention—as Mahaffy did long ago—to the information given us by Plutarch, that the great sophist Hippias of Elis, who lived towards the end of the fifth century, compiled the list of Olympic victors, on no very secure evidence.[1] Dates thus reckoned are therefore no more securely fixed than those which were admittedly calculated by generations.

---

[1] *Life of Numa*, I. Cf. however the discussion of the matter by Wade-Gery in *C.A.H.*, III, pp. 762-4.

CHAPTER IV

KASTOR OF RHODES ON PRE-PHŒNICIAN SEA-POWERS

THE chronologist Eusebios quotes from Diodôros of Sicily a list of " those who ruled the sea, from the fall of Troy to Xerxes' crossing into Europe ". Diodôros must have given the list somewhere in the lost " second volume " (books VI to X) of his forty-book History of the World ; these books covered precisely the epoch to which the List refers. He presumably got his information from the History of Sea-Power of his contemporary, Kastor of Rhodes, the only Greek study of the subject of which we know. The probability is strengthened by the fact that our list concerns itself with Levantine waters only, ignoring the west and such powers as Corinth, Korkyra, Carthage ; for Kastor was an orientalist who also (as Suidas tells us) wrote a History of Babylon.

What Kastor's sources may have been we can, naturally, only guess ; but some of the entries in the list are so surprising as to make it clear that it is not merely an ordinary Hellenistic repetition of earlier Greek traditions, with embroidery, and with the gaps filled in *a priori*. W. Aly has indeed argued[1] that this is just what it is—an artificial construction based on Herodotos, and especially on his catalogues of Greek and Barbarian fleets during the Persian Wars. But it is difficult to collect from the Father of History any justification for the list's statements that Phrygians, Lydians and Thracians had ruled the sea in early times ; while on the contrary a list based entirely on Herodotos would surely mention the three western naval powers named above, and also Chios, which, in addition to a great overseas trade, possessed at one time the most powerful war-navy in Ionia,[2] as Herodotos expressly tells us. This omission alone would make Aly's theory unlikely. Detailed study of that part of the list which deals with historic times (the eighth to the fifth century) further brings to light the fact that the best parallels to the information given by our

---

[1] In *Rheinisches Museum*, LXVI (1911).
[2] Hdt., II, 178, VI, 20.

document are frequently to be found in writers other than Herodotos. In short, Aly's theory that the list is worth nothing, though very cleverly worked out in detail, seems to be both gratuitous and improbable.

Of the quality of Kastor's work we can of course form no conception ; but the singularly inept character of our document, in which one power is always first and "the rest nowhere", and the replacement of one power by another never a gradual process but always a single event, is to be laid to the charge of Diodôros or Eusebios—whichever of them it was who tore from its context this mere date-chart, and gave it to the world entirely without commentary.

We are here concerned only with the six powers alleged in the early part of the list to have ruled the sea before the Phœnicians. The ten entries, nearly all Hellenic, which carry on the tale down to Xerxes' invasion of Greece, fall outside our period and, with a single emendation at a point where the list is known to be mutilated, can be accepted without difficulty.[1] Above this point the information given by the list is as follows :

From the fall of Troy (1172 B.C., according to Eusebios) :

1. The Lydians or Maiŏnians ruled the sea for 92 years (1172-1080)
2. „ Pelasgians „ „ 85 „ (1080-995)
3. „ Thracians „ „ 79 „ (995-916)
4. „ Phrygians „ „ 25 „ (916-891)
5. „ Rhodians ᵢ „ „ 23 „ (891-868)
6. „ Cyprians „ „ 33 „ (868-835)
7. „ Phœnicians „ „ 45 „ (835-790)

Working backwards from the last entry, we naturally find no difficulty in accepting the tradition of a Phœnician sea-power at the end of the ninth century. Indeed, the only surprise is that this "thalassocracy" lasts no longer than it does. From the way in which Greek writers from Homer onwards represent Phœnicians as almost monopolizing Aegean trade before the rise of Miletos, one might expect their command of the sea to cover the whole of the dark age from the tenth century to the eighth.

Of the next power named—that of Cyprus—we know nothing relevant. Of the next, the Rhodians, one is not surprised to hear nautical prowess predicated at any time.

---

[1] I have discussed the later portion of the list in *J.H.S.*, XLVII.

Strabo gives some details, probably from Kastor's account, of just such a " thalassocracy ", when Rhodian mariners sailed far afield " many years before the foundation of the Olympic Games ".[1]   But the idea of a Phrygian sea-power is astonishing, and Greek literature contains no other allusion to any such thing.

The three earliest entries, partly perhaps because we have a few other allusions to them, are still more puzzling.

One does not instinctively think of the Thracians as a nautical people, but there are various tales of their raiding by sea in early times, such as the story of Eumolpos, who invaded Attica from the sea side and helped the men of Eleusis against Erechtheus, king of Athens[2] ; or of Butes, son of the North Wind, whose piratical squadron raided Euboia and the coast of Thessaly, and whose descendants occupied Naxos for two hundred years " before the Karians held it ".[3]   And Samothrace is already " the Thracian Samos " in the Iliad.[4]

But a difficulty arises ; all these raids are explicitly dated before the Trojan War ; for the Karian occupation of the Cyclades comes traditionally very soon after the war, and the Thracians had then already abandoned Naxos, owing to drought.

And so it is with the next entry.

About the Pelasgoi the air was already so thick with theories in ancient times that it is very difficult to make any statement about them that is not open to question.   Originally they seem to have been a pre-Hellenic tribe (if Herodotos is right in his account of their language as spoken in his day) whose home was in the northern regions of Greece.   Here was the only " Pelasgian Land ", Pelasgiôtis, known to history ; here was the Pelasgian Argos[5] ; and not so very far away was the sacred place of the " Pelasgian Zeus " of Dôdôna to whom Achilles prayed.[6]   In these regions they must have been neighbours of the first Achaians, who, by the time when the Catalogue of Ships in Iliad II was drawn up, appear to have taken complete possession both of lands, town, and shrine.   Nothing of the Pelasgoi remains in Homer's Greece except their name, so far as our information goes ; the Pelasgoi themselves seem to have

[1] Str., XIV, 654.
[2] Thk., II, 15 ; Str., VII, 321.
[3] D.S., V, 50.
[4] Il., XIII, 12, 13.
[5] Il., II, 681.
[6] Il., XVI, 233.

been pushed by gradual encroachments into the sea. But they were not extinct; they had taken to the sea under pressure of necessity, as any vigorous and virile race will, and Homer speaks of colonies of them in Crete[1] and (apparently) in the Troad,[2] in the latter of which regions they take their opportunity of striking a blow for King Priam against their old enemies the Achaioi. Fifth century historians knew of them also near Kyzikos,[3] in Lemnos,[4] Imbros,[5] and Samothrace,[6] in the peninsula of Chalkidike,[7] and between the Strymon and the Axios rivers.[8] Such a distribution of the scattered fragments of their nation is in itself sufficient testimony to their activity by sea.

There are also stories of Pelasgoi in Attica[9] and in Boiotia,[10] the former of which is told with much circumstance by Herodotos and was believed by Thucydides; but it contains some suspicious features and may be a myth. It should be remembered that both these writers are deeply influenced by the "Pelasgian Theory" which can be traced back as far as the Hesiodic poets, and which equated Pelasgoi with "pre-Hellenic people" in general. Accordingly Hesiod or a poet of his school makes their eponym Pelasgos a hero of the aboriginal people of primitive Arkadia.[11] It was a very natural theory to adopt with reference to a people who had anticipated the Greeks in so many regions; but it was a most fruitful source of misconceptions.[12]

A Pelasgian "thalassocracy" in the Dark Age after the Trojan War is not impossible; but it would fall more naturally at an earlier date after they had taken to the sea and set out to conquer new homes, but before their nation was broken into fragments.

So we come to the "Lydian or Maiŏnian" entry at the beginning of the list.

[1] Od., XIX, 177.
[2] Il., II, 840 ff.
[3] Hdt., I, 57.
[4] Hdt., IV, 145, VI, 137; cf. Della Seta's excavations there, J.H.S., XLVII, p. 259.
[5] Hdt., V, 26.
[6] Hdt., V, 51.
[7] Thk., IV, 109.
[8] Hdt., I, 57.
[9] Hdt., IV, 145; Thk., l.c.
[10] Str., VII, 321.
[11] See Strabo, VII, p. 327.
[12] On the whole subject, cf. Myres, in J.H.S., XXVII.

If this is indeed to be placed immediately after the Trojan War, it must be clearly identified with that development of sea-power on the Asian Coast which other Greek historians preferred to call Karian.[1] This thalassocracy must in any case have been short-lived, since it was brought to an end by the great outpouring of people from Greece which founded Aiŏlis and Ionia. But if we are not to suppose that the Karian and Maionian sea-powers are alternative versions of the same thing, then the only Greek tradition of " Lydian "[2] sea-power with which we are left are those concerning the migration of the Etruscans.

The Tyrrhênoi are mentioned within the Aegean in historic times in the same two districts as the Pelasgoi, on the coast of Western Thrace. Herodotos speaks of "the Tyrrhenes who dwell above Krêstôn beyond the Pelasgians " ; and Thucydides goes so far as to identify the Tyrrhenoi of Chalkidike with "those Pelasgians who at one period held Lemnos and Athens."[3] Either these fragments of the two nations were in a fair way to become fused, or the name Pelasgoi was being loosely applied by the Greeks, in accordance with their " Pelasgian theory ", to tribes who would have called themselves Tyrrhenes. (One may compare the use of the term " Indians " in America.) Hellanikos and Sophokles go so far as to identify the two peoples.[4]

The first appearance of the Tyrrhenian name in Greek literature is in the post-Homeric epic poets, who know them as pirates in the Aegean and, vaguely, as an important people among the " isles of the west ".[5] Their origin, according to Herodotos, was Asiatic ; the eponyms Lydos and Tyrsênos were said to be brothers, sons of Atys, the Anatolian god.[6] Hellanikos however, having identified the Etruscans of his own day with the descendants of the ancient Pelasgoi, appears to have derived them, probably on *a priori* grounds, from Thessaly[7] ; and Xanthos, the fifth century native Lydian

---

[1] Thk., I, 8 ; D.S., V, 84.
[2] Strictly speaking the use of the Lydian name at so early a date is an anachronism. Cf. the Homeric Catalogue and Strabo's comments on it (XII, 572, XIV, 678). " Maionian " is more accurate.
[3] Hdt., I, 57 ; Thk., IV, 109.
[4] Hellanikos, quoted by Dionysios of Halikarnassos, I, 28.
[5] Homeric *Hymn to Dionysos*, l, 8 ; Hesiod, *Theogony*, l. 1016.
[6] Hdt., I, 94.
[7] Dion. Hal., I, 18 (probably from Hellanikos).

PLATE II

(b)

(a)

Stele of Autiles Feluskes; from Vetulonia,
c. 650 B.C.

(c)

(b) "Hoplite" and (c) warrior with leaf-shaped sword, from Sinjerli, North Syria, c. 1000 B.C.

HITTITE AND ETRUSCAN WARRIORS

[face p. 60

historian, never mentioned Tyrrhenians or their emigration to Italy at all. Herodotos' "Tyrsênos son of Atys" is, according to Xanthos, a corruption of the quite different name Torrhêbos.[1]

Archæology, however, appears to give some support to Herodotos' account of the matter.[2] Numerous resemblances have been traced between Asian art and the earliest Etruscan, even in such important matters as dress, weapons and armour. A type of heavy-armed pikeman, with horse-hair-crested helmet and round shield, who could pass either as an Etruscan warrior or an early Greek hoplite, makes his first appearance in Hittite sculptures[3] of the Dark Age, from North Syria. The Etruscan tracing of descent through the mother, one may here note, is most easily paralleled from Lykia,[4] and their method of taking omens from the entrails of sacrificed beasts was learnt from Babylonia by the Hittites.[5] Even the Etruscan physical type[6] and many of their names[7] are redolent of Asia Minor.

The presence of Etruscans on Lemnos at some very early period is now attested by archæological evidence that is practically conclusive ; not only by the sculptured tombstone, long well-known, the epitaph on which is in a language " at least closely akin " to Etruscan,[8] but also by the weapons and pottery from an extensive cemetery excavated by Della Seta on the island, and datable, by the character of the jewelry found, to the Geometric period.[9]

The date of the migration to Italy is given by Herodotos as before 1220 B.C. His chronology is worth little or nothing, but it is at least clear that he conceives the movement as taking place before the Trojan War, as Hellanikos certainly did. But the archæological evidence seems to indicate

---

[1] Dion. Hal., I, 28.
[2] For a fuller discussion of this, with full references to authorities, cf. Fell *Etruria and Rome*, Part I, 1 ; especially p. 7 and n. 4, pp. 10-12.
[3] Cf. Plate II.
[4] Hdt., I, 173.
[5] Models of sheep's livers, for the use of students of hepatoscopy, have been found in Etruria and Sumer, and nowhere else except at the Hittite capital of Boghaz Keui.
[6] Cf. Weber, *Hethitische Kunst*, Plates 5, 24-27, 41, with Della Seta's *Italia Antica*, Plates 208, 236-8, 240 ; Peake, *Bronze Age*, Plate 3.
[7] Fell, pp. 12-13, 46-47 and n., and authorities cited.
[8] Conway, *C.A.H.*, IV, p. 408.
[9] *J.H.S.*, XLVII, p. 259.

(according to Dr. Randall MacIver's great work, " Villanovans and Early Etruscans ") that the characteristic Etruscan civilization of Italy did not appear before the second half of the ninth century.

There is also the serious difficulty of the silence of Xanthos' Lydian History as to this migration, which must be met.

All the claims of this collection of evidence seem to be satisfied by the following theory.

The Tyrsenoi or Etrusci, the Turski of some Italian dialects, (the latter part of both names being merely ethnic termination) were a tribe of Asia Minor probably inhabiting the district known to the Old Testament as Tiras[1] and to the Hittites as Taruisa.[2] They took to the sea probably, as Herodotos says, under pressure of famine—the famine in Asia Minor which Pharaoh Merneptah helped to relieve[3]—and are mentioned by that Pharaoh, under the form T'r'sh', among the predatory sea-farers, " fighting to fill their bellies daily ", whose attack on Egypt he so bloodily repulsed. Thereafter they remained in an unsettled condition for some centuries, more and more of them gradually leaving the Asian coast, to occupy—after the time of the Iliad, which does not name them—Lemnos and other Aegean islands, where they either fused with Pelasgoi or were confused with them by the Greeks. It is highly probable that some of the " Karians " whose graves Thucydides saw opened in the Cyclades and identified by the Asiatic style of their weapons and armour,[4] were really Tyrrhenes. Finally they migrated in a body to Italy, finding their quarters in the Aegean straitened by the advance of the Greeks. Xanthos does not mention their final movement to the west, because the tribe that migrated had passed out of Lydian history centuries earlier. It is worth noting that he does mention a Lydian expedition that captured Askalon[5]—a clear reference to that migration of peoples from Asia Minor to the borders of Egypt which brought the Philistines into the land of Canaan.

---

[1] *Genesis*, x, 2.
[2] Förrer's identification of this with the city of Troy is vitiated by the fact that there was no such place. The city is invariably called Ilios by Homer. Troia, whether or not it = " Taroisa," is merely the country round.
[3] See Breasted, in *C.A.H.*, II, 165.
[4] Thk., I, 8.
[5] Athenaios, VIII, 346 : Stephanos of Byzantion, s.v. Ἀσκάλων.

To return to the Thalassocracy List; it seems most likely, on the whole, that it is to some tradition of the beginning of this movement overseas from Lydia that Kastor, or his authority, refers when he speaks of Maionian sea-power; but if so, then, once again, the movement ought to be placed before, not after, the Fall of Troy. It is true that after the Trojan War there were still Tyrrhenians in the Aegean, as their introduction into the Hymn to Dionysos shows; but they had long ceased to be in any sense "Lydians and Maionians."

Thracians, Phrygians and Lydians ruling the sea; Phœnicians not powerful until the ninth century; Pelasgoi still so flourishing after the Trojan War; what, one wonders, can Kastor's authorities have been, that they give us a picture of early post-Minoan sea-power so unlike that suggested by other Greek historians? Can he perhaps have been using a document that was not Greek at all?

It is by no means unlikely. Kastor was an Orientalist; and each entry in the List falls naturally into line with our other evidence, Greek and Oriental, if we suppose that he found his Phœnician and earlier entries among the Chronicles of the Kings of Tyre and Sidon—which an Oriental scholar of the Hellenistic Age, writing on the history of sea-power, could hardly fail to consult. That these Chronicles were still extant in Roman times, we know; as also that they were looked after by keepers of the Archives appointed by the Tyrian municipality,[1] that they were available for inspection by research students, and were praised by Josephus for their " exactness ",[2] a quality that one might expect from a Phœnician writer. There was also a Greek summary of them by a certain Menandros of Ephesos,[3] who in his histories of barbarian monarchies made a point of using the " original sources ".

In this case it inevitably follows that the List will start not after the fall of Troy, an event which is not likely to have bulked large in Canaanite eyes, but after the fall of Knôssos— a really epoch-making event, since it involved the collapse of the Minoan thalassocracy, and an event whose results are at once seen in the development of raids by piratical Lykians on

---

[1] Josephus, *History of the Jews*, VIII, 2, 7.
[2] Id., *Against Apion*, I, 17, 20.
[3] Id., *History*, VIII, 5, 3; *Against Apion*, ib.

the coast towns of the Levant.[1]   Previously, Minoan sea-power
seems to have kept them under control. The Age of the
Sea-Raids, which follows, was of profound importance in
Phœnician history, since it ultimately (as we shall see) brought
a vigorous sea-faring population to the Syrian coast, from
whom the Canaanites of the coast towns—" Chnâ " as the
Phœnicians called themselves[2]—of old a mercantile but not,
it seems, a sea-going stock, presently learned to sail a-trafficking
on their own account.[3]

In the early part of the Thalassocracy List I would therefore
propose to see a list of sea-powers compiled by a Phœnician
chronicler, after the manner of the lists of Gentile nations,
Dukes of Edom, and the like, familiar to us from the chronicles
of the Phœnicians' Israelite neighbours and cousins. It covers
the whole age of the sea-raids, in which the Phœnicia of historic
times took shape, and ends with the great age of over-seas
activity of the Canaanites themselves. Kastor took up the
document and carried it on, in his History of Sea-Power,
throughout Hellenic times, down, probably, to his own age,
which was also that of Pompey the Great and his suppression
of piracy. That our extract ends in 480 is, of course, due to
Eusebios' immediate authority being the lost " Volume II "
of Diodôros.

In editing the early part of the list, however, Kastor got into
difficulties in the attempt to square the Greek legends with
his Oriental knowledge. Especially, since, according to Greek
tradition, Minôs lived about the year 1250, and the sea was
clearly commanded in the generations immediately following
his death by Homer's Achaioi, he was unable to start the
list until the year 1184 on Eratosthenes' scheme. This involved
such difficulties as the dating of the Pelasgian and Thracian
power after the Trojan War instead of before it, and also gave
the Phœnicians a bare half-century, only, of sea-power, before
their decline began in the eighth century. With regard to a
sea-power on the Lydian coast, the evidence about Karians
and Tyrrhenians was copious and vague enough to make his
task easier.

[1] *Tell-el-Amarna Letters*, no. 28 (ed. Winckler).
[2] Hekataios of Miletos, frag. 254 in *F.H.G.*, I ; cf. Philôn of Byblos in
F.H.G., III, p. 569.
[3] Woolley, " La Phénicie et les Peuples Égéens " in *Syria*, 1921. Cf. Hall,
in *Anatolian Studies presented to Sir W. M. Ramsay*.

Now if we hypothetically start the list in 1400 B.C., we get the following results :

Thalassocracy-List. " *Rulers* " *of the Sea :*	*Relevant events known from other sources :*
1400-1308. Maionians (i.e., some power based on the coast of Asia Minor).	Appearance in the Levant of Lykian pirates and " Shardana " mercenary soldiers (Tell-el-Amarna Tablets). Extension of Hittite suzerainty to the Aegean.[1]
1308-1223. Pelasgoi (i.e., some tribe from the European side of the Aegean).	Appearance of *Achaians* (if Dr. Förrer's identifications are right) on the coasts of the Hittite Empire. See below, pp. 117-19, 124-30.
1223-1144. Thracians (i.e., northern races now taking to the sea in large numbers).	Sea-raiders support Libyan attack on Egypt about 1221. Northern hordes destroy Hittite Empire about 1200. Great attack on Egypt by Philistines and other fugitive Aegean and Asiatic tribes about 1194. " Sub-Mycenæan " pottery in Philistia.
1144-1119. Phrygians (same people as above, but now settled mainly in Asia).	? Establishment of the Thraco-Asiatic alliance that appears from Homer's Catalogue of the Trojan Allies.
1119-1096. Rhodes (i.e., Achaians : Rhodes, from a Phœnician point of view, their best-known stronghold).	Achaians break up the Trojan alliance by capture of Ilios, about 1120. " Achaian period " in archæology; fibulæ, occasional cremation, leaf-shaped swords : decay of " Mycenæan " style in vase-painting.

[1] On which cf. Hall, " Mursil and Myrsilos," in *J.H.S.*, XXIX.

1096-1065. Cyprus (same people, now pushing their outposts further east).
1065 and throughout the next three centuries : Phœnicians.

About 1050 B.C. Fall of Achaian power. Cessation of trade and general breakdown of communications in Greece, shown by the numerous local styles of Geometric vase-painting. Foundation of Gades and Utica by Phœnicians, eleventh century ; Carthage, about 800.

In short, the list agrees astonishingly well with the rest of the evidence.

This whole scheme is obviously far too hypothetical to be used as evidence in support of any part of our narrative. It will be, however, permissible to refer to it from time to time, but rather by way of adducing the other evidence in support of the theory.

PART TWO

NARRATIVE

οὕτω καὶ τῶν πρόσθεν ἐπευθόμεθα κλέα ἀνδρῶν ἡρώων . . . .

—*Iliad*, **IX**, 524-5.

" Lo, we have heard of old the glory of the kings of the Spear-Danes, how the chieftains wrought mighty deeds. . . ."

—*Beowulf*, **I**, 1.

PART TWO

CHAPTER I

The Rise of Aegean Civilization

Κρήτη τις γαῖ᾽ ἐστι, μέσῳ ἐνὶ οἴνοπι πόντῳ,
καλὴ καὶ πίειρα, περίρρυτος· ἐν δ᾽ ἄνθρωποι
πολλοί, ἀπειρέσιοι, καὶ ἐννήκοντα πόληες·

.   .   .   .

τῇσι δ᾽ ἐνὶ Κνωσός, μεγάλη πόλις· ἔνθα τε Μίνως
ἐννέωρος βασίλευε, Διὸς μεγάλου ὀαριστής.

—*Odyssey*, XIX, 172-4, 178-9.

IN the later years of the fifteenth century B.C., while
Amenhotep the Magnificent reigned in Egyptian Thebes
and ruled also the Amorite country as far as the river
Euphrates ; when Minôs ruled in Knôssos and his fleets were
unrivalled in all the waters of the Great Sea, and before King
Subbiluliuma had made of his Hittites one of the imperial
powers of the world, there dwelt a tribe in Thessaly who were
called the Achaioi. It was a name destined to be famous in
later years, though not so famous as that of one of their
sub-tribes, the Hellenes.

They were a race of mixed descent—the native stock of the
land crossed with an invading people, who had introduced
Indo-European speech in the later centuries of the third
millennium, and whose still remoter ancestors had brought it
into the Balkan peninsula from the steppe and park-land
of its origin. The Achaioi of Thessaly were those of the
Aryan-speaking folk who had remained behind, when others
passed on southward, in the twentieth and nineteenth

69

centuries, to colonize Central and to conquer Southern Greece, and in both to introduce their characteristic pottery, which we call "Minyan", and their language, which we call Greek.

South beyond Othrys and among the marble islands over the sea, momentous events were taking place as the second millennium progressed. Cities and kingdoms were being founded, while a brilliant civilization rose slowly to its height. But of this the Achaioi knew nothing except by hearsay. Within their ring of mountains, they were indeed learning to use tools and weapons of bronze, but in most respects they remained a backward folk, probably despised as such by their kinsmen further south. The sea was still an unknown element to them, and their true landsman's epithet for it, ἀτρύγετος, waste, "uncultivable", probably sums up their feelings about it in these early days. On the fertile grassland of their home they continued to live very much the life of their pastoral and patriarchal ancestors, north of the Black Sea, nearly two thousand years before. Centuries later, amid the brief and stormy splendours of their "heroic" and imperial time, they looked back as to a Golden Age of peace and innocence to the old uncivilized inland life ; and their chiefs still delighted to count "Tamer of Horses ", "Shepherd of the People ", among their titles of praise.

They were probably on the whole a taller and fairer people than the true Mediterraneans of the coasts and islands, and, unlike these latter, great eaters of meat. Their government was aristocratic ; they were ruled by patriarchal petty kings, dwelling in big log-" halls " with a central hearth, round which straggled untidily the chieftain's barns and byres and stables, along with the houses of his retainers and the cabins of his thralls. All or most of these nobles called themselves Aiŏlidai—a race destined to occupy many a throne in the southland in days to come ; either claiming descent from a mythical common ancestor Aiolos, "the Glorious ", or else using the word as yet as a simple adjective, "Children of the Splendid Ones". This, too, was a name with a great future before it, for in historic times it is found to have spread from the nobles to whom Homer applies it to the peoples over whom they ruled. Greek writers use it, very loosely, as an ethnological term, to indicate all those numerous

Greek tribes and dialects which are not obviously Doric or Ionic.

By the fifteenth century the Achaioi would seem to have been increasing in numbers so as to be in a fair way to find the land " unable to bear them ". They were pressing hard upon the neighbouring Pelasgoi of Pelasgic Argos and the Spercheios region, and were ready themselves ere long to play a catastrophic part in the further history of the Aegean world.

It was a very civilized and splendid world.

For unknown thousands of years the dark Mediterranean folk of the Cyclades and Crete had been slowly building up their civilization. For nearly two thousand, metal had been known, introduced about 3400 B.C., apparently from Asia, by one of the rare immigrations of foreigners, a movement which betrays itself by the appearance of broad-skulled folk among the natives of the island.

This immigration was an event of the first importance in Cretan history, for it was probably responsible for the fact that throughout the Bronze Age southern Anatolia and the South Aegean had a common religion and spoke dialects of a common non-Aryan language.

This language was that known to us only through the numerous Greek words which have no Aryan etymology, and which may be presumed to have been picked up by the introducers of Aryan speech from the natives of the land. Plant-names are naturally a numerous class among these ; so, too, are terms denoting civilized inventions or amenities. Among these we notice many which have the sounds -nth- and -ss- in their terminations—two sounds which reappear in a very large number of old Aegean place-names. Knôssos, Larissa (better, Larîsa), Parnassos, Ilissos, are a few well-known examples ; Corinth, Tiryns (in its oblique cases, Tiryntha, etc.), Mount Kynthos, whence the goddess Artemis' title " Cynthia ". In Asia Minor appear corresponding groups of names in -ssos, -sa, and -nda : Sagalassos, Halikarnassos, Labraunda, Alabanda. Among common nouns, thalassa, the sea, and asaminthos, a bath, are two noteworthy examples ; and actually in modern English we have upwards of a dozen of these old Aegean words, taken over by us in our turn from

Greek. Hyacinth, narcissus, acanthus, cypress ; colossus, plinth, labyrinth ; mint, absinthe, turpentine (via Latin, from terebinthos) ; hymn, pæan, dithyramb ; abyss (which in Greek originally meant the depths of the sea) ; these and a few more remain to bear witness of our debt, through the Greeks, to the old Aegean civilization.

The religion in question was the worship of the Great Mother and her Son ; the primitive and unchanging religion of the Mediterranean world, except in so far as Aryan Greek polytheism or the masculine monotheism of the Jew and the Arab may locally and for a season drive it underground. In Crete as in Anatolia, during the Bronze Age, we find the Great Mother depicted as attended by doves, or by lions—a striking detail, this last, for there seem to have been no lions in Crete. The Double Axe itself, the sacred symbol that confronts us everywhere in Minoan art, appears also in Asia. One of the very names of the Goddess, in her stronghold in Lydia —Kўbĕle—is derived from a word, " kybêlis ", meaning an axe.

By the twentieth century Aegean civilization was already high. The distribution of implements and fragments of the obsidian of Mêlos would alone testify to the existence of trade between almost all parts of the Aegean area ; and beyond that area their indirect trade-connections already ramified far and wide. The mainland of Greece, and even Crete, was already receiving amber—that of the Baltic, not the characteristic amber of Sicily ; and Middle Minoan objects found in Bohemia serve to mark the route. They also serve to suggest that Bohemia was the quarter whence the Aegean bronze-founders got their tin. Troy had long been trading with peoples far up the Danube, as well as with Cyprus via the interior of Asia Minor ; and a certain famous lump of white nephrite, which Schliemann found there among the ruins of the Second City— the city which was destroyed round about 1850 B.C.[1]—cannot have come from anywhere nearer than the Kuen Lun mountains on the borders of China ! And Troy was in close contact with the Aegean world, though not itself Aegean in culture ; two Trojan vases of silver, found in the Cyclades, at Syros and Siphnos, bear witness of this connection. A cylinder-seal, made in Babylon from Armenian silver and found on the island

---

[1] For this date, see Frankfort, *op. cit.*, p. 152, n. 3.

PLATE III

Minoan Houses: faïence plaques from Knôssos

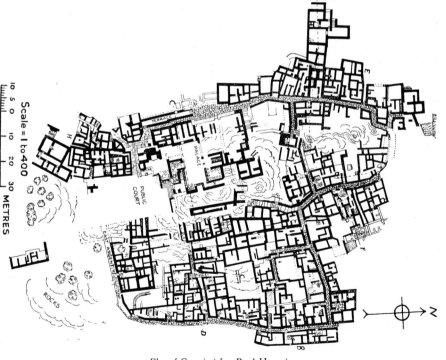

Plan of Gournia (after Boyd Hawes)

A MINOAN TOWN

of Mochlos off the coast of Crete, speaks of contact with the civilized east. Lastly Egypt, as long ago as the reign of King Khasakhemui of the Second Dynasty, in the thirty-third or thirty-second century, had already been receiving gold from north of the Danube. Some place-names on the coast of the Black Sea and the Marmora, with the characteristic Aegean terminations (Odessos, Salmydessos, Perinthos, Apsinthioi) seem to mark a route up the coast to the mouths of the Danube ; probably a route opened up by Aegean sailors after the Second City of Troy had been burnt and while the site lay desolate.

The evidence for the provenance of King Khasakhemui's gold, by the way, is interesting. A gold object found in this king's tomb was covered with a red deposit which proved under chemical analysis to be antimoniate of gold ; but gold and antimony will only combine in the presence of the rare element tellurium. It remained to look for a region in which gold, antimony and tellurium are found together—and geology has hitherto recorded only one, namely Transylvania.

It was to Egypt above all that Early and Middle Minoan civilization was indebted and with which it kept up the closest communication. Middle Minoan vases—and their contents— regularly found their way to Egypt, and Egyptian finds in Crete are many and various. Ornaments of ivory, vases of syenite and diorite—models for the exquisite stone vases which Cretans at an early date were already making for themselves ; scarabs, and bright blue faïence beads ; memorials of personal friendship, like the diorite statuette of an Egyptian, whose name is inscribed on it, found at Knôssos ; ostriches' egg- shells—there was at one time a great vogue for these among wealthy Cretans, for use as vases ; a whole range of designs on seals, perhaps the " trade-marks " of Cretan business houses whose connections lay towards Egypt ; all these tell the same tale of close connection and all-pervading influence. The seals are particularly interesting. One is shaped into the form of an ape ; others show such designs as an ostrich ; a camel, kneeling ; the medicinal silphium herb of the plateau of Kyrene. With these must be mentioned the hippopotamus shown in relief on a weight from Knôssos.

Trade and Egyptian influence had meanwhile suggested the invention of a system of writing ; a pictographic syllabary, from which a linear script had evolved before the end of the Middle Minoan Age.

In art, the ivory seals show the skill of the Cretan craftsmen, the stone vases their skill and their taste. Their painted pottery reaches the same high level ; many lovers of Minoan art consider " M.M. II " its greatest age, as showing a purity of taste that is not always found in the " great palace period " of Late Minoan times. Of work in the precious metals there was much, but for obvious reasons very little survives.

Politically, the age of Knôssian imperialism was not yet. The two great " Middle Minoan " palaces of central Crete, at Knôssos and Phaistos, north and south, might indeed be as has been suggested, " the Windsor and Balmoral of a Cretan potentate " ; but recent discoveries (in 1925) by the French School of Archæology suggest that we ought rather to imagine the island parcelled out into city-states, under dynasts who were both traders on the largest scale and also doubled the parts of High Priest and King. At Mallia, along the coast, east of Knôssos, the French School unearthed the palace of such a priest-king, with the loggia-shrine in which, it may be supposed, he performed sacred rites in the sight of the people assembled in the great court without. Nearby, in a side chamber of this same loggia, were found two " truly regal " weapons. One was a magnificent ceremonial bronze axe-head, its surface chased with a connected-spiral pattern, and its butt end (for once, it is not a double axe) cunningly wrought into the shape of a leopard's head and fore-paws, about to spring. The other was a sword, the largest and by far the finest specimen yet discovered of the tapering Aegean thrusting blade. " Its hilt, 8¼ inches long, had been decorated with finely engraved gold plate and terminated in a long faceted knob of rock crystal with here and there a glint of amethyst. Its length, about 3 feet 5 inches, exceeds by a good fifth that of any Bronze Age sword hitherto known. We have here in truth a Minoan Durendal."[1]

Suddenly and without warning, this brilliant period came to an end in widespread ruin and confusion. A terrible volcanic eruption, towards the end of the seventeenth century, on the island of Thera, overwhelmed a flourishing town with the fate

[1] Sir A. Evans, in *The Times*, December 24th, 1925.

of Pompeii ; and Sir Arthur Evans believes that it was in the first instance a great earthquake, part of the same catastrophe, that shattered the Cretan palaces and towns. But signs are not lacking that political disturbance followed the disturbance of nature. Crete was certainly not invaded from without ; for after the troubles Cretan civilization starts again without interruption " where it left off ", and is still, as before, supreme in the south Aegean. Moreover, after as before the troubles, Cretan towns remain unfortified—clearly relying on their sea-power to keep external enemies at arm's length. But the disaster was followed by a complete re-orientation of the foreign policy of the chief power in the island ; a re-orientation that suggests a shifting of the political centre of gravity from Phaistos close to the south coast to Knôssos on the north. Henceforward, though paintings from the tombs of Egyptian court officials under the Eighteenth Dynasty depict typical Minoan Cretans among bearers of tribute to Pharaoh—and typical objects of Late Minoan art among the gifts that they bring—yet Late Minoan objects are on the whole comparatively scarce in Egypt. Cretan energies have been diverted into a new channel. It was in the years following the earthquake that the first Cretan settlers landed in Argolis.[1]

It is arguable that the Cretan features of the " Mycenæan " civilization now introduced into Greece may have been due to trade and peaceful penetration. They may ; but it seems exceedingly unlikely. The change from the native Helladic to the imported Mycenæan—i.e. Late Minoan—culture is altogether too sudden and too profound. It is rather by colonization and conquest, whether at first fiercely resisted we cannot tell, that so complete a metamorphosis must have been brought about.

The civilization of the Argolid in the succeeding centuries is simply Late Minoan ; Cretan in religion, in language (at least at first, as shown by the script), in art, in social life and amusements, and in dress. Colonization must be postulated to account for all this. And the fact, that certain definite and significant differences are also observable, can best be explained on the theory, inherently probable from what is known of colonization by Mediterranean races in historic times, that the Cretan immigrants intermarried with the more

---

[1] Wace, in *C.A.H.*, I, pp. 597-8.

numerous Greek-speaking natives, who were perhaps called
Danaans ; until, while the higher civilization survived, the
Cretan language and nationality had been almost totally
submerged.

The Cretan colonization seems to have proceeded in two
waves. First, settlements are established at various selected
points north and south of the Isthmus of Corinth, Mykênai
being from the first an important stronghold ; and a couple of
generations of consolidation follow. Relations with the
natives were clearly friendly, almost if not quite from the
settlers' first arrival, and the civilization of the neighbouring
native city-states such as Orchomenos in Boiotia and Minoan
Corinth on her isthmus (the modern Korakou) shows during
these years a strong tendency to imitate that of the newcomers.

Then, about the middle of the sixteenth century, the area
of the Minoan civilization spreads. Evidently the powerful
lords of Mykênai felt their kingdom firmly established and the
time ripe for an advance ; and a strong body of new colonists
must have arrived from Crete. In all directions the advance
is simultaneous, definite, and wisely limited. All the colonies
founded become in a few years strong and prosperous. There
is no such thing as a precariously-held Minoan settlement. The
movement is not the vague " push " of a barbaric people feeling
the need for expansion, but the deliberate and well-conceived
action of a civilized nation proceeding according to a plan.

Colonization is by no means confined to the Argolid. Clearly
Knôssos, while reinforcing Mykênai, has other plans also.
Settlements appear not only at Corinth, and throughout the
Argolid, but also at Thorikos in south-eastern Attica, at Thebes
and Orchomenos, and presently as far as Iôlkos at the head of
its sheltered gulf, under Mount Pêlion, on the coast of Thessaly.
Westward, too, the new sea-borne civilization appears at
selected points round the coast of the Peloponnese ; in Lakonia,
in Messenia, in southern Elis, and in the western isles, at Leukas,
which perhaps then bore the name of Ithaka. The settlements
correspond very closely to the capitals of the kingdoms named
in Homer.

Plentiful finds of the northern amber at Kakovatos on the
west coast of the Peloponnese, in what was later to be Nestor's
kingdom of Pylos, give a clue to the trade by which Leukas
soon grew wealthy ; while ivory at the same site attests the

continuation of the trade-route via Crete to Egypt and " the lands where the elephants are ".

Characteristically Cretan is the formless " agglutinative architecture " as it has been called of the " labyrinthine " palaces of this date at Tiryns and Thebes, in which the northern " megaron " is conspicuously absent. Characteristically Minoan, too, are the frescoes with which artists familiar with the splendours of imperial Knôssos adorned Tirynthian and Theban walls ; and most interesting of all, Minoan is the writing which, before the sixteenth century ended, the men of Orchomenos seem to have been adapting to the purposes of a non-Cretan language. If this language was Greek, it gives us the best of grounds for the hope that the script may some day be deciphered. The Argolid is one of the regions in which it is possible to hope that we may one day find a bi-lingual document ; and indeed, even as I write comes the rumour of an important step in advance, in the shape of a newspaper report that the Swedish archæologists under Professor Persson have discovered there a graffito of eight Minoan words in Greek script, and that their leader has with this assistance been able to identify the Cretan language as akin to the non-Aryan elements in Albanian.

This, then, is the setting into which fit the numerous Greek legends of the cultural and especially the religious influence of prehistoric Crete, and of the civilizing influence of strangers from over the sea. Rather curiously, the eponymous hero Danaos was said in historic times to have come not from Crete, but from Egypt, and Kadmos of Boiotia not from Crete but from Phœnicia ; but archæology shows no sign of immigration at any period from either of those lands. On the contrary, we know that it was from Crete that the founders of new and powerful kingdoms came ; from Crete that a sea-borne settler introduced into Boiotia, as the legend of Kadmos tells, the first writing seen on the mainland. Phœnicia and Egypt have been substituted by later Greeks who knew those countries as homes of ancient civilization, while that of Crete had passed and left hardly even its name behind.

Still, other traditions remain in which the Cretan name has been preserved. The old " Homeric " Hymn to the Pythian Apollo told how the first priests of the oracle of Delphoi had been brought across the sea and up the Corinthian Gulf to the port of Krissa by the especial guidance of the Dolphin-God ; "Cretans from Minoan Knôssos" they were, we are told, "who were bound after business and profit to sandy Pylos in their dark ship".[1]　So the priestly corporation of the Labyades at Delphoi in historic times look as if they were originally Labryades, servants of the Double Axe.　A name reminiscent of the sacred "labrys" occurs also across the gulf, at Patrai and Messene, where in Roman times they worshipped a goddess Laphria, identified with Artemis, and kept a festival called the Laphria in honour of her.　The name was expressly said to be derived from the region round Delphoi[2] ; where votive double-axes of bronze have in fact been found.　The same title recurs in the western isles in Kephallênia, but this time only as an epithet attached to a goddess who has kept her Cretan name, Britomartis,[3] "Sweet Maiden"—for the Mother Goddess is also worshipped under the title of the Virgin.　On the other side of Greece, again, Athens has her legend of the Cretan Bull of Marathôn, and the "Cretan garment" which her chief religious magistrate wore when offering sacrifice.[4]

It was now that the vine and the olive were introduced into Greece ; and in the case of the olive, at least, one of the various legends of its discovery correctly described it as having been introduced from Crete.　There was a Cretan culture-hero of legend whom the early Greeks, after their fashion, identified with their favourite, Herakles.　It was one of the triumphs of Greek criticism in a later, more self-conscious, age that it detected this identification and drew a perfectly correct distinction between the introducer of the olive and founder of the Olympian sanctuary, and the tempestuous Greek giant, chiefly distinguished as a sacker of cities, like the Achaian and proto-Dorian that he was.[5]　Another of the great productive achievements of the colonists was the reclaiming of Lake Kôpaïs, in Boiotia, by well conceived and executed drainage-works, which the historic Greeks (the tunnels having become blocked) never even seriously attempted to restore.

---

[1] Lines 219 ff.　Nor is archæological confirmation of the Minoan origin of the sanctuary lacking ; see C.A.H., III, p. 625.

[2] Paus., IV, 31. 6 ; VII, 18. 6.

[3] Antoninus Liberalis, *Metamorphoses*, chap. 30.　For the meaning of the name, cf. Hêsychios' Lexicon, *s.v.* Βριτόμαρτις.

[4] Julius Pollux, VII, 7. 7.

[5] Hdt., II, 43, D.S., V, 76 (a good and well-reasoned chapter).

PLATE IV

THE KEFTIU IN EGYPT

Frescoes from the Tomb of Rekh-ma-ra

[face p. 78

But for all the flood of Cretan influence, some native traits survive. The old matt-painted pottery of the Greek mainland was still produced, for example, and in some cases even where the decoration of a pot is typically Minoan, it is clear that the mainlanders preferred the graceful shapes characteristic of their own old "Minyan" ware. The kings of "rich Mykênai", known to us in all but name from Schliemann's discovery of their graves, with all their treasure of gold, were in most matters of culture Minoan princes, but not in all. They were bearded, for instance, whereas Cretans were clean-shaven ; and, most significant of all, they were buried in "shaft-graves", after the fashion of the old mainland cist, within the bounds of the old native cemetery. The inference is clear. The Greek legend told how the bringers of civilization from over the sea had taken to themselves wives of the daughters of the land ; here is an example. The Kings of Mykênai had from the first been careful to preserve, in the important matter of burial-rites, for instance, continuity with the dynasty which they were replacing. Within a century, the land was already making its influence felt, and the grandson of a Cretan colonist was in a fair way to feel himself, no longer a transplanted Cretan, but an Argive and a Danaan ; in the language of a later century, a Greek.

CHAPTER II

The Golden Age of Crete

οὐ γὰρ Φαιήκεσσι μέλει βιὸς οὐδὲ φαρέτρη,
ἀλλ' ἱστοὶ καὶ ἐρετμὰ νεῶν καὶ νῆες ἐῖσαι
ἦσιν ἀγαλλόμενοι πολίην περόωσι θάλασσαν·

αἰεὶ δ' ἡμῖν δαίς τε φίλη κίθαρίς τε χοροί τε,
εἵματά τ' ἐξημοιβὰ λοετρά τε θέρμα καὶ εὐναί.
— *Odyssey*, VI, 270-2, VIII, 248-9.

HIS Excellency Rekh-ma-ra, Governor of Upper Egypt
under the great conquering Pharaoh Thothmes III,
built for himself a splendid tomb after the manner of his
country. On its walls he, like other high officials of Egypt
of his time, bade the artists, who were to paint the frescoes,
depict the nations of the four corners of the world, North and
South, East and West, coming to lay their tribute at the feet
of his master, the great king. So there they painted them :
the Semites and the Negroes, and the people of the land of
Punt on the Red Sea, and from the west the men whom the
Egyptians called the Keftiu, "the people from beyond"
from over the "Very Green", the sea.

At the feet of the Vizier they lay their tribute down :
packages oblong and cylindrical, piled high in great earthen-
ware or metal bowls ; works of art in the shapes of animal
heads—a lion, a deer, a bull ; large beads or jewels, strung in
magnificent necklaces. Many apparently bring oil or wine,
in pitchers and amphoras that vary in size and shape ; but the
shapes are uniformly artistic, and the material in some cases
is silver or gold. The vessels themselves were no small part
of the offering. A white-headed Egyptian (Rekh-ma-ra
himself ?) receives their goods, while a scribe at his side makes
an inventory of them. Above is written : "The Coming in
Peace of the Great Ones of Keftiu and of the Isles in the Midst
of the Sea."

80

Now some at least of the offerings—the heads of the bull and lioness, and some of the vases—are clearly objects of Aegean art. This becomes still clearer on inspection of other Egyptian tomb-paintings showing tribute-bearers of the same physical type and similarly dressed, notably those of Queen Hatshepsut's councillor and Minister of Works, Sen-mut. The physical type and dress themselves, observed with the admirable accuracy of the best Egyptian art, suggest the same conclusion. It is a dark, regular-featured Mediterranean type ; their black wavy hair is in part done up in an elaborate curl on top of the head, in part hangs in long strands over the shoulders. The dress is simple ; merely an embroidered loin-cloth, hanging from a belt drawn tight about the slim waist, and soft-leather boots, laced up above the ankle ; boots adapted, as has been observed, for walking through the ubiquitous scrub of an Aegean hill-side.

These were the sea-farers, true brothers to the Cup-Bearer of Knôssos and other Cretans known to us from Minoan art, whose skill as workers in gold and silver, stone, ivory, and the potter's clay, was well-known in the prosperous Egypt of the sixteenth and fifteenth centuries B.C., and whose shipping Thothmes III himself, when in Syria in the year 1467, employed to transport timber from the coast of Phœnicia to the wood-less Egypt. For there was no native Phœnician sea-power in the land of Canaan then.

Thothmes, like other Egyptian monarchs, claimed these Keftiu as subjects and their presents as tribute ; which claim, coming from the non-maritime Egyptians, is merely imperial hyperbole. The " tribute " should rather come under the heading of customs receipts. M. Glotz well compares the jars of wine presented to Agamemnon in his camp before Troy by the Lêmnian traders, before they did business with the host in general.[1]

Minoan Crete traded not only with Egypt, but even, indirectly, with the distant Babylon and " the lands of Sumer and Akkad ". The silver cylinder from Mochlos remains as a relic of this commerce ; and indeed, the oldest reference to the island world in a written document, of which we know, comes from the records of a Mesopotamian king. Twelve centuries before the time of Thothmes and Rekh-ma-ra, the great

[1] *Il.*, VII, 467.

conqueror Sargon of Akkad had stood on the Syrian shore and cast longing eyes towards " Ku-ki, the Tin-Land, which is beyond the Upper Sea ".

The Sumerian and Semitic push to the north-west, in which Sargon's invasion forms an episode, was a movement of the first importance in the history of civilization. Before it began, the merchants of Sumer and Akkad had no doubt for some time been aware that silver came to them, passing from hand to hand among the tribes, from a mountain-range in the north-west, and tin, it would be reported, from a yet remoter land. In the attempt to reach the sources of the supply of these desirable metals, they opened up direct communication with the comparatively distant west, and planted the seeds of civilization both in Asia Minor, afterwards the Hittite country, and in what was afterwards Phœnicia.

Far into the north-western highlands Sargon led an expedition, to show that he had power to defend, even so far off, the agents of Babylonian business houses interested in the silver mines. He met and defeated Pamba, king of Garsaru, who came up to assist the people of the city of Kanis, secured the position of the Babylonian trading-community there, and returned, bringing with him saplings of several northern plants (the vine, the fig-tree and the rose among them) which he introduced into Mesopotamia. The trading community at Kanis later became extremely important, as we know from the several hundred cuneiform tablets found there, mostly commercial correspondence, dating from the age of the Third Dynasty of Ur (about 2400-2200 B.C.). The use of cheques in this long-distance north-western trade introduces a strange note of modernity into our impressions of the advanced Sumerian civilization ; as does the existence of a women's college at Kanis, to give the benefits of a sound Babylonian education to the daughters of the colonial commercial agents and managers of the silver mines.[1]

From Phœnicia we have as yet no such early records, but it is highly probable that here, on the way to Sargon's Tin-land, the same things were going on. Sargon himself has told us of his interest in the Tin-land, and indeed, if we could believe his royal boast, he even crossed the sea to invade and conquer it. It is not impossible that he may have explored as far as Cyprus.

[1] Sayce, in *J.H.S.*, XLIII, pp. 48-9.

The recent discoveries of a Sumerian civilization in the Indus region show us that the pioneers of town life in Mesopotamia were not afraid of long distances. At any rate, since the merchants of Sumer and Akkad planted colonies in and beyond the Taurus in order to get silver, nothing is more likely than that they also occupied the ports to which the sailors of " Kaphtor " brought their European tin.   Here, then, is the probable source of the tradition that Herodotos heard at Tyre, that the city was founded by colonists from the Persian Gulf about 2300 years before his time.[1]   This brings us to 2750 B.C., or just about Sargon's period.   Tyre itself as a matter of fact was probably a much later foundation ; but of the earliest towns on the Phœnician coast the story may well be true. Gebal, the Greek Byblos, was known to the Egyptians as a thriving port in very early days, though the ships that came to it with merchandise seem not to have been its own but those of the Keftiu.

Such, then, was the trade which brought tin, and occasionally Minoan pottery, to Cyprus and the Syrian coast, and silver, and Babylonian cylinder seals, and probably also such perishable things as " goodly Babylonitish garments " from the East to Crete.

Now, in the fifteenth century B.C., Minoan Knôssos was at the height of its prosperity and power ; and if any Egyptian or Babylonian trader had cared to follow the tin-traders of Kaphtor home, instead of waiting for them to bring the precious metal to him, he might well have been surprised not only at the advanced and brilliant civilization, but at the very strength and numbers of the island race.

Getting back from Egypt in a sailing-vessel was a less easy matter for the " tribute "-bearers than going there, for the Annual Winds, as the Greeks called them, blow persistently from the north in those waters, the summer through ; but at last it would be done, not without heavy labour at the oars, and the ship would be beached and drawn up beyond high-water mark, on the south coast of Crete, not far from Phaistos, at that very port which Menelaos in the Odyssey uses, and which Sir Arthur Evans re-discovered not many years ago.[2]

From the southern harbour, the way across the island to

[1] Hdt., I, 1 ; II, 44 ; VII, 89.
[2] Od., III, 291-296 ; Evans, Palace of Minos, Vol. II, Part 1, § 35.

the northern capital lay up the hot but lovely mountain-girdled plain of the Messara, until, after leaving on their right the royal palace of Phaistos on its rocky knoll, the travellers would turn left, northwards, up the hills towards the pass over the mountain backbone of the island. Pack animals carried their goods, no doubt ; but the horse had been known in the island for some centuries, and important visitors could drive in a lightly built chariot more or less at their ease. Here our imaginary Egyptian might have observed that the chariots had their cars scientifically placed over the axle, as may be seen to-day in frescoes from Mykênai ; it was a contrast to the bad Egyptian mode of construction, with axle and wheels at the extreme rear of the car, thus throwing a needless share of the weight upon the backs of the horses.

It was no small achievement even to have built a road fit for wheeled traffic right across the mountain backbone of a large and rugged island ; but the Minoan monarchy had done it.[1] It was no mere track, but a very fine piece of bronze-age engineering, with culverts and short stretches of viaduct where necessary, and probably fortified guard-posts at intervals in the twenty-mile stretch that crosses the hills. Historic Hellas never had such highways.

On went the travellers across the high ridges between Mount Iuktas and the holy peak of Ida with its sacred caves ; and so at last, after their forty-mile journey, almost from sea to sea, they used to descend into the northern maritime plain and see before them, sprawling over valley and hill-side by the rivulet of the Kairatos, the great city of Knôssos. By way of a viaduct along the hillside and a bridge that spanned a tributary ravine, the road led up to the stately southern portico of the palace of the kings.

Here it forked, and a branch, for the use of the general public, led past the palace into the city—giving the royal officers every facility for observing all coming and going between the capital and the interior ; while another branch, trodden by members of the royal household, by ambassadors, and by the king's captains and messengers, led straight ahead into the palace.[2]

Cold water plashed into a horse-trough by the side of the

[1] Evans, *P.M.*, *loc. cit.*
[2] *Ibid.*, §§ 36, 38.

PLATE V

(a) "Bull-Leaping"; from a Knôssian Fresco

(b) The Lion and the Bull
(Seal from Vaphio, near Sparta)

(c) The Minotaur
(Seal from Zakro)

(d) The Palace: a Hall and Stairway

THE PALACE AND THE MINOTAUR

[face p. 84

way, and close by the fork in the road stood a pavilion, which appears to have been a guest-house or inn.[1] Opening off the yard were bath-rooms where the traveller might cool his feet and wash off the fine white clinging dust of a Cretan road. Afterwards as he ate and drank in a room, also opening off the inn yard, where hoopoes and partridges processed in a delicate and lifelike frieze round the top of a wall whose lower frescoes imitated timber pillars, the Egyptian visitor might marvel at his leisure, as he reflected further, on the very highly developed civilization of the " people from Beyond ".

To a stranger from the opposite direction—some hapless barbarian captive from the hills of Greece, for instance, destined for he scarcely knew what fate, once he was herded within the dreaded Palace of the Double Axe—the most striking thing must have been the sheer size of the buildings and the town, and the numbers of the thronging people. Especially awe-inspiring was the palace, two and three stories high, with its courts and magazines and staircases, and its inner rooms where only a deep light-well gave a glimpse of the blue sky, and its endless maze of passages, whose turnings, left and right, and up and down too, seemed designed expressly to mislead the nocturnal footsteps of the slave who had to meet the Minotaur in the morning and who was trying to escape. The town, too, with its tall houses packed together and extending over scores of acres every way, was a very different matter from the largest village or hill-fortress that the slave had ever seen at home in Attica ; for Knôssos was a great bustling sea-port, even by modern standards a large town, and by comparison with any other human settlement in the Europe of that age, gigantic. It could challenge comparison with Egyptian Thebes or with the great towns of Mesopotamia. Its populousness is well illustrated by a fresco of a theatre packed with people, in commenting on which Sir Arthur Evans has given as his opinion that there were in Knôssos nothing under one hundred thousand souls.

Even now, when levelled to the ground, the palace is imposing, and gives a striking impression of the human hive that it must have been in its prosperous days ; with its throne room and its halls of reception opening off the great courts ; with its private living-rooms behind ; with its magazines for all

[1] Evans, *P.M.*, § 37.

manner of stores, and especially for the oil that the king received as tribute from his subjects and traded, after the manner of the great monarchs of that age, by way of exchange of " presents " with his " brother " rulers over sea.   There were plenty of other towns and palaces in Crete, but fifteenth-century Knôssos dwarfed them all.   Its royal archives remain, alas, unread, but nevertheless their study suggests important conclusions.   To quote two distinguished archæologists, the great mass of baked clay tablets includes " inventories of treasure and stores, and receipts for chariots, armour, metal vessels, ingots of copper such as have been found in store at Hagia Triada and singly in Cyprus and Sardinia ; and smaller quantities of unworked gold, by weight.   Other tablets contain lists of persons, male and female ; perhaps tribute paid in slaves, or in person as in the Greek legend of the Minotaur ".[1] There are also " longer documents, which suggest reports or despatches from local governors or representatives abroad ".[2] " Clearly," continues Myres, " we have to do with the details of a vast and exact administration, far more extensive than Cnossus itself would justify " ; and the very bulk of the archives confirms the impression that " the later Greeks were right in the main, in regarding Minos of Cnossus as a monarch who ruled the seas and terrorised the land, absolute and ruthless, if only because inflexibly just ".

This is the setting within which the Greek traditions of King Minôs take their place ; Minôs, as the epics tell us, the " son " or "familiar friend" of the most high God; the great judge and lawgiver, the greatest monarch that this world had ever known ; Minôs, who was also from the point of view of the mainland folk, the subject of a quite different and a bitterly hostile tradition, as " Minôs of the baleful heart ", a tradition preserved to us in full by the " aboriginal " Athenians, but one to which Homer only once, in his one reference to the story of Theseus, deigns to allude.

It was in this hostile tradition of the mainland Greeks, who trembled at King Minôs' name, that the name of the Labyrinth, the king's great palace, which in the Cretan language meant " the Place of the Double Axe "—the sacred symbol that everywhere adorned its walls—came to mean simply a maze,

[1] Myres, *Dawn of History*, p. 184.
[2] Wace, in *C.A.H.*, II, p. 437.

and more especially that particular maze of passages at Knôssos, out of which no prisoner, it was said, had ever yet found his way back home. So, too, Minôs' Bull, the sacred animal over whose splendid horns trained boy or girl athletes vaulted or somersaulted as it charged—or failed to do so and were impaled and gored—while Minôs and the lords and ladies of his court looked on, became for the haunted imagination of the subject folk the Minotaur, a nightmare monster, born of sin, which Minôs kept in a secret lair and fed with the living flesh of those youths and maidens whom he demanded as tribute year by year.

The Greek traditions of Minoan imperialism, and of profound Cretan influence on the culture and religion of all but the most northerly Aegean shores, are indeed particularly varied and widespread,[1] and in many quarters, though not in all, their soundness is proved beyond a doubt by archæology. It is also archæology that with no uncertain voice bids us refer the traditions to the fifteenth century B.C.; for then, *and at no later date*, Crete was in truth the home of a culture whose influence was felt on every side.

" Minôs ", so fifth-century Athens believed, " was the first of whom we hear that he possessed a fleet, and controlled the greater part of what are now Greek waters, and ruled over the Cyclades. . . . And he drove out the Karians and installed his sons as governors ; and he naturally suppressed piracy so far as was possible, so that his revenues might come in better." So, too, Bakchylides of Kĕos tells how Minôs came with fifty ships of war, and colonized the poet's native isle.

Later writers add a few details. Diodôros for example calls attention to the wide distribution in the islands and on the Asiatic coast of the Aegean, of the significant place-names " Minoa " and " Cretan Harbour ". Minôs, he further adds, grew jealous of the reputation for fairness of his brother Rhadamanthys, who was associated with him in the kingship, and sent him abroad in order to be rid of him. So Rhada-manthys became governor of the Asiatic islands, and founded Chios and Erythrai.

Diodôros' use of place-names as evidence has quite a modern sound ; nor is his story of Rhadamanthys at Chios altogether

[1] For references, cf. p. 31 above.

to be despised, for it is local tradition. Erythrai, with its significant name, "Crimson Beaches", was presumably a centre of the purple dye industry and its attendant shellfisheries. In the case of the Cyclades the evidence for actual subjection to a Minoan empire is conclusive. The archæological evidence for the sixteenth and fifteenth centuries B.C. would suggest it even apart from the tradition. Cycladic culture at that time was simply, it has been said, "a colonial edition" of that of Crete. Some "son of Minôs" it will have been, who brought over to decorate his residency on Mêlos that Cretan artist, who there executed the famous wall-painting of the Flying-Fish. The place-name Minoa, which was the name of two ports on the north coast of Crete, recurs in the Cyclades three times—at Siphnos, Paros, and Amorgos. "Cretan Harbour" on the other hand is not otherwise known to us. Probably it was never the name of any town, but only that of various desolate but convenient coves or bays, and so the various extant late Greek geographies and gazetteers have all passed it by. The name of Naxos, too, like that of Lesbian Mêthymna, was also that of a Cretan town.

There was another Minoa on the east coast of Lakonia, whence the builders of Cretan palaces imported the beautiful porphyry stone of the Taygetos hills ; there was a seventh in the Sarônic Gulf, the inshore islet which, as legend said, had been the king's headquarters when he besieged and sacked Nisa, near the later Megara. And thereby hangs a tale—one of the two Greek versions of the story of how a woman betrayed the hero whose "virtue" was in his hair. King Nisos had his magical purple hair plucked by his daughter Skylla, who had fallen in love with Minôs, and fell, as his fate was to fall when that hair was lost. But Skylla escaped less lightly than Delilah in the Hebrew version of the tale ; for Minôs, living up to his reputation for justice combined with cruelty, hung her by the feet from the stern of his galley, and so let her drown. As for Minôs' holding Athens to ransom and levying his terrible tribute in human kind, is it not written in Charles Kingsley's *Heroes* ? But of Theseus and how he delivered the land from its terror, we shall have to treat more fully on a later page.

Eastward of Crete, the island of Karpathos was said to have been settled by "some of Minôs' troops" ; while the southwest coast of Asia Minor had a slightly different history.

Sarpêdon, another brother of Minôs, and his rival both in love and politics, was compelled after a dynastic struggle to flee from home with his partisans, and it was they who, mingling with the native " Termilia ", founded the small but powerful national state of Lykia.   The city of Miletos, whose name is, again, the same as that of a Cretan town, was also said to have been founded by this refugee movement.

Other traditions of Cretan settlement, not mentioning Minôs, existed among other places at Kolophôn, where, as at Erythrai, we are definitely told that the Cretans formed one element in a cosmopolitan seaport,[1] and, of all places, in the Troad. Here, though the archæological evidence shows close contact with the Minoan world, it also shows that the towering walls of Ilios defended a culture that was at bottom quite independent— native Anatolian, with connections also with Thrace and the north-west.   Yet the tradition is strong, and comes to us from an early and usually well-informed Greek poet, Kallînos of Ephesos, who lived in the early seventh century.   He attributed the introduction of the worship of Apollo Smintheus, Apollo the Mouse-God, which, as every reader of the Iliad knows, was strong in the Troad, to a colony of Teukrians from Crete.[2] It is at any rate true that the god's epithet or title has in its termination   the   -nth-   sound   characteristic   of   the   old Cretan, Karian, and South Aegean language ; that Mount Ida in the Troad bears the same name as the Cretan sacred mountain ;   and that at the neighbouring Tenedos, where Apollo Smintheus " ruled in might ", as Homer says, there remained in use as a symbol throughout historic times— figured on coins of the island, and famous in a proverb, with explanatory myth attached to it[3]—the Double Axe of Crete.

Lastly as regards Asia, the rich mythology of Rhodes told how the arts of civilization were introduced there by the

---

[1] Paus., VII, 3, 1 ff.

[2] Il., I, 37-9 ; Strabo, XIII, 604, quoting Kallînos, and supported by the local writer Kephalon of Gergis (quoted by Stephanos, s.v. 'Αρίσβη). Cf. also Nikolaos of Damascus, frag. 17.

[3] For the "axe of Tenedos," as a proverb for brutal abruptness, see Paus., X, 14, 2.   The name of Sarpêdôn also turns up in the north Aegean ; there was a Sarpedonian Crag on the coast of Thrace, whose eponymous hero was said to have been killed by Herakles (Apollod., II, 5, 9 ; Σ on Apollonios, I, l. 216).   Phôtios' dictionary explains it as meaning " great " or " powerful ". Apollo Sarpêdonios and Artemis Sarpêdonia were worshipped on the coast of Kilikia (Str., XIV, 676 ; Zôsimos, I, 57), where there was also another Cape Sarpêdon.   (Str. 670, 682.)

Telchînes, the webbed-fingered mermen-elves of Crete, who
could control the weather and change their shapes ; and the
worship of the gods by the less uncanny Children of the Sun,
whose legend was also told in historic times in Praisos, the last
stronghold of the pre-Hellenic language of Crete. (Cretan
Kourêtes, the famous culture-heroes and legendary priests of
Zeus, were said to have played the same civilizing part on the
mainland of Karia.)   Rhodes was also the scene of the dolorous
tale of Althaimenes, son of Katreus, a Cretan prince called in
the story son of Minôs or of Krês.   Althaimenes fled from
home and colonized Rhodes, in fear of an oracle that he should
kill his father ; and presently Katreus in his old age
longed to see his son, and set sail ; and reaching land after
nightfall, he and his company were taken for hostile raiders,
and in the fighting the prophecy was fulfilled.[1]

But a difficulty arises : the archæological evidence does not
in Asia, as in the Cyclades, confirm the traditions.   In Rhodes,
at Miletos, at Kolophôn, Erythrai, and Phôkaia, and at various
other points along the coast, there have been found plentiful
traces of contact with Mykênai in the fourteenth century, after
the fall of Knôssos; but practically nothing that can be
connected with Knôssos in its prime.[2]

The pure archæologist would therefore bid us let drop the
doubtful evidence of some Greek geographer's report at
twentieth or fiftieth hand, and keep to the solid certainties of
potsherds and their distribution.   But yet, the traditions are
extraordinarily persistent ; and reasons for their invention,
at so many different points along this coast, are lacking ; and
there is no subject on which oral tradition is more likely to be
reliable than on the question, " Whence did our ancestors
come ? "   And to jettison evidence is not the same thing as
critical caution.

On the whole it seems best to accept the traditions, while
taking it as proved, negatively, by archæology that the Cretan
colonies in the Ionian region were, as compared with those in

---

[1] Diodôros, V, 54-60. (All these legends ; suppressing supernatural and
unnatural details, after his fashion.) Webbed hands, Eustathios, *On Homer*,
p. 772. Other details about Telchînes, Nonnos, *Dionysiaka*, XIV, 47 ;
Kallimachos, *Hymn to Delos*, 32 ; Hêliadai, cf. Pindar, *Seventh Olympian*,
36-51.

[2] Cf. the valuable collection of the evidence in the chapter on " Inter-
national Relations " in Glotz' *Aegean Civilization*, and references to original
publications, *ib.*

PLATE VI

MINOAN TYPES

(a) The Cup-Bearer
(fresco from Knôssos)

(b) The Snake-Goddess
(Gold and Ivory statuette in Boston Musuem)

VASES FROM KNÔSSOS

(c) Middle Minoan

(d) "Palace-Style"

the Cyclades, short-lived and small.   It must be remembered that, if founded in the middle of the fifteenth century, at the height of the Knôssian imperial age, they will have had only some fifty years of life before the true Minoan art came to an end and markets were everywhere flooded with the mainland wares, which Mykênai began to produce in vast quantities for export.   At many a Romano-British site that has been excavated, remains of the earliest period known to us from history have been scanty to vanishing point, as compared with those of later generations ; it may be so here, too.   Also the Ionian coast has been by no means thoroughly explored as yet, especially below the surface ; and lastly, we are not told here, as we are elsewhere, that the colonies formed part of a Minoan empire.   They were planted probably by mere groups of traders, living—as some of the traditions expressly say—among a native population that was presumably much larger.   And it is possible to trade without trading either in works of art or in the finest quality oil or wine, such as the gay painted vases may be presumed to have contained.

By way of parallel—we know that the sailors of Knôssos voyaged as far as the islands off the north coast of Sicily, whence they brought back the unique " Liparite " stone to be used by the artist-craftsmen of Crete ; but neither in Italy nor Sicily do any earlier than fourteenth-century Aegean potsherds occur to bear witness to these voyages.   And for all the tomb-paintings of Sen-mut and Rekh-ma-ra and Menkheperreseneb, scarcely an Egyptian object of their age has been found in Crete.   Egypt exported to Crete, among other things, foodstuffs[1] ;   Crete to Egypt, European tin ; Crete to the west, in exchange for tin and liparite and such raw materials, probably such perishable goods as luxury textiles, embroidered or purple-dyed.   None of these goods leave any trace that can ordinarily be discovered by the spade.   The negative argument in archæology seems likely, therefore, to be just as dangerous as the " argument from silence " in the criticism of written records.

To return from this troublesome but necessary digression :

Westward also, beyond the Greek mainland, Cretans were

---

[1] Evans' workmen at Knôssos unearthed some sealed jars of beans of a kind still exported from the Nile to Crete.   They were still quite good after their thirty-three centuries in store.

certainly trading, as we have just seen. A Minoa on the island of Corfu looks like an advanced post on the Adriatic sea-way towards the Bohemian tin-land and the amber-coast of the still remoter north. Beyond the Lipari islands, too, at least one daring voyage brought 'Aegean pottery to the region of Marseilles.

Towards the end of the fifteenth century, then, the Minoan dynasty ruled an empire covering at least the Cyclades and southern Sporades, while its fleets terrorized and held to tribute some sections of the mainland coastal regions by their raids. (There is a perhaps significant absence of Minôs-legends in connection with the neighbourhood of Mykênai and the powerful fortresses of Argolis.) Beyond, lay an outer ring of small Cretan colonies and trading stations and factories extending the cultural influence of Knôssos still further, but not subject to the empire politically ; probably in very much the relation of a historic Greek colony to its metropolis, and sometimes potentially hostile, like Lykia under its Sarpêdon-dynasty, or like the now powerful—over-powerful ?—Mykênai. But danger from any of these quarters can never have seemed particularly pressing ; too securely, over all the south Aegean, had the Minoan octopus spread his tentacles.

The navy that had accomplished all this was manned by Leleges, the natives of the empire's island provinces and of the Karian coast-region, who being a poor and hardy maritime folk rendered this service to Minôs in lieu of tribute. They were apparently uncivilized enough to be tractable under Cretan leadership, and probably retained their warlike spirit better than the peaceful townsfolk of the larger island.

Behind their " wooden walls ", the princes and princesses of the Minoan house, and the lords and ladies and captains and rich merchants of the ports, lived delicately in their unwalled open towns. Even at the capital, a guardhouse of no great dimensions was the only fortification thought necessary for the royal palace on the side towards the sea. The palace itself, a huge shapeless conglomeration of haphazard walls and roofs, can have had few claims to architectural dignity except perhaps when approached by the southern portico ; but it was not with a view to external appearances that it had been built. It had been built, or rather had grown up over a period of centuries, with a view to internal convenience ; and no doubt that object was attained. New wings, new blocks, new walls and passages and staircases, were built as they were wanted without reference to other considerations. A palace is meant, the practical Minoan would have said, not to be looked at but to be lived in. A Greek of a thousand years later might have been disposed to argue the point ; but the Minoan Cretan would have had little respect for the opinions of a people content to live so uncomfortably—without proper drains, for instance— as the later Greeks in many respects did. For his own part, he devoted all the powers of his quick and fertile brain to the service not of ideals but of his own comfort. He had his reward. His applied science at all events was far above the Hellenic or even the Hellenistic level. Out of doors we see it in his roads and bridges, both in Crete and in the Argolid ; indoors, in the bathrooms and latrines and drainage system of the great palace, which, the situation being complicated by the fact that the palace lies partly on the slope of a hill, gave him full scope for the exercise of his skill in hydraulic engineering. It is an amazing contrast to the primitive and malodorous discomfort in which the builders of the Parthenon were content to live.

So it was also with the Minoan and his art. He built no Parthenon ; nor did he ever carve a life-sized or colossal statue out of marble. He preferred a quicker medium. Nearly always, too, his art is domestic, intended to gladden the eye of the owner in his house ; seldom or never to express the spirit of a whole people, under the sky. So the glories of Minoan art are its gold repoussé cups and inlaid dagger-blades, its splendid bull's head rhyton and its dainty ivory statuettes. Very appropriately it is in painting and in the art of the statuette—not in architecture nor in full-sized sculpture—that Minoan art most completely comes into its own, in the beauty of that demure ivory of the Goddess with the Snakes, or the extraordinary grace of the little athlete from Knôssos, in the act of swinging clear over the horns of the charging bull. In painting, nothing could surpass the satisfactory purity of the best Minoan plant designs, stem and leaf and flower, on some Middle Minoan or " great palace period " painted wall or vase, or the vividness of the picture of marine life in the fresco of the dolphins at Knôssos or of the flying-fish from Mêlos, or the vase from Mêlos with the slender water-flower whose stalk almost seems to sway before the gazer's eye in the slow movement of the current. Even the slimy octopus becomes attractive, treated as the Minoans treated him. Nor less satisfying to the eye are the ornamental mouldings of their ceilings or their frescoes of themselves It is, after all, first and foremost through these great wall-paintings with their charging bulls and flying limbs, their fashionable court-ladies and dapper prince or page, that we seem to know the " Minoan race " as men and women who really lived and moved.

Of the Minoans' higher thought and literature we can know nothing ; but it is not probable that there was ever much to know. Their religion seems to have remained very much the same through a full two thousand years, and their government a theocratic despotism throughout that period. As to their language, it vanished with little resistance and almost without trace before the superior claims of Aryan Greek. Sir Arthur Evans has guessed at the existence of a pre-Homeric Minoan epic, on the somewhat flimsy ground that certain Minoan seals *may* represent scenes from the " heroic " legends ; but a language that possessed a literature of any merit ought surely to have offered more resistance to an invading tongue ? Short poems one can well imagine to have been quite in the Minoan vein, but it is little likely that that practical and comfort-loving nation ever launched out upon the bitter waters of persistent thought.

Even Minoan taste could lapse at times. It is unwelcome news that the steatite vase from Hagia Triada was formerly covered over with gold leaf. The carven stone needed no such cosmetics. Nor, it appears from finds in the later palace at Knôssos, was the Minoan mind troubled by the knowledge that the surface of the apparently marble slab before him was as a matter of fact only of cunningly painted stucco—an anticipation of what may be termed the Grand-Hotel Style in architecture that one discovers with regret. In other respects, too, before the fifteenth century was out, some weaknesses were making their appearance in Cretan civilization. The latest " palace period " art, fine as it is, has passed its greatest stage. Palace art had long ceased to have its roots in the national life ; swift changes of style bear witness to self-consciousness and to the influence of fashion, not tradition ; and now, in " Late Minoan II ", the changes are in a direction that was ultimately to be disastrous. There is a tendency towards formalism ; "the artist, anxious to give free rein to his fancy, abbreviates certain essential details, for instance, the heads of human figures"; and simultaneously the freshness, reserve, and eye for detail of the earlier art "gives way to broader designs, executed freely and with a grand carelessness. The marine motives of octopuses, shell-fish, dolphins and the like . . . are still in use, but in a degenerate form. The patterns are no longer reserved in zones or restrained within natural limits ; they all—cuttle-fish, lilies, and other naturalistic motives—run riot over the surface of the vase in the grand manner of incipient baroque ".

Apart from these intangible "things of the spirit" there were perhaps already other signs of darkening skies. At Gournia, for example, the site in eastern Crete where the narrow streets, that wind between the houses up the side of the hill, give so vivid an impression of a Minoan provincial town—there was no Second Late Minoan period. Gournia was sacked and burnt. It looks as if the Minoan navy was no longer the only sea-power in the Aegean ; as if there were others—some predatory maritime folk, who were fully alive to the possibility that the Minoan fleet might be taken at a disadvantage, off its guard, or that circumstances might arise when it would need, and would not be able, to keep guard everywhere at once.

CHAPTER III

The Destruction of Knôssos

"Shall not the isles shake at the sound of thy fall, when the wounded groan, when the slaughter is made in the midst of thee ? . . . How art thou destroyed that wast inhabited of seafaring men, that wast strong in the sea—she and her inhabitants, which caused her terror to be on all that haunt it."

—Ezekiel xxvi, 15, 17.

THE question whether Minoan civilization was doomed, whether, as we vaguely put it, the race was "decadent", is as difficult to answer as such questions usually are. Clearly the Cretan had for two centuries been extraordinarily active, as sailor, explorer and colonist, as trader and manufacturer, as conqueror and organizer, as artist and builder and engineer. It was an outburst of energy on the part of a small people as remarkable as any in history; after 1400, the people of Crete never again showed any sign of such talent. But the nature of genius, in nations as in the individual, remains obscure, and still more so the nature of degeneracy. Certainly it is not unlikely that the great movement of Cretan colonization oversea had left the stock at home the weaker for the removal of so many thousands of its most vigorous individuals; as also, that the almost complete cessation of warfare within the island of Crete for something like two centuries, under the rule of a strong centralized monarchy with command of the sea, may have led to a decay of the military qualities in at any rate the town populations. As we have seen, the Knôssian rulers, like the Athenian and Florentine republics in their later stages, were now employing less civilized foreigners to do their fighting for them, and the tough Karian mercenaries, who under the banner of Minôs had become the most formidable sea-rovers of their day, must at once become a terrible danger if success should desert Minoan arms. And we have even one suggestion of a more perilous practice still. A fresco from a house near the Palace shows a Minoan captain followed by a line of spear-men *who are coal-black*. Apparently the house of Minôs had learned from the Pharaohs to depend in part for guardsmen on its black mamelukes, recruited via Egypt from among the uncouth and dreaded negroes of the far Sudan.

It all looks—and the conclusion is most of all suggested by the suddenness of the collapse—as though the Minoan Empire, like its palace-art, was out of touch with the national life ; as though it was no longer the self-expression of an expanding people, but merely that most vulnerable of all political organisms, a dynasty, an army and a bureaucracy, for which the rest of the population exists only to be taxed.

Even the swollen size of the population, especially that of the great city, may have constituted a potential danger. Crete is neither a very large nor a very fertile island, and the numerous Cretan colonies may well, like those of historic Greece, have been intended in part to relieve the pressure of over-population. We know at any rate that some foodstuffs consumed in Knôssos were imported from the Nile ; it might soon go ill with that teeming populace if anything should happen to disturb the regularity of its receipt of supplies from oversea.

In the last resort, we can only note as a phenomenon the historical fact that the Empire broke down, finally and completely, as the result, it seems, of a single disaster, when at the very height of its apparent prosperity and power. Certainly at the court of Knôssos there can have been no presage of the future, as the Great Palace Period progressed to its final stage. The last great enterprise of Minoan as of Athenian imperialism was also its farthest afield.   At home life under the Sea-Kings continued cultured, peaceful and secure ; cultured with a refined and delicate luxury almost worthy of China, and like nothing that the West was to know again for over a thousand years. Knôssos led the Aegean world in every refinement of daily living, of the fine arts, and apparently of vice[1] ; and the life of the capital continued—the relics make it perfectly clear—gaily and without foreboding up to the very morning when, with appalling suddenness, the crash came.

The " True-Cretans " of Praisos, who, as inscriptions show, still in Hellenic times spoke their pre-Hellenic language, said that the Fall of the House of Minôs began with the Sicilian

[1] Athenaios, XIII, 602, quoting Timaios.

Expedition. Their story is mentioned by Herodotos and preserved to us in full by Diodôros.[1]

The legend goes, that some great artist of the Minoan court (in the story it is of course the famous Daidalos himself) had become involved in the most terrible scandal by which that court had ever been set aghast—and a scandal that involved no less a lady than the queen. When it came to light, he fled oversea (flew, so the legend says) out of reach, as he hoped, of the wrath of the great king. No shore of the Aegean would have been safe for him; he took refuge far away, in Western Sicily, where at the city of Kamikos reigned a powerful chief, Kôkalos of the Sikanoi. Kôkalos was nothing loth to shelter and employ the great craftsman. His subjects might be barbarians, but Cretan sailors had ere now made their way so far west, and the king was at least veneered with Aegean culture.[2]

But the arm of the Lord of Crete was long, like the tentacles of the octopus that adorns some of his government's standard weights. Presently it was stretched out to recover and take vengeance upon the person of the refugee. Minôs himself appeared with a fleet, and demanded his extradition. Kôkalos temporized, and returned a courteously evasive answer. He proposed a conference within the walls of Kamikos, and offered Minôs entertainment. The temptation was severe, to a Cretan prince accustomed to every luxury, now, after a long and uncomfortable sea-voyage, camped beside his long-boats on a barbarous shore. Minôs took the risk and went up to the castle, where, in good Aegean fashion, Kôkalos offered him the bath of welcome.[3] The chief's own daughters were bidden attend to the bathing of the honoured guest. There Minôs perished, drowned in the hot water of that same

---

[1] Sources for this chapter : Hdt., VII, 169-171 ; D.S., IV, 77-79. (Cf. Σ on Pindar, *Nem.*, IV, 95) ; Plutarch, *Theseus*, chap. XIX, quoting various Atthidographers.

[2] Cf. Evans, *Scripta Minoa*, I, 95, on Cretan analogies in Western Sicilian religion. At Eryx, for instance, the Mother-Goddess is worshipped at a shrine with sacred pillars, on which doves perch, and the Swastika sign is prominent.

[3] This detail is important, since the custom of offering visitors a bath is *not* Hellenic, and *is* old-Aegean ; cf. *Odyssey*, IV, 48-9, etc., and also the fact that Minoan bath-rooms tend to be near the front door. The mention of this custom, therefore, along with what seem to be genuine pre-Hellenic names (Kôkalos, Kamikos) makes it likely that we are indeed dealing with a genuine Cretan tradition, and not with a late Greek compilation.

bath, by order of the treacherous Sikan.   Simultaneously, the Cretan ships along the shore were attacked and fired ; and few, if any, of Minôs' leaderless followers made their way home again.

From Crete, a great armada set sail to avenge the murder of the king, though even at this crisis there are said to have been Cretans who were slow to move and cities that, on this pretext or that, sent no contingent.   Still, it was a powerful armament that reached Sicily ;   but reverses dogged their operations in this distant land.   They encamped before Kamikos, but could make no impression on its fortifications, where Kôkalos and his Cretan artificer conducted the defence. Storms battered and crippled their fleet, and as the siege dragged on famine thinned their ranks.   And in their absence, irretrievable ruin befell the cities of Crete.

Who it was that sacked the palace of Knôssos, we do not know.   Sir Arthur Evans speaks of a revolution, an upheaval of " submerged elements within the island ".   But to most writers it has seemed that the destruction is too universal and the resultant alteration in the whole balance of power in the Aegean too complete for this theory to find favour. An external enemy, it is almost certain, must have done the damage.   But the problem still remains, from which side of the Aegean that enemy came.

Egyptian records show that one immediate consequence of the shattering of Minoan sea-power was the appearance as predatory sea-raiders of the Shardana and Lykians, the former probably, the latter certainly, a people of the Asian coast. There even survive in late Greek authors one or two hints— hopelessly fragmentary and vague—of an early Greek tradition of " Sardanians " being connected with an attack on Minôs.[1] Alternatively, M. Glotz[2] ingeniously suggests that the arrival of mainland Mycenæan pottery in Egypt at this very time and simultaneously at Mykênai that of a whole consignment of Egyptian faience ware, marked with the royal cartouche of Amenhotep III, marks the conclusion of an agreement between the Pharaoh and the Greek mainland dynasts to trade direct and cut out the exorbitant middleman's profits of the House of Minôs.   Such an agreement would be quite in the spirit of the very commercial diplomacy of the Tell-el-Amarna letters ;

[1] For references, see next chapter, pp. 111-112, and notes.
[2] *Civ. Egéenne*, p. 245.

and it could not be put into effect so long as Minoan sea-power remained in being.

It is certain, anyhow, that Mykênai reached the height of her power as Knôssos fell, and that the culture of the Greek mainland now begins to influence that of Crete, instead of being influenced by it as for centuries past ; a consideration which points to the mainland as on the whole the most likely source of the attack.

The fourth century Atthidographers, those assiduous collectors and systematizers of Athenian and Attic local legend, knew a fine and romantic story of Theseus the Athenian and Troizenian hero, who slew the Minotaur and escaped from the Labyrinth, by the love of Ariadne the daughter of Minôs the king. There was also a sequel, which told how the hero returned later with a fleet and army, seeking his revenge. Such material cannot be criticized as history, especially since what at first sight seems a good and unexaggerated version of a legend in the late Greek historians on further inspection usually appears to be merely a rationalizing version. Such are the well-meaning " histories " that turn the Minotaur into an Admiral Bull of the Minoan navy, against whom Theseus fought a fleet-action. Yet even here, beneath the masses of poetic romance and learned rationalization, there did exist a sub-stratum of genuine ancient tradition. Philochoros for example told how Ariadne fell in love with Theseus when she saw him in the arena, and comments " for it was customary in Crete for women as well as men to look on ". It was, as we know from many Cretan wall-paintings ; but that Philochoros, over a thousand years later, should know it is surprising. Nothing but the existence of a tradition based on *early* poems or stories can account for it. Philochoros' evidence is the more valuable because he records the detail with such obvious surprise. Contemporary Athenian custom was the exact opposite. Certainly no historic Athenian invented that episode.

This being so, one is the more willing to accept as tradition, not imaginative construction, Kleidêmos' account of the making of the war-navy with which the mainland prince made his attack on Crete. There was much secret shipbuilding at Troizên in Argolis, Theseus' other principality, and at the desolate harbour of Thymoitadai. Then the golden opportunity is given by the Minoan disaster in Sicily. The new squadrons with their creator put out to sea and make their dash for Crete.

The ruins at Knôssos at several points showed the excavators how fearfully complete was the surprise. The people of the great city had scarcely time to fly ; none at all in which to save their property. That morning, a sculptor sat down in his workshop to work on a stone vase ; but the vase was left unfinished when the alarm summoned the craftsman to fight or fly. At the royal chapel, attendants set out the holy vessels and libation-jars for a service that was never performed. Some rooms in the palace were being re-decorated ; the unfinished frescoes remain, in the too-flamboyant style of the latest Palace art. Perhaps it was an hour, from the moment when the coastguards sighted strange ships in the offing until they grounded in the shallows at the mouth of the Kairatos and the tide of armed men came pouring over their bows.

In ordinary times the very size of the city and its population would have made it hazardous to raid the place, even if the trained Lelegian " regulars " were absent on a campaign. The invader had chosen his time well, when Crete was drained of its best fighting-men for the great struggle in Sicily. And even so, the capital of the sea-kings did not fall wholly without a fight. Kleidêmos tells how a young prince, king Minôs' son, rallied the household troops ($\delta o \rho \acute{v} \phi o \rho o \iota$, the word used of a ruler's personal guard) and tried to hold " the north gate of the Labyrinth ". These Guards, who would probably include the black spearmen, were presumably the only troops present on the defending side. They had a good position round the old guard-house and the narrow entrance-way ; the palace was no castle, but it had been built partly with an eye to defence against a riot or a sudden raid. But the odds were too over-whelming. The defence, if it consisted solely of the Guards, had no reserves to bring up. The resistance may have been desperate, but it cannot have been long. The prince Deukalion was killed, the outnumbered Minoan troops broken and driven backwards, and the half-civilized Greek invaders burst their way in.

Then the greatest city and most splendid palace of the Aegean world was given up to the sack. Most thoroughly the looting was done. Hardly a vestige of silver or gold was found by the excavators in all the extent of the ruins. There

was no need to leave any corner unsearched through haste ;
there was no revanche to fear.   The remnants of the defenders
had fled to the hills ; the dreaded Cretan-Cycladic fleet had
gone to its destruction on the rocks of the far west.   Minôs
lay dead in Sicily and his son somewhere between the guard-
house and the shattered doors of the north gate.   There was
smashing and destruction, too ; too well had the name of
Minôs been hated and feared by the mainland folk ; and
presently, out of the plundered building the flames roared up.
Billowing clouds of smoke rose, and sheets of flame of intense
heat, as the oil in store in the royal magazines took fire.   It has
even been suggested that the clay tablets of the Knôssian
archives owe their preservation, in a soil by no means so dry
as the sands of Egypt, to the exceptionally thorough firing
that they thus received.   Walls cracked, floors foundered and
roofs crashed in as the burning beams gave way ; there were
mountains of débris everywhere afterwards, when people
could venture back on to the smouldering site.   Under it in
places, protected by some fragment of wall or half-burnt beam,
still stood the relics of a people caught unprepared—the
libation jars in the chapel, and in the stone-cutter's workshop
the unfinished vase—to tell their pathetic tale to the
archæologist after more than three thousand years had gone.

The firing was wanton, not deliberate ; for in places a floor
seems to have collapsed under it before the plundering was quite
complete.   It was the expression of the hatred of those who had
trembled for so long before Minôs and his conquering fleets and
his human tribute and his fabled monstrous Minotaur.

As it was at Knôssos, so it was, a few days or a week or
two later, as the case may be, at every other notable city of the
great island.   Phaistos, Zakro, Palaikastro, all suffered the
same fate, which Gournia had suffered a long lifetime before.
Afterwards a pestilence devastated the land, as though the gods
were not yet satisfied with the abasement of the pride of Crete.

And presently at the capital, when the raiders had
departed with their spoils and their prisoners, the survivors
of a once thronging population returned to the blackened ruins,
and with rough stone walls made habitable again as best they
could—dividing up its stately rooms into squatters' shelters—
so much as was left of the beautiful, terrible palace of the
Minoan kings.

PLATE VII

(a) The Postern Gate

(b) A Royal Tomb

(c) The King's Death-mask

MYKĒNAI

[face p. 102

CHAPTER IV

THE SILVER AGE : MYKÊNAI AND HER NEIGHBOURS

- - - - Ἀμφίονά τε Ζῆθόν τε,
οἳ πρῶτοι Θήβης ἕδος ἔκτισαν ἑπταπύλοιο
πύργωσάν τ᾽·ἐπεὶ οὐ μὲν ἀπυργωτόν γ᾽ἐδύναντο
ναίεμεν εὐρύχορον Θήβην, κρατερώ περ ἐόντε.
—*Odyssey*, XI, 262-5.

THE sack of Knôssos inaugurs the last period of the old
Aegean civilization, Late Minoan III ; on the Greek
mainland Late Mycenæan. It is a long period, covering at
least two centuries, and to the modern student it is clear at a
glance that it is the age of the decline and fall of Minoan culture
throughout the Aegean world. Starting with nothing worse
than a vulgarization of that culture, it culminates in widespread
confusion, about 1200 B.C., everywhere from the Vardar to the
Nile ; and the end of the succeeding Sub-Mycenæan period
(which seems to be the Achaian " Heroic Age ") saw the
powerful mainland settlements fall by fire and sword.

But it does not follow that the men of the fourteenth century
B.C., like Homer in the ninth, considered themselves inferior
to the great ones of the past. On the contrary we may be
sure that they did not. The builders and rulers of " rich
Mykênai " with its frowning walls, " piled by the hands of
giants for godlike kings of old " as the later Greeks believed—
for it was surely a superhuman feat to build with stones so
huge—Mykênai with its Lion Gate, through which a king
standing erect in his chariot might drive, and its secret passage
underground to the hillside spring, whence water might be
drawn in time of siege—these men were not afflicted by doubts
or consciousness of decadence. They, too, as well as the
Cretans of old, had their potters and vase-painters and wall
painters and cunning artists in gold ; they, too—or perhaps it
may have been their predecessors of two hundred years before
—had their architects, the builders of the great hillside tombs
such as the so-called " Treasury of Atreus ", with its forty-five

foot dome—built without use of the keystone, and perfect
to-day.   Even more wonderful than this great dome, perhaps,
is the lintel of the stately doorway by which one enters it ;
a vast slab, poised a full twenty feet above the level of the
passage floor, and calculated to weigh over one hundred tons.
It is a greater feat—though a smaller object—than an Egyptian
pyramid, that tomb and the others like it.   The lords of
Mykênai must yield place to Pharaoh in the amount of slave-
labour at their command ; but their architects possessed an
engineering and calculating skill that not even the great temple-
builders of Egypt could despise.

Nor were industry and commerce, in the two generations
following the fall of Knôssos, less progressive than architecture.
The art of the period, as seen both in frescoes from the mainland palaces and in vase-paintings, may be " decadent " in the
sense that it is stylized and conventional, but it is vigorous
enough as yet, and more restful to the eye than that of Crete
a century before.   But it is in craftsmanship and commerce
that archæology shows us the most definite progress.   The
potting of fourteenth century mainland vases is definitely
superior to that of the fifteenth century Cretan product ; and
their fragments are found over a wide area—on every part of
the Aegean coast-line, and even sporadically far inland in Asia
Minor.   And what we know of industry and trade in the case
of ceramics, we have the right to conjecture in the case of more
perishable products.   Aegean civilization, the tyranny of Crete
removed, had entered upon an age of unprecedented expansion.
South-eastward, Ialysos in Rhodes was developing as a thriving
and populous sea-port, and further afield the great island of
Cyprus and perhaps even parts of the adjacent coast were
colonized by what must have been a very numerous band of
settlers ; settlers who spoke the " Arkadian " Greek dialect
of the contemporary mainland.   Northward, the Achaians of
Thessaly came under the spell of Minoan culture for the first
time ; and even the wild chieftains of Thrace took a fancy to—
and succeeded in buying—the long thrusting swords of Argolis.[1]

In short the fall of Knôssos must have seemed at worst an
event of purely political significance—a victory of the Lion of
Mykênai over the Cretan Bull, marked by the appearance of
mainland influence in Crete instead of vice versa—and at best

[1] S. Casson, in *Man*, November, 1923.

the welcome destruction of a paralysing tyranny. There was a less satisfactory side to the situation, but for some decades this was apparent to few if any.

The civilization and social life of Mykênai, Tiryns, Orchomenos and the other mainland settlements, was Minoan —but Minoan with certain differences ; differences due in part to adaptation to the conditions of mainland life, in part perhaps already to intermarriage between the colonists and the vigorous barbaric mainland Greeks. Ladies dress their hair in the Cretan style, and wear as full dress the Cretan flounced skirt and open-breasted jacket ; but men wear beards, instead of being clean-shaven, and tunics instead of the loin-cloth. The palaces of the more important barons are shapeless and " labyrinthine " enough, and good Late Minoan frescoes adorn their walls ; but by this period we find, as the central feature of each, a " great hall " of northern type, as at Troy, with pillared porch at one end, and a permanent hearth in the centre, on which a great log-fire blazed in the severe winter weather.

So, too, in religion there is both likeness and difference ; the sacred pillars of Crete were revered also on the mainland— a famous example, between its guardian beasts, adorns the Lion Gate ; but on the other hand the Shaft-Graves, where Schliemann's treasure was found, resemble the native " cist " ; and amber was popular, probably for its supposed magical qualities, on the mainland but not in Crete.

Again, in the important matter of sport, we find that the lords of Tiryns no less than those of Knôssos delighted in watching the bull-leaping game and liked to see frescoes of it if they were not watching the real thing ; but they had also the opportunity—indeed, it was almost necessary for them— to take part in the manlier sport of big game hunting on foot with spear and sword. Wild boars that laid waste the crops or lions that came down from the hills in winter against the cattle, must be fought and killed ; and the delight of the lords of Tiryns and Mykênai in this dangerous and genuinely " sporting " contest, in which the beast not infrequently killed his man before he died or escaped, appears in the art they patronized. In fresco we see the wild boar in the brake in full career, driven by hounds right on to the ready spears ;

on the famous inlaid dagger-blade, the furious turning at bay of a wounded lion. The foremost hunter is in deadly danger, knocked off his feet and weaponless. His four comrades rush forward—but will they be quick enough to save him ? It is a brilliant piece of work, that dagger-blade; reminiscent in its workmanship of the shield, inlaid with scenes of human life in peace and war, that the Fire-God made for Achilles, and, in the subject depicted, of the great lion-similes in the Iliad. The boar, too, is a favourite subject for Homeric similes, and always depicted as the most valiant and impetuous of beasts ; it will not give way even to a lion, if they meet at a mountain spring. Individual beasts of both species even make a name for themselves in saga—the Lion of Kithairôn, the Lion of Nemea, the Wild Sow of Krommyôn, the Boars of Erymanthos and of Kalydôn. The last of these was only laid low by an army of hunters gathered from far and wide, for it had already "sent many men to the hateful funeral-pyre ".[1] Such heroes as Theseus, Meleagros, Herakles, count victories over beasts as well as men among their titles to fame.

And lastly—most noted of all differences between the Minoan and the mainland world—the Cretan cities are unfortified, while all those of the mainland are heavily walled. The fact speaks for itself. Not only were there repeated wars between the kings of one stronghold and another, and more especially between those north and south of the Isthmus[2]—there were also fierce tribes of predatory hillmen still surviving untouched by Minoan culture, against whom the more civilized coast-landers waged a not always successful warfare. Homer mentions casually a few such tribes : the hairy men of Pêlion whom Peirithöos and Kaineus smote in the days when Nestor was young,[3] and the up-country Arkadians whom Nestor's own Pylians had fought under his leadership ; whose champion " fought not with bow nor spear, but with an iron club he brake the battalions ".[4] Meanwhile Thebes and Orchomenos, apart from hostility to one another, are both alike endangered by

---

[1] *Il.,* IX., 523.
[2] Cf. for example the very circumstantial episode narrated by Pausanias, II, 6, 1-4, among the voluminous traditions of Sikyôn ; the story of an invasion of Sikyônia by the Kadmeians of Thebes, under Nykteus, to recover his daughter carried off by Epôpeus, king of Sikyôn.
[3] *Il.,* I, 262 ff. ; II, 743-4.
[4] *Il.,* VII, 132 ff.

PLATE VIII

(a) A Girl Rides Out

(b) Hound in Leash

Frescoes from Mykênai

(c) The Lion at Bay. (Dagger-Blade from the Shaft-Graves)

(d) Hittite Seal from a
grave near Mykênai

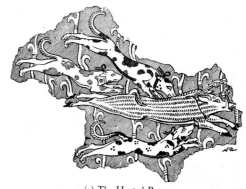

(e) The Hunted Boar
(Fresco from Tiryns)

LIFE AT TIRYNS AND MYKÊNAI

[face p. 106

the raids of Tảphians and Têleboans, presumably from the neighbourhood of Mount Taphiassos, against whom Amphitryon in Hesiod leads his punitive expedition,[1] and of the Phlegyai " those violent men, who dwell upon earth caring not for Zeus, in a fair vale near the Kêphisian Marsh ".[2] Later tradition had a good deal to say of these Phlegyai ; it was for fear of them that Zêthos and Amphion fortified Thebes, for instance ; but nevertheless they sacked it, under their king Eurymachos, after the sons of Antiope were dead.[3]

Not for nothing did Mykênai and its fellow-settlements, then, crouch behind their fortress walls.

Still, the picture suggested to the imagination is on the whole a pleasant one. If wars are frequent, at any rate defences are strong, out of all proportion to the means of attack ; nor, at most periods of human history, has an insecure life necessarily ceased to be a merry one. The connotation of the adjective " Homeric " bears sufficient witness to that ; and the outlook on life of Homer's heroes was probably very like that of the men who dwelt in the frescoed palaces within those heavy fortress walls, amid the increasing turbulence of the Silver Age.

It is not quite the society described by Homer, this with which we are dealing. Two hundred years were to introduce some changes between the beginning of the Silver and the beginning of the Heroic Age ; some progress in the art of war, some fading of Cretan before Northern religious and other influences, and the rise of parvenu Achaian Aiolids to political power in many cities. Already we seem in the frescoes to see the life of the Iliad and Odyssey—a healthy country life out of doors, and within doors a fair standard of magnificence and even luxury, for kings and their families. A princess drives out in her chariot with a girl companion, on a Tirynthian fresco, driving with her own horses, just as does Nausikaa in her mule-waggon when she and her maidens go out for their picnic

---

[1] *Shield of Herakles*, 1.56. For wars between Thebes and Orchomenos, cf. the story of Erginos, king of Orchomenos, in Str., IX, 414; D.S., IV, 18; Paus., IX, 37. 2.

[2] Homeric *Hymn to the Pythian Apollo*, 278-80. Cf. *Il.*, XIII, 302, for the Phlegyai as favourites of the War-god.

[3] Σ on *Il.*, *loc. cit.*, citing Pherekydes. Cf. *Od.*, XI, 263-5.

N.B. that though it is likely that all these events, which struck the imagination of posterity, really took place, we can say no more of their dates than that they took place before the Trojan War and perhaps long before it. To attempt to base an absolute chronology on legendary genealogies we have seen to be illusory.

and laundering expedition in the Odyssey ; and the great hounds so proudly depicted, hunting the boar or held in leash by a squire, are evidence of the good " Aryan " companionship of man and dog. One is reminded of Odysseus and his dog Argos—" Swift "—that he left at home young when he departed to Troy, and which in extreme old age knew him and died, when he returned after many years, a beggar, unrecognized and alone.

The political map, too, is beginning to resemble that of Homer's world. From Rhodes and Cyprus to Thessaly and Ithaka, Aegean civilization covers just the area held by the Achaians and their friends ; and as in Homer, it has contact with Egypt, the Syrian coast, Lykia, Troy, and Thrace ; while the Sikans and Sikels of the west are in both periods, though in Homer only vaguely, known through trade.[1]

We must turn to consider what was going on east of the Aegean during the great days of Mykênai.

Here we find the first ominous symptom of the confusion that was to come—though it is no more than a symptom as yet. Since the fall of Knôssos, piracy has been becoming increasingly frequent in all parts of the Levant. If Amenhotep III really intrigued with the mainland Greeks against the house of Minôs, he may have had some inkling, before his death in 1375, that he made a ruinous mistake. The disappearance of the Minoan navy ended the effective policing of the seas for nearly a thousand years, and such hardy maritime tribes as the Lykians and Leleges—of late employed by Minôs *against* piracy, but now deprived of that employment—took full advantage of the fact. Before Amenhotep was dead, he had to arrange for the protection of the Delta coast itself against their depredations[2] ; and in the reign of his son, the " heretic pharaoh " Akhnaton, the king of Alasya (Cyprus, or the plain of Tarsus) complains that the " Lykki " yearly sack one village after another along the coasts of his land.[3]

So much for the second in fame among the non-Greek races of the Iliad. As to the most famous of all, the Trojan kingdom also was increasing in strength and in importance. It had

[1] *Od.*, XX, 383 ; XXIV, 211 ; both references to the slave trade.
[2] See Breasted, in *C.A.H.*, II, p. 98.
[3] *Tell-el-Amarna Letters*, ed. Winckler. No. 28.

already two centuries of prosperity behind it, since, in the sixteenth century, as archæology shows, the founder of Laomedon's and Priam's kingdom re-fortified the hill of Hissarlik. The position had then been crowned by no fortress worthy of it since the "Second City" perished at the hands of an enemy nearly three hundred years before. It was now once more surrounded by an enceinte, of enormous strength and enclosing a much larger area than of old. The walls are twenty feet high and sixteen feet thick at the base; and this mighty stone embankment (for its sides lean back a little from the perpendicular) was topped by a vertical stone rampart six feet in height and thickness.

"Dardanos first" (Aineias tells us in the Iliad[1]) "was begotten of Zeus the Cloud-Gatherer, and he founded Dardania, for not yet was holy Ilios built in the plain as a city of mortal men, but still they dwelt on the hillside of Ida of the many springs. And Dardanos begat a son, Erichthŏnios the king, who was richest of mortal men, and had three thousand mares at pasture in the water-meadows. . . . And Erichthonios begat Trôs, lord of the Trões, and from Trôs three noble sons were sprung, even Ilos and Assarakos and godlike Ganymedes; he was most beautiful of mortal men, and the gods carried him away to be Zeus' cup-bearer, for the sake of his beauty, that he might be among the immortals. But Ilos begat a son, noble Laomedon, and Laomedon begat Tithônos and Priamos . . . but Assarakos begat Kapys, and he Anchises, and Anchises begat me, but Priam the goodly Hektor."

Such a pedigree, from the pen of a foreign poet, can have little that is historical in the strict sense about it, excepting perhaps some of the last few names (especially those that are not Greek); but it presents several points of interest. Even the eponyms at the beginning of the list show us what Homer believed about the Trojan nationality. The Trojans, Trões, are a sub-tribe of the nation of the Dardanians; and the fortress of Ilios is a comparatively late affair; it has a shorter history than Dardania as a whole, or even than the "Trojan" sub-tribe. It is incidentally worth noting that there is a contingent of Trões in the Iliad who are not inhabitants of Ilios but of another city, Zĕleia[2]; and that, although Aineias

---

[1] *Il.*, XX, 215 ff.
[2] *Il.*, II, 824 ff.

is in the pedigree called a descendant of Trôs, his men are
Dardanians indeed, but not Trojans, and expressly distinguished
from them.[1]

As to the origin of the Dardanian people, they were probably,
as Homer clearly believed, indigenous inhabitants of the
district where we find them. Most modern writers seem to
conceive of them as immigrants from Europe—part of the
" Thraco-Phrygian " movement which reached its height as
late as 1200 B.C. ; pointing by way of evidence to the existence
of another tribe of Dardanians in north-west Bulgaria, who
survived to be a thorn in the side of the Macedonian monarchy
a thousand years later. Against this it may be argued that
Homer everywhere distinguishes between Trojans or Dardanians
and Phrygians, and that a later epic poet expressly tells us
that their languages were different.[2] Since epic always tends
rather to ignore differences of language than the reverse, this
passage is important. To use the names " Phrygian " and
" Trojan " interchangeably appears, therefore, to be merely a
piece of Roman bungling. The Phrygians appear not to have
entered Asia Minor before 1200 B.C. ; the Dardanoi were
certainly there about 1280, when the Hittites employed them
as mercenaries, and if, as Homer says, they were the builders
of Ilios, then they were on the spot much earlier still—not much
after 1600. And as recent excavations in Macedonia seem to
be making it clear that in the early part of the second millennium the current of migration had been from rather than into
Asia Minor, it seems better to regard the European Dardanians
as colonists from Asia, rather than vice versa.

However this may be, we can form a fairly clear picture of
the character of the Trojan people during the four and a half
centuries for which Ilios stood. They are essentially a hard-
headed sturdy folk, as befits the holders of a key-position where
land-ways and sea-ways intersect. They were the men who
built, and their princes the men who planned, the famous walls
by which they secured themselves in possession of the wealth
they won as commercial middlemen ; for though Dr. Leaf's

---

[1] *Il.*, II., 819 ff.
[2] Homeric *Hymn to Aphrodite*, 111-116.
    Archæology confirms this view; in painted pottery, the pot-hook spiral
ornament, which Frankfort believes to have been introduced into Asia Minor
from Europe by the Phrygians, is not found in the Troad. Frankfort, *Studies
in Early Pottery*, etc., pp. 170, 173.

pleasing theory, that Troy was the scene of a great annual fair, is unsupported by evidence, it is abundantly clear from archæology that the Trojans did exploit the advantages of their position. The finds tell of contact, direct or indirect, with lands from Cyprus to the Danube ; while from the east came silver, mined by the Halizônes of Alybe,[1] a people friendly to Troy, and on the south-west Aegean civilization influenced and was influenced by that of Dardania. There is even an early and not unsupported tradition, as we have seen, of Cretan settlers among the Tröes. They are not an aggressive nor a particularly daring folk, these Trojans ; they rarely travel by sea, and do not engage in aggressive wars ; but they can fight with desperate tenacity in defence of their homes and their prosperity. Lastly, it is noteworthy that when attacked by the predatory Achaian confederacy they are enabled to hold on for so long by the help of allies from every side ; even the distant Paiones, Lykians, Paphlagŏnians. Troy, it seems, had made herself not only rich, but useful and respected ; moreover she is able to subsidize her allies out of her reserves of wealth.[2]

Lastly among the Aegean peoples prominent in the fourteenth century, we must mention the Shardana—a warlike tribe, than whose name none is more prominent in the troubled history of the years that follow.

We hear of them first (and indeed, only) in Egyptian records, where they appear at this time as mercenaries—twice mentioned in letters to Akhnaton from Rib-addi, Governor of Byblos.[3] A little later, we may see them depicted for us on stone ; for they played a great part in Egyptian history, being good servants and most formidable foes. Their defensive armour is unlike that of Minoan Crete, and an improvement on it. Whereas the Aegean warrior has only his helmet and his huge leather shield—" like a tower ", " covering the whole man ", " reaching to the feet ", as Homer says—the Shardana carry a round shield, "equal every way", as Homer, who knows both types, puts it, and are further protected by a rather complicated type of corselet. This item of equipment is formed of long overlapping bands of metal, perhaps on a leather

---

[1] *Il.*, II, 856-7. Sayce, quoted by Allen, *ad. loc.*, in *J.H.S.*, XXX, suggests that Alybe (or Halybe)=Hittite " Khaly-wa,"=Halysland.
[2] For maintenance and subsidizing of allies by Troy, cf., *Il.*, XVII, 225-6.
[3] *T.A. Letters*, ed. Winckler, 77 and 100.

backing; the general effect has often been compared to the armour of a lobster. It is also curiously like that of the Roman legionary. Therewith the Shardana wear a helmet adorned with horns and a high metal crest, and carry thrusting swords like those of the Aegean, but larger—sometimes of enormous size. The blade is invariably very broad at the hilt, and has two straight edges, tapering to a point. They certainly are not suitable for a slash, as is sometimes asserted.

But the origin of these warriors is a mystery. "Shardana of the Sea" the Egyptians sometimes call them; but, with their usual ignorance of lands lying beyond the "Great Green", give no further clue. To Sardinia it is not impossible that the tribe ultimately found its way, but the archæological evidence from that island makes it hardly possible that they were already there. Sardis has been suggested as their home; but we are assured by a learned ancient geographer that the city was not in existence until after the Trojan War.[1] Moreover, if they were dwelling in any part of Asia Minor, they must have come into contact with the Hittite Empire; yet not only are they not mentioned in any Hittite document at present known, but they actually fight for Egypt against the Hittites, at a time when the Hittites have mobilized practically the whole sub-continent, as far as Lykia and Dardania, on their own side. It is hardly possible that at such a time the Hittites could afford to allow a people within their own sphere of influence to go on fighting for Egypt; or that any tribe in Asia Minor could afford to do so, in face of the likelihood of Hittite vengeance.

On the other hand, if the Shardana hailed from anywhere within the Greek area, it is extraordinary that they have left absolutely no trace of themselves either in place-name or legend; and there is also the non-Minoan armament to be considered. The corselet, if anything, points to Asia; it is an oriental invention, still almost unknown in Greece in the fourteenth century, while in Asia Thothmes III of Egypt, in his victory over the allied Syrian kings at Megiddo, is said to have captured two hundred of these pieces of armour.[2]

On the whole it seems best to suppose the Shardana natives of the Hermos region, where Sardis and the neighbouring

[1] Strabo, XIII, 625.
[2] S. A. Cook, in C.A.H., III, 329.

Sardianian[1] plain *may* preserve their name ; also a Mount
Sardêne,[2] overlooking Kyme at the mouth of the river, which
is mentioned in an Ionian epic tag.   But during the migration-
period their fame as mercenaries and raiders suggests that they
were straitened for territory at home, while the fact that not
the Hittites but their enemies employ the Shardana as soldiers
makes it unlikely that they were still living on the Asiatic
mainland ; it looks as if they were at that time living an
uncomfortable life somewhere in the islands ; until finally,
before the age of which Homer writes, they seem to have
gathered all together and, like the Greeks of Phôkaia, ages
later, in the same part of the world, sailed away to find a less
troubled home in the Western Mediterranean.   In spite of
some differences, it is generally agreed to be quite likely that
the bronze statuettes of early Iron Age warriors, found in
Sardinia, represent their descendants ; the more so that these
Sardinians, even in early Hellenic times, had not altogether
forgotten their sea-raiding habits.   Strabo (V, p. 225) had
heard accounts of their piratical descents upon the coast of
Etruria.

The Iliad and Odyssey nowhere mention the tribe, unless
their name underlies the proverbial phrase " Sardanian (not
" Sardonic ") laughter " ; which of course we cannot, with the
ancient Romans, derive from the honey of Sardinia.   One
early Greek legend seems to have connected it with the myth
of Talôs, the Bronze Man of Crete, whom Hêphaistos made for
Minôs.   He is said to have leapt into a furnace with, and so
destroyed, " the Sardonians who refused to ferry him over to
(or against) Minôs ".[3]   " Sardonic laughter " is explained as
grim or bitter laughter, from the contorted faces of the victims.
The story can be traced back to the sixth century B.C., and is

---

[1] Σαρδιανὸν πεδίον : not Σαρδικόν.   Str., XIII, 626.
[2] " *Homeric Epigram*," I, quoted in the late-Hellenistic " Herodotean "
Life of Homer.   Modern editors read Σαιδήνη, from Stephanos' gazetteer ;
but as MSS. of the " Life " unanimously read Σαρδήνη—twice over !—
the change seems quite gratuitous.   If Stephanos means the same place,
it is probably he, when copying from the " epigram," who made the mistake.
The name seems to have gone out of use at an early date ; Strabo does not
mention it.
[3] Zenôbios, *Proverbs*, 5, 85 ; Phôtios, *Lexicon*, s.v. Σαρδόνιος γέλως.
Both quote Simonides.   Σαρδάνιον (γελᾶν), *Odyssey*, XX, 302.   Of Talôs,
Hêsychios, *s.v.*, says that he was a sun-god ; Apollodôros (I, 9, 26) gives the
ordinary account of him as a bronze man, " but some say he was a bull ".
Cf., the Phalaris story.   Kinaithon, the cyclic poet, makes him son of Krês
and *father* of Hêphaistos !   Paus., VIII, 53. 2.

probably older than any Greek knowledge of the western Sardinia ; nor is there any obvious reason why Sardinians in the modern sense should be brought into contact with Talôs the fire-demon or with the ancient king of Crete.[1]

Beyond all these, from the point of view of a Greek observer, lay, in the heart of Asia Minor, the capital of the powerful empire of the Khatti, whom we call Hittites. Now, in the early fourteenth century, they were at the height of their power, under the able and vigorous ruler who rejoiced in the name of Subbiluliuma. In the course of the century, from their home in the east of the central tablelands, the Hittites penetrated to every part of the peninsula, extending their sphere of influence as far as the Lykian and the Dardanian country, and leaving their characteristic crudely vigorous rock-hewn monuments to mark their passage, along a route from the Upper Halys valley, via the Upper Sangarios, to Mount Sipylos, overlooking the Hermos valley and not far from the sea.

With the stormy history of this people we are not here concerned, except in so far as the Hittites came into contact with the nations of the Aegean ; but such contacts are numerous and important. Occasional direct intercourse

---

[1] In this context it may be worth while to draw attention to an obscure allusion in Villon (*Testament*, 641 ff). After naming several "lords of old time" ruined by love—Samson, Orpheus, Narcissus—he continues :

> " Sardana le preux chevalier
> qui conquist la regne de Cretes
> en voulut devenir moullier
> et filler entre pucelletes."

The commentaries usually say : "Sardana ; Sardanapalus"; which is not helpful. Sardanapalus did not " become a woman " for love ; he was not a "preux chevalier"; he has nothing to do with Crete ; nor did his famous effeminacy extend to doing anything so useful as making clothes.

It looks as if Villon has got hold—through a mediæval romancer ?—of a version of the Asiatic story, which in Greek mythology has become attached to Herakles. That hero, at the court of Omphale, daughter of Iardanos of Lydia, does " become a woman " and work as we are told here. But what about Sardana and the conquest of Crete ? If the story could only be traced at any rate back to its Roman or Byzantine source, it might prove very interesting.

In connection with the myth of Herakles in Lydia, it is worth noting that Dionysios of Halikarnassos (I, 27, 1-3 ; but cf. I, 28, 1-2) makes him become, by Omphale, the father of Tyrrhênos, whom Herodotos calls a son of Atys. It really looks as if the androgynous god or "hero" Atys, the eponymous hero of the Tyrrhenian and Sardanian sea-rovers, and the "Lydian Herakles" of the Greek versions of the story, had in the original form of the myth been very closely connected.

between Hittites and Mykênai itself seems to be proved, when citizens of Mykênai use inscribed steatite seals of Hittite manufacture.[1] It is worth noting, too, that an art practised in the Argolid but never in Minoan Crete—that of relief-sculpture on stone—is also an art for which the Hittites were and are famous. Such monuments as the Lion Gate relief, or the grave stone crudely adorned with a chieftain in his chariot in full career, can be most easily paralleled from Asia Minor.

The Hittite sphere of influence certainly extended to the Aegean. Effective control, it seems probable, rarely reached so far ; Hittite monuments are rare and of isolated occurrence in the west, and the kings were usually preoccupied campaigning in the opposite direction. Whether a Hittite conqueror ever went further than the Aegean coast, we cannot tell. *A priori*, it seems unlikely. The Hittites were no sailors. Still, speculations as to the possibility of such expeditions have been made[2] ; and Greece had its stories of " Amazon " incursions from Asia Minor even into Attica. Less nebulous, however, than such tales as the Amazon legends in Plutarch's *Theseus*, is the tradition concerning the fortress walls of Tiryns ; a tradition deserving of the more respect from the fact that it was attached to a definite and extremely solid relic of antiquity. These walls were believed to have been built by giants from Lykia, at the time when Proitos, king of Argos, driven from his kingdom by his brother Akrisios, had taken refuge with his friend and father-in-law, the Lykian king ; and the latter presently sailed with a fleet and army and restored him to his throne.[3]

---

[1] Cf. Plate VII.

[2] E.g. by H. R. Hall in *J.H.S.*, XXIX (" Mursil and Myrsilos ").

[3] Apollodôros, II, 1, 2 ; cf. Strabo, VIII, 372 ; *Iliad*, VI, 170 (on Proitos' relations with the Lykian king).

CHAPTER V

ἆ ξεῖνοι, τίνες ἐστέ; πόθεν πλεῖθ' ὑγρὰ κέλευθα;
ἦ τι κατὰ πρῆξιν, ἦ μαψιδίως ἀλάλησθε
οἷά τε ληιστῆρες, ὑπεὶρ ἅλα, τοί τ' ἀλόωνται
ψυχὰς παρθέμενοι, κακὸν ἀλλοδάποισι φέροντες;
—*Odyssey*, III, 71-4.

SO much for the actors in the drama of the fourteenth and
thirteenth centuries.

The situation, then, some twenty-five years after the fall
of Knôssos, was that, freed from Minoan tyranny, Aegean
civilization appeared to be stronger than ever before ; Khatti
and Egypt, too—the one in warfare, the other in art and
thought—were showing every symptom of free and vigorous
development. It would have taken a clever prophet to foresee
that, before two centuries were out, Hittite civilization would
be lying in ruins, and both Aegean and Egyptian far gone in
decay. There may have been merchants of Crete or of Mykênai
who felt misgivings over the growth of piracy on the Asiatic
coast, and regretted the passing of the house of Minôs ; but
even they cannot have foreseen the dimensions to which the
menace was to grow within a few generations.

Nor, it would seem, need the menace have been allowed to
grow. There are times in history when man is manifestly the
sport of circumstances as cruel as Homer's gods ; but this is
not one of them. There is no obvious reason why civilization
in Asia and in the islands at any rate—if not in mainland
Greece—should not have been saved, had the time of crisis
brought forth the man.

But, to say no more of the might-have-been, it appears that
the crisis was not recognized and tackled. The lordship of the
sea, wrenched from the hands of the Cretans, was seized by—
no one ; or if anything, left to the Lykian pirates and
" Shardana of the Sea ".

True, the kings of Mykênai, to say nothing of the lords of Pylos and Lakedaimon, or of the Kadmeians and Minyans north of the Isthmus, or even the invader who now dwelt in his palace, of mainland type, at Knôssos, and ruled over still wealthy Crete—all these must have had ships as well as men at their disposal, and have been interested in maritime trade ; the distribution of Late Minoan potsherds, and especially the frequency of the occurrence of mainland pottery in Rhodes and Cyprus, would alone show that.   But none of them singly had power to police the seas as Minôs is said to have done ;   and both Greek legend and the great number of small palace-citadels of this age in Greece—several even within so small an area as Boiotia, or Attica, or Argolis—suggest that there was a complete lack of political unity among the Minoized Greeks, and that now as ever "fractionalism" was the bane of Greek civilization.[1]

Egypt, too, had everything to gain by the seas being kept safe, as well as free ; but the young Pharaoh Amenhotep IV, son of the old Amenhotep the Magnificent who had had dealings with Mykênai, was not the man to take an interest in such matters as encouraging the forces of order and peaceful commerce, by subsidy or even moral support, among the distant "isles of the Danaans".   Of a singular personal beauty—in his youth at any rate—and of high intelligence ; poet, dreamer, visionary, patron of a new sincerity in art and religious reformer as he was, he was emphatically not the cunning and ruthless soldier and diplomatist that a Pharaoh of Egypt in that age had need to be.   Before he had been six years on the throne he had introduced and was trying to enforce his monotheistic sun-worship, changed his name to Akhnaton in honour of his one God, and embarked on his famous and lifelong struggle with the powerful priesthood of Amen-Ra.

Subbiluliuma, King of the Hittites, was an entirely different character, an exponent of the most Machiavellian real-politik

---

[1] There was however in Hellenic times an ancient "Amphiktyony" of maritime cities which worshipped the Sea-God at the Island of Kalaureia in the Sarônic Gulf.   The members were Hermione, Epidauros, Athens, Aigina, Nauplia, Prasiai (on the coast of Lakonia) and Minyan Orchomenos.   Later, Argos and Sparta took over the membership of Nauplia and Prasiai.   As the League ignores such great maritime powers of historic Greece as Corinth, Megara, Chalkis and Eretria, it has been suggested that it dates from pre-Hellenic times ; so perhaps we have here a survival of an attempt at union for defence against piracy dating from the troubled times with which we are dealing.   (On this league, see Strabo, VIII, 374 ; and cf. Myres, in *C.A.H.*, III, 650.)

of his age, and if he had chosen—since fight he must—to lead
his victorious armies towards Lykia and Dardania and bind
those regions more firmly to his empire than his dynasty in
fact ever did, he would have given to the now anarchic Aegean
world an element of stability which it badly needed. But the
natural tendency of the Hittite raider was to look southwards
and eastwards where the richest spoils were to be won, and
thanks to Akhnaton's personal character the Egyptian empire
in Syria offered opportunities not to be missed. So the West
was left to itself, and Subbiluliuma obliterated his ancient rival,
Egypt's ally, the kingdom of Mitanni in the bend of the
Euphrates, and invaded Syria, and fomented rebellion against
Egypt in Palestine and Phœnicia. Among the invaders of
Palestine we seem to hear the name of the Hebrews—Khabiru.
Meanwhile, Egypt was rent by discord, and governors and
native princes of the Egyptian party addressed despairing
letters, still to be read among the Tell-el-Amarna Tablets, to
the deaf ears of a Pharaoh who cared for none of these things.
The reproaches and entreaties of Rib-addi of Byblos are
echoed by Abdi-Khiba of Jerusalem, as the situation grows
always more desperate ; until, writes Abdi-Khiba :
"The king has no longer any territory ; the Khabiru have
wasted all the lands of the king. If the royal troops come this
year, then my lord the king's territory will be saved; but if no
troops come, then the territory is lost unto my lord the king."
And the summer ended, and the troops did not come.

Akhnaton died about 1360, none too soon for his country's
good ; and before the decade was ended, the young Tutankhaton
had made his peace with the priests and changed his name to
Tutankhamen. The monotheist heresy was at an end.
Subbiluliuma " mounted the hill ", as the Hittites put it, about
the same time, and after a few years taken up with dynastic
troubles in both kingdoms his son Mursil concluded a treaty
with Egypt which ended the wasteful Syrian wars for the time
being. Horemheb, the tough old soldier who reorganized
Egypt and founded the Nineteenth Dynasty, wisely recognized
the fact that his country was in no condition for a war with
the formidable northerners, and accepted the situation as it
stood, ceding practically the whole of the Eighteenth Dynasty's
Asiatic conquests.

PLATE IX

AEGEAN INFLUENCE ON FOURTEENTH-CENTURY SYRIA

Ivory relief of the Mother-Goddess as Corn-Giver and Mistress of Beasts, in typical Aegean costume and attitude ; lid of a casket found at Ras Shamra, along with numerous other objects which appear to attest close contact between the Aegean, Cyprus and Syria, in the fourteenth century B.C.

[face p. 118

During the years of peace with Egypt, Mursil was at last free to attend to affairs on less remote frontiers of his empire. He reduced to vassalage the kingdom of Arzawa in the south of Asia Minor, and extended his suzerainty as far as the borders of Lugga, which is probably Lykia. It may well be more than accident that his name (among other non-Greek names) was borne by more than one Greek of Lesbos in historic times.

And in the course of his conquests, he came into contact with certain persons and places whose names have suggested to many scholars that we have here references to Homer's Achaians in the Hittite texts from Boghaz Keui.

The references in question are as follows :

About 1336 Mursil assisted a certain Antarawas, king of Akhhiyawa, against the kings of Arzawa and Millowanda ; which may be Milyai in Lykia. The treaty which followed makes mention of " the god of the city of Akhhiyawa, who is the god of the city of Läasba ".

About twelve years later Akhhiyawa is mentioned again, when its new prince, called in the clumsy Hittite script Tawagalawas the Ayawalawas, or something of the kind, supplicates Mursil for a grant of the title of king, in return for military services rendered to Lugga.

It is certainly very tempting to see in the name of Akhhiyawa the name of the Achaioi—Akhaiwoi, as they seem originally to have been written, with the insertion of a digamma. But the implications, if we accept the identification, as many scholars have done, are somewhat startling. These Achaioi under their chieftains Andreus (?) and Eteokles the Aiolian (?) are not, as we should expect, sea-rovers active on the coast, but occupants of one or more cities on the mainland of Asia, which can be attacked by the king of Arzawa and delivered by the king of Khatti. And Tawagalawas clearly stands towards Mursil in the relation of a vassal to his overlord.

This is in itself enough to rule out the rash identification of Läasba with the island of Lesbos, which is nowhere near Arzawa, and which in the Iliad is still held by non-Greek people ; it is called the " home of Makar ", a native name (Il., XXIV, 544), and is hostile to the Achaians (Il., IX, 129). We should place the city of Akhhiyawa, whether Achaian or not, rather in Pamphylia or the modern Cilicia, within Arzawa's sphere of influence. Some years ago, before the

Achaian identification had been suggested, Professor Garstang showed reason to identify it with the Anchiale of Greek times.

However, a "city of Achaia" somewhere in the south of Asia Minor in the days of Mursil is not an impossibility. The recent sensational discoveries by the French at Ras Shamra show strong Aegean influence on Phœnicia even as early as the fourteenth century ; the archæology of Cyprus, too, seems, as we have seen, to show that it received its Arkadian-speaking Greek colonists not long after the fall of Knôssos, if not even before ; and as the same Arkadian dialect was spoken by the semi-Greek population on the coast of Pamphylia in Hellenic times, it is quite possible that parts of this coast were colonized at the same time.[1] The griffin-slaying warrior on an ivory mirror-handle of this period, from Enkomi in Cyprus, carries what looks like that characteristically "Homeric" weapon, the cut-and-thrust leaf-shaped sword.

Already in the Tell-el-Amarna letters we may read a report from Abimelech, king of Tyre, to the Pharaoh, that the king of D-n-y-n is dead and that his son has succeeded peacefully to the throne (letter no. 151). If, as is often suggested, this is a reference to the Greek Danaoi, then presumably there were Danaoi also, as well as Achaioi, in the Levant. The king of Tyre is reporting on the *local* situation and would hardly

---

[1] See Meillet, "Place du Pamphylien dans les dialectes grecques", in *Rev. des Etudes Grecques*, XXI, pp. 413 ff. On Akhhiyawa=Anchiale, cf. Garstang in *Supplementary Papers of the British School in Jerusalem*, 1923.

It is necessary to labour this point—that Akhhiawa is clearly on the mainland of Asia—owing to the fact that several popular works by well-known scholars have roundly identified Akhhiawa with Greece, Achaia, and write of Antarawas as a king of "wandering sea-peoples" "active on the coast of Asia Minor". This is not only to ignore the context, as summarized above, but to suggest the existence of a context that is entirely different. The citizens of Akhhiyawa are not "wandering sea-peoples", and there is no suggestion of nautical activity in the passages under discussion.

Nor is it possible that the kings of Arzawa and Khatti attack and protect lands beyond the sea. It may be taken as certain that Khatti had at no time any sea-power at all ; otherwise their very competent generals would not have left the Egyptians, who were no Vikings, free to make use of the sea entirely undisturbed, for communication between Egypt and Phœnicia throughout the whole period of their wars.

There is a Greek tradition of an Andreus, son of the Thessalian river-god Pêneios, who had a son Eteokles, and who was said to have founded the Minyan Orchomenos (Paus., IX, 34. 6). The story is quite irrelevant to our present context, however ; the pair are nowhere mentioned except in this local tradition, and certainly never ruled over the whole of Achaia and had dealings with the Hittite king ; if they had, then folk-memory, since it preserves their names, would certainly remember that they had been people of such unique importance.

For other discussions of this subject, cf. note on p. 135, below.

trouble himself about a people so distant as the Danaoi of the Aegean.

A name resembling that of Akhhiyawa and Achaia was still attached to the south-east corner of Asia Minor many centuries later. The name of the district in Assyrian times—Kuweh—preserves the same consonants; and about 658 B.C. the Assyrians were having trouble somewhere in the Taurus with a motley horde of barbarians under a leader named Andaria, which is very like the Hittite Antarawas. More interesting still, Herodotos (VII, 92) tells us that the Kilikians in Xerxes' army were descended from Greeks who had come thither in the Heroic Age, and " were of old called Hypachaioi ". This name, " Lower Achaians " or " Lesser Achaians " is reminiscent of the " Hypothêbai " in the Iliad (II, 505), the " Lower Thebes " whence the Boiotians came to the Trojan War, at a time when the great Kadmeian citadel was lying waste.

Whether or not it was a " Lesser Achaia ", Akhhiyawa was certainly a very important state at one time ; its kings are addressed by the Hittite emperors as "brother", and it is even mentioned in the following century (see below, p. 135) in the same breath with Egypt, Babylon, and Assyria. One is reminded of the tradition in Solinos that before the rise of the Assyrian Empire, Cilicia was one of the four great powers of Asia.

And there we must leave the matter ; a question that can never be answered with certainty until excavations are possible in this corner of Asia Minor.

Early in the reign of Mutallu, the successor of Mursil, about the year 1310, we hear of a treaty concluded with another chief who bears a suggestive name—Alaksandus of Uilusa ; he may well be a Greek Alexandros of Ialysos—Homer's Iêlusos—the very important " Mycenæan " settlement in Rhodes.

It all tends to show how strong, already at this date, was the tendency to migration from the Aegean to the south-east. To the following century (about 1308-1223) belongs, if our theory concerning Kastor's History of Sea-Power is correct, the dispersion of the Pelasgoi over the length and breadth of the Aegean ; and indeed, whether or not that theory is sound, it must have been now or earlier that they were thrust into the sea, from their old home in Pelasgiôtis and round the Pelasgian Argos, by the advance of the Achaioi.

Also, about 1300 the movement was given a fresh impetus by natural causes, in the shape of a curiously sudden break in the climatic conditions of Central Europe.

The patient work of de Geer, in counting the layers of annually-deposited mud in the bottom of Lake Ragunda in Sweden, which was accidentally drained in 1796, seems to have dated the end of the Quaternary Ice Age fairly certainly, not more than 8,500 years ago.

Since then, the fluctuations of European climate have been less violent. It seems to be established, however, that fluctuations have taken place, and the story of the deduction of their history from evidence of the most diverse character, geological, archæological, and for recent millennia literary, makes fascinating if not altogether easy reading.[1] On the whole the evidence from Irish peat-bogs and Central European lakes, Norwegian and Alpine glaciers and their moraines, agrees together remarkably well. The " climatic optimum " of post-glacial time appears to be fairly securely dated round about 1800 B.C., at which period Mr. Brooks, after an exhaustive discussion, comes to the conclusion, somewhat astonishing to the layman, that the North Polar ice sheet (though not the ice of Greenland or of Antarctica) temporarily broke up altogether. As a result of this " the sub-tropical anti-cyclones would extend much farther north than at present " and " storminess, especially along the present north temperate storm-belt, would be greatly diminished ". Under these favourable conditions the European Bronze Age civilizations reached their height.[2]

Round about 1300, however, there was a catastrophe—a sudden and unexplained rainfall maximum, of no great duration ; a foretaste of the much more serious climatic break early in the last millennium B.C. During the preceding climatic Golden Age, Gams and Nordhagen, the leading authorities on the history of climate in Central Europe—" the ideal combination of a Swiss and a Norwegian " geologist, to quote Mr. Brooks,[3]—believe many of the so-called Lake-Dwellings of the

---

[1] Cf. C. E. P. Brooks' *Climate throughout the Ages*, on which this and the following paragraph is based.
[2] *Op. cit.*, pp. 162-3, 410-11.
[3] In *Discovery*, December, 1926.

Alpine region to have been established not in the lakes themselves but on peat-bogs now covered by their waters. Now, in the Feder See basin and around many other lakes of Central Europe, there was a " high-water catastrophe ", which overwhelmed the villages of the Lake-Dwellers on every side.[1] A whole population was homeless ; and not here only, but in many another district of marsh, now growing wetter, or mountain region where clouds meant snow and severe conditions, must there have been a tendency for individuals, groups, or even in places tribes, to set out to seek their fortune under sunnier skies.

Having noted which, we shall be less surprised at what followed.

An increase in the rainfall would matter comparatively little to the Mediterranean agriculturist ; it might even be welcome ; but traditions exist that seem to show that not far to the north of Greece, in the valleys of Pindos and on towards the wild hills of Illyricum, the climatic break was felt as a disaster. Aristotle, in a curious and characteristic essay on climatic change,[2] alludes to a tradition that the name of Hellas first came into use " around Dodona, where Deukalion's flood was worst ". It is a most suggestive remark. That it is indeed in this region that the name appears earliest and in various primitive guises we know ; as also that it was from the adjacent regions that the Hellenic dispersion was said to originate.[3] " Deukalion's flood " gives us the occasion if not the cause of the migrations.

For though the climatic break was probably directly responsible for certain tribal movements of the following century, there can be little doubt that in Greece the coming of the Heroes was largely the product of nothing else than the spirit of adventure. As Mr. Peake,[4] modifying Ridgeway's " Nordic

---

[1] Brooks, *Climate*, pp. 338-9.

[2] *Meteorology*, I, chapter 14.

[3] Cf. discussion of the point by Strabo, VII, p. 328, who quotes the form Helloi or Selloi from *Il.*, XVI, 234 ; also Hell-op-ia (cf. Dryopes, Dolopes, etc.) from a Hesiodic catalogue-poem, as a name for the land round Dodona. Cf. Thk., I, 3 ; Str., VIII, 383, for Phthiôtis as original home of Hellenes and Achaioi respectively ; both passages based on inference from *Il.*, II, 684, no doubt. Cf. also *Il.*, XVI, 595, for Hellas in the narrow sense.

Even from Leukas comes evidence of disastrous floods, in the shape of prehistoric walls half washed away by a torrent—presumably swollen by unusually heavy rains.

[4] *Bronze Age*, pp. 106 ff.

theory " of the Achaians, has observed, it was less an invasion than an infiltration. Repeatedly, he points out, in Greek story the hero arrives alone or almost alone at a city, distinguishes himself in service against an enemy, human or animal, and often ends by marrying the king's daughter and succeding to the throne. Perseus, Theseus, Amphitryon, Tydeus, Alkathöos of Megara, will serve as examples. Very probably it was in some such way that the men of the leaf-shaped sword rose to power in Argolis.

Some of the earliest northerners may well have made their appearance as slaves ; there is a serving-man in one Tiryns fresco whose flesh is painted white—not red, the conventional Minoan colour for men ; and Sir Arthur Evans convincingly suggests that he is a northern captive. So did the Germans make their way to Rome ; first as slaves, later as mercenary soldiers, presently as conquerors.

The genealogies of most of Homer's " Zeus-born kings ", as is often pointed out, are short, and probably imply that the rise to greatness of these families—or perhaps their arrival in the country—was recent. But there was a tradition about some earlier Achaians, which does not seem to be a myth, since it explains nothing and flatters nobody, and the names are not eponyms. These earliest Achaioi known to Greek legend are named Archandros and Architeles. Nothing was known of their date or parentage ; they are said to have appeared in the land "in the time of Danaos "—which means nothing but "long before the Trojan War " ; they are called sons of the eponym Achaios himself ; and their chief exploit, character-istically enough, is the waging of an indecisive war against King Lâmedon of Sikyôn.[1]

The process by which the Achaioi reached the thrones of so many kingdoms, by the help of their strong right arms, seems to have been helped by the existence in pre-Hellenic Greece of some form of matrilinear succession, perhaps intro-duced by the non-" Aryan " Cretans along with the worship of their Mother-Goddess, whose son-consort seems to occupy such a definitely subordinate position. Such a system would be of great assistance to the immigrant warriors, as ensuring that to win a throne one need not murder the occupant ; one need only marry his daughter. That such a matriarchal

[1] Hdt., II, 98 ; Paus., II, 6. 5.

system existed (still, in historic times) in Lykia, on the edge
of the Minoan area, is well known.[1] Whether it did in fact
exist in pre-Hellenic Greece has been much argued, and the
weight of modern authority seems on the whole to be of opinion
that it did not. There are, however, some facts which accord
much better with a matriarchal than with a patriarchal system ;
for example, one may examine the genealogy of the kings of
Lakedaimon in Homer (Kings printed in heavy type) :

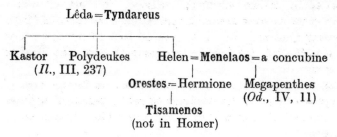

Here the kingdom twice passes to a son-in-law, during the
life of a son or sons—though in one case the son is base-born.
Before Tyndareus and Lêda we have no authentic information ;
the accounts are numerous and conflicting. But if it is true
that Tyndareus was son of Periêres, an Aiolid from Thessaly,
then it looks as if he, too, must have succeeded to the throne *iure
uxoris*, like his own successor Menelaos; certainly not *iure suo*.

Another genealogy that is worth quoting once more for the
way in which it brings out the idea, is that of the kings of
Nisa ;[2] though in this case the earlier steps are all obviously
mythical and of no authority.   (Kings in heavy type, as before):

Pylas =   ?
        |
    daughter = **Nisos,** son of Pandion of Athens.
            |
        Iphinoe = **Megareus,** son of Poseidon.
              |
          Euaichme = **Alkathôos,** son of Pelops.
                |
            Periboia = **Telamon,** son of Aiakos.
                  |
                Aias (claimed as a king of the Megarid by
                    local tradition)[3]

[1] Hdt., I, 173.
[2] Paus., I, 39-41.
[3] Σ to *Il.*, II, 557.

Probably the fact is that the laws of succession were thoroughly vague in the Aegean at this time. It is likely enough that the Minoan Cretans reckoned it through the mother and introduced their system on the mainland ; but there it must have met and conflicted with the presumably patrilinear system of the Aryan-speaking native Danaans, so that it may never have been the invariable rule there. In any case during the Achaian period one may assume that in this matter as in others—clothing, religion, the art of war— Achaian customs were gradually prevailing over those of Crete.

However that may be, there was no lack of adventure, on either side the sea, for thirteenth century heroes who liked to seek for it.

Occasionally adventure came unbidden, as in the case of Bellerophon, whose story contains so many points of archæological interest that it will be worth our while to translate it *in extenso*.

Bellerophon's date cannot be given with any confidence, even in terms of generations, reckoning back from the Trojan War ; for we come up against a conspicuous example of the way in which the laboriously-secured mutual consistency of the legendary genealogies breaks down when tested.[1]

Here, however, is the story, as Glaukos the Lykian told it to Diomêdes son of Tydeus on the plain before Troy :

" Great-hearted son of Tydeus, why ask my race ? Even as the race of leaves is the race of men ; these leaves the wind scattereth to earth, and others the green wood putteth forth, when the season of spring is at hand. So of men, this generation groweth up, and that passeth away.

" But if thou wilt learn this also that thou mayest know my lineage—many there are that know it ;—

" There is a city Ephyre in the heart of Argos the pasture of steeds ; there Sisyphos dwelt, most cunning of men, Sisyphos Aiolos' son ; he begat a son Glaukos, and Glaukos begat the good Bellerophon. To him the gods gave beauty and lovely manhood ; (but Proitos devised evil for him in his heart, and drave him from home, for Proitos was mightier far among the Argives ; for Zeus had made them subject to his sceptre ;)— and Proitos' wife, the fair Anteia, lusted after him, to lie with him in secret love ; but she in no wise persuaded wise

[1] See p. 24, above.

Bellerophon, the upright of heart. Then she with lies addressed the king : "Mayest thou die, Proitos—or kill Bellerophon, who was fain to lie with me against my will." So she spake, and anger took hold on the king at the tale. Kill him he would not, for he was ashamed to do that ; but he sent him to Lykia, and he gave him grievous signs, scratching on a folded tablet many baneful things ; and he bade him show them to his[1] father-in-law, that he might perish.

"Then he went to Lykia under the good guidance of the gods ; and when he came to Lykia and the stream of Xanthos, then the lord of wide Lykia greeted him well. Nine days he set hospitality before him, and sacrificed nine oxen ; but when on the tenth day rosy-fingered dawn appeared, then he questioned him and would see his token, even what word he might bring from Proitos his son-in-law. And when he had received his son-in-law's evil token, first he bade Bellerophon slay the horrible Chimaira. Now she was of breed divine and not of men ; a lion before, and a serpent behind, and a goat in the midst, and breathing forth the dread might of burning flame.

"Her he slew, by obedience to the portents of the gods. Then second he fought with the proud Solymoi ; that, he said, was the sternest battle he ever was in. And third he slew the Amazons, a match for men. But as he was returning, the king devised yet other cunning guile against him ; picking the mightiest men out of broad Lykia, he set an ambush ; but they returned not home, for all of them did noble Bellerophon slay. Then when the king knew him for the valiant child of a god, he kept him there, and plighted to him his daughter, and gave him the half of all his kingly honour ; and the Lykians set apart for him a demesne, exceeding fair beyond all others, with vineyard and ploughland, that he might till it.

"Now the princess bare three children to wise Bellerophon ; —Isandros and Hippolochos and Laodameia. With Laodameia lay Zeus the Giver of Counsel, and she bare godlike Sarpêdon of the helm of bronze. But when he also became hateful to all the gods, then verily he wandered alone along the Alêian plain, eating out his heart, shunning the paths of men. And Isandros his son, him Ares greedy for battle slew, in battle with the proud Solymoi ; and his daughter, Artemis of the

[1] *i.e.* Proitos' father-in-law ; Anteia's father.

golden reins slew her in wrath.   But Hippolochos begat me, and his seed say I that I am ; and he sent me to Troy, and laid many a command upon me, ever to play the warrior and to be excellent among all men, nor to dishonour the race of my fathers, who showed themselves exceeding valiant men, both in Ephyre and in broad Lykia.

"Of this lineage, then, and of this blood I boast myself to be."[1]

The narrative is a curious one, and not quite like anything else in Homer.   It is clearly not put in out of delight in story-telling, for the stories of Bellerophon's adventures are not *told ;* they are merely made the subject of allusions.   Sand-wiched between the fine poetry of the first five and the last five lines we have, not a " short story " with or without a moral, like Nestor's reminiscences or Odysseus' " yarns ", but the outline of a whole " Bellerophon's Saga," containing far more episodes than there are in the main plot of the Iliad itself ; " providing ", as Aristotle would say, " material for many tragedies ".   The allusive style in which the Lykian king and his daughter are not even named, and phrases like " by the gods' good guidance ", " but when he also was hated of all the gods ", which are not explained, are more reminiscent of the " Catalogue " of personages whom Odysseus saw in Hades than of anything else, and seem to indicate the existence of an audience which enjoyed merely being reminded of stories which it knew.   The same thing is indicated by the extraordinarily free use made of the personal pronoun, which would be intoler-able to anyone who did not know the story already.   (There are even fewer proper names in the original than in the translation here given ;   nor are the Greek pronouns here less ambiguous than the English.)

However the chief interest of the story in the present context lies in the light it sheds on conditions in the Aegean at the very beginning of the Achaian period.

The age depicted is one of free intercourse with foreign lands, as we should expect from the character of " Mycenæan " pottery—painted in exactly similar style whether we find its sherds in Argolis, Boiotia, Crete, Asia Minor, Thessaly or Cyprus.   Of the three actors in the first episode, Bellerophon

---

[1] *Il.*, VI, 145-211.

PLATE X

(a)

(b)　　　　THE CHIMAIRA IN HITTITE ART

Reliefs, (a) from Sinjerli, c. 1000 B.C., (b) from Carchemish, rather earlier

is an Aiolid, and therefore by later Greek ideas a Hellên by descent; Proitos' lineage on the other hand goes back to Danaos, who came from the south oversea and was a grandson of the sea-god; and Anteia is a princess of Lykia, with a pedigree presumably going back to Sarpêdon, the brother of king Minôs of Crete (see p. 87). The unnamed king of Lykia, whose relations with Proitos are taken for granted, like everything else in the chronicle, is of course he whose expeditionary force restored the Danaan prince to his throne when driven out by his brother, and who was credited with the building of the walls of Tiryns. These walls are far older than any probable date for Proitos; but his Lykian allies if they did not build may have repaired and reconstructed them.

The " Potiphar's wife " story told of Anteia is one of several favourite " plots " common to Hebrew and Greek mythology (see p. 160).

The next lines are famous and important, as containing Homer's only reference to writing. In the following Book, when the heroes draw lots for the right to meet Hektor in single combat, they only mark their lots, and one man cannot recognize another's mark (VII, 175-189).[1] Homer has no verb meaning " write ", for γράφω merely means " scratch " and except here is used only of weapons (e.g. Il., XVII, 599) or of thorns (Od., XXIV, 229). Here, he refers to " grievous signs " or " tokens ", " life-destroying things ", and " the token, whatsoever he might be bringing from Proitos ", rather as if he did not understand what he was describing and suspected magic. In fact, as the Aegean world in historic times uses our familiar alphabet, the " Phœnician letters ", with their Phœnician individual names—unlike Greek Cyprus, which uses a syllabary descended from the Minoan script—it seems very likely that writing did really become a lost art in the Aegean amid the increasing barbarism of the later heroic and earliest Hellenic periods; and as if both the Heroes and their poets were illiterate. That there is nothing impossible in this theory has been shown by evidence from more recent times among the South Slavs; in Bosnia the bards used to remember without any extreme difficulty bodies of verse considerably longer than the surviving works of Homer.

The fact of the tablet being folded (and doubtless also

[1] A fact curiously ignored by Bury, *C.A.H.*, II, p. 508.

sealed) makes it clear that the reference in this passage is to real writing which unauthorized persons (such as Bellerophon) might have read if the letter had been open.

So Bellerophon comes to Lykia and, with the charming politeness of the Aegean world, is entertained first and asked his business afterwards—like Têlemachos by Nestor and Agamemnon's emissaries by Achilleus. The fact that, after reading the " soul-destroying things " in the letter, the father of the alleged injured lady still does not have Bellerophon murdered out of hand is probably due to the same cause as Proitos' own similar forbearance ; Bellerophon was now his guest. So like Saul in a similar predicament he tries to let his enemy's own high spirits cause his death, by sending him on a desperate quest ; but Bellerophon, like David with his collection of Philistine trophies, returns alive and triumphant, having killed the chimaira.

The description of the Chimaira, " a lion before, but a serpent behind ", is well known. It is not so well known that a beast of this description was probably to be seen in Asia Minor in Bellerophon's time, and can be seen in Syria at the present day. A Hittite relief from Carchemish shows us a veritable Chimaira ; a winged lion, with its tail raised aloft and ending in a serpent's head, and a human head in a conical helmet rising from the lion's shoulders, in place of that of the goat. Once Hittite art had evolved an effective composite monster of this type, it was a short step to the point at which stray heroes from the Aegean who had penetrated beyond the Asian coast claimed over their wine, when at home again and bragging of their experiences, that they had met the beast in the flesh, and killed it too. They had had special interviews with the immortal gods who gave them a winged horse (or winged sandals and a cap of darkness) to help them rid the world of a pest. But they were not able to bring these home to show their friends, because Athene (or Hermes, or the Nymphs) wanted them back afterwards.

Pêgasos, by the way, and his partnership with Bellerophon, is described in Hesiod (Theogony, ll. 281, 325) and was presumably known to Homer, though not mentioned in this brief synopsis. There is a winged quadruped among the Hittite reliefs of Sinjerli whose head and neck might be meant for those of a horse, though it has a lion's legs and paws. In this case as in that of the Chimaira, since we know that the Hittites imagined such monsters in their Syrian period (about the tenth century) and that the Greeks pictured them as existing in Asia about the twelfth or thirteenth, it is a probable hypothesis that the conception, both in Greek poetry and Syrian art, derives from the art of Anatolia in days when the empire of Khatti still stood.

The Solymoi, victims of Bellerophon's next exploit, are a perfectly historical people. They were the aboriginal hillmen of the Lykian hinterland, and as such waged perpetual war with the lowlanders and coast-dwellers, with their foreign kings and contact with foreign civilization. The few facts we hear about them bear sufficient witness to their prowess : they gave Bellerophon the hardest struggle of his life, in the next generation they killed his son, and centuries later, as we hear from an inscription, they were still carrying on the same warfare against the Rhodian colonists of Greek Phasêlis.[1]

The very persistent Greek tradition of Amazons in Asia Minor is difficult to account for. Possibly it is a mistake, originally based on the existence of a hairless and fleshy male type among the Anatolian peoples, a type represented in Hittite art. Alternatively, there may really have been female warriors in Asia ; there is possibly a reference to them in a cuneiform tablet, containing part of a code of laws, from Boghazkeui.[2] An old theory was that the original " Amazons " were armed priestesses, corresponding to the effeminate eunuch-priests, of one or other manifestation of the Asiatic mother-goddess—for instance the war-goddess Ma (whose name does not require interpretation) at Kŏmana. Evidence that such *armed* priestesses existed is lacking, however.[3] In any case, one or two travellers' tales, handed on into the Aegean via Troy or Lykia, of women warriors on the plateau, would naturally give rise to whole nations of Amazons by a simple process of exaggeration.

Then at last, after Bellerophon has come successfully through all these adventures, does the King of Lykia in desperation try to kill his guest by direct methods—and fails

---

[1] *Lindos Temple Chronicle*, Entry No. 24.
[2] *Keilschrifttexte aus Boghazkoï*, VI, 3. Cf. Sayce, *J.H.S.*, XLIII, p. 48.
[3] Sayce's statement that they are mentioned by Strabo (*J.H.S.*, XLIII, p. 47), is incorrect.

again ; at which, recognizing him for a favourite of the gods, he gives it up, promises Bellerophon his daughter to wife (the usual ending) and one imagines that they will all live happily ever after.   But not quite.   A final and even more than usually cryptic allusion is made to a story of how "he also came to be hateful to all the gods " ; it looks like a story of the madness of Bellerophon, on the lines of the Old Testament story of the madness of Nebuchadrezzar.   The Alêïan plain, however, where he wanders " shunning the path of men " is probably that of Tarsos,[1] the Elisha of Hebrew and probably the Alasya of Egyptian geographers ; a locality of which we shall hear more anon.

Sarpêdon, the leading Lykian chieftain in the Iliad, holds his throne by matrilinear succession as far as the pedigree here given goes.   He is son of the *daughter* of Bellerophon by the *daughter* of the previous king and queen.

That is one picture of life in the Aegean at the time when the Aiolid heroes were beginning to "discover" Asia.   As a pendant to it—a picture not of individuals but of populations beginning to move by sea—we have the sundry and confused accounts of the wanderings of the Pelasgoi[2]; wanderings which ultimately brought fragments of their race to Crete, to the Troad, to the coast of Thrace, to the islands of the north Aegean.[3]   There were also traditions of them in the foundation stories of Lesbos, Chios, Knidos, and, on the mainland of Asia, Klazomenai.[4]   Whether they spoke a dialect of Greek we cannot tell ; we only know that in Herodotos' time the language of their descendants was unintelligible to him, and there- fore " barbarous ".   If the place-names Larîsa (or Larissa) and Argos, both found so commonly both in Greece and Asia, were native to the Pelasgian language, then obviously that language, like that of the Minoan Cretans, was primitive Aegean.[5]   But in any case, driven out from their old " Pelasgian Argos " in

[1] So Myres, *C.A.H.*, III, p. 644.
[2] See Myres, " History of the Pelasgian Theory," in *J.H.S.*, XXVII.
[3] For references, see pp. 58-9.
[4] D.S., V, 81 ; Str., XIII, 621.
[5] The Pelasgoi of the Trojan War come from Larissa, *Il.*, II, 841.   The name probably means " the Castle "—possibly the syllable " Lar " is the same as the well-known Etruscan word meaning " lord " ; combined with the termination-sa or-ssa meaning " place." Argos apparently means " plain "—so Strabo, VIII, p. 372.

Thessaly they became for the time a wild race of landless pirates —one more danger to civilization—with their hand against every man.

Meanwhile Egypt and Khatti were busy in Syria, drawing each other's blood again.

In 1313 after the short reign of Rameses I, Seti I succeeded to the kingdom restored to health by Horemheb, and immediately broke the treaty with Khatti. The honour of a Pharaoh, he seems to have felt, demanded a war of revenge for the aggressions of Subbiluliuma ; and so he and his successors followed the will-o'-the-wisp of prestige into the bog of a new Hittite War.

It is at this point that the very important recent excavations at Beth-shan in the Jordan Valley begin to throw light on the history of Aegean influences in Palestine.

There were no considerable Hittite forces nearly so far south ; resistance to the Egyptian advance was feeble, and Seti, with his army newly organized in the four great " legions " of Amen, Ra, Ptah and Sutekh (as we learn from a stele found at Beth-Shan itself), overran Palestine in one campaign. In the absence of any formidable enemy he was even able to divide his army and move in several columns ; and the legions of Amen, Ra, and Sutekh occupied Hamath,[1] Beth-shan and Yenoam on the self-same day.

Seti's army included a considerable force of those Shardana who had already figured as Egyptian mercenaries in the " Amarna Age " ; and we now meet with valuable evidence of their Aegean origin. In the remains of the temple which Seti proceeded to set up at Beth-shan, after completing his re-conquest of Palestine and Transjordania, the excavators claim to have discovered several cult objects of unmistakably Aegean type ; and the most obvious, indeed the only theory of the way in which these were introduced is that they are relics of Seti's mercenaries. The excavators believe, in fact, that the mercenaries did the actual building of this temple, save for a few pieces of highly skilled work. It looks as if a small permanent garrison of mercenaries was left on the spot, who worshipped the gods of the land in the temple that they themselves had built for their Egyptian master.

Having in a further campaign pushed forward against the

[1] Not the famous Hamath in North Syria, evidently.

Hittites, fought a battle with them and probably been disagreeably surprised at the solidity of their power in Syria—for they were actually colonizing the land—Seti had the sound sense to abandon thoughts of further conquest and renew the treaty, contenting himself with little more than Palestine out of the great Asiatic empire of his predecessors. But his son and successor, the ambitious, vigorous, and not very clever Rameses II, must needs renew the war, one of the most futile military struggles in history.

A preliminary compaign gave Rameses the Phœnician coast, by means of which the great Eighteenth Dynasty conquerors had been accustomed to keep open communications with Egypt by sea. The Egyptian was no great seaman, but the Hittite was no seaman at all, and sea-transport, for limited numbers of troops, was safer as well as quicker than land-transport. However, as Professor Breasted has pointed out, this campaign gave the enemy warning of the coming offensive, and when in the following year Rameses moved against the country further north, which the Hittites had not only conquered but colonized, all preparations had been made against him. The veteran king Mutallu had come down in person with the full levy of his empire and its subject kingdoms, as well as bands of mercenaries from the warlike nations further west; Dardanians and Lykians, "M-s-", who may well be Homer's Mysians, and "K-r-k-sh", who may well be the Kilikes, Andromache's people in the Iliad, dwelling south of the Dardanoi, about the Gulf of Adramyttion[1]. With them also were a people whose name is variously read as that of the Maiŏnians or men of Ilios or of Oroanda. Of these the first identification is the most probable, and the second much the least so. Ilios (never Ili*on* in Homer) was a small though a wealthy and strongly fortified town, and not likely to send a contingent worth mentioning. If any Ilians or other Troes figured in Mutallu's army, they are probably included among the Dardanian contingent. The Maiŏnes on the other hand, who, like the Lykioi, figure among the Trojan allies in Homer, seem to be quite an important tribe; and they hail from the later Lydia—just that central district of Western Asia Minor where the westernmost Hittite rock-sculptures, at Sipylos and

---

[1] An alternative identification—since there is only one Egyptian character for l and r—might be Gergithes; on whom see below, pp. 153-4.

Kara-bel, mark the limits attained by the conquests of Mursil. Consequently the reading " Maunna " or the like, rather than " Iliunna ", is to be preferred.

Altogether it was a formidable host. The Hittite king, says the Egyptian epic poet who celebrated the valour of Rameses, " had left not a nation on his way, that he brought not with him. . . . He had left neither silver nor gold to his people ; he had taken all their wealth and possessions to give them to the people who marched with him to war ".

Rameses for his part had not been idle in preparation ; he had with him the four " legions " of the Egyptian regular army as reorganized under Seti, with probably the black Sudanese troops who had been a feature of Pharaoh's armies from early times, and a large force of the redoubtable armoured Shardana. So important an element in the army did these now form that " the footmen, the chariots, and the Shardana " has become a natural periphrasis for the whole army.

These " Shardana ", when named as a contingent in the Egyptian army, probably include troops levied among the sea-peoples generally. Some at least of them were prisoners of war, we find, whom Rameses had incorporated in his own army ; they must have been captured in unsuccessful raids on the Delta coast.[1] It sounds a dangerous expedient ; but even when, in later years, these troops were pitted against their own countrymen, their discipline or loyalty stood the test.

The armies met in the hard-fought Battle of Kadesh, where some forty thousand men must have been engaged on this side and that ; the most interesting of Egyptian battles since the sources are full enough to let us see something of the cleverness with which Mutallu lay in wait for Rameses. The latter, sweeping northward by forced marches, remained all unsuspecting until the whole mass of the Hittite chariotry thundered out from behind the town of Kadesh, falling upon the flank of his marching columns as they straggled over the plain. We can see, too, how, by desperate fighting, Rameses and the wreck of his two leading divisions struggled out of the trap ; while the fact that practically the whole of Palestine proceeded to revolt from Egypt, and had to be reconquered once more, shows how ill-founded was the Pharaoh's claim to reckon his

[1] For such lenient treatment of captured pirates, cf. the story of the sea-raider in *Odyssey*, XIV ; quoted below, pp. 180-83.

escape as a victory.   But neither with this nor the succeeding campaigns in which, by fifteen summers more of arduous fighting, Rameses carved his way into central Syria, are we here immediately concerned.   The appearance of the sea-peoples and western Asiatics in the ranks of the opposing armies is of more importance for our present purposes than the result of the campaign.

Like his father, Rameses II built a temple at Beth-shan, utilizing the labour of his mercenaries ; and some of the bricks are marked with signs identical with characters of the Minoan script.   Both this and some other indications confirmed the excavators in the belief that the builders were certainly of Aegean and not improbably of actual Cretan extraction.   The building may have been done either in the intervals between campaigning seasons or after the end of the war.

For at last, in about Rameses' twentieth year as king, a peace was signed, apparently on the basis of the *status quo ante bellum*, between him and Mutallu's brother and successor, Khattusil III ; a peace presently confirmed by the marriage of Khattusil's young daughter to the middle-aged polygamist of Egypt.   Even Rameses had had enough of the war.   His persistent battering had seriously shaken the Hittite Empire, but he had not loosed its hold on Syria ; and the resources of Egypt for a war of aggression were coming to an end.

In the following generation the sea-peoples began to venture on attacks on both the late belligerents ; no longer mere acts of piracy, but operations on a considerable scale.   The damaging and evenly-contested war between the two great powers must have had a deleterious effect on the prestige of both, among the sea-peoples ; very much the same effect as modern European wars, from 1854 to 1914, have tended to have among Asiatics.   And the habitual employment of islanders and western Asian peoples as mercenaries on this side and that served to give these nations a high idea of their own warlike prowess, and also to keep them well informed about the state of affairs in the east and south.

The earliest great sea-raid of which we hear is directed against the Hittites.   Some time after the middle of the century, Attarissiyas, or Attarsiyas, of Akhhia, was making war with a large armament in the south-west of Asia Minor, where he drove from his throne the native king, Wadduwattas,

Adyattes as the Greeks would have called him. Hittite royal troops, however, sent by the new king of Khatti, Dudkhaliyas III, restored Adyattes, and gave Dudkhaliyas a chance to boast of his victory. The fact that he addresses Attarsiyas as " brother " in a letter, however, suggests that the Hittite victory might have been, to say the least of it, more complete. Attarsiyas was in fact not discouraged from making a second attack with a fleet of as many as a hundred sail,[1] about 1230. He was again defeated, in a pitched battle, and driven back towards his base, but appears from the language of the tablet, to have continued to hold some portion of the Pamphylian coast ; and he was also still strong enough to fall a few years later upon Cyprus, which he devastated.[2]

The " Achaia " from which this sea-rover was operating, if it is not the same as the Akhhiyawa or Lesser Achaia of which we have already heard, was probably the island of Rhodes, where Diodôros[3] tells us that the city of Ialysos at one time bore the name Achaia, and where well-known finds of " Mycenæan " graves testify to colonization from the Greek mainland before this date.

The name of Attarsiyas (" -T-r-s-y-s ") himself is identified by his discoverer, Dr. Förrer, with "Atresas", an uncontracted form of the familiar name Atreus ; Dr. Sayce, however, shows reason to prefer " Pterseus ", " the Destroyer ", the older form of the more euphonious name Perseus. The initial vowel then represents a Hittite attempt to render the awkward Greek double consonant. He further suggests a connection between this episode and the founding of Tarsos (called Tersos on its coins) ; and draws attention to the statement of a late historian[4] that " while Bĕlimos reigned over the Assyrians ", " Perseus son of Danæ arrived in his country with a hundred ships." Certainly, whether or not we may connect Bĕlimos with some such Hittite name as "Subbiluliuma", there is no

---

[1] So, Förrer ; Sayce doubts the reading " ships ".

[2] On this important epiosde, see the following, among other discussions : *Die Griechen in den Boghazköi Texten* in *Orientalische Literaturzeitung*, XXVII (1924), col. 113-118, and *Vorhomerische Griechen in den Keilschrifttexten von Boghazköi*, in *Mitteil. d. Deutsch. Morgenl. Gesellsch.*, 1924 ; Glotz and Cohen, *Histoire Grecque* (in the *Hist. Generale*), I, p. 92 ; Sayce, in *J.H.S.*, XLV, pp. 161 ff., and in *Antiquity*, II, pp. 207-8, where he rejects some of his earlier views.

[3] V, 57. There was also an " Achaians' Point " in Cyprus ; Str., XIV, 682.

[4] Eusebios' *Chronikon*, I, p. 62 (ed. Schoene), quoting Kephalion.

doubt that the very early Achaian hero Perseus' adventures were traditionally placed in the East; it was here that he slew the monstrous Gorgon and here—on the coast of Syria, at Joppa, it was said[1]—that he rescued Andromeda from the sea-dragon. It would be quite in the manner of folk-memory and of the epic tradition to transmute the historical chieftain of a fleet and army into a legendary slayer of dragons all alone.

The Empire of Khatti was indeed rocking towards its fall. The strain imposed by Achaian raids following on Egyptian wars was intensified by a disastrous famine about 1225— probably to be connected with the return of dry conditions after the "rainfall maximum" early in the century. It is interesting to hear that Merenptah of Egypt sent shiploads of grain to help in the work of famine-relief[2]; so it was still possible for a strong Egyptian convoy to sail along the coast of Syria in spite of the sea-raiders. Shortly afterwards the Pharaoh found to his disgust that peoples whom he reckoned as Hittite subjects were leaguing themselves with the Libu (Libyans) to threaten an invasion of the western Delta. These peoples were the ever restless Lykians with the Sh-k-l-sh (Shakalsha ?— perhaps Sagalassians ; but the historic Sagalassos was inland) and the T-r-sh, who are clearly the people of the Hittite Taruisa and Old Testament Tiras, and probably identical with the Tyrrhenoi or Tursci, whom we call the Etruscans—still at this date a people of Asia Minor.[3] With them, and probably not from the Hittite area, were bands of Shardana and -k-w-sh-, whose name is usually vocalized as Akaiwasha and identified with that of Homer's Ἀχαιϝοί, Achaians.

The Pharaoh might well feel aggrieved at being attacked by old allies of the very kingdom to which he was just selling the corn that they sorely needed, but the probability is that the Hittite king could no longer control them. The remote and almost amphibious Lykians can have been but precariously "subject" at the best of times, and the career of Attarsiyas shows that in the outer regions of his empire the Hittite king's writ no longer ran even so firmly as of old. Also the raiders, like the native Khatti themselves, were hungry, as Merenptah

---

[1] Strabo, XVI, p. 759.
[2] Breasted, *Ancient Records of Egypt*, III, 580, l. 24.
[3] See above, p. 62.

tells us, and their reason for fighting was a pressing one—
" to fill their bellies daily ".

It was a powerful confederacy, but the threatened storm
did not burst at once, and Merenptah had time to carry out a
campaign in Palestine, chastising rebels among whom Israel
makes its first appearance in a contemporary document, before
turning his steps westward. The invasion came in or about
1221. The Pharaoh was ready for it. He had fortified
Heliopolis and Memphis, but his best defence was the very
effective field army which he was holding in readiness,
and with which in the early days of April he marched to
seek out the enemy in the western Delta. There the battle
was joined.

From the first it was a one-sided affair. The allies were
numerous and brave, but their masses of swordsmen on foot
were ill-matched against a combination of archery and mounted
troops. For six hours the Libyans and the sea-raiders tried
to press home their attack, while the Egyptians poured their
shafts into the crowded ranks. It was an ancient Omdurman.
Then at last the assault wavered, and the Pharaoh counter-
attacked. His chariotry, held in reserve till this moment,
charged in terrifying style, rank on rank, with archers shooting
from the cars as they came, as we may see in Egyptian battle-
pieces of their old Hittite wars ; and the enemy line dissolved
in irretrievable flight.

The rout was very bloody. Some 2,500 of the sea-raiders
were killed, 6,500 Libyans, six sons of the Libyan king.
Prisoners were nearly as numerous. The Libyan camp was
captured with a splendid spoil, looted and burnt. Nine
thousand bronze swords were taken up on the battlefield—but
no bows ; evidently the allies had none, to their cost.

Egypt was saved for a generation. It was well, for the
Nineteenth Dynasty virtually died with Merenptah, and a
period of confusion seems to have followed. Merenptah,
already an ageing man when he succeeded his father, the long-
lived Rameses II, had shown the vigour without the rashness
of his father's youth, and had deserved well of his country.
It was, it will be remembered, one of his short-lived successors,
Seti II, who set his cartouche upon an object of the utmost
importance for Aegean archæology—a bronze sword of the
Danubian leaf-shaped type ; the captured sword of some

ill-fated sea-raider. But there was no further serious threat until the twelfth century had begun, by which time a soldier, Rameses III, once more sat upon the throne of the Pharaohs.

It was well that it was so ; for about 1200 the storm burst finally over the tottering Hittite Empire.

CHAPTER VI

The Great Migrations : about 1210-1190 b.c.

"THE isles were restless, disturbed among themselves; they poured out their people all together. No land stood before them, beginning from Khatti—Kode,[1] Carchemish, Arvad and Alasya; they destroyed them and assembled together in their camp in the midst of the Amorite country. . . . They marched towards Egypt with fire prepared before them. P-l-s-t, Z-kk-r, Sh-k-l-sh, D-n-y-n and W-sh-sh were their strength. These lands were united; they laid their hands upon the countries as far as the circle of the world. . . . The countries which came from their isles in the midst of the sea, they advanced upon Egypt, their hearts relying upon their arms."

Thus wrote the scribes of Rameses III, describing the most formidable invasion that had endangered Egypt for three hundred years, since the passing of the Shepherd Kings. The Hittite records confirm the news, by their silence. Dudkhaliyas IV, their last king of whom we know, came to the throne about 1210, and during his reign came the catastrophe. The great stronghold of the City of Khatti—Khattusas, "the Silver Town" which is now called Boghaz-keui—came to an end as an imperial capital, and the tablets in its record office lay scattered and neglected until our own times. We know nothing, nor are we ever likely to, of the last campaigns of the Hittite army or of the disastrous battles somewhere along the Halys or in the pass of the Sangarios Gap. An allusion in a subordinate clause by Rameses III's scribe above-quoted, and, negatively, the cessation of the Hittite records; these give us our only notice of the fall of one of the great powers of the older world. And when next we have news of the interior of Asia Minor, from Assyrians and Greeks, it is news of Aryan-speaking peoples, the Phryges and the Moschoi, under their Midas and Gordios kings—those Phrygians who first appear

[1] = Modern Cilicia.

in Homer as allies of the old Mysian and Dardanian tribes. As for the Hittites, with their strange half-Aryan group of languages, they still hold Carchemish and their other Syrian strongholds ; but their very name has perished out of Anatolia.

The Phrygians, who thus penetrate to the centre of Asia Minor between 1200 and the date of the Trojan War, almost certainly came from the Balkan Peninsula.[1] The refugees of the older nations, fleeing before them, move to the south and east, by land through the Taurus mountains into Syria and Palestine, and by sea from " the isles ", that is, the shores of the Aegean, into the Levant. And thus by land and sea together, the wave of migration breaks upon the coasts of Egypt.

Working back from the well-known to the less-known, it will be best for us to see first how the hordes of the migration fared at the hands of Rameses III, and afterwards to examine the rather copious Greek and Lydian traditions which appear to refer to these important events.

It was not a mere piratical raid, this time, like that incursion of sea-folk who had fought against Merenptah along with the Libyan migrants. The whole of Asia Minor seemed to be moving, disturbed by the same shock that ruined the Hittite power ; all except a few tribes such as the Lykians and the Dardanoi, left, as though in a backwater of the stream of migration, in the far west of the peninsula.

Egypt had fought the Sh-k-l-sh before, but the other contingents of the horde bear names that are unfamiliar. The W-sh-sh *may* be men of Oassos in Karia or Oasos in Crete ; the D-n-y-n *may* be Danaans[2] ; for archæology shows that the Aegean civilization-area, as well as Anatolia, recruited this movement. The Aegean, however, unlike Anatolia, suffered

---

[1] Cf. the following passages of Herodotos : VII, 73 (Phrygians were called Briges before they went from Thrace to Asia Minor) ; VI, 45 ; VII, 185 (mention of a tribe called Brygoi in Thrace under the Persians) ; VII, 138 (rose-gardens of king Midas (!) at Mount Bermios in Macedonia). Cf. also Strabo, VII, 330 (Briges held Bermion in their pre-Asiatic days), VII, 326 (Brygoi, a tribe in Epeiros) ; also Stephanos, *s.v.* Βρύξ.

Casson, *Macedonia, Thrace and Illyria*, pp. 102-3, also collects a large number of place-names common to the Balkan region and the historic Phrygia. His note on p. 105 traverses Beloch's and Hiller von Gärtringen's denial of this tradition.

[2] These D-n-y-n are probably the same as those in whose land the peaceful accession of a new king is reported in the Tell-el-Amarna letters ; see above, p. 118.

no wholesale displacement of populations. The gradual decline of Late Minoan civilization continued without any abrupt break ; and even such notable sea-wolves as the Lykians and the Achaioi took no part in this enterprise.

The name of the Z-kk-r is variously transliterated and vocalized : Thekel, Zakkar, Zakkal, Djakaray, to quote a selection. One may reasonably connect them with a region called Zikhria or something like it, conquered by the Hittites in the reign of Mursil. There are highly suggestive Greek traditions about the tribe called the Teukroi, an ancient people found in Crete and in the Troad (see pp. 87, 153); but the initial letter of the Egyptian word—some kind of modified dental—presents us with a difficulty.

Lastly, the P-l-s-t are certainly the Philistines, whose most important achievement in history was to be the welding into a nation of the hill-tribes of Israel. Of their origin, at least, we can speak with some confidence, on the strength of the representations of them on the walls of Rameses' temple at Medinet Habu. Here we see them, armed with the tapering sword, round shield and laminated lobster-like corselet of the Shardana. The corselet is worn only by some, not all, Philistines however ; and instead of the prominent apparently metal crest of the Shardan helmet, the Philistines, like the " T-r-sh ", have their headgear surrounded by a circlet of feathers. It is this equipment that enables us to trace them with fair certainty to the south-west of Asia Minor. The feather crown is " as worn " by a procession of Ionian and Karian warriors in an Assyrian relief, and by the Lykian contingent in Xerxes' fleet[1] ; the feather crown and round shield appear together among the hieroglyphics of the Phaistos Disk, a document found in, but clearly not native to, Minoan Crete ; and the crown, with a different type of shield, semi-cylindrical like a common Roman type, seems to reappear in the battle-scene on the fragment of a silver vase, the " Siege Vase ", found at Mykênai. The Philistines in short were not Minoans, but were in touch with Minoan civilization.[2]

---

[1] Hdt., VII, 92 ; cf. Hall, " A Note on the Phaestos Disk " in *J.H.S.*, XXXI, and figures from an Assyrian relief of the time of Sennacherib, fig. 7, *ibid.*

[2] On the whole question of Philistine origins, cf. Hall, in *C.A.H.*, II, pp. 275-295.

Not mentioned by the inscription, but added by the great Papyrus Harris to the list of Rameses' enemies, there was also among the migrants a contingent of Shardana.

The situation was complicated for Rameses by the fact that, in spite of the great victory won by Merenptah, the Libyans were already once more threatening the Delta from the west ; and to make matters worse, the sea-peoples knew quite well what was going on and were prepared to concert operations with them. That the Libyans should again be moving, and in very large numbers, within a generation after the fearful punishment inflicted on them by Merenptah, argues pressure of economic circumstances—more shortly, of famine. This agrees well enough with several Greek traditions, with Merenptah's reference to famine among the Hittites in his time, and with the evidence cited by Mr. Brooks on conditions in Central Europe. The great and widespread increase of rainfall about 1300 had spelt disaster to inhabitants of the European mountain-zone ; but in more arid districts, such as the Greek islands and the steppeland of the Libyan coast, increased rainfall must have meant increased fertility and increased population. Now, with the gradual return to dry conditions, from about 1250 onwards until 1000, the shoe pinches ; but there is " corn in Egypt ", thanks to Abyssinia and the Nile, and towards Egypt press both Libyan tribesmen and Asiatic refugees.

The sea-farers had planned an attack on Egypt from two sides ; the main army and fleet, convoying the enormous waggon-train that carried the women and children, moved southward from their camp " in the midst of Amor ", while the Libyans, supported by an allied contingent, struck in from the west. But to synchronize operations so far apart was beyond their power, and Rameses was able to engage them in detail. Rameses' army was of the now usual Egyptian type : strong in archers and chariotry, but relying for heavy infantry almost entirely on mercenaries drawn from among the sea-peoples themselves ; the Shardana, as usual, the Tursha or Tyrrhenians who had fought against Merenptah, and a Libyan contingent. It was very much the same type of army as that of the Persians in the time of Alexander, with its eastern cavalry and archers, but relying on its Greek mercenaries for

PLATE XI

RAMESES DEFEATS THE SEA-RAIDERS

A scene from the huge sculptured battle-piece on the walls of the temple at Medinet Habu. On the left the Egyptians, armed with bow and club, are about to board a Philistine ship, of whose crew the arrows have made havoc. On the right a ship of the Shardana (in horned helmets) is in danger of fouling that of their Philistine allies; men on both ships gesticulate and shout warnings. The Egyptians are already confident enough to be taking prisoners (see bottom, l.). The laminated body-armour of the sea-peoples can be clearly seen.

[face p. 144

stubbornness and solidity.   But there was not an Alexander among Rameses' opponents.

Near the rising ground on the edge of the desert, called " the Mountain of the Horns of the Earth ", just where Merenptah's chariotry had at last checked their pursuit in the battle nearly thirty years before, Rameses and his men made a still more dreadful slaughter of the Libyans and their allies. The sea-rovers, like the Achaians at Troy, were driven to the water's edge where their ships were beached ; and even their fleet, or much of it, was burnt or captured.   A thousand prisoners were taken, and nearly thirteen thousand enemy dead were counted on the field.   The western danger was at an end.

Then, moving by the coast into Palestine and accompanied by a powerful fleet, which he had collected to meet that of the sea-peoples, the Pharaoh marched against the main body of the northerners.   Shardana   fought   Shardana,   and   the mercenaries of Egypt won, breaking through the enemy's attempt to defend his vast unwieldy convoy and plundering the slow two-wheeled ox-waggons that carried the women and children and other possessions of the horde.   And finally, as his " crowning mercy ", Rameses somehow managed to trap the opposing fleet between his own fleet and army, in one of the harbours of north Syria or of the Delta.   This is the fight of which so spirited a picture still exists, in the reliefs on the temple walls of Medinet Habu.

Once again it was an archers' battle.   At long range the first Egyptian arrows sang through the air, and as the fleets came   together   the   heavy-armed   men,   who   crowded   the northerners' decks and fighting-tops, fell in heaps beneath them.   There was no escape to be had on to the land, for there was the Egyptian army under the Pharaoh ; and a desperate attempt by the northerners to force their way out by sea only hastened their destruction.   " They were trapped like wild-fowl ", says the exultant Rameses.   " As for those upon the sea, a full flame was before their eyes in the harbour mouths, and a wall of bronze upon the land enclosed them. . . . They were slain and made heaps from stern to prow of their galleys; and all their goods were cast upon the waters, for a remembrance of Egypt."   All was confusion among the Philistines before ever they could get near enough to board. On the temple walls the scene still lives before us : men

gesticulating, shouting orders and counter-orders; ships
fouling one another—one has capsized; the arrows pick off
the chiefs from deck or crow's-nest; and then finally the
southern fleet crashes into them and the Egyptians leap, mace
in hand, over their galleys' lion-headed prows, to complete
the work.

Egypt was saved, and Rameses was also confirmed in his
sovereignty over the southern portion of Syria, where he now
graciously permitted the surviving Philistines, "Zakkaray",
and their allies to settle; the Zakkaray at and north of Dor
in the neighbourhood of Mount Carmel, and the Philistines
in what now for the first time became the land of Palestine.
He also left, like his predecessors, a permanent mercenary
garrison at the stronghold of Beth-shan.

After one more campaign in which he penetrated into north
Syria, and one more victory over the hapless Libu, who were
driven on by other tribes from behind, Rameses was able to
spend the rest of his reign of thirty-one years in well-earned
repose.   In the wall-paintings of certain tombs of this period,
in Egypt, appear some Aegean vases of "Late Minoan III"
type.   It is almost the last trace of trade, or of any but hostile
contact, between Egypt and the Aegean peoples for over
five hundred years.

Archæology, in Cyprus and in Palestine, preserves numerous
traces of the movements of these eventful years, and shows, as
we have said, that some at least of the invaders of the Levant
were people who had been in close touch with Minoan civilization.   The characteristic " Philistine Vase "—a type of pottery
found on all the undoubted early Philistine sites, and on no
others in Palestine—is already familiar to archæologists from
thirteenth-century finds in Argolis, Rhodes, and Cyprus[1]; and
the brooch or safety-pin, which in the previous century had
been coming into vogue in the Aegean, now seems to have
become commoner in Cyprus, and, in a slightly different form,
makes its first appearance in Palestine.[2]   Cyprus seems to
have suffered considerably from the passing of the horde;
Alasya was one of the lands that " stood not before " the sea-
raiders; and accordingly in Cyprus, where Apollo Alasiôtes

[1] Phythian-Adams, in *B.S.J. Bulletin*, 1923.
[2] Blinkenberg, *Fibules*, pp. 62, 284.

was worshipped in Hellenic times,[1] we find that at this very date the important Aegean settlements all appear to suffer destruction, and two of them—Salamis and Kition—when rebuilt in the following years, are rebuilt on different sites.[2]

One interesting relic of the times was found at Gaza, in the shape of a tapering sword of bronze,[3] of exactly the type carried by the Shardana and Philistines on the temple walls of Medinet Habu. It is of considerable size, and may be compared with the enormous weapons of some of Rameses III's mercenaries in the sculptures. In the course of the thirteenth century swords—and helmets—had developed with a rapidity that tells its own tale ; probably in the effort to resist the " great Thracian sword " that does such execution in Homer's battles.[4] Three leaf-shaped swords from Egypt and one from Cyprus point the moral.[5] The Shardana would have done well to adopt this weapon, but their conservatism evidently shirked a change that would have necessitated a complete alteration in their style of fencing. They preferred to go on enlarging, to the point of unwieldiness, swords of an old type in which the weight is all close to the hand. This facilitated clever wrist-work and the use of the point ; but the fact that the trend of migration was all from north to south shows that their sword-play was on the whole no match for the furious onrush and whole-hearted slash of the warriors of the Homeric or Danubian school.

The Danubian sword made its way south through Asia Minor as well as by sea—as indeed one would expect from the double land and sea migration. The Hittite warriors of north Syria, early in the last millennium B.C., are girt with leaf-shaped swords of great size, as may be seen from the sculptured dado-slabs from Sinjerli in the Berlin Museum.[6] These weapons belong to the fully-developed Iron Age ; but since the leaf shape is not particularly suitable for iron, and essential if a heavy blow is to be delivered with a blade of the more brittle bronze (a long, straight blade of bronze would be

---

[1] Inscription quoted by Meister, *Griech. Dialect.*, II, p. 171 ; Farnell, *Cults of Gk. States*, IV, p. 477.
[2] Myres, in *C.A.H.*, III, p. 636.
[3] Hall and Burchardt, *Proceedings of the Society of Antiquaries*, 1914.
[4] e.g., *Il.*, XIII, 576. Cf. Miss Lorimer in *Liverpool Annals*, XV.
[5] Peake, *Bronze Age*, Plate XII, Nos. 6, 7, 8, 11. No. 8 is the all-important specimen dated by the cartouche of Seti II (1209-1205).
[6] Plate II (c).

shivered by such use)—it is probable that like the historic Greek and Roman swords, these Syrian weapons owe their shape to bronze-age originals.

Greek traditions of the migrations of 1200-1190—the outpouring from Thrace, the overrunning of Anatolia, and the invasion of Palestine from the Aegean and the west of Asia Minor—are fairly numerous, and are worth collecting ; less because they add anything to what we already knew of the period than because they show how solid a core of history, if only we can get at it, the most unpromising legend reported by a Hellenistic historian may contain.

First, as to the movement from Thrace ; we have already quoted traditions confirming the probability that the Phrygians who destroyed the Hittite Empire came from Thrace. There are also other traditions which give us some idea of the activities of raiders from Thrace, both among the islands of the Aegean and in Greece.

The thalassocracy-list, on the theory here adopted, would date the great development of Thracian sea-power about 1223 ; which corresponds sufficiently closely with the date of the first great concerted attack of the disturbed Asian and Aegean peoples upon Egypt, under Merenptah in 1221. But this is by no means the only Greek reference to Thracian sea-power at the time of the Greek " Heroic Age."[1] The most detailed story that we possess is that in Diodoros, of the Children of the North Wind, a Thracian war-band which occupied Naxos and spread its devastations far and wide. Repulsed in a descent on Euboia, they supplied themselves with women by carrying off a number who had been celebrating religious rites on the coast of Thessaly ; for their own viking expedition had consisted of men only. They were said to have continued to hold Naxos for two hundred years, after which they abandoned it owing to drought and the island was afterwards reoccupied by Karians.

Samothrace also received its northern colonists at an early date ; it is already in the Iliad called the Thracian Samos. And Eleusis in Attica had an old legend of one Eumolpos, a prince of Thrace who was also in some fashion a son of the Sea-God, a fighter and medicine man, who in true sea-raider

[1] For references in the following paragraphs, see p. 58 n.

fashion lent his sword to the Eleusinians for their war with Erechtheus king of Athens and was slain by him.[1] Eumolpos has all the appearance of a historic personality. A clan of Eumolpidai, priests of the Mysteries, preserved his name down to historic times ; and since neither they nor their ancestor were in any particular sense " sweet singers ", as the name implies, it is probable that that ancestor is a real person and not a mythical creation. The names of two of his daughters, Saisara and Pammerope, are also recorded, and that of a son, Immarados[2] ; and these names are not Greek at all—a striking contrast to the conventional Kreusa's and Iphinoe's that we find in a genealogy that has been patched up by the "logographers ". Mr. T. W. Allen suggests that since Eumolpos' children are not Greeks by language, their father should presumably bear a non-Greek name too ; and that possibly the name by which we know him may be a Hellenization of some Nordic name ending in -ulf.[3]

By land, too, as well as by sea, Thracian bands pressed into Greece, and the traditions of a short-lived Thracian kingdom as far south as the region of Parnassos are too numerous and circumstantial to be reasonably ignored. The grim old fairy-tale of the Nightingale and the Swallow, who for ever lament a deed of blood done long ago, is attached to a Thracian kingdom in Daulis[4] ; and presumably from this same kingdom the raiding bands penetrate further yet. They stormed and sacked the Minyan Orchomenos,[5] so the Greeks of the fifth century believed ; they defeated the Thebans under king Labdakos, by treachery, somewhere among the spurs of Kithairon, after an earlier battle by Lake Kôpaïs in which the Thebans obtained a hard-won victory[6] ; they strengthened themselves against Thebes by an alliance with the men of

---

[1] Apollodoros, III, 15. 4 (=subject-matter of Swinburne's *Erechtheus*). Cf. allusions in Strabo, VII, 321 ; Thucydides, II, 15.

The fact that the king of Athens in this story is Erechtheus, a much earlier ruler than Theseus, according to the traditions, is no objection to our introducing the story of Theseus on pp. 98-9 and the story of Eumolpos here ; since, as we have seen, "folk-memory " remembers names, personalities, and picturesque stories, but is notoriously weak in chronology. Cf. Chambers on the Teutonic heroic cycle of the early centuries A.D., quoted on p. 25.

[2] Paus., I, 5. 2.
[3] *Homer, the Origins*, etc., p. 49.
[4] Thk., II, 29 ; for the story, see Apollod., III, 14. 8.
[5] Hellanikos, frag. 71 (Müller).
[6] Str., IX, 401, quoting Ephoros.

Athens[1] ; they extended their power even into the Megarid,[2] and colonized Euboia from the mainland.[3] These numerous stories are highly suggestive, in view of the strong evidence for northern influence on the Heroic Age of Greece.

To the fall of the Hittite Empire, there is only one possible allusion in Greek saga ; it is the story of Pelops.

Pelops was, we are told, the son of Tantalos, king of the Paphlagones,[4] or Enetoi,[5] or Phrygians[6]—that is, evidently, of some Asiatic folk whose very name had perished. The alternative traditions make it quite clear that Pelops was *not* a genuine Phrygian, one of the invaders of Anatolia from Thrace. High gods were angry with Tantalos and smote him with hunger and thirst—a reminiscence of the great drought of the late thirteenth century ? ! Then his "autochthonous" native dynasty was attacked and overthrown by a Trojan and Phrygian invasion led by "Ilos, son of Trôs". Tantalos died, and his son Pelops abandoned the country, passed over to Greece with some retainers and a great treasure, and arrived at Thebes where he was kindly received by the ruling Kadmeians.[7] With their backing, before the end of his life he had carved himself out, by conquest, treachery, and politic marriages, the nucleus of a new kingdom in the western Peloponnese, at the very time when another prince of the same royal house was similarly winning himself a new throne in Philistia.

It all fits in very exactly with what Aegean and Philistine archæology and Egyptian history would lead us to infer. Allusions to disastrous drought in Asia and the Aegean during the Heroic Age are also fairly numerous in the Greek tradition, and may be compared with the Egyptian evidence for famine in Asia Minor and persistent emigration from Libya into the Delta. Herodotos speaks of a drought in Lydia, more than five hundred years before king Gyges, which drove the

---

[1] Thk. and Apollod., *loc. cit.*
[2] Paus., I, 41, 8.
[3] Str., X. 445.
[4] Ap. Rhod., II, 358, and Σ, *ibid.*, and on l. 790.
[5] *Ibid.*
[6] Paus, II, 22. 4 ; V, 13. 4. This tradition seems to have become as it were the "vulgate" version, but the existence of the other versions make it certain that it is wrong. Pelops is always regarded as of Asian family, and never as an invader from Thrace.
[7] N.D. frag. 17.

Tyrrhenoi oversea, on a migration which brought them at last to Italy.[1] Diodoros repeats local traditions of similar famine causing migration from Syme[2] as well as from Naxos; and it was a famine that came upon the northern branch of the Minyan tribe which occasioned the famous Voyage of the Argo, the legends of which deserve to be studied in some detail.[3] Mr. Brooks' collation of such evidence with that from Central Europe enables us to see these disasters in historical perspective, as episodes during the recession from the curious rainfall maximum of 1300 back to dry conditions in the last generations of the millennium.

The Hellenistic historians repeat several stories mostly derived from Lydian sources, which we can confidently connect with the Philistine migration. Of these the most detailed is that of the foundation of Askalon, which is variously given. Xanthos, the early native Lydian historian, who seems to have had access to some sort of written Chronicles of the Kings of Lydia,[4] tells us that the founder, Askalos, was a brother of Tantalos and general under a western Anatolian king named Akiamos[5]; with which may be connected the legend that Derkêto, who elsewhere appears as a Lydian nymph married to the river-god Kaÿstros,[6] was drowned in the lake of Askalon by Mopsos or Moxos, an Aegean hero.[7] Another version of the Moxos story makes him a mighty and popular warrior in the Lydian region, who overthrew the hated tyrant Mêles and won great glory by many warlike expeditions. The most famous of these was against the city of Krabos, which he took after a long siege, and—with a piety which he had already shown by his offerings to the gods after the fall of Mêles—drowned all the inhabitants " as atheists " in the neighbouring

[1] I, 7 and 94.
[2] V, 53.
[3] See below, pp. 187-195. On the famine, see Apollod., I, 9. 16.
[4] N.D. frag. 49, §42, commenting on the absence of any account of a king Spermes (eighth century ?) from the " Royal Records".
[5] Frag. 23 (Müller), quoted by Stephanos s.v. Askalon. For the name Akiamos, cf. (1) Akia, a fourteenth century king's messenger, whose passport, written by some prince of Western Asia, is among the Tell-el-Amarna letters; (2) Akhiyawi—or Akhiami ?—in the Taanach tablets of the same period; (3) also a whole group of names known from the newly discovered tablets from Katna, a Mitannian town in North Syria, which contain the element Aki-, "offering": Akizzi, Aki-ia, Aki-Teshub, Ak-bite. Cf. Ch. Virolleaud, in Syria, 1928, pp. 90 ff; Antiquity, 1929, p. 314.
[6] Etymologicum Magnum, s.v.
[7] Athenaios, VIII, p. 346.

lake.[1] The last detail is as unexpected as it is striking. It is interesting to find that religious atrocities even at this early date are not confined to the Jews and to peoples under their influence.

The same account adds the detail that there was a great famine at the time of Moxos' expeditions.

These legends were known to the Greeks at a fairly early date. The Hesiodic school had already a story of the foundation of Kolophôn in which Mopsos figures as the prophet who out-prophesied Kalchas, meeting him when the latter was on his way home from Troy.[2] Kalchas died of the shock. And in Kallînos, the early and learned elegist, there seems to have been a full account of Mopsos' march overland, leading his army through the defiles of the Taurus to find new homes in Syria.[3] The place-names Mopsos' Hearth and Mopsos' Fountain, near Tarsos, remained to mark his passage in Hellenic times ; and a tomb of Mopsos (this time said to have come that way as the seer of the Argonauts) was shown at Kyrene.[4]

Disregarding the Greek attempts to attach the story, in the usual cyclic manner, to the Tale of Troy or to the Argonaut legends, we are left with a very convincing picture—all the more convincing because so alien to any Greek poetic ideal—of a stalwart Asiatic warrior, pious and upright according to his lights, popular with his own folk, to his foes fanatical and cruel ; just such a leader as must have been needed to combine into an army the motley hordes of the Philistines and their allies, and to arrange the combined operations against Egypt, from Libya, Palestine and the sea, whose results we have already seen. Under the circumstances it seems highly probable that the invader of Syria and the hero buried at Kyrene are one and the same.

The variant forms of the name, Mopsos and Moxos, pre-sumably result simply from the varying use of the letter ψ in different early Greek alphabets to denote ps and x.

The name seems to appear also in certain place-names in Greece—Mopsion in Thessaly, Mopsŏpia a district in Attica.[5]

---

[1] N.D., frag. 19.
[2] Quoted by Strabo, XIV, p. 642.
[3] *Ibid.*, p. 668 ; cf. 676, where Mopsos is said first to have been allied with, but afterwards to have fought Amphilochos of Argos, who comes by sea ; on whom cf. also Hdt., VII, 91.
[4] Ap. Rhod., IV, 1518.
[5] Str., IX, 443.

As the former place is in Pelasgiôtis, it may well be that
Mopsos is a Pelasgian name. We have already seen what
a blend of European and Asian elements it was that founded
Philistia ; and the suggestion has even been made, several
times, that " Philistine " and " Pelasgian " are in some way
the same name.[1]

The story of the drowning of the people of Krabos in their
own sacred lake is of such an unusual character in Greek
literature that it is probably to be taken as literal history ;
but the variant that makes it not the people but their goddess
that was thrown into the temple pond, to be devoured by the
sacred fish, is due to a confusion of historical legend with
religious myth. Derkêto, or Atergatis, as her name is alternatively given, is a manifestation of the mother-goddess in
mermaid shape, worshipped as a patroness of fish[2] ; hence the
sacred fishponds attached to her temples, in Cyprus as in Syria,
and hence the hieratic myth according to which she drowns
herself in the pool at Askalon or Hierapolis as the sequel to a
love-chase, and is metamorphosed into a fish.[3] A variant of
this story, with some of the cruder details Hellenized away,
appears in Crete, with Diktynna, the Lady of the Fishermen,
also called Britomartis "the Sweet Maiden", in the heroine's
rôle, and Minôs in that of the amorous pursuer[4] ; and yet other
versions referred the legend to Aigina or Kephallenia.[5]

Such being the local cult, it is natural to find localized in
this same part of the world the romance in which Perseus,
coming from Achaia, rescues the king's daughter Andromeda
from being sacrificed[6] ; finding her exposed to be devoured
apparently by this same Fish-Goddess' sacred crocodile. And
here again we find a legend localized in Palestine and also in
the Aegean—the doublet this time being the tale of Herakles'
rescue of Hêsione, whose name means simply the Maid of Asia,
from a similar fate.[7] It is a story as old as Homer and as
modern as the legend of St. George.

[1] Cf. e.g., Macalister, *Philistines*, p. 2 and n.
[2] Lucian, "*On the Syrian Goddess*," c. 14.
[3] D.S., II, 4.
[4] Kallimachos, *Hymn to Artemis*, ll. 189 ff.
[5] Antoninus Liberalis, c. 30.
    For a general discussion of the Derkêto and Britomartis legends, cf.
Macalister, *op. cit.*, pp. 93-99.
[6] Str., XVI, 759 ; Pliny, *N.H.*, V, 13 (69).
[7] *Il.*, XX, 145 ; Apollod., III., 12. 7.

Derkêto, by the way, is not the only Palestinian deity to appear also in Lydia. The god Marnas (explained as being Zeus the Cretan-Born, and apparently the Virgin-born), who was especially the god of " Minoan " Gaza,[1] is also named on coins of Ephesos in Roman times as "Marnas of the Ephesians". The recurrence of the name is usually dismissed as a mere coincidence[2] ; but that there should be two such coincidences seems unlikely. Probably, therefore, we have here one more item of evidence on the highly composite origin of the Philistines.

Lastly, it is worth while to collect the evidence of Greek writers on the geographical distribution, in prehistoric and in historic times, of three ancient tribes of the Asian coastlands.

The " Cilicians "—Kĭlĭkĕs—appear in Homer[3] as a tribe of the southern Troad ; Andromache, Hektor's wife, was daughter of the king of Thêbe, one of their towns. It may be they who had already appeared along with Lykioi and Dardanoi as allies of the Hittite king at Kadesh. Anyhow, their next appearance seems to be in the Assyrian (late eighth century) references to " Khilakku ", a district now apparently in the centre of the peninsula, bordering on the Assyrian province of Kuweh which is the modern Cilicia. Khilakku in these documents appears as being threatened and raided from the west by Mita, King of the Mushki or Moschoi, who has been long recognized to be the fabled Midas of Phrygia ; which gives us a hint of the agency by which, like Goths pushed on by the Huns, the Kilikes have been pushed so far to the east. Presumably they were still north of the Taurus when, as Strabo tells us,[4] the Kimmerian raiding bands from the north were cornered and destroyed in Kilikia by Lydians and Assyrians.

By Herodotos' time the movement from north-west to south-east is almost complete. The Kilikian name has replaced that of the Akhhiawa of the Hittites, the Kuweh of the Assyrians, the Hypachaioi of the old times referred to by Herodotos ; yet even now, there were still some Kilikes north of the Taurus,

---

[1] S.B., s.v., Γάξα "which is also called Minôa after Minôs. Hence they worship Zeus Marnas, that is to say Cretan-born ; for the Cretans call virgins ' Marna ' ". Cf. Macalister, *Philistines*, pp. 107-113, for the evidence of inscriptions and of Mark the Deacon's *Life of Porphyrios* (fifth century, A.D.).
[2] Head, *Historia Numorum*, p. 498 ; cf. Macalister, *op. cit.*, p. 107 n.
[3] *Il.*, VI, 397.
[4] I, p. 61.

if one may trust the old historian's accuracy when he makes the upper Euphrates the boundary between Kilikia and Armenia.[1]

Strabo, in discussing this migration, mentions a Thêbe and a Lyrnêssos in Pamphylia as well as in the land of Troy,[2] and a tradition that the Kilikes had driven out a " Syrian " population from the Kilikia of historic times.[2]

The movement of the Kilikes is typical of the shifting of populations across Anatolia by land ; with the Teukroi we find ourselves among the peoples of the sea. They are not mentioned by Homer, but Kallînos believed that they had carried the worship of Apollo the Mouse-God from the Cretan to the Trojan Mount Ida [3]; and Teukros the brother of Aias is said by post-Homeric writers to have been so called, according to a regular Greek custom, as being the son of Telamôn by a Teukrian captive woman.[4] By him, the genealogists said, was founded the Teukrian Salamis of Cyprus, which certainly was always connected in men's thought with the Salamis of the Sarônic Gulf.[5] And also—a valuable confirmation of the belief that we have here something more than a mere Greek logographer's piece of pedigree-faking—a long line of priest-kings of a brigand tribe in Pamphylia still in Hellenistic and Roman times boasted their Teukrian ancestry, " and most of the priests were called Teukros or Aias ".[6] If it is phonetically impossible to identify the Teukroi with the Zakkar or Djakaray, all that can be said is that it is a pity.

And thirdly, the obscure but ancient Asiatic tribe of the Gergithes have a similar distribution, showing coastwise movement from the Aegean into the Levant ; and their traditions connect them somehow with the Teukrians. Herodotos in fact, naming them among the races of the Troad[7]—where there was a place called Gergithion[8]—calls them definitely " the remnant of the ancient Teukroi ". There were other Gergithes

[1] Hdt., V, 52 ; VII, 91.
[2] Str., XIV, 667, 676.
[3] See above, p. 87.
[4] The legend does not however seem to be traceable earlier than Sophokles, who may have invented it.
[5] Aristotle, Peplos, No. 7, which shows that Teukros' tomb was shown in the Cyprian Salamis.
[6] Str., XIV, 672 ; cf. inscr. apud Heberdey and Wilhelm, Reisen in Kilikien, in Denkschr. der K. Akad. der Wiss., Wien, 1896 (XLIV).
[7] Hdt., V, 122.
[8] Str., XIII, 589.

in Strabo's time near Kyme in Aiolis[1] ; in Miletos in the sixth century B.C., forming apparently a "submerged" serf or proletarian class[2] ; and yet others in Cyprus, said to be ultimately of Thessalian origin, and to have been brought to Cyprus by Teukros.[3] And if, as Dr. Cowley has conjectured, the Hivites—Ha-Khiwwi—of the Old Testament can legitimately be connected with the "Akhaiwoi", then it is a far from hazardous suggestion that these Teukrian Gergithes are the Old Testament Girgashites[4] and perhaps also the New Testament Gergasenes.[5]

This early Greek interest in the north-east corner of the Levant seems, by the way, to have introduced the name "Asia" into geography. The name makes its first appearance, in the form Asy, as that of a remote land named along with Keftiu in a triumphal inscription of Thothmes III[6] ; and its second, probably, in the famous Homeric simile of the clamorous wild fowl in "an Asian mead".[7] In Hesiod "Asia" is first personified as a nymph,[8] and Herodotos refers to a legend, apparently well-known, that made her the wife of Prometheus, son of the Titan Iapetos.[9] Another version makes her marry Iapetos himself.[10] The district of "Asy" at this date is evidently still some part of southern Asia Minor, and the association of its eponymous nymph with Iapetos is interesting ; for Iapetos is apparently none other than ancestor of the peoples of Asia Minor and the Isles[11]—of Kimmerians and Medes and Ionians and Moschoi and "Tiras"—Japhet, the friend of everyone's childhood, out of Noah's Ark.

---

[1] Str., XIII, 589.
[2] Ath., XII, 533, quoting Herakleides.
[3] Ath., VI, 255, quoting Klearchos of Soloi.
[4] *Genesis* X, 16, etc.
[5] *Varia lectio* in *St. Luke* VIII, 26.
[6] See Hall, in *C.A.H.*, II, pp. 279 ff., esp. 281.
[7] *Il.*, II, 461.
[8] *Theog.*, l. 359.
[9] IV, 45.
[10] Apollod., I, 2. 2.
[11] *Genesis* X, 2.

CHAPTER VII

The Sea-Raiders in the Levant : the Twelfth Century and After

> "Woe unto the people of the sea-coast, the nation of the Cherethites; the word of the Lord is against you, O Canaan, land of the Philistines."—*Zephaniah*, II. 5.

RAMESES III died in 1167, and within the decade the sea-raiders settled along the Syrian coast had ceased to pay the slightest attention to the desires of the Pharaohs. From the excavations at Beth-shan it appears that the Aegean colony, originally planted there as a garrison by the Pharaohs of the Nineteenth Dynasty, continued to exist as an independent city-state, one of a large number, mostly on the coast, extending from Sidon, Arvad and Byblos on the north to the famous Five Towns of Philistia on the south. Between these two groups, the Phœnician and the Philistine, lay the less famous central settlements, of which Dor and Taanach are perhaps the best known. All the cities regarded themselves as completely independent ; so much so that when one of the puppet-kings of the Egyptian Twentieth Dynasty—Rameses IX. about 1140—ventured to send some ambassadors along this coast, the lord of Byblos took it into his head to detain them, and did so, for the rest of their lives—a period of some seventeen years.

In every case, the oversea settlers eventually became completely Semitized by contact with the more numerous natives, but it was a long process. Roughly speaking, the non-Semitic element in the population seems to have been weakest in Phœnicia and strongest in Philistia, where a self-conscious nation survived long enough to be named by Greek writers and fluently cursed by the Hebrew prophets.

In Phœnicia, traces of a non-Semitic immigration are scarce, and it is sometimes denied that the Phœnicians were anything but a pure Semitic race ; but even here the goods from several graves excavated in the Lebanon, now in the museum of the

American College at Beirut, are clearly Aegean, and of thirteenth or twelfth century date, and the fact at least of strong Aegean influence is now confirmed by the finds at Ras Shamra.   It seems likely that the Phœnicians took to the sea only under the influence of these Aegeans ; for though Byblos had been a port from very early times there is no evidence earlier than Homer for Phœnicians trading by sea on their own account. When Thothmes III in the fifteenth century required shipping, he turned not to Phœnicians but to the Keftiu.   It is true, however, that the sea-raiders in Phœnicia were absorbed the earliest and have left the least trace in archæology and tradition.   Hogarth drew attention to the fact that, in the matter of writing, Phœnicia was using Babylonic cuneiform at a time when a signary based on the Aegean linear script was still in use in Philistia.[1]

Rivalry developing into hostility existed between the northern and the southern settlements, and ultimately a war broke out and was fought to a finish, between the king of Askalon and the king of Sidon.   The Philistines were victorious and captured Sidon, refugees from which fled to Tyre and seem to have contributed largely to that city's future greatness.[2] But even though weakened by such internecine feuds, the sea-raiders were quite strong enough at first to hold their ground against the Hebrew mountaineers of the hinterland, and even to expand at their expense, thanks no doubt to their Asian armour and weapons, but more especially to their possession of " chariots of iron ".

The areas in southern Syria within which Aegean remains are found do in fact correspond fairly closely with the areas which the Hebrews, in the more candid portions of their traditions of the conquest, admit that they could not master ; they comprise the greater part of the coast and the few valley areas that run up into the hill-country, notably the plain of Jezreel, from Beth-shan to Mount Carmel.   "These are the nations which the Lord left, to prove Israel by them   . . .

---

[1] *Ionia and the East*, p. 95.
[2] Justin, XVIII, c. 3, who is, of course, wrong in saying that Tyre was *founded* in the twelfth century by these refugees ; it is mentioned in Egyptian documents much earlier.   But since Menandros of Ephesos, the translator of Phœnician documents, likewise regards this period as somehow marking an epoch for Tyrian history (see Josephus, *Ant.*, VIII, 3. 1), the story appears to be in the main correct.

only that the children of Israel might know, to teach them war, at the least such as beforetime knew nothing thereof : the five lords of the Philistines, and all the Canaanites, and the Zidonians, and the Hivites that dwelt in Mount Lebanon, from Mount Baal-hermon unto the entering in of Hamath."[1] The pious author's explanation of Yahweh's purpose in omitting to do quite all that was expected of him is entertaining. "And Manasseh did not drive out the inhabitants of Beth-shan and her towns, nor of Taanach and her towns, nor of Dor and her towns . . . nor of Megiddo and her towns ; but the Canaanite would dwell in that land. . . . And the Amorites forced the children of Dan into the hill-country ; for they would not suffer them to come down into the valley."[2] "And the Lord was with Judah, and he drave out the inhabitants of the hill-country ; for he could not drive out the inhabitants of the valley, because they had chariots of iron."[3] At Dor, on the central part of the coast, we accordingly find in the Golenischeff Papyrus (of which more hereafter) a vigorous and hard-headed sea-faring population of the tribe of the Zakkaray.

It is, however, of the strong southern Philistine settlements that most is known, and here that we can see, from the Old Testament historical books themselves, how profound was the influence of the Aegean immigrants on Israelite civilization.

The culture of the Philistines is known to us, though very incompletely, both from its concrete remains and from Hebrew allusions. Their architecture, like their pottery, is reminiscent of the Aegean. Houses excavated at Gath and at Gezer show " the characteristic Cretan lightwell " ; a model shrine found at Beth-shan shows a building with three storeys, reminiscent of the upper floors of Minoan houses. Here we find the prototype of the palace at Samaria from whose upper-floor window King Ahaziah accidentally fell,[4] and of that at Jezreel from which Queen Jezebel was thrown. So, too, Aegean prototypes have been suggested for the palace at Gaza where Samson met his end, with its theatral area where the blinded giant " made sport " and its roof supported on two pillars

---

[1] *Judges* III, 1-3.
[2] *Ibid.*, I, 27, 34.
[3] *Ibid.*, 20.
[4] 2 *Kings* I, 2.

which, like those at Knôssos, can be dragged off their bases. It has even been suggested that the Philistines introduced the all-important vine and olive into the land.[1]

With the coming of the Philistines, too, dawns definitely in Syria the Iron Age.   It has long been observed that weapons on Rameses III's monuments are painted blue ; and more recent discoveries confirm the belief that his weapons were in fact, whenever possible, of iron.   Tutankhamen's dagger, with its blade of iron—and very good iron, too—shows that as early as the fourteenth century there were smiths to whom the working of the metal presented no difficulties ; henceforth, the only problem for Egypt was to obtain access to a supply. Unfortunately the chief known sources of the supply, in the Taurus mines, were controlled by the Hittites.   One ceases to wonder at Egypt's lack of success in her Hittite wars ; and even after the treaty of 1271 the Hittite kings remained chary of sharing their valuable possession with others.   About 1260, a letter from Khattusil III expresses diplomatic regret at being unable to supply the iron for which Rameses II has been asking, on the distinctly unlikely ground that there is no iron-working going on in the province of Kissuwadna just now.   Iron only becomes really common in North Syria after 1200, evidently introduced by the same Land-Raiders who introduced cremation of the dead and who sacked the first city of Carchemish.[2]   So also in the south, iron and cremation seem to be introduced together by the Philistines.   All doubt as to the extensive use of iron by the Philistines has been laid finally to rest by Sir W. Flinders Petrie's excavations at Gerar and Beth-pelet, in 1927 and 1929.   Here the earliest use of iron was datable not later than the fourteenth century ; while in the twelfth century furnaces for smelting are found, and large tools being manufactured—plough-irons, a seven-pound pick, large hoes, and swords.

All this while it remains very rare in the Aegean.   It seems, in fact, that the late-Minoan " Achaian " world had fallen seriously behind the times in this important matter.   It is probably significant that Asia and the Balkan mainland, in both of which iron was coming into use in the twelfth century,

---

[1] Glotz, *Civ. Eg.*, p. 451.
[2] Woolley, in *Liverpool Annals*, VI, p. 51 ; Hogarth, *Kings of the Hittites*, p. 29.

PLATE XII

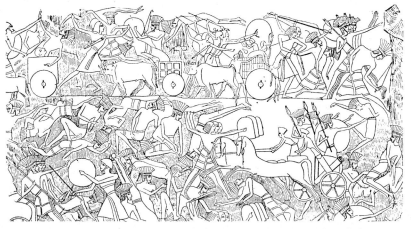

(a) Egyptians and Shardana defeat the
Philistines (p. 143). From Medinet Habu

(b) "Horns of Consecration"; from a late Minoan
Vase from Cyprus

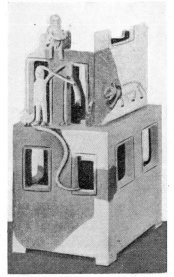

(c) Model Shrine of the Mother-Goddess
as Mistress of Beasts and Snakes: from
Beth-shan

(d) Pair of Gladiators, from a Minoan
Seal. (cf. 2 Samuel II. 16)

THE SEA-RAIDERS IN THE LEVANT.

appear in Homer as united in a great defensive alliance against the predatory Achaians. The Homeric world knows something of iron and of how it is wrought[1] ; but only small objects, such as knives, are made of it ; swords are still of bronze, and it is only among Trojans, or among Achaians after they have plundered the Trojan villages,[2] that the metal is at all common. It is a supply, not the knowledge, that is lacking. Archæology agrees with tradition, that iron had been known in Crete, as a rarity, since very early times.[3]

Many passages in the Old Testament also suggest Philistine influence on the Chosen People in manners and customs, and even in the externals of religion. The tree- and pillar-cults of early Israel,[4] the heretical bull-worship, or rather calf-worship,[5] and the " horns of the altar ",[6] like those that decorate Cretan shrines, are all reminiscent of the Aegean and probably derived from it through Philistia ; for a triple coincidence is not likely. Israelites seem also to have picked up, along with other " abominations of the heathen ", a taste for the gladiatorial shows that we may see depicted on the Cretan " boxer vase ". The mixed crowd of men and women on the roof, who " beheld while Samson made sport ", seems to surprise the Jewish writer no less than the Greek narrator of the story of Theseus (cf. p. 98 above) ; but when Joab and Abner, the rival generals in the time of David, meet in friendly fashion, a gladiatorial show is given for their delectation. " And Abner said to Joab ' Let the young men, I pray thee, arise and play before us.' And Joab said ' Let them arise.' Then they arose and went over by number ; twelve for Benjamin and for Ish-baal the son of Saul, and twelve of the servants of David. And they caught every one his fellow by the head and thrust his sword into his fellow's side ; so they fell down together."[7] There is a Cretan seal that shows two swordsmen stabbing each other mutually, by exactly the movement here described.

It even seems likely that Aegean literature or traditional story-telling (of which we know nothing) has left its mark on

[1] Cf. the epithet πολυκμητός, Il., X, 379, etc.
[2] Il., loc. cit. (Dŏlon the Trojan), VII, 473 ; XXIII, 826-835.
[3] Cf. Parian Marble, l. 22.
[4] 1 Kings XIV, 23 ; 2 Kings XVII, 10 ; XXIII, 14 ; etc.
[5] 1 Kings XII, 28 ; 2 Kings XVII, 16 ; etc.
[6] 1 Kings II, 28, etc.
[7] 2 Samuel II, 14-16 ; cf. Plate XI.

that of Israel. It is, at any rate, a fact that the motifs of no less than four famous Hebrew stories are to be found also in the mythology of, among other races, the Greeks.

The motifs are (1) that of the betrayal of the hero whose strength lies in his hair[1]; (2) that of the father commanded by a God to sacrifice his child, and of the substitution of an animal at the last moment[2]; (3) that of a father's rash vow to sacrifice the first living creature to meet him on his home-coming, and of its disastrous sequel—the " Jephthah's daughter " story[3]; and (4) the " Potiphar's Wife " motif.[4] In any one of the four cases, taken separately, one would be inclined to suppose that the same good motif has occurred to story tellers in the two countries independently ; but four such coincidences are unlikely, especially when we have the best of evidence for important migrations from the one area to the other.

The language of the Philistines, like their national con-sciousness, survived in Palestine for several centuries, existing as a local patois in Ashdod, if as nothing more, as late as the time of Nehemiah.[5] But the steady progress of Semitization seems to be shown by the number of Philistine chiefs named by the Assyrian conquerors who bear Semitic names ; and though the non-Semitic names in the Old Testament have been closely scrutinized, it seems unlikely that they will ever throw much light upon the pre-Hellenic languages of the Aegean. The only result obtained appears to be the suggestion that the apparently common Philistine name Achish may be identical with the Dardanian Anchises, the name of the father of the pious Aeneas.   In this context it may be worth while to observe that an obscure chieftain from the edge of the Philistine low-lands, mentioned in the book of Joshua—one Piram of Iarmuth[6] —bears a name more famous still ; it is the very same as the

---

[1] With the story of Samson and Delilah, cf. that of Nisos and Skylla (p. 86 above) and also that of Pterelaos, whose daughter Komaitho betrayed him by plucking his magic hair when he was attacked by Amphitryon—Apollod., II, 4, 7.
[2] Story of Isaac ; cf. that of Iphigeneia.
[3] On Idomeneus' rash vow, when caught in a storm on his way back from Troy, cf. Servius, *ad. Aen.*, III, 401.
[4] There are at least three Greek versions of this story ; that of Bellerophon in Iliad VI (see p. 124, above), that of Hippolytos as given in Euripides' play, and that of Tennes of Tenedos—Paus., X, 14, 1 ff.
[5] *Nehemiah* XIII, 24.
[6] *Joshua* X, 3 ; XV, 35.

name Priam, which the Aiolic Greeks who dwelt in and around the Tröad rendered as " Perramos ", and with which we may compare the name Pyramus, borne by the ill-fated hero of an Asian love-story, and well-known to the modern world through its handling by Ovid[1] and Shakespeare.

So much, and very little more, we know of the people whose later history consists for us of their efforts to maintain their independence, against heavy odds, among the more numerous surrounding tribes; Hebrews from the first, and, later, Egyptian and Assyrian imperialism.

"And it came to pass ", says the book of Judges, " when Israel was strong, that they put the Canaanites to task-work and did not utterly drive them out."[2] The lines refer to the dealings of the north-central Israelite tribes with the Canaanites of the valley of Jezreel, from Beth-shan to the port of Dor. From the point of view of the Zakkaray and the other Canaanites, the same situation might be described by saying that the surly and untameable highlanders, new arrivals from the unknown desert beyond Jordan, levied blackmail on their lowland neighbours whenever they were not kept in check. In any case, the stage was set for a struggle which could only end with the complete victory of one or the other side.

For a time a sort of deadlock seems to have been reached, as we see from the statements of the Hebrew writer. The tribes of Israel had overrun the mountain-zone, but on the plains could never face the sea-peoples with their stalwart pikemen like Goliath, and their chariots, very terrible to the undisciplined hill-men if met on level ground. Goliath's panoply, it has often been remarked, is almost that of a Homeric man-at-arms, with his bronze scale-corselet, like the " lobster " armour of the Shardana, his bronze helmet and greaves, his heavy shield carried for him by a squire before action, and his heavy sword capable of severing a man's head. And Goliath has, too, what the Homeric warriors had not, a massive spear-head of iron.[3]

For a time highlander and lowlander let one another alone, and the earliest border-wars of Israel when settled in the Promised Land were, if we may trust the order of events

[1] *Metamorphoses*, IV, 55 ff.
[2] I, 28.
[3] 1 *Samuel* XVII, 5, 6, 7, 51.

given in the book of Judges, fought against the Trans-Jordan nations of the desert-edge. But at last the " tribute ", which the Israelite regarded it as his right to levy on the Gentile, became intolerable, and the Canaanites of the valley of Jezreel, under a vigorous leader—the famous Sisera—made a determined attempt to subdue the neighbouring portions of the hill-country once for all.

At a venture, this episode may be dated round about 1100 ; it is apparently a considerable length of time after the first settlement of Israelites and of sea-raiders in the distracted land of Canaan, and a considerable time before the wars of the southern Philistines against Saul and David. The result of the movement is described in two of the most famous and splendid chapters of Hebrew poetry and narrative ; here we need only indicate baldly and prosaically the chief facts that seem to emerge from the Old Testament epic. At first the Canaanites met with a considerable measure of success ; whole tracts of the highlands are pacified—" mightily oppressed " as the Hebrews put it—and considerable quantities of their not easily replaceable weapons confiscated ; "Was there a shield or spear seen among forty thousand in Israel ? " But in due course the Israelites also find a leader, Barak, " the Lightning ", who with the backing of a prophetess of Ephraim raises a considerable army. Most of his men naturally came from the surrounding district, from Zebulon, and from his own tribe, Naphtali ; but though the more distant Israelites were not interested, all the four central tribes—Issachar, Benjamin, Manasseh (Machir) and the powerful Ephraim—seem to have sent contingents.[1]

Sisera marched by Taanach and " the waters of Megiddo " to disperse the rebel concentration on Mount Tabor ; and there Nemesis befell him for his attempt to follow the Israelites into their hills. So far as can be seen from the magnificent but obscure allusions of Deborah's Song, a sudden storm burst over his line of march, bringing the hill-streams down in furious spate ; and then as his great column of chariotry labours along the stony slopes among the roaring gullies, with the storm came Barak and his half-armed fighters, driving the whole array, with its prancing terrified horses, downward to hopeless ruin in the swollen waters of the Kishon. Sisera, as the famous

---

[1] *Judges* V, 14-16.

story runs, escaped alone and on foot, failing to extricate his chariot from the jammed confusion by the river ; escaping only to be treacherously murdered, in violation of every tie of hospitality known to the desert code, by a Bedouin woman whose family had remained neutral so long as the issue hung in the balance.

Thus ended abruptly Sisera's attempt to pacify Mount Ephraim ; "the land had rest" for the conventional forty years. But we are not told that Israel thereafter captured any of the Canaanite cities ; probably the central group of the oversea settlers came to depend henceforth more and more upon the help of the Philistines ; certainly in their wars with Saul we find even the inland Beth-shan regarded as a Philistine outpost.[1]

The later Philistine attempt to pacify both the central and lowland regions of Israel—Ephraim and Judah—was a more serious affair and won a less short-lived success. Here again the story has been told once and for all in the Old Testament of how two men of the tribes chiefly threatened—Saul of Benjamin and David of Judah—began and carried to completion the movement for Israelite independence. As literal history, the narrative teems with difficulties, and in one or two places flatly contradicts itself[2]; but there can be no question that in broad outline it appears to tell us very much what must in fact have happened, quite apart from its literary merits as one of the finest stories ever told by man.

It is clear at any rate that the effort to be rid of the Philistines made of Israel for the first time a nation and a state, and not merely a group of tribes. It is also beyond reasonable doubt that the Philistine danger stimulated a spontaneous demand on the part of the tribesmen for a king to lead them and rule them ; hitherto they have been content with the universal primitive form of government, that of the head of each family, that of the village elders in council, and that of some self-appointed and more or less widely accepted war-leader in a time of crisis.

[1] 1 *Samuel* XXXI, 10 ff.

[2] Two well-known instances being 1 *Samuel* XVI, 14 ff, where David becomes Saul's favourite musician and armour-bearer, and XVII where David is a simple country lad, unknown to Saul, at the time of his encounter with Goliath ; and again, 1 *Samuel* VIII, 1-8, where the demand for a king is condemned as a sinful rejection of the theocracy, and IX, especially v. 16, where God chooses Saul as the divinely-appointed saviour of his people.

Samuel the priest, says a rather awkward and self-contradictory narrative, more or less unwillingly acceded to the demand for a king, which implied among other things dissatisfaction with the administration of justice by Samuel's sons[1]; and he proceeded to anoint Saul, a Benjamite, a man with fully-grown sons but still in the full vigour of manhood, and a person of magnificent physique and presence. Saul makes a brilliant start, silencing envious criticism by a crushing defeat of an Ammonite foray, and showing himself in the hour of victory not less generous than brave.[2]

But in spite of this the new king was not at all points psychologically fitted for his position. By nature he was shy,[3] sensitive, and liable to black hours of melancholia; and he was afraid of Samuel and of the occult powers that Samuel represented. He could and did beat the Philistines, with the help of his valiant son Jonathan; but when he fell foul of Samuel over such matters as sacrificing in person when Samuel failed to keep his appointment to do so, or sparing the life of a captured Bedouin chief whom Samuel had marked down for slaughter (and did slaughter, in cold blood) then Saul cringed and cowered; and when he is met by curses and assurances that his kingship would end in disaster, his self-confidence gives way and he is at once ready to believe that " an evil spirit from the Lord " is troubling him.

Samuel's method of atoning for his first mistake in the choice of a king was to assure himself, against his better nature,[4] that it had all been Saul's fault, and to anoint— secretly, for the best of reasons—another candidate, assuring him that it was God's will that he should be the future king. The recipient of these seditious communications was David of Bethlehem, an attractive and unscrupulous young soldier with a talent for music, fighting, and the leadership of men. The splendid group of adventure-stories of which he is the hero assures us, however, that he remained loyal to his king and to Jonathan, his sworn comrade, until Saul, jealous of his rising fame and popularity, had more than once attacked him murderously, in one of his black moods, and at last definitely proscribed him.

---

[1] 1 *Samuel* VIII, 4, 5.   [3] X, 22, 23.
[2] X, 27; XI, esp. 12, 13.   [4] XV, 34; XVI, 1 ff.

Then follow the episodes of David's career as a successful brigand in the cave of Adullam and elsewhere in the wilderness of Judah, until after numerous hair-breadth escapes he finally goes over to the enemy and rises high in the service of Achish, the lord of Gath.

David's defection, or banishment, brought temporary disaster to the nationalist cause in Israel; for though David himself contrived, throughout sixteen months' service with Achish, never to do violence to any Israelite, the band of gallant desperadoes who had followed him over the border could ill be spared, and the defection of larger bodies of men was not unknown.[1]

Presently the Philistines attacked the now weary and disillusioned Saul again, marching this time not by the direct route into the highlands to the scene of their former defeat at Michmash, but round by the north through the friendly territory of the vale of Jezreel. David and his band marched with them, with the contingent from Gath, and we read of how part of Manasseh went over to him as the army passed through their territory in the course of this very campaign.[2] It seems almost certain that David must already have been making some pretensions to be something more than an exiled brigand chief.

Achish trusted David implicitly, but the other Philistine chiefs, perhaps fortunately for themselves, refused to risk his presence in a battle against his countrymen; so he and his followers were sent back to their frontier-post in the south, found it sacked and burnt by the Bedouin in their absence, and were engaged in a desperate pursuit of the spoilers into their native desert while the last act of Saul's tragedy was played out to its end.

Weakened by desertion and led by an embittered neurotic, no longer the Saul of yesterday, the national levies were scattered by the Philistine chariots and archers on the slopes of Mount Gilboa. Saul and his sons fought gallantly : " From the blood of the slain, from the fat of the mighty, the bow of Jonathan turned not back, and the sword of Saul returned not empty " ; but it was to no purpose, and presently the king, " sore wounded of the archers ", was constrained to fall on his

[1] For a list of these, see 1 *Chronicles* XII, 1-22.
[2] *Ibid.*, v. 19.

sword, above the bodies of his sons, while the rout fled past, "and lo, the chariots and the horsemen followed hard after him ".

David, having lamented in beautiful and moving verses the disaster which he had done so much to hasten, immediately gave point to his lament by moving up into the hill-country and allowing his fellow-tribesmen of Judah to proclaim him king in Hebron, in the far south, in opposition to the house of Saul in the person of Ish-baal, his youngest son.

It was the darkest hour for Israelite national hopes since the struggle against the Philistines had started. At the beginning of Saul's reign there had been a Philistine garrison at the strategic point of Geba[1]—Jonathan's capture of the post had been the first action of the successful rebellion—and Israel had been to a great extent disarmed[2]; but things were far worse now. The body of the king hung mutilated and naked from the walls of Beth-shan, until rescued by some of those whom he had delivered from a cruel fate long ago[3]; and the vassal of a Philistine lord ruled in Hebron with Philistine acquiescence and carried on war against the remnant that still clung to the house of Saul. Beyond Jordan, and in the north, and in the fastnesses of the Ephraimite highland, Abner, Saul's marshal, still kept an army together on behalf of Ish-baal; but even this territory was being gradually diminished by warfare that went on the whole in favour of David, and by the desertions that had long since affected even Benjamin, Saul's own tribe. It is noteworthy that the historian refers always to Ish-baal's side as "Israel"; their enemies are merely "the servants of David ".

This was the high-water mark reached by Philistine arms and diplomacy; for before long, Abner himself had deserted to David and been murdered by Joab the marshal in satisfaction of a blood-feud, and the hapless Ish-baal himself was at last killed by two of his own men. Then Joab, by a daring *coup-de-main*, took the independent stronghold, Jerusalem of the Jebusites, and David made it his capital; he was now acknowledged king of all Israel, reigning from an all but impregnable fortress in the heart of the hills, and the Philistines

---

[1] 1 *Samuel* X, 5; XIII, 3, 4.
[2] XIII, 19-22.
[3] *Ibid.*, XXXI, 8-13; cf. XI.

recognized the fact that he might well prove more dangerous to them than Saul had ever been. While he dwelt at Hebron, within easy reach, they had let him alone, thinking of him no doubt as their catspaw. Now they attacked him, but he was already too strong for them. Two successive invasions of the hill-country met with disaster in the valley of Rephaim, at the place thence named by David Baal-perazim ; and in a third campaign David carried the Hebrew arms for the first time down into the plain of Philistia.[1]

Baal-perazim is the decisive battle of Philistine history ; after it the losers were never again a danger to the independence of their neighbours. Beth-shan and the whole plain of Jezreel, too, were lost and became an integral part of the Hebrew kingdom ; and the wars of the Philistines henceforward are defensive. It is clear, however, in spite of the Hebrew historian's claim that David " subdued " the Philistines, that the latter long remained independent within the territory of their original Five Cities. In the tenth century their fortress of Gezer passes into the hands of Solomon, but only as the dowry of his Egyptian bride, and after being taken with difficulty by a Pharaoh of Lower Egypt.[2] In the eighth century Amos prophesies and Uzziah of Judah campaigns against them,[3] and even the great Assyrian conquerors count a Philistine campaign worthy of a place in their records. Nehemiah records, as we have seen, the late survival of at least a Philistine patois ; and Amos, echoed by Joel centuries later, bears indirect witness to Philistine activity in commerce. An active slave-trade passed through the Philistine as well as the Phœnician ports, and Joel heaps curses upon both as having " sold the children of Judah and Jerusalem to the sons of the Grecians, that ye might remove them far from their border ".[4]

As late as Roman imperial times, as we have already seen, the men of Gaza were proud to claim their " Minoan " descent by the legends on their coins ; and they continued far into the Christian era to worship Marnas, " Zeus the Cretan-born "[5]. In a word, the Philistines were a civilized people, proud and

---

[1] 2 *Samuel* V, 17-25 ; VIII, 1.
[2] Josephus, *Antiquities*, VIII, 6, 1.
[3] *Amos*, I, 6 ; 2 *Chronicles* XXVI, 6 ff.
[4] *Joel* III, 4, 6.
[5] Stephanos, *s.v.* Γάξα.

tenacious of their civilization ; while as to their warlike prowess, one other instance of it may be given—in addition to the bare fact of their survival, in a fertile plain among numerous and covetous neighbours. After their wars with David were over, David was glad to recruit his bodyguard from among the " Cherêthites and Pelethites "—Cretans and Philistines— of the coast ; and they for their part, with the same readiness to sell their swords that their ancestors had shown in the service of the great Rameses long before, had no objection to serving under their late enemy. The Pelethites and Cherêthites were indeed the *corps d'élite*, the professional house-carles, of David's establishment ; their command was a most important post, held by the great warrior Benaiah, whose adventures are recorded in the Catalogue of David's mighty men[1] ; and it was they under one of their own officers, Ittai, one of a regiment of six hundred men who followed David from Gath, who stood loyally by him, even though offered free and honourable discharge, in the dark hour when David's own people rebelled against him under Absalom.[2] Ittai is thereafter found, along with Joab and his brother Abishai, in command of a third part of the army.[3]

We cannot conclude the history of the Sea-Raiders in their settlements in the Levant without some mention of an all-important invention dating from these centuries, though its precise origin is still matter for discussion : the invention of our alphabet.

As compared with such earlier scripts as cuneiform or the Egyptian and Aegean syllabaries, the alphabet combines simplicity with precision in an extraordinary degree. As an instrument of the advance of culture it has been hardly less important than the Aryan languages themselves with their marvellous beauty and exactness. With the twenty-odd letters of one of our Greek scripts before him, no longer need the scribe spend the energy of his most impressionable years in acquiring the art of notation alone ; no longer need kings and merchants be dependent on the services of a not always competent secretary at every turn ; no longer need the art of

[1] 2 *Samuel* VIII, 18 ; XX, 23 ; XXIII, 20-23.
[2] *Ibid.*, XV, 18-22.
[3] *Ibid.*, XVIII, 2.

writing itself be a mystery hid from ordinary men. With the perfecting by the Greeks of this older Levantine script, a great stride forward was taken towards the freeing of the human reason for systematic speculative thought, and towards the creation of what will one day exist, an educated public. It is not too much to say that the alphabet is third, along with Aryan speech and the age-old perfection of Aegean craftsmanship, among the pre-existing human achievements that made possible the " Greek miracle ".

It is beyond reasonable doubt that the Greeks took over the rudimentary alphabet from the Phœnicians, the sea-going " Canaanites ", as they called themselves, of Tyre and Sidon. The tradition that in its earliest form it was introduced by Kadmos is worth little, since most of the blessings of civilization associated with that hero are such as we know to have come from Minoan Crete. If " Kadmos " really introduced writing, it was one of the old Minoan syllabaries. But we are given unimpeachable evidence by the names of the letters themselves, meaningless in Greek but significant in Phœnician, and often recognizably descriptions of an early form of the letter concerned ; Aleph " ox ", Beth " house ", and so on. The alphabet, too, in a primitive form and written, as, at first, in Greece, from right to left, can also be traced back further in Syria than in the Aegean ; the Moabite Stone was until recently the oldest important inscription in it known to modern times. The one very important improvement which the Greeks, characteristically, made for themselves, was the transmutation of certain breathings and auxiliary signs, such as the " Jot ", Iota, into the vowels that we know. It was this step that perfected as a true alphabet what had hitherto been in reality simply a very simple syllabary, in which with every consonant any vowel might, but need not, be understood.

Beyond the last millennium B.C. we seek for certainty as to the origins of our alphabet in vain. Did the Phœnicians— least original of folk—invent it entirely for themselves ? And if not, whence did it develop ? Various suggestions have been made, none of which can as yet be finally accepted. The forms of several of our letters, notably H, are anticipated in the Minoan linear script ; possibly the sea-peoples made an advance in the direction of simplifying this. Again, certain inscriptions from Serabit el-Khadim in the Sinai peninsula, an ancient Egyptian mining district, show a remarkable resemblance to the alphabet in several points ; so much so that many scholars regard the Sinaitic as our parent script. But two things we know : first, that if the usually accepted date be accepted for the construction of the recently-discovered coffin of Ahiram, prince of Byblos, then the Phœnician alphabet dates from the age of the Sea-Raids ; and second, that in the Golenischeff Papyrus we meet, about 1118 B.C., a chief of the sea-peoples of Syria who keeps, duly filed, his father's business accounts, and can turn up entries in them for himself. By his time, at any rate, some simplified script is in existence ; but perhaps it is only the simplified " alphabetic cuneiform " of Dr. Schaefer's discoveries at Ras Shamra.

So much for the fortunes of the Sea-Raiders after their establishment on the coasts of the Levant ; valiant, hard-headed men, to whom we are perhaps indebted for the ease with which we read and write. Zakar-Baal of Byblos, consulting the ancestral ledgers and importing his papyrus from Egypt, is already more a " modern " Phœnician than a figure of the older world. It is time to pass on ; and conditions in the Levant during the Dark Age of the tenth and ninth centuries must form the subject of a later chapter.

CHAPTER VIII

THREE STORIES

ἀνδρῶν τε πτολέμους ἀλεγεινά τε κύματα πείρων.
—Homer, Il. XXIV, 8.

THERE exist three short stories of adventure by sea in the
Age of the Sea-Raids, dating from that age itself or
from little later, which in addition to their intrinsic interest
are among our most important sources in any attempt to form
a picture of life at that time. One is the Golenischeff papyrus,
being the report of an Egyptian ambassador, sent by the
High Priest of Amen to the Phœnician coast to buy timber
for the sacred barge of the god, concerning his journey and
misfortunes. The effusive style and voluble account of every
detail sound as if the report emanated from a person in fear of
condign punishment ; probably it is intended to explain his
return to Thebes, late and empty-handed, without either the
timber or the money entrusted to him wherewith to pay for it.
The other two are stories told in the Odyssey, which are not
so widely known as they deserve to be ; for they contain some
of the best story-telling in the poem, and some of Homer's
best touches, such as the obvious satisfaction with which the
swineherd settles himself in his corner, to inflict his auto-
biography on at least one listener who has not heard it before,
and the dream-picture that the grown man paints of the home
of his baby years, before he was a slave.

The summary of Wen-Amen's report, which supplies our first
story, is conflated chiefly from the published versions of
Flinders-Petrie,[1] Macalister[2] and Breasted.[3]

I. THE STORY OF THE INCOMPETENT EGYPTIAN

Wen-Amen set out from Thebes on the sixteenth day of
the eleventh month[4] of the fifth year of Pharaoh Rameses XI,

[1] *History of Egypt*, Vol. III, pp. 197-201. This version, published in
1905, is to some extent superseded by more recent translations, but still useful
in conjunction with them.
[2] *The Philistines*, pp. 29-35.
[3] *Ancient Records of Egypt*, §§ 557-591.
[4] =April 6.

to fetch cedar wood from Lebanon for repairs to the barge User-het, the sacred barge of the god Amen-Ra. He did not set sail at once in a ship bound for Phœnicia, for the Upper Egyptian boatman was no salt-water sailor, and moreover the Delta region did not own the sovereignty of the High Priest of Thebes, nor yet that of the puppet Pharaoh whom the High Priest rather ruled than served. Lower Egypt was ruled by Nesubenebded, prince of Tanis, married to the great lady Tentamen, who was apparently of the blood royal. To this friendly but independent chief came Wen-amen with a letter of introduction from Hrihor the High Priest—a passport, in fact. Nesubenebded and the lady Tentamen could not read, but their scribe read out the letter to them " and they said, ' Yea, yea, I will do all that our lord Amen saith ' ". They entertained Wen-amen graciously, but they did not go to the length of sending him direct to Phœnicia in a specially-chartered ship. They merely placed him in charge of a sea-captain of Tanis, named Mengebti, bound on a trading-voyage, and so let him sail.

Mengebti's ship weighed anchor and set sail from Tanis on the first day of the twelfth month (=the twentieth of April) and creeping up the coast of Syria put in at Dor, not far from Carmel. Here Badyra the governor politely sent the ambassador " much bread, a jar of wine and a joint of beef ". But here, also, disaster happened ; a member of the crew stole the money that Wen-Amen had brought to pay for the timber, and deserted ; he was not seen again. The loss consisted of some vessels of gold to the weight of five deben (about $1\frac{1}{4}$ lbs.), some vessels of silver, and a bag of smaller pieces of silver— 31 deben weight of silver in all. It was apparently all the money that Wen-Amen had.

Next morning Wen-Amen went up and interviewed Badyra. " I have been robbed in your harbour ", he said, " and it is your business as king to investigate and find the money. It belongs to Amen-Ra, and to Nesubenebded, and to my lord Hrihor, and to Warati, and Makamaru, and to Zakar-Baal, lord of Byblos." (The last are clearly the destined recipients of the money.)

In spite of this array of important names, Badyra not unnaturally flatly refused to accept responsibility for the misbehaviour of a foreign sailor. " Your excellency ", he replied, " I know nothing about this matter. If the thief were one of my people, I would repay the money out of my own treasury until we had found out who the thief was. But now, the thief is from your ship. However, wait a few days and I will have investigations made."

Wen-Amen waited for nine days, but the thief had not yet been detected, and it began to seem unlikely that he would be. At last he decided to go on, relying on a powerful fetish that he had with him—an image, representing " Amen of the Way ", alleged to be wonder-working and to have the property of conferring life and health. Hrihor had apparently entrusted him with this in order to supplement with its blessings the distinctly meagre sum in gold and silver which was all he was prepared to pay ; but as we shall see, the business-like, not to say materially minded, semi-European sea-raider folk were not so much impressed with Wen-Amen's fetish as the Egyptians hoped and expected.

After this point the papyrus fades away into deplorable tatters. The surviving fragments however allow us to reconstruct the general course of the story :

. . . he said to me " Silence ! " . . .
. . . and they went away and sought their thieves . . .
. . . and I went away from Tyre as dawn was breaking . . .
. . . Zakar-Baal, lord of Byblos . . .
. . . and there I found 30 deben of silver and took it . . .
. . . your silver is deposited with me . . .
. . . I will take it . . .
. . . they went away . . .
. . . the harbour of Byblos . . .
. . . to Amon ; and I deposited his goods in it. And the lord of Byblos sent a messenger to me, [saying " Depart from] my harbour " ; and I sent him a message . . .

From the sequel it is possible to guess the sense of the lost words enclosed in brackets. When the continuous narrative begins again, Wen-Amen has arrived at Byblos, but has not recovered his money, and has apparently recouped himself by stealing a bag of silver from somebody else. The

Egyptian apparently suffered from an idea that one barbarian was much the same as another, and that it was reasonable to take this sort of line, since the prince of Dor had given him no satisfaction. Perhaps Egyptians had been accustomed to treat the natives in this cavalier fashion in the days when Egypt was an imperial power ; but those days were long past now, and the ancestors of the Phœnicians and grandchildren of the sea-raiders were by no means disposed either to respect an Egyptian as such, or to tolerate high-handed behaviour by a foreigner who had lost his property. There is indeed no more striking contrast in the story than that between the modernity of the sea-folk and the pitiful mixture of feebleness and bluff displayed by the fetish-ridden theologian in whose hands the prestige of the ancient civilization lay.

Zakar-Baal of Byblos was unsympathetic, granted the Egyptian no audience and, as we have seen, bluntly bade him depart. Wen-Amen did not do so, but dallied helplessly about, down by the harbour, waiting for something to turn up ; while Zakar-Baal, who did not lack a sense of humour, contented himself with repeating once a day his suggestion that the ambassador should go away. At last, after waiting, as he says, for nineteen days, Wen-Amen gave it up. Mengebti's ship had gone on, long ago, but there was another vessel in the harbour, bound for Egypt, and in her he booked a passage. He then waited for nightfall before going on board, lest profane eyes might rest upon his sacred image of Amen of the Way.

Then suddenly the whole situation was changed. As Zakar-Baal was sacrificing, one of the young men of his court was seized by a religious frenzy, danced, and "prophesied ". It is the earliest example on record of this not uncommon Palestinian phenomenon. " Bring up the god ! " he cried ; " bring up the messenger of Amen ! Send him on his way ! " And consequently, when Wen-Amen was on the point of departure, he suddenly found himself greeted by an armed guard who said that next morning the prince would see him. "Then why ", protested Wen-Amen irritably, " have you done nothing all this time but tell me to go away ? I am going." " No ", said the guards ; " you must stay and see the chief." Wen-Amen seems to have suspected that it was all a plot to let the ship go off with his luggage and leave him stranded on the quay. He sent a message to this effect to the chief, who replied by sending an order to detain the ship as well.

So at last, next day, after the morning sacrifice, Zakar-Baal gave audience to Wen-Amen, in his castle looking down to the sea. "And I found him sitting in his upper chamber, while the waves of the great Syrian sea beat upon the shore behind him. I said 'Amen be gracious to you'. He said ' How long is it since you left the land of Amen ? ' I said ' Five months and one day so far '."

Characteristically the sea-king goes straight to business, spending no time on the salutations dear to Egyptian diplomacy. Wen-Amen's reply shows us why he was so anxious to get back to Egypt at once ; his adventures between Dor and Byblos, described in the lost part of the papyrus, had taken up the whole summer. He had set sail in April ; it was now September and Zakar-Baal's sudden change of front had lost him practically his last chance of getting home by sea before the equinoctial gales suspended sailings for the winter. Since the journey by land was a dangerous and expensive business for which he was not equipped, there seemed every prospect of his being left in Syria till next year.

" Well ", went on Zakar-Baal, " if you are a true man, where is the letter that the High Priest of Amen gave you ? "

" I said to him " (continues the papyrus), " ' I gave it to Nesubenebded '." Clearly the envoy should have asked for it back again before leaving Tanis.

" Then he was very angry. ' What ! ' he said, ' you have no letter to show ? Well then, where is the ship in which Nesubenebded sent you ? Where is its crew of Syrians ? I am sure he never trusted you to this [Egyptian fool] who would have drowned you ; —and where would they have looked for your god and you, then ? ' "

Some of Zakar-Baal's words have been " bowdlerised by the hand of time ", as the saying is ; but the context makes it clear that the point of his remark was a hit at Egyptian sailors and seamanship. Wen-Amen protested : " There are indeed Egyptian ships and Egyptian crews belonging to Nesubenebded. He has *no* Syrian crews."

" He said to me ' There are twenty ships in my harbour which are in connection with Nesubenebded ; and at Sidon, where you want to go, there are ten thousand ships, in connection with Berket-el '——

"Then I was silent in that great hour. And he said 'On what business have you come here ? '

"I said 'I have come for the timber for the great sacred barge of Amen-Ra, king of the gods. Your fathers sent it, and so will you '."

This attempt to demand timber, in the manner of an Egyptian of the great conquering days, was a total failure. "Quite true ", said Zakar-Baal, "they did ; and when you pay me I will do it too. Certainly our agents transacted the business ; the Pharaoh sent six ships laden with Egyptian goods, which were unloaded into our store-houses."

"And then ", Wen-Amen continues, " he had the account books of his ancestors brought in and read them before me. They found a thousand deben of every kind of silver, which was recorded in the ledger. And he said 'If the king of Egypt were lord of my property, he would not send silver and gold; he would command me : " Do as Amen bids you ". It was not a tribute that they received from my father. I am no servant of yours nor of your master's. If I speak the word to the Lebanon, here the logs will lie, on the sea-shore. But what then ? Where are the sails that you have brought to transport the logs ? Where are the cords you have brought to make them fast ? . . . I admit that Amen equips all lands ; he equips them, having first equipped your country of Egypt. Craftsmanship and civilization came forth from Egypt to this country. Why then have they sent you in this miserable fashion ? ' I said to him ' Impious knave, I am not travelling in miserable fashion. There is no ship on the river that is not Amen's ; and his is the sea, and his is Lebanon which you claim as yours ; and for his sacred ship the cedars grow ; for he owns every ship. It was Amen-Ra, king of gods, who bade Hrihor my lord send me, bearing [the image of] this great god. And you have kept this great god waiting for twenty-nine days [here Wen-Amen improves by ten days on his former account] although you knew he was here. Assuredly he is still mighty as of old, while you stand here bargaining about the Lebanon with Amen its lord. And as for these former payments in gold and silver that you mention, if our kings had then sent life and health they would not have sent

the money ; they sent your fathers the money instead of life and health.   Amen-Ra, king of the gods, is lord of life and health, and he was lord of your ancestors, who spent their lives offering to Amen ; and he is your lord too.   If you say to Amen " I will perform thy command," and do perform it, you will enjoy long life and health and prosperity, you and all your people ; but you must not covet that which belongs to Amen-Ra the king of the gods ; for the lion loves his own '."
. . .

Wen-Amen harangued on and on, like a papal legate before a refractory mediæval potentate ; but about this point he apparently realized from Zakar-Baal's expression that he was not producing the desired effect, for he abruptly changes his tone.   His speech ends to this effect :

" ' Now let my scribe be brought, so that I may send him to Nesubenebded and Tentamen, the rulers to whom Amen has committed the north of his land, and they will send everything that I order ; and when I return to the south again I will send you all these trifles that you want.'   That was what I said."

Thus the interview ended—a distinct success for the office ledger as opposed to the wonder-working image.   Wen-Amen wrote his letter, and it was sent, and in less than two months the reply came, in the shape of a consignment of goods on account—four vases and a basin of gold, seven vases of silver, hides, rope, fish, lentils, linen, and five hundred rolls of papyrus —an important item to these keen business-men with their carefully posted account-books.   Then the prince " rejoiced " —canny man—and gave Wen-Amen three hundred men with three hundred oxen, to look after the felling and transport of the trees.   At last, some eight months after Wen-Amen had started from Thebes, the cedar logs lay ready on the sea-shore, and Zakar-Baal, accompanied by Pen-Amen, his Egyptian butler, who held the state umbrella over him, and by Wen-Amen himself, proceeded down to the harbour to hand them over in due form.

Even at this point, though they had no objection to selling him cedar-wood at a sufficient price, Zakar-Baal and his attendants were quite ready for a laugh at the expense of the envoy and his ridiculous pomposity.   The shadow of the state umbrella happened to fall upon Wen-Amen ; at which the butler remarked, " The shadow of thy lord Pharaoh falleth upon thee ! "   The point of this witticism probably is " even if you are Pharaoh's servant, you are in our king's power while you are here ".   Zakar-Baal however reprimanded Pen-Amen sharply ; evidently he felt the remark to be in bad taste, either in itself, or at any rate in the mouth of a servant.   The latter seems the more likely, for he proceeded to make much more pointed remarks, to exactly the same effect, himself : " Well ", he said, " I have now done what my fathers did, though you have not paid me as well as your ancestors used to pay.   Here is the timber, all ready for you to do what you like with it.   But never mind the terrors of the sea for a moment.   Just look at me.   Rameses IX sent some ambassadors to me once ; and they stayed here for seventeen years. Show him their graves ! "

" No, please ", said the terrified Wen-Amen ; " I would much rather not see them.   Besides, they had no god with them.   Why do you not erect an inscription to record for all time that ' at the bidding of Amen-Ra I sent timber to Egypt, and I prayed for ten thousand years of life, and it was so ? ' "

" A lot of value that sort of evidence would have ", sneered Zakar-Baal.

Even now Wen-Amen's troubles were not at an end.   He was just getting his cargo stowed, when there appeared in the offing eleven ships of the Zakkaray, who showed every sign of hostility.   They apparently claimed to be some sort of sea-police—a good Minoan institution—and it further seems that Wen-Amen had already been in their hands once, and was badly wanted by them for his theft of silver earlier in the summer.

Wen-Amen collapsed on the shore in tears, and the chief's secretary came and asked him what was the matter.   " Don't you see these sea-fowl ? " was the answer ; " Here they are, for as long as they like to stay, and when ever will they go ? It is all over with me, and they have come to take me again ! "

The secretary bore the news to Zakar-Baal, who on hearing it wept also—or so Wen-Amen says. , Certainly in this crisis he behaved very fairly ; after all, Wen-Amen was a customer, and the chief wanted the balance of his price which by the contract would be due when Wen-Amen and the timber reached Egypt in safety.   The secretary presently reappeared, with

Zakar-Baal's advice to be of good cheer, and some concrete aids to cheerfulness in the shape of a sheep, two jars of wine, and the loan of an Egyptian singing-girl, whose name was Tentnut.

Next morning Zakar-Baal held an assembly of his people and gave audience to the Zakkaray, asking them on what business they had come. They said : "We have come after the ships which you are sending to Egypt, for we are the guardians of the helpless". Zakar-Baal replied, "I cannot arrest an ambassador of Amen in my own territory. You must let me see him started, and then you may pursue him and try to catch him ".

So away went Wen-Amen over the sea (with or without his heavy freight ?). He was not caught by the Zakkaray, but he sailed straight out of this trouble into a southerly gale, which blew him miles out of his course, and ended by piling up him and his ship upon the coast of Alasya—whether this be Cyprus or the neighbouring mainland. Here the people seized him and dragged him off—intending to kill him, as Wen-Amen fully imagined, until they fell in with Hatiba, the ruling queen of their city, whom they met as she was passing from one palace to another.

"Does anybody here speak Egyptian ? " cried Wen-Amen. A man stepped forward, and through him Wen-Amen made his appeal to the queen : "Say to my lady : 'I have heard as far as Thebes, the abode of Amen, that though injustice is done in every city, yet justice is done in the land of Alasya. But I find injustice being done here daily '". She said, "What is this ? " I said "There was a storm at sea, and the wind bore me to this land. Please do not let them kill me. I am an ambassador of Amen, and now there is always somebody after me ! And as for the King of Byblos' sailors, whom they were going to kill—their master will certainly catch ten crews of yours and kill them in return ".

The queen evidently saw that Wen-Amen was on the verge of collapse, and answered kindly, bidding him lie down and get some sleep, and giving orders for his crew to be summoned. And at this point the Golenischeff papyrus breaks off, and we are left in ignorance as to how Wen-Amen reached Thebes again and sat down to write his report to his lord Hrihor, the High Priest of Amen-Ra.

II. THE STORY OF THE SEA-RAIDER

(*Odyssey*, XIV, 199-359)

This is the story told to the faithful swineherd of Odysseus by the wandering beggar whom he has entertained, who is Odysseus himself in disguise. The whole tale is an elaborate lie, but all the better on that account ; it is not merely the story of what the poet alleges to have happened in one unusual case, but that of the sort of thing that might happen to anyone —and probably the sort of thing that did happen several times in the course of the twelfth or eleventh century.

" From the broad lands of Crete I boast my race to be, the son of a wealthy man ; and many other sons of his were bred and born in his hall, true-born sons of his wife ; but my mother was his concubine bought with money ; yet he honoured me equally with his true-born children, did Kastor, Hylakos' son, whose son I boast myself to be. He then was honoured like to a god among the folk of the Cretans, for his good fortune and riches and his gallant sons. But the fates of death bore him off to the house of Hades, and his proud sons divided his substance and cast lots therefor, and to me they gave but a very small portion and house to dwell in. But I married a wife of a wealthy family, for my own valour's sake, for I was no worthless one, nor a coward in war ; but now all that prowess is ended ; it is but the dry stalk of a man that you see here, I think ; for indeed abundant grief is upon me.

" Now the gods, Ares and Athene, gave me a sanguine heart, and might to lay men low. When I picked my best men for an ambuscade, preparing ill for my foes, my proud spirit had no foreboding of death, but first by far I would rush on and slay that foeman whom I might overtake. Such was I in war ; but work did not delight me, nor home-keeping that brings up fair children ; but my delight was in oared galleys, and wars, and smooth-shafted javelins, and arrows, those grievous things, whereat other men shiver. But my delight, doubtless, was in such thoughts as God put into my mind ; for different men take pleasure in different occupations. For before the sons of the Achaians set foot in Troyland, nine times I had chief command among men and swift-faring ships, abroad among foreign folk ; and great possessions came my way. Of them

I chose out to my heart's content, and much also fell to my share by lot; and soon my house was enriched, and I was feared and respected among the Cretans.

" But when far-seeing Zeus devised that woeful journey, that relaxed the limbs of many a man, then they bade me and the noble Idomeneus to command their ships that went to Ilios ; nor by any device could a man hold back, but the fear of ill report among the people constrained me.   There for nine years we warred, we sons of the Achaians ; and in the tenth we sacked the city of Priam and started homeward with our ships, and some god scattered the Achaians.

" But for unhappy me, Zeus the counsellor planned misfortune ; for I stayed but a single month enjoying myself with my children and my wedded wife and my possessions, and then straightway my heart bade me fare oversea to Egypt, having well arrayed my ships, with my godlike comrades.   Nine ships I made ready, and quickly the folk gathered.   Then for six days my trusty comrades feasted, and I gave many a victim to sacrifice to the gods and to make their own meal of ; and on the seventh day we put out from spacious Crete, and sailed with a fresh and fair north wind, easily, as though downstream ; none of my ships had trouble, but unscathed and without sickness we sat at ease, and the wind and the helmsmen sent the ships on their way.

" On the fifth day we came to well-watered Egypt, and in the River of Egypt I beached my oared galleys.   Then I bade my trusty comrades to bide there by the ships, and guard the ships, and scouts to go to spy out the land and return ; but they, giving way to over-confidence and obeying their whim, immediately began to plunder the fair lands of the Egyptians and led captive their women and little children, and slew the men ; and soon the cry of it reached a city.   And hearing the shouting they came, at dawn ; and all the plain was filled with horses and men and the flashing of bronze.   And Zeus the Thunderer made a panic to arise among my men, and not one of them would abide the onslaught ; for ill was about them on every side.   There they slew many of us with the edge of the sword, and others they took alive to work for them perforce. As for me, Zeus set a thought in my heart—oh, would that I had died and met my fate there in Egypt ; for there was yet more sorrow in store for me.   Straight I put off from my head the well-wrought helmet, and the shield from off my shoulders and let fall the spear from my hand ; and then I made for the chariot of their chief, and embraced his knees and kissed them ; and he saved me and took pity on me, and set me in his chariot and brought me to his house, weeping. Many of them brandished towards me their ashen spears, desirous to kill me, for they were very greatly angered ; but he kept them back, and was mindful of the anger of Zeus, the stranger's god, whose indignation is most kindled by evil deeds.

"Then for seven years I abode there, and won much wealth among the Egyptians ; for all men gave to me. But when the eighth year came round, then came a Phœnician, a deceiver, a greedy scoundrel, who had wrought much harm among men. He persuaded me by his cunning to go with him, until we came to Phœnicia, where his home was, and his possessions. There with him I dwelt for a full year ; but when the months and days were fulfilled of one circling year, as the seasons came round, then he set me upon an ocean-going ship to go to Libya, giving me deceitful counsel to go a-trading with him, so that he might sell me beyond the sea for a great price. I went with him in his ship, perforce, though I guessed the truth ; and the ship ran before a fresh and fair north wind, outside Crete, over the open sea ; but Zeus was planning their destruction. When we were leaving Crete behind, and no other land was in sight, but only sea and sky, then Zeus brought a black cloud above the hollow ship, and darkened the sea beneath ; and straightway he thundered, and cast his bolt upon the ship ; and she staggered through all her length beneath the shock of the thunderbolt, and was filled with sulphurous fumes ; and the men fell overboard. Like sea-birds they showed swimming among the waves around the dark ship ; and God took from them their home-coming.

"But Zeus brought my way, troubled as I was at heart, the huge mast of the dark-prowed ship, into my hands, that I might yet escape disaster. To it I clung, and was borne by baneful winds. For nine days I was borne, and on the tenth dark night the great rollers brought me near to the land of Thesprôtis. There the hero Pheidon, king of the Thesprotians, took care of me without recompense ; for his dear son, coming upon me worn out with cold and weariness, took me by the hand and raised me up, and brought me home to his father's

house, and clad me in tunic and cloak. There I heard news of
Odysseus " . . .

(The details of the false report of Odysseus that follows are
of no particular interest.)

" And the king sent me on my way ; for there chanced to
be a ship of the Thesprotians sailing to fertile Dulichion. He
therefore strictly commanded them to bring me to king
Akastos ; but they preferred an evil counsel concerning me,
so that I might be yet further grieved with sorrow. When
the ocean-faring ship was far out from land, then did they
bring the day of slavery upon me ; they stripped me of my
tunic and cloak, and cast about me some other wrap and
tunic, threadbare—these, which you see before your eyes.
That evening they came to the country of far-seen Ithaka ;
then they bound me within the benched ship, tightly, with a
well-twisted rope ; but themselves they disembarked and
hasted to take their supper on the sea-shore. Then for me
the very gods themselves loosed my bonds, easily ; and
covering my head in my rags I climbed down the smooth
steering-oar until my breast was in the water, and then struck
out with my hands, swimming ; and soon I was away clear of
them. Then I crept up, where there was a thicket of the
flowering woods, and lay there peeping out ; and they ran this
way and that with cries of dismay ; but since it seemed to
them not worth while to seek me further afield, they embarked
again on their hollow ship ; and the very gods themselves
kept me hid, easily ; and they have brought me to the farmstead
of a prudent man. So it is still my fate to live yet longer."

III. THE SWINEHERD'S STORY
(*Odyssey*, XV, 363-492)

The stranger in the swineherd's hut, who is Odysseus himself,
has asked as though casually after Odysseus' parents (though
in fact he already knows of his mother's death). This leads
to the swineherd's telling the story of his life. He starts with
a reminiscence of the kindness his old mistress showed to the
little slave-boy from oversea :

" . . . For she brought me up along with Ktimene of the
long robes, her fair daughter, the youngest of her children ;
with her I was brought up, and her mother paid me but little

less attention. Then when we both came to the prime of lovely youth, they gave her away in marriage over in Same for a great price ; and my lady clad me in good clothes, cloak and tunic, and gave me shoes for my feet, and sent me off to the country. She was a good and true friend to me. But now I have lost those friends ; but as for myself, the blessed gods give increase to my labour, and thereof I eat and drink and give to strangers. But of Penelope there is no good news to hear, either of word or deed, for there is evil in her house, namely insolent men ; yet thralls have a great desire to speak before their mistress and to discover everything and to eat and drink, and thereafter to carry something off to the country, of such things as ever delight the heart of thralls."

Then Odysseus of the many devices answered him :

"Ah, swineherd Eumaios, at how tender an age you were carried far away from home and parents. Tell me this, now, truly—Was your wide-wayed city of men taken in war, the city wherein your father and mother dwelt ? Or, when you were alone with the sheep or the cattle, did cruel men kidnap you and sell you oversea into this man's house for a sufficient price ? "

And the swineherd, that prince among men, answered him again :

"Stranger, since you ask me this, hear me now in silence and take your ease, as you sit and drink your wine ; these nights are ages long—there is time to sleep, and time to enjoy a yarn, and there is no need to go to rest too early. Too much even of sleep is wearisome. Now any of the others who will may go outside and sleep ; and at dawn after breakfast he shall go with the pigs to our master's hall. But we two will sit in the hut drinking over our supper, and take pleasure in the tale of one another's bitter woes, hearing them called to mind ; for a man enjoys even his troubles, afterwards, when he has suffered much and wandered far. And this that you ask me, I will tell you :

"There is an island called Syria, if you have heard of it, beyond Quail Island, at the rising of the sun ; an island of no great size, but a good land—good pasture, rich in sheep, a land of corn and vineyards. Famine never visits the people, nor does any other grim plague come upon hapless mortals ; but when in that city the people grow old, Apollo of the Silver

Bow, with Artemis, comes and kills them with his gentle shafts.[1]
There are two cities there—the whole island is divided in
two—and my father was king over both of them, Ktêsios,
Ormenos' son, a godlike man.

"Thither came certain Phœnicians, those famous seamen,
—greedy knaves, bringing countless trinkets in their black
ship. Now there was a Phœnician maid in my father's house,
a fine strapping woman and skilled in handicrafts ; and the
crafty Phœnicians beguiled her. First, when she was washing,
one of them lay with her beside the hollow ship, in love, that
beguiles the wits of even good women. Then one asked her
who she was and whence she came, and straight she told them
of her father's high-roofed house :

"'From Sidon rich in bronze I boast myself to be, and I am
the daughter of Arybas exceeding rich ; but Taphian pirates
kidnapped me when coming home from the country, and sold
me here oversea into this man's house for a sufficient price.'

"Then her lover answered her again :

"'Then would you come home again with us, to see your
father's and your mother's high-roofed home, and themselves
also ? For they are still alive, and men call them rich.'

"And the woman answered him again and said :

"'Yes, that I would, if you, sailors, will please to swear
me an oath to bring me home unharmed.' Thus she said, and
they all swore as she bade them ; and when they had made an
end of taking the oath, the woman spoke again among them,
and said :

"'Now, be silent, and let none of your company address a
word to me, if you meet me in the road or at the well ; or
someone who comes to the house may tell the old man, and he
may guess the truth and keep me fast bound and plot your
destruction. But keep my words in mind, and speed the sale
of your merchandise ; and when your ship is laden with
goods, then let word be sent to me at the house at once, and I
will bring some gold with me, whatever I can lay my hands on.
And I would gladly bring something else, too, to pay my
passage : I look after the master's little boy in the house—
a fine child, who runs beside me when I go out. I could bring
him on board ; and he would fetch a big price when you sell
him among foreigners over the sea.'

---

[1] The ordinary Homeric phrase for a "natural death".

" With that she went away to the beautiful house.

"Now the men stayed with us for a whole year in their hollow ship, and did a brisk trade. But when their ship's hold was laden, so that they could return, then they sent a messenger to tell the woman. A cunning man came to my father's house, with a gold necklace, hung with amber pendants. And while my mother and the maid-servants were handling and gazing at it, and making offers for it, he nodded to the woman privately. With that, he departed to the hollow ship, and she took me by the hand and led me out of the house. On the verandah she found cups and tables, where men had sat at meat, who were in attendance on my father ; they had gone to the place of session and of public audience ; and she quickly took three cups and hid them in her bosom[1] and carried them off ; and I went with her, not understanding. And the sun set, and all the roads grew dark ; and we came to the famed harbour, hurrying ; and there lay the swift ship of the Phœnicians. Then they embarked, and sailed the sea-ways, having taken us on board ; and Zeus sent them a fair wind. For six days we sailed, by night and day ; but when Zeus, son of Kronos, brought the seventh day, then the archer Artemis smote the woman ; and with a splash she fell into the bilge, as a sea-bird dives. They threw her overboard to be the prey of the sea-beasts and fish ; and I was left alone in my grief. And wind and wave bore them to Ithaka, and there Laertes bought me with his possessions. And in this fashion I first set eyes on this land."

And divine-born Odysseus answered him :

"Eumaios, surely you have moved me with all this tale of the griefs that you have suffered. And yet beside your sorrows Zeus has given you happiness, in that after all your trouble you came to the house of a kindly man, who gives you meat and drink in plenty ; and you live no bad life ; but as for me, in wandering through many cities of men am I come hither."

---

[1] i.e., into the capacious and useful fold formed by a loose tunic caught up at the waist with a girdle. The passage is one of those which show us the great difference between Minoan and "Homeric" costume ; this passage would certainly not fit the former.

CHAPTER IX

The Cruise of the *Argo*[1]

οἴη δή κείνη γε παρέπλω ποντοπόρος νηῦς
Ἀργὼ πᾶσι μέλουσα . . .
—*Odyssey*, XII, 69-70.

Ὠκεανοῦ παρὰ χεῖλος, ἵν᾽ ᾤχετο θεῖος Ἰήσων
—*Mimnermos.*

WHILE in the Levant the sea-raiders were consolidating their power in Syria and Cyprus and teaching the Canaanites of Sidon the handling of ships, other adventurers, setting out from ports in the Aegean, were exploring the North. One famous tale of twelfth or thirteenth century adventure in the Black Sea has survived, though unhappily there is no complete version of it that is removed by less than seven hundred years from the event ; it is the story of the *Argo*, the first ship in the world to become famous among posterity by name. However, the story was well-known to Homer,[2] and several details in it seem to indicate that here, as usual, the epic tradition was " founded on fact ". Other details on the other hand seem to be part of a nature-myth. Taking all together, we are presented with an unique opportunity of observing the growth of a legend, by the blending of elements of myth and popular story with a genuine tale of exploration.

It was Jason the Minyan, so the old epic said, which the rhapsodes used to recite at Ionian street-corners, who sailed from Iôlkos to explore the Unfriendly Sea ; and he sailed in the ship *Argo*—" *Swift* "—the first long-ship (i.e. the first ship of

---

[1] A pleasing study of this legend is Miss J. R. Bacon's *Voyage of the Argonauts* (London, 1925), to which however the present chapter is not indebted.
[2] In view of such passages as *Il.*, VII, 467-9 ; *Od.*, XII, 69-72, with Σ *ad loc.*, quoting Hesiod ; Hesiod, *Theogony*, 992-1002 ; Mimnermos, frag. 11; —Mr. Allen's remark (*Homer, the Origins*, etc., p. 108) that " no tradition exists before Pindar," of this exploit, is somewhat surprising.

fifty oars ?) that a Minyan ship-yard had produced. Jason was Aisôn's son, and rightful heir to the throne of the Minyan principality ; but Pĕlias, his wicked uncle, who had usurped the kingdom, urged him when he grew to manhood to prove himself by a daring deed—namely, to bring home the Golden Fleece from the land of Aia where it lay. Pelias would have killed him, had he not feared the odium of such a deed ; and so, like Saul with David or the king of Lykia with Bellerophon, he tried to get rid of him by sending him on a desperate quest.

So Jason set out on his long voyage to the eastward, with his little band of adventurers, fifty strong. They passed by Lemnos and across the north Aegean, up the Hellespont past the frowning citadel of Troy, and through the Propontis and the Bosporus, meeting with many dangers by the way— adventures with savage hill-tribes on the coasts where they put in to camp or water, adventures with the Harpies, the storm-fiends that haunt the dangerous Salmydessian shore, whose wreckers in later ages won an evil fame. These Harpies caught the imagination of the Greeks, who portrayed them as demons in monstrous winged half-human form. But along the coast of Asia Minor the Minyans pressed on undaunted until at last they came to the land of Aia, which later Greece identified with Kolchis in the far south-east of the Black Sea ; a mountainous country beside the river Phasis, bordering on the iron-country of the Chalybes and on the towering range of " Caucasus at the end of the world ". The voyage out was accomplished ; but the Golden Fleece was yet to be won.

Anxious days followed. King Aiêtes was suspicious and inclined to be hostile, and by no means inclined to part with the prize. There was even some fighting,[1] in which no doubt the heroes acquitted themselves manfully ; but it was not by such methods that they could gain their end. The Kolchians were no mere savages, to be cheated or overborne. They were well-armed and numerous, formidable both by land and sea ; the little band of Europeans down on the beach must get their way by negotiation or not at all.

They seemed likely to fail, when Mêdeia, the king's daughter, fell in love with Jason, and the whole position was changed. By her help Jason satisfied the conditions, intended to prove

---

[1] So our oldest extant complete account of the Quest : Pindar, *Fourth Pythian*, ll. 212-13.

impossible, which her father had laid down ; and then, before Aiêtes should think of further difficulties to create, they determined to steal the Fleece and be gone. Mêdeia guided them, after nightfall, to the grove where the treasure hung, and helped them to drug and kill the giant snake that guarded it. Absyrtos, her brother (so one version says)[1] came upon them while they were making their escape, and was killed before he could give the alarm. Then, with Mêdeia and the Fleece on board, *Argo* slipped her cable and dropped quietly away down the river in the darkness before dawn.

To avoid the certain pursuit of Aiêtes' navy, and almost certain capture, the Minyans did not take the direct route home ; and according to some versions of the tale, it was only now that their real difficulties began. It was now, for instance, according to the Odyssey, that they met with the Wandering Rocks—the terrible Blue Bergs that clash together and threaten to crush ships that pass between.[2] And it was on their homeward way that, as every account of their wanderings says, they came to a place where their ship could go no farther, and whence they must drag her on rollers for twelve days overland. How they came home, the ancients had no idea ; their stories are various and wild ; but all are agreed that they reached the uttermost parts of the earth, " where the sun turns back again "[3] ; and all are agreed upon the detail that they had to man-handle their ship in one place from sea to sea. It seems almost certain, however, that it was they who first told the Aegean of the Kimmerians, in their gloomy northern land, which we still call the Crimea.

At last, however, after months if not years of wandering and hardship, they found themselves back again in their home-harbour of " Iôlkos by the sea ".

The sequel, as told in the old epics, appears to have been that Mêdeia made Aisôn, Jason's father, young again by her magic arts, and paid Pelias out by encouraging his daughters to attempt a similar experiment on him, but purposely omitting to tell them some important details ; after which she and Jason

---

[1] Sophokles, *Kolchides* (Σ to Ap. Rhod., IV, l. 223).

[2] παρ' Αἰήταο πλέουσα, *Od.*, XII, 70 ; not, as most later accounts say, when outward bound. The attempt to distinguish between the Planktai and Symplegades found in some later writers (e.g., Apollonios) is a clear case of formation of a " doublet ".

[3] *Od.*, XII, 3-4.

no doubt " lived happily ever after ".   But there is also a much
later and much truer and finer version of it ; that of Euripides'
Mêdeia, which for the first time in history handles the
tragedy of the barbarian girl and the European sailor.   Jason,
says this " modern " story, had to flee from Iôlkos to escape
the consequences of Mêdeia's habit of bringing his enemies
to a violent end.   He settled at Corinth ; and while he was
there, there appeared a heaven-sent chance of restoring his
fortunes.   The king of Corinth was old, and had one child
only, a daughter.   He could wish for nothing better than a
son-in-law with such a brilliant reputation as Jason's, and one
who, having now no principality of his own, would be willing
to devote himself whole-heartedly to his wife's kingdom.   The
king offered the explorer his daughter's hand ; and to both
parties it seemed an ideal match.

So Jason and the princess were married, and Jason did his
best to make things tolerable for poor Mêdeia who naturally
would now have to retire into the background ; for of course
there could be no legal sanction to a civilized man's union
with a barbarian woman.   But Mêdeia herself had other plans.
Turned into a fury by jealousy and her resentment of Jason's
ingratitude and injustice she struck, not at Jason himself,
but at those nearest to him.   She butchered her own children,
as being his ; she sent the princess a robe smeared with caustic
poison, of which the princess died in agony, with her father
who tried to save her ; and when an infuriated crowd came
seeking her blood, she had gone beyond their reach, to Athens.

As for Jason, middle-aged and alone, he went back to his
ship, that lay on the shore at Iôlkos, rotting, like Jason himself.
He used to hang about her and think of the past ; and one day
when he lay asleep in the shade of her now ancient hull, the
stern-post fell out, and hit and killed him.   Thus ended the
ship and the man that had accomplished the quest of the
Golden Fleece.

To return to the oldest part of the story—Jason's adventures
—the grounds for believing that the legend embodies the
distorted memory of a real voyage are several.   It is in any
case probable that Aegean ships did sometimes penetrate the
Black Sea, both from archæology[1] and from the evidence of

[1] Cf. Evans, *The Shaft-Graves and Beehive Tombs of Mycenae*, pp. 43-48.

PLATE XIII

(a)

(b)

(c)

(a) and (b) gold gems, (c) fragment of silver vase (the " Siege Vase "), all from Mykênai.   In (c), archers, slingers and spearmen (old men ?) are drawn up in support of a sortie from the hillside town, on whose walls women shriek and gesticulate.   For the large non-rigid (leather ?) shields, cf. the lion-hunters on plate viii.

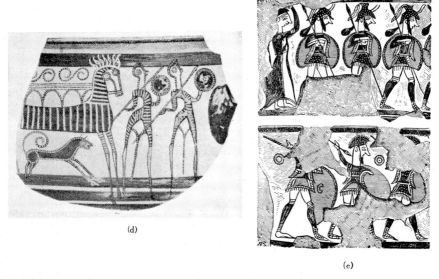

(d)

(e)

"Sub-Mycenæan" (twelfth century ?) sherds, (d) from Tiryns, (e) from Mykênai (the " Warrior Vase "), showing warriors with smaller shield and (in e) clumsy " bell-shaped " corselet.

MINOAN AND ACHAIAN WARFARE

place-names such as Odessos, Salmydessos, with their Aegean termination, on the way from the Bosporus to the mouths of the Danube. It is also certain that the shores of the Black Sea, north as well as south, had their own well-developed and artistic copper and bronze age civilization.[1] Even the name Kolchis is very probably mentioned in the Hittite documents, in the form Khalki, " wheat-city " ; a name from which it has also been suggested that the Greek " chalkos ", not an Aryan word, may be derived.[2]

The type of winged demon, seen in Greek representations of the Harpies, may well be native to Asia too, like Pegasos and the Chimaira ; like them, it occurs in connection with a tale of adventures east of the Aegean, and like them it occurs in Hittite and Assyrian sculpture.

So it is also with those adventures of the Argonauts which Homer took over bodily into his Story of Odysseus. The Kimmerians, for example, are mentioned in the same episode of the Odyssey that tells of Kirke the witch, " own sister of Aiêtes the baleful-hearted ", on her " Aiaian Isle " ; " Aia " is the name of Kolchis in the earliest versions of the legend. Hence, too, Homer must surely have heard that traveller's tale of the far north, where " a man that needed no sleep might earn double wages, . . .   for hard by one another are the paths of the night and day ".[3] This land, where the evening almost overlaps the morning, and where the cannibal Laistry-gŏnes dwell, also seems to be not far from the Aiaian Isle, which is the scene of the next adventure ; and evidently it is far enough north for the short summer nights to have been noticed and exaggerated.

The Blue Rocks that clash together are clearly ice-bergs or floes. Very thick ice does form in severe winters on the Black Sea ; in the late autumn of 1920 A.D., the Red Army outflanked the defenders of the Crimea by the daring night march of a picked body of troops across a corner of the frozen sea of Azoff, and ice of such thickness could easily endanger a wooden long-boat of the *Argo's* type.

[1] Cf. Rostovtzeff, *Iranians and Greeks in South Russia*, early pages, especially 17, 18.

[2] Cf. Tubalcain " forger of every kind of cutting instrument of bronze " in the Hebrew tradition (*Genesis* IV, 22) with Tubal-ki, somewhere in the Caucasus region, in the Hittite texts.

[3] *Od.*, X, 82 ff ; Aiaian isle first mentioned, *ibid.*, l. 135.

It is, therefore, a reasonably convincing rationalization of the Argonaut legend to say that it is the record of a treasure-hunting expedition to Kolchis, which on its return journey followed the north shore of the Black Sea, in order to evade pursuers following the direct route. After being endangered and badly frightened by the floating remnants of the previous winter's ice, the expedition finds itself in the *cul-de-sac* of the Sea of Azoff. Prospecting by land, its members discover open water to west of them beyond the Isthmus of Perekop ; and accordingly, rather than face the passage of the melting ice-fields again, they make the laborious but perfectly feasible portage from sea to sea.

As to the Golden Fleece itself, it, too, is not a mere product of romantic imagination, but apparently, like the clashing rocks, a traveller's tale of something that really did exist. There may never have been a treasure of this name that could be stolen and carried away ; but there was of old, and also in modern times, within the memory of men living, a method of treasure-hunting, in which " golden fleeces " figured, in that part of the world. It was the primitive " grease-process " of mooring fleeces at points where a gold-bearing stream crosses a gravel-bed, and collecting the alluvial gold grains that collect upon them.[1]

Of the date of the voyage, nothing can be said. Homer places it in the generation of the Trojan War, in which Jason's son, Eunêos of Lêmnos, is a " friendly neutral ". This, however, may be merely an example of the epic tendency to compress all the heroic stories into a space of a couple of generations. Eunêos, " Ship-man ", a very appropriate name for Jason's son, may have been made up by the poet as he made up the names of scores of his " supers " ; and if Homer knew merely that the kings of Lemnos before the Pelasgoi came there had been of Minyan descent, the fact would give him an opportunity for alluding to an old story in his favourite manner. Probably, in fact, the exploit is very much older than the Trojan War, for the story seems to have been handed down orally, before the poets " fixed " its form, long enough to have lost practically all its proper names. The names of the chief personages in the story as we have it do not sound like those of real people ; and the naming of famous non-Minyan heroes (Herakles,

[1] Strabo, XI, p. 4-99 ; cf. Myres, in *C.A.H.*, III, pp. 661-2.

Peleus, and so on) as members of the crew is generally considered to be a late development.

Along with the details that suggest genuine tradition are others that seem to be such stuff as myths are made of. As the background of the story, lexicographers like Apollodoros tell a barbarous old tale of famine and human sacrifice and a fairy bride : Athamas, one of the old Aiolid kings, they said, had wooed and wedded a Cloud-Nymph ; but afterwards he married another wife who ill-treated the children of the Cloud ; and forthwith the Cloud departed to her sisters, and they all forsook the land. Then there was drought and famine, and at last men determined on human sacrifice to placate the gods ; and their wicked stepmother turned this plan against the children of the Cloud, and they would have been sacrificed had not a Golden Ram appeared, sent by their mother, and borne the children away safe on its back, through the air. Now it was the skin of this Ram (says the fully developed form of the legend) that Jason had to bring home, and thereby to lay to rest the uneasy ghost of Phrixos, his kinsman, who had died far from home in the eastern land to which the Ram had carried him.

It is in keeping with a story of this type that the land to which Jason went, and its ruler, have no proper names. Aia is merely " the land " ; Aiêtes " the Man of the Land " ; and for the rest, we are only told that the place is hard by the sunrise—" where the sunbeams lie stored in a chamber of gold ", as the elegist Mimnermos put it—and that the King himself is a son of the Sun-God by a daughter of Ocean,[1] that outermost River that encircles the whole world. His daughter is merely Mêdeia, " the Cunning Woman ".

This gives us a clue to a version of the story as old as Simonides[2] in which the object of the Quest is not a Golden but a Purple Fleece. The Golden or Purple Fleece, sent by the Cloud-Nymph and on which her children rode away—the Fleece, to find and win which a man must go to the farthest end of the earth and the rising of the sun—is clearly the golden or purple mist of morning, that parts in fleecy clouds before the brightening day. Jason in this myth is, as his name implies,

---

[1] *Od.*, X, 138.
[2] Σ on Euripides, *Mêdeia*, l. 5.

Iasôn " the Healer ", who goes to bring back the clouds to his parched and thirsty country.

There are thus two strands interwoven to make even the earliest form of the story as known to us ; a genuine tradition and a weather-myth. It is not a simple theory, but the facts for which we have to account are notoriously complicated, and no simple theory, however ingeniously worked out in detail, seems to account satisfactorily for more than a selection of them. The poet responsible for combining the two probably imagined *Argo's* voyage " round the back of beyond " as going actually round the world, where the sun goes when we cannot see him. This would account for the way in which most of our versions—all, excepting that of the fifth century humanists, Hêrodôros and Sophokles[1]—contrive to bring the heroes, across land and sea, into the Western Mediterranean before they can get home.

Of the two principal proper names in the story, that of Jason, being significant and appropriate, most probably belongs to the weather-myth, the fairy-tale ; but it was not as " the story of Jason " that the legend was usually referred to. Its usual name comes evidently from the true saga ; the story is called the story of the *Argo's* Sailors ; and this is as it should be ; the tradition of the first opening-up by Greeks of the Unfriendly Sea was regarded as the tale not of an individual but of a ship, a voyage, and a crew.

With these two strands intertwined, the story was complete in essentials ; but it still could be, and has been, embellished by the addition of other incidents and other famous names. Inserted in it, for instance, we find the effective old fairy-tale of the Sowing of the Dragon's Teeth, which is also attached, in a more detailed form, to the Kadmos legend. The fact that the two stories are doublets is naïvely recognized in one version, where we are told that all the teeth came from one dragon, that killed by Kadmos ; for Athene carefully reserved half of them, leaving Kadmos to sow the remainder, while she carried off her selection in a bag and gave them to Aietes (we are not told why) in case he should ever want to raise a similar crop.[2]

[1] Σ on Apollonios, IV, 259 and IV, 284.
[2] Pherekydes, in Σ on Apollonios, III, 1178.

As to the addition of other names, post-Homeric fancy glorified the expedition, as it glorified the Hunting of the Boar of Kalydon, by introducing into it every hero of the " pre-Trojan " generation ; Orpheus, Herakles, the Dioskouroi, Peleus, Theseus and Peirithoös, Telamon, Meleagros—even Atalanta finds her way on board. Nothing need be said of most of these names, except to note that in some versions the story approximates to the type of folk-tale, widely popular in Germany and elsewhere, in which the hero wins through his trials by the help of companions each of whom possesses some superhuman gift. Thus in these fully-developed versions of the legend, the crew includes the Strong Man, in Herakles ; the Winged Men, in the Dioskouroi ; Keen-Eye, in Lynkeus who, as an old epic said, from a hill-top took in the whole Isle of Pelops at a glance, and saw his enemies hiding in a hollow tree[1] ; in Tiphys, the perfect helmsman ; in Orpheus, the perfect musician, who outsang the Sirens and charmed the Snake, the Guardian of the Grove, to sleep ; and in Mopsos, the perfect seer, who, like Melampous and Siegfried, can understand the language of beast and bird.

---

[1] *Kypria,* ap. Σ to Pindar, *Nem.* X, 114.

CHAPTER X

The Aegean under the Achaians

... ἀνδρῶν ἡρώων θεῖον γένος, οἱ καλέονται
ἡμίθεοι, προτέρη γενεή κατ᾽ ἀπείρονα γαῖαν.
καὶ τοὺς μὲν πόλεμός τε κακὸς καὶ φύλοπις αἰνή,
τοὺς μὲν ὑφ᾽ ἑπταπύλῳ Θήβῃ, Καδμηΐδι γαίῃ,
ὤλεσε μαρναμένους μήλων ἕνεκ᾽ Οἰδιπόδαο,
τοὺς δὲ καὶ ἐν νήεσσιν ὑπὲρ μέγα λαῖτμα θαλάσσης
ἐς Τροίην ἀγαγὼν Ἑλένης ἕνεκ᾽ ἠυκόμοιο.

—Hesiod, *Works and Days*, ll. 159-165.

OF what was happening in the Aegean after the fateful
decades about 1200 B.C., archæology tells a melancholy
tale. Civilization is not merely, as in the great age of Mykênai,
somewhat vulgarized as compared with the best Minoan
ideals; it is, at least on its artistic side, already foundering.
"Sub-Mycenæan" art is the art of the Warrior Vase and the
Warrior Stele, and of that famous and interesting potsherd
that shows two "Homeric" warriors with spear and round
shield, with their chariot and their faithful hound. Not only
is the drawing like that of a child of six, but the dog's tail,
which is about a yard long, is gaily rolled up into the artist's
favourite spiral ornament. It is neither the realistic art of
Knôssos nor the fully-developed "geometric" of the tenth
century; it is half-way down the decline that leads from the
one to the other, and has all the puerility of geometric art
without the dignity that the latter obtains from the very
strictness of its conventions. There are descriptions in Homer
of realistic art in metal; but we are not told that the Achaians
could produce such work. The shield of Achilles is the work
of a god, and presumably the poet is thinking of such objects
as the Vaphio cups or the Mykênai dagger-blades, the products
of an earlier age. The silver bowl that Menelaos gives to
Têlemachos is likewise Hêphaistos' work, and a present to
Menelaos from the King of Sidon, whom Minelaos had visited;
here the poet may well have had in mind an early example
of those silver bowls, decorated by the clever Phœnician

craftsmen in their weird unoriginal mixture of Egyptian and Assyrian styles, which later Phœnicia exported both to Greece and to Etruria. But of creative artists among the Achaians themselves we hear not a word.

Writing, too, has disappeared; the Achaian gentry are neither traders nor diplomats. Descendants of the old Aiolid families as many of them are said to be, they hail from backward Thessaly, where the art had never been known. They neither keep their accounts like Zakar-Baal, nor write letters to their brother-kings like the old king of Tiryns in the Bellerophon story. When the chieftains at Troy mark their lots, one man, as we have seen[1], cannot recognize another's mark. Like the Goths in the Roman empire, the Achaians are chivalrous illiterate barbarians, squandering the resources of an advanced and ancient civilization.

Homeric clothing helps to remind us that we are no longer in a Minoan but in a Greek world. Men wear the tunic and plaid instead of the loin-cloth ; women, instead of the elaborate flounced skirt and open-breasted jacket, have the loose and graceful but extremely simple " Doric chitôn ", as it is rather misleadingly called—a mere blanket, girdled at the waist, whose bosom can make a very serviceable pocket. Garments are perishable and leave no trace for the archæologist ; but a visible sign of the change of style in dress does remain for us amid the relics of this Achaian or latest "sub-Mycenæan" age, in the shape of numbers of the newly-invented safety-pin brooches. These, it is true, are believed by some authorities to be a true Aegean invention, and not, as was once thought, an importation from the north. Still, their use is evidence of the appearance of the loose Homeric style of dress, a style that has spread not from the higher to the lower civilization by way of "culture contact", but into the civilized Aegean from the barbaric north, in a way that shows a movement of population. It is the effect of the raids from Thrace and immigration from Thessaly of which the Greek traditions speak.

In details, dress in Homer is, as we should expect in such a transitional age, no more invariably uniform than defensive armour in the same period. Usually it is loose and fastened with a safety-pin ; but one chieftain wears under his plaid

[1] p. 127 and n.

a kind of skin-tight vest of some smooth and sheeny material, "like an onion-skin "[1]; and some ladies still fasten up their robes with the old straight pin that could on occasion be used as a weapon. To caress incautiously a Homeric lady's shoulder might mean scratching one's hand quite badly.[2]

Trade, like the fine arts, is left to foreigners, like the Phœnicians, or the Taphians, somewhere to the west of Greece and a people as ready to swindle or kidnap their customers as the Phœnicians themselves. The Achaian gentleman despises such things ; to call a man a trader is to him an insult.[3] His delight, like that of his predecessors, the older kings of Mykênai, is to hunt the lion and the boar, or to feast in hall while a divine minstrel sings of the glorious deeds of men ; and his chief business in life, for all that he is no berserk and will readily confess that he is afraid, is war. War, piracy, and cattle-raiding are indeed the Achaian's only industries ; to be asked if he is a pirate is *not* an insult.[4] Repairs to the fortress walls of Mykênai, and the ominously rapid improvement in weapons and armour, testify to the insecurity of the times ; and yet, even now, though not unacquainted with iron, the Achaian is too conservative or too contemptuous of trade to import it systematically from the east, where it was in general use, and make his weapons of it. The Taphian captain in the Odyssey[5] is represented as shipping a whole cargo of it to Těměse, wherever that may be ; but the Achaian warriors still cling to their ancestral weapons, the Danubian leaf-shaped sword fashioned in bronze. No less than seven of these Homeric swords have been found in Greece—two in Crete, four in Argolis, one in Boiotia—in addition to the one from Cyprus and three from Egypt mentioned on an earlier page.[6]

Society is aristocratic ; no commoner ever rises to a high place by merit, in Homer, though doubtless in so turbulent an age such things did happen in fact. Broken men in Homer do sometimes rise again to fame, but always we are told that they were born of princely family. At the head of each state, great or small, stands a king of the ancient European type—

[1] *Od.*, XIX, 232 ff.
[2] *Il.*, V, 422 ff.
[3] *Od.*, VIII, 159 ff.
[4] *Od.*, III, 71 ff. ; cf. Thk., I, 5. 2.
[5] *Od.*, I, 179 ff.
[6] Peake, *Bronze Age*, Plate XII, cf. p. 145, above.

judge, warlord, and sacrificer on behalf of the people. He has certain privileges and prerogatives, marks of respect in social life rather than powers, and is thought of as reigning in some sort by right divine[1]; but in practice his power depends on his force of character. Above all things he must be a good man of his hands—fighter, carpenter, ploughman—or his turbulent nobles, who like him are called " princes ", will have no respect for him. An old man who feels his powers failing will often abdicate in favour of his son, like Laertes; and if the king disappears, like Odysseus, leaving a widow and a son not yet of age, the other princes do practically what they will, even to the point of importuning his presumed widow and living at free quarters in his house. The young Têlemachos counts for nothing, and when he attempts to assert himself the nobles plot his murder.

So, too, Achaia as a whole forms a loose confederacy under the King of Mykênai as overlord. The overlord, of the dynasty of Pelops, is explicitly said to hold his position by divine appointment,[2] and is unquestioned leader among the chiefs of the confederacy in time of war[3]; but though Agamemnon is no mean spearman he is an unlovable character, and the chiefs do not hesitate to cross him in matters both personal and of state.

All the " kings ", in short, are social equals, and any of them if he marries into a ruling house may become a ruling chief. The real gulf is fixed between nobles and commons, the latter being wholly at the mercy of the former. No commoner is named in the Iliad except the would-be demagogue Thersites, first of a long line of stupid aristocratic caricatures. When the swineherd in the Odyssey plays a prominent and sympathetic part, we are carefully informed that he is really a king's son. Odysseus is praised for ruling " gently as a father ", and rulers are called " shepherds of the people "; but there is ample evidence that the shepherds considered themselves quite justified in preying on the flock to their heart's content. The quiet and easy-going Menelaos offers perfectly casually to turn a village-full of his subjects out of hearth and home, to make room for an old comrade in arms to

---

[1] e.g., *Il.*, II, 206.
[2] *Ibid.*, 100-108; IX, 99.
[3] *Il.*, I, 78-9; IX, 69, etc.

migrate thither with his kinsmen and household[1] ; and even the famous generosity of Alkinoös and his nobles is based on the comforting knowledge that after loading Odysseus with presents they can recoup themselves at the expense of the people.[2]

Arbitrary and often oppressive rule, the decay of trade, and general insecurity of life and property thus appear to the prose historian as the leading characteristics of the Achaian age. Its attractiveness when depicted by Homer is due first and foremost to the poet's genius. In so far as it belongs to the age itself, it is simply the attractiveness of a vigorous open-air physical life in which appetites are hearty and unrestrained, manners generous and unaffected, women free and held in honour, and men's minds little affected by either of those arch-troublers of the human race—superstitious fear of the supernatural, and self-conscious questioning about the duty and destiny of man.

For Homeric religion is as little consistent as the Homeric descriptions of armour are often said to be. All one can say definitely is that the heroes do not allow it to worry them. One can see at a glance both that the old Minoans had been a profoundly religious folk, and that in post-Homeric Greece there was still much anxious placating of ghosts and deities— spirits of springs and woodlands, of the weather, the corn, the vine, the cattle—even down to the fifth century. But from all this, Homer's Achaian chieftain stands aside. The only gods he recognizes are the beautiful anthropomorphic super-human Beings that have made " a Greek god " a phrase implying physical perfection and nothing else. And of these beings themselves he by no means stands in awe.

In the Viking Age in northern Europe, the same phenomenon may be observed. Ancestors of the Vikings had lived a settled life in Norway and placated Odin and Thor ; their descendants were to live a settled life in Norway or Iceland as members of the Catholic Church ; but between the two lie the very unsettled generations, during which severe practical tests had tended to show the help of heaven to be less efficacious than that of a man's own strong hand. In this age, not a few characters in the sagas are surnamed " the Godless " ; and

1 Od., IV, 174-7.
2 Od., XIII, 14-15.

even other men, Christian or pagan, allow their religion to sit only very lightly on them. So also the Achaians, lifted in station above the cares of peasant religion, and living, like the Vikings, in an unsettled age, are punctilious in the external matters of libation and sacrifice, but rarely if ever restrained by religious considerations from doing anything that they have decided to do.

Homeric religion is not entirely unethical : the Fury that Walketh in Darkness avenges offences against the family[1] ; Zeus is the protector of the stranger within a foreigner's gate— an important point, for the stranger has none other that fighteth for him ; but the fear of Zeus is not always an adequate protection.[2] Lastly, and very important, Zeus is believed to punish with plagues, such as heavy rain in the harvest season, unjust men " who by violence give crooked judgments in the assembly, and drive out the right, and reck not of God's wrath to come ".[3] Yet alongside of this almost Hebrew conception we have to set the reference to Autolykos, who " excelled mankind in thieving and perjury ", by the help of the god Hermes to whom he sacrificed,[4] and is apparently admired for his skill. In the last resort Homeric morality, such as it is, depends on no sanction whatever, but simply on the innate bias towards goodness of the human heart—the kindliness that made Eumaios' lot as a slave so tolerable, and those two great forces that sustain the morality of our own day too ; Aidôs and Nemesis, Honour and Public Opinion, or, as Myres has pleasantly said, " My feeling that I can't do that sort of thing " and " People's feeling that that sort of thing is not done ".

Throughout the period, sea-raiding and wars of aggression continue to be frequent, within the Achaian world itself as well as on its borders ; and accounts of several such wars occur among the manifold stories of Herakles.

Herakles himself is the subject of too great and complicated

---

[1] *Il.*, IX, 454 and context, 571 and context.
[2] Cf. Odysseus' words to the Cyclops : " Zeus regardeth the suppliant and the stranger," etc. *Od.*, IX, 269-271 ; but cf. also the phrase ἀτίμητὸς μετανάστης, " a stranger without rights," i.e., who can be wronged with impunity, without paying a fine (τιμή) in *Il.*, IX, 648 ; XVI, 59, where Achilles complains that he has been treated like one.
[3] *Il.*, XVI, 385-8.
[4] *Od.*, XIX, 394-6.

a mass of legend for any satisfactory rationale of the whole to be possible ; but as with King Arthur, all the legends seem to fall under one or other of two heads—ætiological culture-myths, a vast mass of which has gradually collected round the name of a famous hero, and genuine traditions of a human warrior who lived in a troubled age   Arthur, who in the oldest account is not a king but a war-lord appointed by the Keltic chiefs to fight the Saxons,[1] seems to be a combination of a Briton, perhaps bearing the good Roman name Artorius, with a Keltic culture-hero of myth.[2] So Herakles, whose name, formed from that of a goddess, is emphatically that of a man and not of a god, seems to be, as some of the Hellenistic scholars suspected, a conflation of a similar culture-hero with the personality of a cadet of the House of Perseus in Argolis ; a troublesome pretender to the throne of Tiryns, restless, brutal, and immensely strong, the most destructive sacker of cities in a destructive age. The stories of his beneficent labours during his servitude to his cousin Eurystheus, King of Tiryns, clearly belong to the culture-hero[3] ; those of his warlike expeditions, to the man Herakles, son of Amphitryon and Alkmêne, who probably lived in the twelfth century B.C.

His expeditions reach every part of the Aegean world. Old Nestor in the Iliad remembers how, when he was a boy, Herakles killed his brothers and left him alone : " Few were we and hard bested in sandy Pylos, for the mighty Herakles had come upon us and beaten us, in the former years, and all our best were slain."[4] In the north of Greece he sacked Oichalia in Thessaly, as a post-Homeric epic told. From Kadmeian Thebes, where his father had sojourned and where he seems to have dwelt when thrown out of Argolis, he led an army against the Minyans of Orchomenos, who had claimed overlordship over the Kadmeians[5] ; and it was said to have been in the war that followed that Herakles blocked the great Minoan tunnel that drained the Lake Kôpais. Certainly the tunnel did cease to function about this time, never to be restored by Greeks ; weakening the once rich Minyan city for ever,

---

[1] *Historia Brittonum*, c. 56.
[2] So Rhys, *Arthurian Legend*, p. 48.
[3] But this as well as the other part of his career is known to Homer ; cf. *Il.*, XV, 639-40 (subjection to Eurystheus) ; *Od.*, XI, 617-626 (labours for Eurystheus, especially the bringing up of the Hound of Hell).
[4] *Il.*, XI, 689 ff.
[5] Str., IX, 414 ; D.S., IV, 18 ; Paus., IX, 37, 2.

and turning miles of fertile cornland into stagnant and pestilential pool and fen.[1] Across the sea, Homer tells us that he raided and plundered even the strongly fortified Ilios, coming "with but six ships and a handful of men "[2] ; (but perhaps this story is only a doublet of that of the great Trojan War ?) and the cyclic poets said that he had attacked the Amazons too.[3] On his way across the Aegean he finds time for depredations among the islands, attacking and devastating Paros, where a "Minoan" dynasty still existed[4] ; and at Kôs, "the city of Eurypylos "[5] whither he was carried by contrary winds on his way back from Troy, he again came to blows with the inhabitants. Separated from the bulk of his little armament he was for a time in great danger[6] ; he kills the king Eurypylos but is himself wounded by Chalkodon,[7] and is probably lucky to get safe back again to Argos.

He seems to have been on good terms with the wild tribes of the north-west ; for when he died his children took refuge among these tribes from their father's numerous enemies. They were said to have intermarried with the chiefs of a mixed horde of wanderers from the Illyrian border, now temporarily settled in the Pindos valleys and in a fair way to become a nation ; the Dorians, the names of whose three tribes give a hint of their origin. These are the Hylleis, a section of whom were still to be seen in southern Illyria in Hellenic times[8] ; the Dymânes, the termination of whose name is like that of the Akarnânes, Ainiânes, and other north-western tribes of classical Greece ; and the Pamphyloi, the mixed multitude that might be expected to be found among a horde of semi-barbarians on the move.[9]

To judge by the dialects of the Dorians and Achaians of the classical period, both belonging to the same "west-Greek" family, the Achaian lords were no very distant cousins of the

[1] Polyainos, I, 3. 5.
[2] *Il.*, V, 642.
[3] Paus, I, 2. 1, quoting Agias of Troizen.
[4] Apollod., II, 5. 9. 3-5.
[5] *Il.*, II, 672.
[6] *Il.*, XIV, 250 ff. ; XV, 25 ff.
[7] Apollod., II, 7. 1.
[8] Skymnos, ll. 403 ff., quoting Timaios.
[9] These have, of course, nothing to do with the Arkadian-speaking Greeks of Pamphylia in Asia Minor, on whom see p. 118 and n.
  On the origin of the Dorians cf. Hdt., I, 56 ; our oldest authority ; but even he is not unaffected by the tendency to theorise.

Dorians away in the north ; but politically they were divided by all the difference that separates " haves " and " have-nots ". It was imperative that the Achaians should in their own interest constitute themselves guardians of the Aegean civilization, debased as it was, which they now enjoyed, and defend, on principle, the civilized world against the outer barbarian. Actually, the Achaians, as might be expected, did nothing of the kind.   Aggression they knew, and reprisal they knew, but the defence of a country, as contrasted with that of a single fortress, was beyond them. The plunder of the Aegean interested them more than defence against the north ; and their warlike energies, in the decades immediately following Herakles' death, were devoted first and foremost to the ruin of the great city that had been the northern capital of Minoan civilization on the mainland.

We have seen something of the way in which Thebes, behind king Amphion's powerful fortifications, had held its own, not without difficulty, against the north-western tribes.[1] Herakles' father had commanded the Kadmeians[2] and the warriors of the neighbouring settled districts in one punitive expedition hardly half a century ago. Now, the Achaian lords of the Argolid looked with envious eyes at the treasures still in the hands of the alien Kadmeians ; and when the two sons of Oidipous failed to agree about the succession, it was easy for the dispossessed prince Polyneikes to raise an Achaian army to restore him to his throne.

Atreus, king of Mykênai, a son of the Asiatic Pelops, was not enthusiastic ; he would have been delighted to join, he said, but was forbidden by an oracle.   He had married a princess of the Perseid royal house and, when the childless Eurystheus came to grief in an expedition beyond the Isthmus, which Atreus himself had cannily refrained from accompanying, quietly occupied the vacant throne.[3] Possibly he felt that for himself to go on an expedition north of the Isthmus might suggest undesirable analogies to other adventurers. Agamemnon in the Iliad remembers Polyneikes' recruiting-tour when he was a child, but no prince of Mykênai marched to Thebes.[4]

---

[1] pp. 104-5.
[2] " Boiotians " in the Hesiodic poem (*Shield of Herakles*, l. 24) is simply an anachronism.
[3] So Thk., I, 9. 2.
[4] For Atreus' excuses, cf. *Il.*, V, 378 ff.

Other chieftains however joined with alacrity. Adrastos the powerful king of Argos was universally recognized as the leader, and with him went the great warrior Kapaneus, Amphiaraos the seer and fighter, persuaded by his wife, for a bribe, to go, though not without gloomy foreknowledge of the end,[1] Tydeus, son of Oineus, exiled from Kalydôn, little of stature but terrible in battle,[2] and other heroes of renown. It was a formidable array that the famous Seven Captains led into the plain of Boiotia, where they defeated the Kadmeians in battle and drove them within their walls. So elated were the invaders that they dared a general assault on the fortress with firebrand, axe and scaling-ladder, and with the almost inevitable result of a disaster immediate and complete. Six of the Seven Captains fell ; the Kadmeians also lost several of their chiefs.[3] Adrastos, saved only by the speed of his horses from sharing his comrades' fate, returned home a broken man.

The death in the battle of both pretenders to the throne settled the question of the Theban Succession in favour of a third party, but it did not save Thebes from further Achaian attacks. A point of honour had been added to the motive of covetousness and desire for plunder ; and a short generation later a second expedition was set on foot, as tradition said, by the seven sons of the seven ill-fated champions—Diomedes, son of Tydeus and son-in-law of Adrastos,[4] Sthenelos, son of Kapaneus, Diomedes' friend and comrade-in-arms, Alkmaion, son of Amphiaraos, and others ; and this time success was won, as the ancients read in the old epic sequel to the Thebaid, the lay of " the After-Born ".[5] The Kadmeian citadel was very thoroughly sacked, and for a generation there was no Theban

---

[1] *Thebaid*, paraphrased by Pindar, *Ol.*, VI, 15. For Homeric references to his story, cf. *Od.*, XI, 326-7 ; XV, 246-8.

[2] *Il.*, V, 801.

[3] To this cycle belongs the story of Tydeus, who, as Professor Murray puts it, "would have been made immortal, owing to his many merits, had not his own tribal war-goddess, Athena, seen him eating an enemy's head on the battlefield and after that preferred to let him die ". To say "eating" is as a matter of fact a little unkind to Tydeus ; it was not a case of cannibalism, but of barbarian rage, when his retainers brought him the head of the man who had mortally wounded him (Σ to *Il.*, V, 126, quoting Pherekydes). There is a curiously exact parallel in Giraldous Cambrensis (*Expugnatio*, I, 4) who tells how Dermot, king of Leinster, disgusted his Norman allies by picking out after a victory the severed head of a rival and tearing at its nose with his teeth.

[4] *Il.*, V, 412-15.

[5] Cf. Sthenelos' boast, *Il.*, IV, 405-10.

fortress, but only a Lower Thebes[1]—the suburbs of the old city, spreading down the slopes of the hill. Legend said that a remnant of the Kadmeian people took refuge out of reach of their foes among the north-western tribes on the borders of Illyria[2]—adding one more contingent to the enemies of the Achaians in that quarter.

The virtual disappearance of the Kadmeian nation left a vacuum ; and the result was ominous—the vacuum was filled from the north-west, by a new people, the Boiotians, who now appear for the first time in the land that was to bear that name.[3] They were said to come from Arne, somewhere in the foothills of Pindos ; possibly their name is connected with those of Boion, in Dôris, and of the Boian Mountains on the Epeirote border ; and they moved south under pressure from another new people, the nation that was to give its name to Thessaly.[4] In any case, they are essentially a people from beyond the pale of Aegean civilization. The language of their descendants in historic times, as seen on inscriptions, is closely allied to Doric.

This migration gave considerable trouble to later Greek historians, whose general impression of ancient history was that the Great Migrations, which replaced the Homeric by the historic map, took place a couple of generations after the Trojan War, and that the Boiotian movement was an early event in the Great Migrations. This theory—in broad outline probably correct—did not square with the presence of Boiotians in the Iliad, so a special reservation had to be made : " but there must have been a division of them there already, who sent the contingent to Troy ".[5] It is fairly clear that in reality, however, the Great Migrations were longer drawn-out and a less swiftly cataclysmic process than Greek folk-memory would give us to understand, and that at the time of the Trojan War *they were already under way*. Asia Minor and the Cyclades had not yet begun to be Hellenized, and the map of the Peloponnese in Homer is that of Minoan times ; but in central Greece, where Boiotia, Lokris, Phôkis and Aitôlia are already taking shape,

---

[1] *Il.*, II, 505.
[2] Hdt., V, 61, etc.
[3] The Iliad uniformly speaks of Kadmeioi when referring to the Theban Wars, Boiôtoi when referring to the contingent sent to Troy. Cf. *Il.*, IV, 385, 388, 391 ; V, 804, 808 ; contrast II, 494, 510 ; XVII, 597, etc.
[4] Thk., I, 12 ; Polyainos, I, 12 ; VIII, 44.
[5] Thk., I, 12.

and also in parts of the southern Aegean, the " Conquest-Peoples " are beginning to appear.

Of conditions in the Aegean during the Achaian period, we know less than of either the Greek mainland or the Levant. Greek tradition speaks of Karians, once subdued by Minos, pushing westward into the Cyclades again after the disappearance of his fleet ; their dominance lasted until the Aegean was finally swept by Greek-speaking bands at the time of the Dorian Migrations. Archæology testifies to the great importance of the Mycenæan settlement at Rhodes. There may possibly be allusions to these two salient facts in the references of Kastor's " Thalassocracy-List " to Rhodian and " Phrygian " sea-power in the latter part of the sea-raid age.[1] For the rest, we hear only of such raids as that of Herakles on Kôs and Minoan Paros, and presently, not long before the Trojan War, of the migration of Greek bands under Herakleid princes to the southeastern Aegean isles. By that date, Rhodes has passed under the rule of Tlêpolemos, a son of Herakles by Astydameia, a northern woman from Ephyre on the Sellêeis River[2] ; while a contingent from the neighbouring islands, Nisyros, Kôs, Kasos, Karpathos and the Kalydnai, is under Pheidippos and Antiphos, who are Herakleids and also in some sort Thessalians : " the two sons of Thessalos, the prince, the son of Herakles."[3] It is the first appearance of the Thessalian name in literature ; though, as we have seen, tradition had it that the pressure of Thessalian tribes had played its part in causing the Boiotian migration.

The arrival of the Herakleid at Rhodes seems to have been marked by something of a catastrophe. In the fourteenth and thirteenth centuries it had prospered, and it had more than once already received Greek colonists—one such was Phorbas the Lapith, of whom a dragon-slaying story is told,[4] apparently an early version of that of Deodato de Gozon, the dragon-slaying Knight of St. John, in the same island over two thousand years later. But now, though Homer emphasizes the prosperity of Rhodes under Tlêpolemos, the number of

---

[1] Alternatively, these Phrygians may be sea-raiders from Thrace, now domiciled in Asia Minor.
[2] Il., II, 653-70.
[3] Ibid., 676-80.
[4] D.S., V, 58.

ships that he brings to Troy is conspicuously small—only nine, as against thirty under Pheidippos and Antiphos; a mere fraction of the number provided by one of the powerful mainland kingdoms.

In Crete, a much-quoted passage of the Odyssey[1] gives a still more striking sign of the times—Homer's one specific mention of the Dorians by name, though it is quite possible that the Herakleid settlements in the south-east Aegean may have included Dorians. The question arises, from what part of the Aegean coast these had sailed; and a very probable answer has been suggested. In the Trojan War, Agamemnon's confederacy stretches as far as the northern borders of Thessaly; Priam's stretches westward through Thrace to the Vardar, Homer's " Axios, most beautiful of streams ". But between the two there is a blank; and here, on what was later the Macedonian coast, appear two place names—Dion and Pydna— which reappear as Dia and Hierapytna in Crete. Here, it is suggested, the independent Dorian tribes were already taking to the sea.[2]

Homer's picture shows us, in short, not so much a stable *age* as a *moment* in the gradual decline of Aegean culture— a moment immediately before the final collapse. It is everywhere the very latest pre-Dorian remains that best illustrate the manners and customs and material civilization described in the Iliad. It is therefore not surprising that remains dating from a definite period of any appreciable length, which we could identify with the Heroic Age, are seldom easy to find. " If anything ", remarks one recent writer, " the Achaian seems to be a proto-Dorian " ; and so far as the archæological evidence is concerned, the statement is true. Dr. Mackenzie has described certain remains in Crete that can probably be ascribed to the Heroic Age; they are definitely transitional in character, between the " Mycenæan " and the " Geometric " or Iron Age cultures. In them, fibulæ and the burial-rite of cremation make their appearance together; and with them, for the first time in the Aegean area, weapons of iron.[3]

This brings us to one final point, deliberately omitted from our sketch of Achaian society : the fact that no trace of a

---

[1] XIX, 196.

[2] Myres, in *J.H.S.*, XVII, pp. 177 ff. Cf. Strabo, X, p. 475, quoting Andron, who says that the Dorians of Crete came originally from Thessaly.

[3] *B.S.A.*, XIII, pp. 423 ff.

Bronze Age burial with the rites so exactly described in Homer has yet been found in the Aegean.

Burial rites have varied considerably in the Aegean during our period. The Minoan Cretans and the early lords of Mykênai inhumed their dead unburnt ; during the sea-raid ages cremation is introduced at several points in the Aegean, but never becomes universal. Its introduction, like that of the brooch, was formerly believed by archæologists to be a sign of immigration from the Danubian region ; fuller knowledge, however, has cast doubt on the theory. The points at which cremation first appears are in Karia and in the islands ; not at points easily accessible from Central Europe. It seems, therefore, quite as likely that the rite came from the east as from the north.

Homer, however, describes, uniformly,[1] disposal of the dead by cremation, followed by burial of the remains, often in an urn, under a barrow ; and such burials have hitherto only been found dating from the fully-developed Iron Age.[2] This can only mean one of two things. One of them is that Homer, as Ridgeway thought, purposely used the archaic and poetic word " chalkos " for the metal of which weapons were made, though in reality they were made of iron. The other—a less startling theory to believe in—is that, as we should naturally expect from a study of the Homeric map, Homeric society is in process of rapid change ; that the interval between the introduction by Achaian chiefs of cremation as their burial-rite and the appearance everywhere of iron weapons was very short ; and that our poet, living a generation or two later, has described a state of affairs of which no relic happens to have come to light ; or conceivably, has actually been in error in this detail of his archæology.

THE TROJAN WAR

The siege and sack of Ilios was the most spectacular as well as the last of the great destructive achievements of the Achaian confederacy ; but its permanent importance in human history consists first and foremost in the fact that it forms the theme of Homer's poetry. Nevertheless, the fact that it is the only

[1] pp. 51-2.
[2] e.g., at Halos : Childe, *Aryans*, pp. 52-3.

one of the great sea-raids which has been depicted for us in
some detail by the men who took part in it makes it worth
our while to deal with it even at somewhat disproportionate
length. We have as sources Homer's account of an episode in
it lasting a little over a fortnight, with his incidental references,
in both Iliad and Odyssey, to the other salient events of the
war ; and also our late epitomes of the early post-Homeric
cyclic epics, supplying sequels and prelude to Homer's works,
and the late version by Diktys of what seems to be an independent account of the matter, from Crete where Homer's poems
were little read.[1]

These accounts, it is generally believed, may be read as the
poetically embroidered accounts of a real war fought by real
men, among whom the names of at any rate the more important
leaders are faithfully preserved by the epics. It is noteworthy
that among Homer's Trojans, while the names of many are
Greek and probably fictitious, the names of not a few of the
most important figures—Priam, Paris, and the leaders of
several of the allied contingents—are native and therefore
probably historical. Still, the poetical embroidery covers
most of the fabric. In dealing with particular incidents we
cannot discern fact from fiction ; excising occasional intrusions
of the supernatural, we must needs narrate the one with the
other, since we cannot discriminate ; one thing only we can
say, namely that the old poet exaggerates both the length of
the war and, as one would expect, the size of the armies. As
the father of critical history pointed out long ago, a large force
could not have been provisioned with the resources of the time.[2]
Neither, we may add, could the small though powerful fortress
of Troy accommodate the fifty thousand Trojans and allies
of which the poem once speaks ; while the way in which one
hero will seek or shout for another—with success—in the
midst of the mêlée, betrays the fact that the armies in fact
were small. So also, Homer speaks of a ten-years' war, but
notoriously the first nine years contain a remarkable dearth
of incident, and it is probably significant that " Diktys "
makes the war last through only two winters, and the siege
through only one ; in itself a sufficiently remarkable feat of
endurance on the part of the Achaians.

[1] Cf. pp. 7-8 above.
[2] Thk., I, 10, 11.

King Atreus died away from home in Crete,[1] and his younger son, Menelaos, who with the family talent for such matters had married a princess and succeeded to the kingship of Lakedaimôn, went thither to look after the interests of the family in connection with the succession. While he was away, Paris, son of the king of Ilios, in the course of a more or less friendly tour round the Levant and the Aegean, in the course of which he ranged as far as Sidon,[2] abducted his queen and departed with all speed, reaching Troy on the third day.[3] Menelaos, returning home to find his dovecote rifled, resorted to his elder brother Agamemnon of Mykênai, who, failing the restoration of the lady, summoned all the vassal princes of his great feudal confederacy for an invasion of Dardania.

Elated at the prospect of sacking a wealthy city, the Achaians mustered readily, and in the second summer after Paris' escapade a powerful fleet was mustered at Aulis in Boiotia, under the chiefs made famous by Homer's verses.[4] All the great chiefs of the confederacy were there with their whole force of " Companions ", as an Achaian chief's housecarles were called : Idomeneus of Crete, Menestheus of Athens, Diomedes of Argos, with his friends the sons of Kapaneus and Adrastos ; Nestor of Pylos, vigorous at sixty though inclined to be garrulous, with his two tall sons ; Menelaos and Agamemnon themselves, with their own troops and a horde of the wild highlanders of the Arkadian hinterland. Smaller contingents, whose leaders by force of personality took rank with the greatest, were those of Aias of Salamis, the giant freebooter,[5] and Odysseus of the Western Isles, famous for his cool and calculating brain. Thither, too, came the Lokrians and Boiotians, perhaps hardly Achaians strictly speaking, but willing followers of Agamemnon's banner. Aias " the Less " of Lokris was admitted to the inner council of the Achaian chiefs, but the five lords of Boiotia, in spite of the great size of their contingent, the most numerous in the whole army, won no such recognition. Achilleus, the fierce and passionate

---

[1] Diktys, I, 1, and *Kypria*, epitomised by Proklos. The following paragraphs follow these sources except where references to Homer or other writers are given.

[2] *Il.*, VI, 289-291.

[3] *Kypria*, quoted by Hdt., II, 117 ; *aliter*, Diktys and Proklos.

[4] *Il.*, II, 494-759 : — " the Catalogue ".

[5] Hesiod ; Berlin Papyrus 10560, ll. 4-11.

young son of Peleus, commanded his father's contingent, the " Myrmidons and Hellenes and Achaioi " of the old Achaian homeland in the Spercheios basin. The Herakleid chiefs of Rhodes and Kôs and Karpathos came, and many others— Minyans of Orchomenos, Minyans of Iôlkos, Phôkians, Aitôlians, Magnêtes and other mountain tribes from the outpost baronies, as far as the Peraiboi and Ainiânes of the land " of the bitter winters " around the sanctuary of holy Dôdôna. The report of this great mustering reached even to the sea-raider communities in distant Cyprus, where king Kinyras—the name is not Greek : compare Sisera, Badyra, Debir[1]—hastened to announce his benevolent neutrality, and sent Agamemnon the costly present of a " lobster " corselet of the type that the old Shardana used to wear.[2]

No island prince, indeed, could afford not to be friendly to the lords of such a fleet as the Achaians could raise ; but on the mainland, both of the Balkan and the Asian peninsula, sympathies were with the Trojans. They, too, could raise no mean army when the forces of all their allies were added to their own. To the Tröes proper could be added their neighbours on every side : Pelasgoi from a Larisa somewhere in the Troad, under the two sons of Lêthos, son of Teutamos—two more native names[3] ; Dardanians, under Aineias the son of Anchises, Priam's kinsman, who might have been more enthusiastic if Priam had not been accustomed to treat his family with a coldness that argues jealousy and suspicion[4] ; and the nearest tribes of Thrace, both Thrakes proper and Kikones from Ismaros, the tribe on whose coast Odysseus conducted a raid that met with disaster after Troy had fallen.[5] From further away, from the west came the Paiŏnian archers of the Axios valley ; from inland in Asia, the Mysians, the Phrygians of

---

[1] King of Eglon in *Joshua* X, 3 ; cf. the name Ben-D'b'r in the " list of Keftian names " on an Egyptian writing board, as read by Peet (*Essays presented to Sir A. Evans*, pp. 96-7).

[2] *Il.*, XI, 20-25 ; that it was a " lobster " corselet is an inference from 24-5.

[3] Teutamos occurs as a name in historic times both in North Syria (Sayce, in *J.H.S.*, XLV, p. 163, cf. Tutamu king of Khattina, a Hittite prince of the Assyrian age) and in Macedonia—e.g., the captain of Alexander's *corps d'élite*, the Silver Shields, about three years after his death ; Plutarch, *Eumenes*, 13, 16 ; D.S., XVIII, 59, 62. If the three names are really the same, they form one more grain of evidence on the extent and direction of the great migrations.

[4] *Il.*, XIII, 460-1.

[5] *Od.*, IX, 39-61.

" far Askănia ", which may be the Biblical Ashkenaz, and the Halizônes of Alybe " where the veins of silver are ". Along the Black Sea coast came the Paphlagŏnes under the " wild heart Pylaimenes, from Enete, where the wild asses breed ".[1] From the south came the Maionians of Mount Tmôlos and the shores of the Gygaian Lake, and the Karians of Miletos and Mykale, and last but not least the redoubtable Lykians, who sent a strong force commanded by both their kings. Many of these allies are expressly said to be mercenary bodies attracted by Trojan " subsidies ",[2] as in the old days when they fought for the Hittite kings[3] ; but the help sent from Lykia seems to be something more than this. Possibly the prominent part in the war played by Sarpêdon, Glaukos, and their followers is the part of men who felt themselves menaced by the Herakleid occupation of Rhodes and the neighbouring islands.

But not all of the Trojan allies marched at once. There are numerous references in the Iliad to some who, like Rhesos or Euphorbos, have just come in at quite a late stage in the war. Those whose territory fronted the Aegean Sea, indeed, probably dared not march until they were certain that the whole Achaian force was definitely established before Ilios ; for the Achaians could move swiftly and silently, thanks to their command of the sea, and might, before striking at Ilios, raid any part of their opponent's long coastline.

That the Achaians realized the strategic possibilities of their position is shown by the fact that this is precisely what they did. A little south of the Troad, on the river Kaïkos, lay the kingdom of the Kêteioi,[4] possibly a surviving enclave of Hittites, as Gladstone suggested long ago. They were reputed to be dangerous fighters and the Achaians preferred to meet them alone rather than in company with the Trojans and their other allies. So before invading the Troad the fleet bore up into the Gulf of Adramyttion and landed its warriors there.

The fighting that resulted was some of the most severe in the whole course of the war. The Kêteian resistance was even

---

[1] Literally "wild mules", *Il.*, II., 852; perhaps the wild pony, "Przevalsky's Horse " depicted on the South Russian Maikop Vase, which however is claimed to be very much earlier than the Trojan War.

[2] *Il.*, XVII, 225-6.

[3] p. 133.

[4] Strabo, XIV, 678.

fiercer than had been expected. Têlephos their king fell badly wounded and Teuthranios his brother was killed, but the Achaians too lost heavily. Here, among others, fell Thersandros, a Kadmeian exile, son of the renegade Polyneikes and last survivor of the house of Oidipous. The raid was so far successful that it did temporarily knock out Têlephos' kingdom as a force to be reckoned with ; it was not until Troy was already in desperate case that his son Eurypylos—which possibly is the Asian name Urpalla—at last led a band of his countrymen to help in her defence.[1] But the Achaian forces too had been so severely handled by battle and by storm at sea that, instead of moving triumphantly on Ilios, they were glad to patch up a truce with Têlephos and return to Aulis to refit.

In this manner the winter passed. Diomedes was sent on a recruiting tour through Greece, and the Achaian fleet was strengthened by fifty ships especially intended for raiding the hostile coasts. Then at last, in the third spring after the Trojan prince's fateful sea-faring, the great armada sailed direct for Ilios.

The landing was forced, not without loss. A prophecy, of the safe type familiar in later Greece, foretold that the first man to spring ashore would be killed ; it was fulfilled in the person of the brave Prôtesilaos, a mountaineer from the north, who fell even as he leapt from the prow of his ship,[2] with a Trojan arrow through his heart. The Trojans, however, finally retired within their walls, and Agamemnon, having at his disposal not nearly the force necessary for investing Ilios, beating off attacks by allies from outside, and maintaining communications with his ships, proceeded with what Greek generals in all ages regarded as the second-best plan—that known as *epiteichismos*, or the system of the " counter-work ".[3] This consisted simply of building one's self a semi-permanent fortified post in the enemy's country from which his territory can be wasted, his resources worn down, his fighting-men exhausted by being always on the *qui vive*, and opportunities

---

[1] *Od.*, XI, 519. For Urpalla—the name of a king of Tyana in the Assyrian age—see Allen on the Trojan Catalogue, in *J.H.S.*, XXX.

[2] *Il.*, II, 701-2.

[3] So in the Peloponnesian War, when Athenian sea-power makes investment, of the kind successful at Plataia, impossible before Athens, a " counter-fortress " at Dekeleia is the most damaging measure that Sparta can take.

for collusion with traitors within his gates expeditiously taken.[1]

This the Achaians did. There are references in Homer to assaults on the walls of Ilios,[2] but the strength of the fortifications—even at their weakest point, on the west—is so great that the attack can hardly have been very dangerous. The really deadly weapon in Agamemnon's hand, though not one that could deal an immediately fatal blow, was the raid on outlying portions of the enemy's territory. These raids served three purposes ; they provisioned the Achaian host with cattle " lifted " from the hill pastures, they damaged the enemy, and they prevented the fighting men of the coastal villages from concentrating at Ilios, where, united, they might have been dangerous. Their sea-power continued to give the Achaians the initiative. They had nothing but one fortified camp to defend, and could strike where they would along the nearest two hundred miles of shore.

Achilleus, by temperament, and Aias of Salamis, by experience, were marked out as suitable leaders for these glorified cattle-lifting operations. Aias went out to the northward, Achilleus to the south, where he harried the whole coastland and even the hill-country in a raid or series of raids to which there are numerous allusions in the Iliad. The defence of islands—Lesbos or little Tenedos—was bound to fail, and was duly broken by Achilleus and the villages sacked and burnt.[3] Then came the turn of the mainland. The Kilikes of the southern Troad, close allies of Ilios,[4] were overwhelmed after a brave resistance ; Thêbe fell, its king Êëtion and all his seven sons being killed in its defence, and a rich and varied booty won,[5] and then Lyrnêssos, where Achilleus slew " Mўnes and Epistrophos, the spearmen wild "[6] and captured, after killing her husband and brothers, Brîsêis,[7] of whom more was to be heard later. Pêdasos, of the Leleges, perched on its impregnable rock, was a harder nut to crack, but fell because the defence

---

[1] Homer's insertion of an account of the fortification of the Achaian camp in his account of Achilleus' quarrel with Agamemnon, much later, is clearly, like his similar insertion of the catalogue of *Ships* (not of men), a re-arrangement of history in the interests of literature.

[2] *Il.*, VI, 435 ff.

[3] Lesbos, IX, 128 ff. ; Tenedos, XI, 625.

[4] If as Homer says their king's daughter had married Priam's son.

[5] *Il.*, I, 369 ; VI, 414 ff. ; IX, 186 ; XVI, 153 ; XXIII, 826 ff.

[6] *Il.*, I, 691-3.

[7] XIX, 291 ff.

ran short of water.[1]   And in the course of these same operations, by a swift march inland, the Myrmidons captured a huge herd of cattle which had been driven up into the glens of Ida, cutting them off from Ilios and heading man and beast alike southward to a final round-up in the neighbourhood of Lyrnêssos on the coast.   Two sons of Priam were here captured,[2] among the guards set over the herd, and Aineias, son of Anchises, just and only just escaped within the walls of Lyrnêssos, in time to take part in the unsuccessful defence, and to escape again, somehow, in the confusion of the final assault and storm.[3]

Aias meanwhile, though he has not had the good fortune to be adopted by Homer as his favourite hero, had won almost as great if not as spectacular successes.   Landing in the Gallipoli peninsula, he overran much of it, forcing the local chieftain, whom the Greeks call Polymêstor, to abandon Priam's alliance and pay the Achaians a heavy ransom in gold and— more immediately important—corn ; after which he carried his arms east of Troy into Phrygia, where a chief named Teuthrans met him in battle and was slain.   One thing however he had not done ; he had not broken the Trojan hold on the famous Narrows of the Dardanelles by the capture of either of the twin fortresses, Sêstos and Abydos,[4] east of which Ilios could still communicate direct with her European allies. However, with this exception the preliminary stages of the campaign had been brilliantly successful.   Achilleus in Homer claims that no less than twenty-three Trojan villages had fallen to his spear.[5]   Nor had hostilities been relaxed, stalemate though the position might be, before Ilios itself.   At some point in the siege Achilleus had captured one young Trojan prince within a few hundred yards of the city, cutting osiers for repairs to a chariot's body by night[6]—evidently to do it by day would have been completely out of the question—and Trojan women could no longer wash clothes at the familiar place by the spring quite close outside the walls.[7]   The whole scheme of warfare is under the circumstances exactly that dictated by common-sense, and gives a very " modern " impression.   It is in fact exactly summed up in Marshal Foch's favourite phrase, " catching the enemy by the throat and hitting him with your

[1] Σ on VI, 35.
[2] XI, 101 ff.
[3] XX, 188 ff.
[4] II, 835-6, cf. XI, 228.

[5] IX, 328-9.
[6] XXI, 35 ff.
[7] XXII, 256.

PLATE XIV

WALLS OF TROY: THE WATER-TOWER

[face p. 218

free hand ".   Agamemnon with the main body kept the main enemy forces pinned, while the " free hand ", the bands under Aias and Achilleus, attacked in detail those who tried to defend the outlying villages.

After an absence of some weeks the " flying columns " returned to the camp, loaded with booty, which according to custom was distributed among the whole army, with special shares for the overlord and for the chiefs under whose command it had been captured.   Nestor and Idomeneus were appointed commissioners to deal with Achilleus' booty, and Odysseus and Diomedes with that captured by Aias.   Male prisoners were " sent oversea "—the usual euphemism for being sold into slavery ; the women were kept as concubines in the Achaian camp.   The neutral Minyans of Lemnos found the war a source of very profitable trade ; we hear of them supplying the camp with wine, no doubt at exorbitant rates, in exchange for bronze, iron, hides, cattle, slaves[1]—all of them commodities which must have been plentiful enough to glut the market, after the recent forays—and of one case where the Lemnian king sells a high-born prisoner back to his friends at a clear profit of 200 per cent., even after buying him fairly dear.[2]

Two factors, however, were sure to operate in favour of the Trojans as the summer wore on.   Their own forces were still growing as the allies came in ; for there were no Achaians east of Ilios except an occasional marauding party, and formed bodies of armed men could enter unopposed, whether from Askănia[3] or from Thrace[4] ; in the latter case they would march in overland from the east side, after crossing the water at some point east of Sêstos and Abydos.[5]   Also the condition of the Achaian troops in their camp on the beach was not improving ; and their entrenchments, unlike the walls of Ilios, were not impregnable.   On the other hand, the resources of Troy were already feeling the strain ; the giving of " presents " to allied chiefs and sustenance to their men could not go on for ever.[6] The question, as it appeared to the most vigorous of the Trojan leaders, was whether the war must end with the complete exhaustion of the wealth of Troy, or whether before that an attack with every available man might not drive the

[1] VII, 467 ff.
[2] XXI, 79-80.
[3] XIII, 794.
[4] X, 434.
[5] XI, 227 ff.
[6] XVIII, 288 ff. ; cf. XVII, 225-6.

Achaians out of their cramped position into the sea.[1]   In short, the strategically defending side was compelled by circumstance to adopt a tactical offensive, while the invaders could well afford to abstain from attacks on the towering walls confronting them.   Hence the chief events of the latter part of the war are a series of furious Trojan assaults on the Achaian lines, always repulsed, though once or twice they came very near to success.

Late in the summer, after unsuccessful peace-negotiations and another great foray by Aias against the eastern and central districts of the Troad, the Trojan opportunity seemed to have come.   The Achaians were becoming both diseased and demoralised.   Pestilence broke out in their no doubt extremely insanitary camp on the shore ; and though it was presently checked by a spasm of unwonted cleanliness,[2] it led to developments which might have been even more serious.   Casting about in their minds to find what god they could have offended, they decided that it must have been Apollo, a local priest of whom had recently been sent away empty and with ignominy by Agamemnon, when he begged for the restoration of his daughter, captured at Thêbe.   Agamemnon had taken the girl to be his concubine and had no intention of releasing her ; he announced publicly that on the whole he preferred her to his wife ; but a majority, headed by Achilleus, urged that the manifest displeasure of Apollo must be allayed.   The atmosphere of petty spite which a summer's discomfort had produced in the Achaian council is well shown by what followed. Homer admits that tempers were lost on both sides, but the less elaborate, less poetically dignified version followed by Diktys says that matters were even worse.   Sooner than surrender, Agamemnon was ready to turn the swords of his own troops against those of his vassals, when suddenly the Trojans, who had heard the tumult, swept down upon their camp in battle array.   If they had come a little later they might have succeeded ; as it was, they were repulsed. Agamemnon now consented to give up Chryses' daughter ; but he meanly paid Achilleus out by annexing his favourite captive, Brîsêis, instead, and this wholly discreditable personal squabble over women very nearly wrecked the whole expedition.   It was Achilleus' turn now to think of attacking

---

[1] *loc. cit.* ; and cf. Hektor's whole speech from l. 285 to 304.
[2] I, 313-14.

the rest of the Achaians, but he found them not unready for
such behaviour, and discretion triumphed ; he contented
himself with abandoning active participation in the war.
Hektor the Trojan had meanwhile been watching his opportunity to launch another attack and a general battle resulted,
after which the Trojans retired within their walls, and the
active campaigning season came to an end.

Even the winter, however, was not entirely inactive. Aias
extended his ravages into Phrygia. Hektor soon after his
return surprised the Achaian camp and succeeded in firing
some of the ships. The situation was critical, and overtures
were made to Achilleus, who put himself entirely in the wrong
by refusing to be placated. Without him, however, the
Achaians managed once more to save the day, Aias striking
down Hektor with a great stone ; and after one more unsuccessful assault, delivered by the Thracian allies of Troy, a truce
was made which lasted until the spring.

It was now, according to the non-Homeric version, that
overtures were again made to Achilleus, with amends and the
restoration of Brîsêis ; aud this time the Myrmidon chief
accepted the offer.

Spring came round, and active hostilities began again ; while
King Priam expended his last and dearest treasures in the
hope of summoning yet more allies. Several battles were
fought. Patroklos, the squire of Achilleus, killed Sarpêdon
of Lykia, but was himself killed next day by Hektor. Hektor
in turn fell in an ambush while on his way to meet an allied
contingent. Antilochos, son of Nestor, was slain by Memnon,
the dark man from the east, of whom Arktînos of Miletos wrote
in his " Aithiopis ". Achilleus killed Memnon, and drove the
Trojans with great slaughter into the town ; but pressing on
headlong in pursuit was shot by Paris from the tower beside
the Skaian Gate. Eurypylos, son of Têlephos, arrived, the
last hope of Troy, and the redoubtable Kêteians once more
inflicted a severe check on the invaders[1] ; but at last Eurypylos
also was defeated and killed.[2] Paris had already fallen to an
arrow from the bow of a northern baron, Philoktêtes, from
the borders of Macedonia. There seemed likely to be no

[1] On which, in addition to Diktys and Proklos (Lesches, *Little Iliad*), cf.
Pausanias, III, 26. 7 ; IV, 3. 2.
[2] *Od.*, XI, 519 ff.

end to the weary struggle; but it was ended at last—by treachery. The stratagem of the famous Wooden Horse was effective enough when backed by insincere offers of peace. In this manner at last Ilios fell, Priam was killed, Helen recaptured, and the streets of the citadel saw re-enacted the scenes that had already been witnessed in the sack of a score of neighbouring towns.

Then, oppressed with the feeling that they had done an ill deed, the Achaians sailed homeward; it was on no colonizing enterprise that they were engaged.[1] And in Troy, Aineias, who had once more managed to escape from the sack, was left to found a new dynasty[2] in the devastated and depopulated land, free from the irksome presence of a senior branch of the House of Dardanos. It was not as the result of the Achaian sea-raid that Troy finally disappeared as a national state, but as the result of a new wandering of peoples from the Balkans— a new wave of Phrygians, coming from Thrace.[3]

[1] Contrary to the statements of some modern historians. If the war had been a colonizing movement, there can be no sort of reason why the national poet of the war should casually, but definitely, imply that it was not. Cf. reference in following note.

[2] *Il.*, XX, 306-8: Poseidon prophesies; Aineias and his children's children after him are to reign in Troy, in place of the accursed house of Laomedon.

[3] Str., XII, 572; XIV, 680, quoting Xanthos of Lydia.

CHAPTER XI

THE IRON AGE

νῦν γὰρ δὴ γένος ἐστὶ σιδήρεον· οὐδέ ποτ' ἦμαρ
παύσονται καμάτου καὶ ὀιζύος, οὐδέ τι νύκτωρ
φθειρόμενοι· χαλεπὰς δὲ θεοὶ δώσουσι μερίμνας·
ἀλλ' ἔμπης καὶ τοῖσι μεμείξεται ἐσθλὰ κακοῖσιν.
—Hesiod, *Works and Days*, ll. 176-9.

"THE Achaian chief", remarks a modern historian,[1] "counted his wealth by the number of generations it would last ; the richest hoped it might last for ten." In other words, he comments, they were living on their capital ; and " our traditions say, in the second generation after Agamemnon the deluge came ".

The " Heroic " World could not in the nature of things have been long lasting. The Achaian nobles were probably never very numerous in the Peloponnesian kingdoms that were the centre of their power. Families in Homer are small, and only sons not uncommon ; and, to paraphrase in modern terms a remark of Hesiod's, they were committing race-suicide by way of perpetual warfare. "Some before seven-gated Thebes in the Kadmeian land, fighting for the flocks of Oidipous, and some crossing the sea for deep-tressed Helen's sake ", war destroyed the flower of the Achaian chivalry.[2]

Meanwhile the northern barbarians were always tending to overflow their boundaries. They were as well armed as the Achaioi, possibly better ; for the knowledge of iron was spreading across the world and there is, as we shall presently see, strong archæological evidence for contact between Macedonia and the tribes which were opening up a new and plentiful supply of it in Central Europe. The guardians of what was left of Aegean civilization did not even present a united front ; the house of Pelops itself was divided by internecine feuds which flared up during and after the Trojan War. Aigisthos, son of

---

[1] Wade-Gery, in *C.A.H.*, II, p. 518.
[2] *W.D.*, 162-5.

Thyestes, in the absence of his cousin Agamemnon seduced Klytaimêstra, Helen's sister, to whom Agamemnon was none too happily married,[1] and on the latter's return treacherously slaughtered him and his most trusty followers, as the Odyssey has finely told.[2] Orestes, the king's young son, escaped into exile, to return when grown to manhood and carry out his duties under the feud, by the slaughter of Aigisthos. He also slew his mother, from a stern sense of duty, leaving the question whether the sense of duty makes his deed less or more horrible to interest tragedians and moralists for ages to come.

Firmly settled on the throne, Orestes married his cousin Hermione, daughter of Menelaos and Helen, and their son Tisamenos, being on both sides an Atreid and on both sides a Tyndarid, and without any legitimate rival, apparently succeeded to both thrones. But the strength of his kingdom was not proportionate to the blueness of the monarch's blood nor to its territorial extent.

In the north, the intrusion of new peoples had, as we have seen, begun already before the Trojan War. It continued steadily ; its extent and limits can be seen from a comparison of the Homeric with the classical map of north Greece. The great difference is that in the meantime Hellenic Thessaly has taken shape, covering the whole of the great inland plain. The name of the Myrmidons, like that of the Lapiths, also prominent in Homer's Catalogue, has perished, and the northern Achaioi have become a vassal people pushed aside into the hills. The Magnêtes likewise have become dependent on the new conquerors, the Petthăloi as their own inscriptions call them ; while the Peraiboi and Ainiânes have been driven south-eastward from Dodona, and the famous oracle and sanctuary left isolated among tribes whom the Greeks never recognized as genuine Hellenes.

The north-Achaian states cannot have long outlasted the Trojan War ; for the Thessalian nation, or at least a " Thessalos, son of Herakles ", is as we have seen known to Homer, and the Thessalian was believed to be connected with the Boiotian movement as cause with effect. And at this time there took

---

[1] Cf. his disparaging remark in *Il.*, I, 113-5 ; quoted above, p. 218.
[2] *Od.*, III, 255-75, 303-10 ; XI, 405-434 ; XXIV, 24-34, 94-6 ; the poet keeps harking back to the story curiously—possibly in order to set off the better by contrast Penelope's fidelity and the happy ending of Odysseus' wanderings.

place also another movement, ominous for the future ; the movement of a branch of the Dorian tribe from Macedonia to the southern valleys of Mount Oita, where in classical times three small cantons still preserved the Dorian name[1]; but the majority of the migrants had not been long in their new home before they turned covetous eyes towards the green valleys and unplundered palaces of the lands where Tisamenos ruled.

It is possible now, as it used not to be, to speak definitely of the quarter from which the Dorians came ; for the excavation of several sites in Macedonia by the British School at Athens has confirmed at most points theories based formerly on the sole evidence of certain obscure passages in ancient writers,[2] passages not themselves believed to be altogether above suspicion.

At Buboshta, in western Macedonia, not far from the Albanian frontier, was found one most interesting site : that of what seems to be a genuine proto-Dorian village-settlement. Here had dwelt, uneventfully, from about 1500 to 900 B.C., a simple, backward little peasant-community, belonging to one of a group of tribes whose characteristic types of matt-painted pottery are found in the Pindos glens, from western and central Macedonia, to the Spercheios valley in Thessaly. (So here again it seems impossible to distinguish between the culture of the primitive Dorian and of the primitive Achaian.) At most sites, however, the culture of these mountain-dwellers is found to have been influenced by contact with the Aegean world ; at remote and backward Buboshta it is not so. And here, most significantly, occurs the meander-pattern as a popular decorative motive for painted pottery—a motive which appears abruptly and becomes very common in the pottery of Greece proper in the tenth century and after.[3]

Here, then, was a glimpse of undisturbed proto-Dorian culture. Elsewhere in Macedonia, at Vardaroftsa, the same excavator—W. A. Heurtley—had a year earlier found evidence

---

[1] Wade-Gery (" The Dorians," in *C.A.H.*, II) casts doubt even on the association of these with the more famous Dorians ; but the tradition is as old as the seventh century (Tyrtaios, fr. 2, Diehl) and is surely of just such a sort as a barbaric people would be likely to preserve.

[2] Especially Hdt., I, 56.

[3] Excavations of spring, 1927 ; cf. *B.S.A.* for that year, and summary in *J.H.S.*, XLVII, pp. 243-4. A general summary of the results obtained by all the excavations in Macedonia, up to 1929, is given in Heurtley's communication to the Academy of Athens, 21 Feb., 1929, published in *Antiquity*, 1929, pp. 318 ff.

of the causes that set these primitive mountain-tribes wandering. Here the traces of a late Bronze Age settlement ended ominously with a burnt layer one-and-a-half metres thick. Sherds of sub-Mycenæan pottery showed that the sack of the ill-fated village took place rather before the end of the Heroic Age in Greece. There was every trace of a violent disturbance, while the occurrence among remains of the new settlement, built on the blackened ruins, of new types of pottery showed whence the disturbance came. There could be little doubt that the pottery of the invaders was of a central European, type, though its exact provenance is not known ; and it resembles that of the "Seventh City" at Hissarlik—the village that grew up on the ruins of the Homeric fortress—thus confirming the ancient report that Aineias' dynasty was ultimately destroyed by invaders from Thrace.[1]

The next style at Vardaroftsa, contemporary with the end of the Greek Heroic Age, is of further interest. It is not the invader's pottery pure and simple, but a mixed style, formed by a fusion of local with northern elements, showing, presumably, a similar racial fusion of the Danubian invaders with the local Makednian population. After this, it has been suggested, the northerners passed into Thessaly, taking this mixed style with them ; out of which, as a result of further contact with Sub-Mycenæan and local Thessalian styles, arose the Thessalian variety of the universal geometric style of the Early Iron Age.[2]

The evidence from Vardaroftsa thus appears to reconcile satisfactorily the theories, each with some facts to support it, that the Dorian invasion came from no further than Macedonia, and that it started much further north.

A puzzle connected with the origins of iron-working in Greece has also been solved by recent archæological discoveries. It had long seemed likely that iron as the common metal for tools and weapons was introduced into Greece by the Dorian Invasion ; but an objection was that the earliest Central European iron industry, that of Hallstatt, could not, without doing violence to the data, be made to appear to antedate that invasion. Now, however, the discovery at Vardaroftsa of pieces of iron slag in Bronze Age deposits hardly later, it is claimed, than 1600 B.C., shows that iron working was indeed further

[1] Cf. p. 220 n.
[2] A. M. Woodward, in *J.H.S.*, XLVI, p. 233.

advanced in the north than in the Aegean ; while the discoveries at Velem, near Szombathely, in Western Hungary, have shown us a Central European iron industry in full swing going back at least to the twelfth century ; and evidence of contact between this locality and the Dorians who invaded Greece is not lacking.[1] Mention has been made earlier in these pages of that characteristic Dorian ornament, the so-called " spectacle "-fibula ; the brooch in which the springs at each end of the pin have been exaggerated into two great flat spirals of wire, forming the pin's only ornamentation. Such pins are found in early Iron Age Sparta, and far to the North-West. They have been found also at Velem.[2]

It is presumably this Central European iron that appears in the most picturesque if not the most important of the finds in Macedonia—that of the early Iron Age cemetery at the mound of Chauchitza.[3]

On this site was found a Bronze Age village, which apparently had a long and undisturbed history, coming to an end at very much the same time as that at Vardaroftsa. A very few traces were found of a short Iron-Age occupation; after that, the site was deserted; the destroyers did not linger, but passed on southwards.

The neighbouring cemetery was fairly large—thirty-seven graves were found—but of only one period, that of the destruction of the village. Here had been laid to rest, pro-tected against wolves by cairns of stones, warriors of the earliest Iron Age, buried lying at full length, uncremated, with their weapons and gear. Their sword-blades, knives, and sickles were of iron, not very skilfully tempered ; beads and ornaments were usually of bronze ; shields, too, were of bronze, but in some cases had been riveted, when broken, with iron rivets. Some bronze shield-centres were found, probably for attachment to shields of leather. They had glass beads, and gold plaques were laid over the mouths of the dead. Most of their pottery and some of their bronze ornaments were of types previously unknown ; those that were recognized were of Illyrian and Danubian types ; the " spectacle "-fibula occurred again here. Swords were in all cases of the northern type, adapted not for thrusting but for a slash.

[1] On Vardaroftsa, see Heurtley, *loc. cit.*, p. 322 ; on Velem, the report on their work by von Miske and von Bandat in *Illust. London News*, March 2, 1929.

[2] *Illust. London News, loc. cit.*

[3] Casson, *Macedonia, Thrace and Illyria*, pp. 148 ff. ; figs. 48-60.

So much archæology tells us of the people who, as Greek tradition said, poured down upon the Minoan south while king Tisamenos reigned. They were led by renegade Achaians—the children of Herakles the mischief-maker. The traditions of what they did are late, contradictory in detail, and largely artificial[1] ; but their outlines may be shortly given for what they are worth. They had already made one grand attack on the south, so one story says, soon after the Trojan War, and been defeated at the Isthmus of Corinth by the valour of Echemos, an Arkadian king.[2] Traces of repairs, conducted in frantic haste, to the walls of Mykênai, show that the civilized or semi-civilized governments were at last awake to their danger ; but it was too late now.

A horde of Dorians and Aitolians crossed the Corinthian Gulf, and swept the west and south of the Peloponnese; the Greeks had a popular derivation of the name of the port Naupaktos on the Lokrian coast as " the place where they built their ships ".[3] The Epeian and Pylian kingdoms went down before them, and a new and predatory Aitolian state arose in the fertile lowland that they called the Hollow Vale[4]—Wâlis, or Elis—whose southern border was pushed steadily southward to where Olympia lies. Dorian Sparta, too, was clearly founded from the north—perhaps by a band coming from the north-west into the Eurôtas valley, over the water-shed. Sparta was long an obscure and humble settlement ; southward her territory for generations stretched scarcely beyond her gates, the way down-river being blocked by Achaian Amyklai, a bare three miles away.[5] Lastly, the late and elaborated story says, Argolis was attacked from the rear by the Herakleid king Têmenos and swept from south to north. Tiryns and Mykênai fell, and their splendid palaces were sacked and burnt. The tradition cannot tell certainly whether the last of the house of Atreus fell in battle or fled, with a remnant of his followers, out of the land.[6]

---

[1] Cf. Wade-Gery, C.A.H., II, chapter XIX.
[2] Hdt., IX, 26 ; Apollod., II, 8. 2 ; D.S., IV, 58, etc.
[3] Str., IX, 426, quoting Ephoros.
[4] Paus., V, 4. For the name " Hollow Elis," cf. Thk., II, 25. 2, etc.
[5] Str., VIII, 364, quoting Ephoros.
[6] Killed, Apollod., II, 8. 3 ; fled to the historic Achaia (north coast of Peloponnese), Paus., II, 18. 7 ; VII, 1. 3. It is a good example of the completely unauthentic character of most of the details in these post-Homeric legends.

Argos became the Dorian capital, and though new settlements grew up within the ancient walls of Tiryns and Mykênai, these strongholds were never great and populous again. It was from the vale of Argos that in the following years the war-bands went out to attack the neighbouring villages ; so, Sikyôn, Phlious, Epidauros fell.[1] The men of Aigina on their island held out longer ; from the remains found there, it seems that the old civilization here lasted for as much as another two centuries, before it was destroyed by an attack from the mainland. It is a fact which serves to confirm the ancient tradition that the main body of the destroyers came across the Peloponnese from the west.

There were other Dorians, however, who moved by sea. In this fashion Corinth fell, to a band under the Herakleid Alêtes, " the Wanderer ", son of " the Rider ", Hippotes, who descended upon the east coast at the village of Solygeia, and established an *epiteichismos* from which he wore down the Aiolians of the citadel[2] ; and the evidence of place-names and the distribution of certain tribes along the east coast of Greece in historic times seems to indicate a good deal of movement down this coast from north to south.[3] All Peloponnese had now suffered conquest except the mountainous centre—where the Arkădes were now completely cut off from the sea—the central portion of the north coast, where a fragment of Agamemnon's kingdom preserved the Achaian name, and a small and shrinking area in the south-west, held by the " Three Peoples " of Triphylia until, in historic times, they were all but exterminated by the repeated harryings of the Aitolians of Elis.[4] As the last act in the period of the conquest, according to a story which there seems no sufficient reason to doubt, Attica was attacked by way of the Isthmus. Kodros, the gallant king of Athens, fell in battle and became a national hero,[5] but his city was not conquered and after devastating the

[1] Sikyon, Paus., II, 6. 4 ; Phlius, *ibid.*, 13. 3 ; Epidauros, *ibid.*, 26. 1. 2 ; Troizen, Str., VIII, 389, quoting Ephoros. Aigina, Hdt., V, 83 ; Paus., II, 29. 5.

[2] Thk., IV, 42.

[3] Cf., e.g., the name Histiaia in Euboia with that of Hestiaiôtis in Thessaly ; also the discussion of the origin, and migration from north Greece, of the Dryôpes of Hermione and Asine, in Strabo, VIII, 373, quoting Aristotle.

[4] Hdt., IV, 148 ; Str., VIII, 355 ; Paus., VI, 22. 4.

[5] Hdt., V, 76 ; Lykurgos, *Against Leôkrates*, c. 20 ; etc.

country the invaders withdrew. They did, however, permanently conquer the northern portion of the Isthmus, where the old city of Nisa ceased to exist and a small and poverty-stricken Dorian community occupied its site. The new acquisition was scarcely a state ; politically it belonged to Corinth or at least was claimed by her[1] ; and the village had not even a name of its own, but became known to later generations as Megara or " House-steads ".

As to the date of all this we know little. The evidence of the genealogies, as we have seen, must be used with care ; on the archæological side, there is no certainly datable evidence of contact with Egypt from the age of the great sea raids until Hellenic colonization begins. The excavators of Sparta believe that the ancient national temple of Artemis Orthia can hardly have existed before the middle of the tenth century ; its foundation, perhaps, marks the epoch at which the invading Dorians began to think of themselves as a settled population.[2] This date agrees well, as we have seen, with that suggested by the Spartan royal genealogies.[3] It was probably, therefore, during the period between the middle of the tenth century and the middle of the eleventh that the splendours of " Mycenæan " Argolis finally passed away.

In the south Aegean also the Dorian movement made itself felt. Crete became almost entirely Dorized, perhaps by swarms that came, like their earlier forerunners, direct from Thessaly by sea ; but the rest of the southern islanders in historic times claimed descent from the conquerors of the Peloponnese. Mêlos and Thêra claimed to be Spartan colonies[4] ; the south-eastern islands, with the towns of Knidos and Halikarnassos on the mainland, were said to have been populated mostly from Argolis.[5] Greek historians make little or no mention of

---

[1] Plut., *Greek Questions*, XVII.
[2] *B.S.A.*, XVI, 11. Cf. also the important discussion of the matter in C. W. Blegen's *Korakou*.
[3] p. 50.
[4] Melos, Thk., V, 84 ; Thera, Hdt., IV, 145-9.
[5] Knidos is said to have been colonized from Sparta, Hdt., I, 174. Kôs, Nisyros and the Kalydnai from Epidauros, Halikarnassos from Troizen, *ibid.*, 99 ; the three cities of Rhodes from Argos, Thk., VII, 57. Epidauros seems to have been a very active colonizing centre at this time. Cf. the part played by Epidaurians also at Aigina (p. 227 n.) and in Ionia, especially at Samos (Hdt., VIII, 99).

the older and weaker Thessalo-Herakleid settlements known to Homer's Catalogue.

The distribution of the Dorian states on the map of classical Greece shows how the invaders, true to their predatory instincts, made straight for the Minoan or Minoïsed south, no doubt in order to enjoy palaces that they builded not and vineyards and oliveyards that they planted not. In the central and northern Aegean they made no permanent settlement ; and thus in this direction a way of escape lay open for the populations that they and the other invading tribes swept before them in their onward march. Thus in north-western Asia Minor, the Aiolis of historic times came into existence. At its greatest extent it counted twenty cities, before the number was reduced by internal and external wars ; six on Lesbos, one each on Tenedos and in the " Hundred Isles ", and twelve on the mainland, of which Kyme and Smyrna were the most important ; and there was also a small detached group in the region of Mount Ida, where the Trojan kingdom had ere now been destroyed by a new wave of Phrygian immigrants from Thrace.[1] In this region grew up in the following centuries a vigorous branch of the Hellenic race, turbulent, adventurous, aristocratic, lovers of fighting and of music, preserving in the structure of their society, with its freedom of women and its bitter feuds, something of the spirit of the Heroic Age. From general probability and from the evidence of dialects it would seem that the Aiŏlians were in origin a mixed horde of refugees from central and northern Greece ; but dwelling as they did in the lands where the sons of Atreus had campaigned, they took, as their poetry shows, a deep interest in the Tale of Troy, and delighted to claim descent—the Lesbian nobles, at least—from an otherwise unknown Penthilos, son of Orestes ; while they connected even that strain in their ancestry which came from Thrace with two alleged descendants of Agamemnon the king.[2]

Far the most important of the refugee settlements in Asia,

[1] Cf. p. 220 above. On Aiolis and its cities, see Hdt., I, 149-51.

[2] Str., XIII, 582. Orestes himself is claimed as leader of the colonists in one version (Pindar, N., XI, 34). For references to Penthilos and to Atreid pedigrees, cf. Alkaios, frags. 43, 48 (Diehl), Sappho, frag. 70 ; interest in the tale of Troy, Alkaios, frag. 74 ; Sappho, 28, 35, 55, especially the last. There was a king named Agamemnon ruling at Kyme in the eighth century ; Pollux, IX, 83. For a Thracian element in Lesbos, cf. the name Pittakos— borne by a Thracian, Thk., IV, 107.

however, were those of the central, the Ionian, group. These also, in historic times, had, like the Dorians and the Aiolians, a flattering but unhistorical heraldic fable to repeat about their own origin. As the Dorians traced the descent of their early kings from Herakles and the Aiolians from Agamemnon, so did the Ionians from Nêleus, Nestor and Kodros, the heroes of pre-Dorian Pylos and of Attica. But it was quite well-known to those fifth century Greeks who troubled to find out, that the Ionians, too, were in fact a race of very mixed descent. Herodotos,[1] in dealing with the Twelve Cities of the sixth-century Ionic League, wrote a concise and important contribution to the subject, which it is worth while to quote :

"The idea that these Ionians are more Ionian than the others, or truer-born, is perfectly ridiculous ; a considerable proportion of them are Abantes from Euboia who do not even claim the Ionian name ; and there are Minyans of Orchomenos mixed up with them, and Kadmeians and Dryopes and a branch of the Phôkians, and Molossians and Pelasgoi of Arkadia and Dorians of Epidauros, and many other tribes, too ; and the ones who started from the prytaneion of Athens and think themselves the most genuine Ionians— even they did not bring any women to their new home, but took to themselves Karian women whose parents they had killed. On account of this blood-guilt these women adopted a custom which they bound themselves by oaths to keep, and which they handed down to their daughters, never to sit at meat with the men nor for a woman ever to call her own husband by name ; it is because [the invaders] had killed the women's fathers and husbands and children and then after all this taken the women for wives. This happened at Miletos.

"As to their kings, some of them set up Lykian princes descended from Glaukos the son of Hippolochos, and some Kaukônes descended from Kodros the son of Melanthos, and some both together.[2] All are Ionians who originated from Athens and keep the Apatouria[3] ; and they all keep this festival except the men of Ephesos and Kolophôn. These

---

[1] I, 146-8.
[2] One might perhaps compare the double kingship at Sparta.
[3] This festival perhaps= ὁμοπατόρια (cf. ἄκοιτις, from ὁμο, κοίτη)=the Festival of the Family Ancestors ; cf. the Latin Parentalia at which the ghosts of the clan were placated.

alone of the Ionians do not keep the Apatouria, because of some trouble about blood-guilt."

Herodotos goes on to speak of the Pan-Ionian Sanctuary at which the assembled Ionians—dimly conscious of a common origin and interests, though the cities fought bitter wars against each other—united to worship Poseidon Helikônios. The title of the god is probably a reminiscence of the famous hill of that name, sacred to the Muses as well as to the sea-god, where the ancestors of some of the colonists had worshipped their gods in what was now the Boiotian land.

In the turbulent early days of the migration there were wars not only between Ionian and barbarian, but between Greek and Greek ; we hear details of one piece of treachery by which Ionia cut short the southern boundaries of Aiolis, and Smyrna became an Ionian city. Strabo quotes a few lines from Mimnermos, the seventh-century Ionian elegist :

" And we, leaving Pylos, Nêleus' city, came in our ships to the fair land of Asia ; and to lovely Kolophôn with conquering arms we came and settled, we authors of cruel violence ; and thence we rose up beside the eddying river and by the counsel of the gods took Aiŏlian Smyrna."[1]

Herodotos explains the phrase about " the counsel of the gods " for us, by describing the rather inglorious way in which it was done :

" This is how the Aiŏlians lost Smyrna. They gave a home to some men of Kolophôn, who had got the worst of a faction-fight and been driven out of their native city ; and some time after, the Kolophônian exiles, watching their opportunity, at a time when the Smyrnaians were keeping a festival to Dionysos outside the walls, shut the gates on them and seized the city. All the Aiŏlians gathered to the rescue ; but they came to an agreement, that the Ionians should surrender all the movable property and the Aiŏlians abandon Smyrna. So then the other eleven cities (of Aiolis) divided the men of Smyrna among themselves and made them citizens."[2]

At the other end of the Ionian coast-line, we hear of an attack on Samos, momentarily successful, by Androklos, the powerful founder of Ephesos,[3] and of a short-lived city of

[1] Strabo, XIV, 634.
[2] *lot. cit.*, c. 150.
[3] Paus., VII, 4. 3.

Mĕlita which became so powerful as to alarm the neighbouring states and was destroyed by them; its territory, opposite the island of Samos, was divided by Samos and Priene.[1] We have even a few traditions about the very earliest days when the settlers were no more than the holders of a fortified camp on the sea-shore, engaged in a long and doubtful warfare with the tough and well-armed Asian native tribes. In Aiolis, at Kyme, men still pointed out in Strabo's day the site of the New Castle, from which base a band of Greeks from Mount Phrikion near Thermopylai wore down the resistance of the Pelasgians of a neighbouring Larissa[2]; and of Phôkaia in northern Ionia there is a detailed foundation-story, which, from the fact that it preserves a couple of genuine Asianic names, seems to be a genuine tradition.[3]

The original Phôkaians, says this story, were a more or less Ionian horde, of mixed descent, from the region of the Minyan Orchomenos. Driven from their homes, they crossed the Aegean and seized an islet lying inshore at the mouth of the river Hermos, from which they might try to win themselves a territory on the mainland. The natives were ready for them, and gathered to oppose the invasion, under a king Mennes who reigned at the neighbouring Kyme. Fighting broke out immediately, and after a severe battle the Ionians had won their way only as far as a rocky ridge a few hundred yards inland. Here they seem to have come to a complete standstill, holding on with difficulty against heavy barbarian attacks. Failure, which to the homeless men meant starvation, stared them in the face.

They were delivered by the villainy and self-seeking of Mennes' brother, Watias—another good Anatolian name.[4] This prince coveted his brother's crown and cared little for the means so long as he could get it. He now made overtures, promising the sea-raiders all that they could possibly desire—

---

[1] Vitruvius, IV, c. 1. Cf., Hiller v. Gärtringen, *Inscr. v. Priene*, No. 37; also *C.I.G.*, II, 2254.

[2] Str., XIII, 622.

[3] N.D., frag. 54 (Müller).

[4] Cf. the feminine form, Watialis, found on a tombstone of early Christian date from Isauria, by A. M. Ramsay (*J.H.S.*, XXIV, p. 283). With the name Mennes one may compare those of Tennes of Tenedos (p. 160 n), and Onnes in the next fragment of Nikolaos; and incidentally such Etruscan or Roman names as Sisenna, Porsenna, Rasenna. Watias is identical with the Roman name Vatia.

PLATE XV

(c) From Rhodes ; L.M. III.
as "Mycenæan," *c.* 1300

(b) From Knôssos ; L.M. II,
"Palace Style," *c.* 1400

(a) From Gournia ; L. M. I., *c.* 1500

DECLINE OF AEGEAN ART : I.

friendship, intermarriage, as much land as they required—if they would help his cause. The Ionians naturally closed with the offer, and Watias came over to them with a considerable force of his partisans.

Now a real offensive was possible. The unfortunate Mennes was defeated and captured, and stoned to death by "the natives"—that is to say, clearly, his brother's partisans. Watias was made king, and succeeded in persuading his people to give up to the Greeks the land on which they built the afterwards famous city of Phôkaia.

Such was the colonization of Ionia, and such the Ionians ; a people with a common self-consciousness, coming mostly from central Greece, especially Attica, though many of their chiefs were Pylian-born. The tradition of Attic origin is early,[1] and almost certainly genuine, and the four primitive "tribes" or septs of the Ionian race are common to Ionia and Athens in early historic times[2] ; but homogeneous they certainly were not. Even the Ionic dialect, as Herodotos[3] tells us, was divided into four different sub-dialects within the Asiatic Ionia itself—not counting Attica or the Ionian Cyclades. But to tell of the settled life that grew up in the Ionian towns, of the replacement of monarchy by oligarchy, and of the brilliant and uniquely original civilization that was presently created by this race of "splendid mongrels"— descendants of the few and fit survivors of this age of confusion and war—this is not part of our present purpose. The story of the Ionian Renaissance is the opening chapter of the history of the great age of Greece.

With the Dorian and Ionian migrations the age of the Sea-Raids, which the Greeks called the Heroic Age, draws to an end. The piracy universal in the society which Homer describes had ended by killing the goose that laid the golden eggs. The age of the great "Sackers of Cities", as they proudly called themselves, ends for lack of civilized cities and

---

[1] Cf. Sŏlon's phrase "(Attica) the oldest Ionian land," in l. 2 of the passage quoted by *The Athenian Constitution*, chapter 5.

[2] Hdt., V, 66. A part from Attica they are mentioned in inscriptions as existing at Delos, Tĕos, and the Milesian colonies of Kyzikos and Tŏmoi ; also at Samian Perinthos.

[3] I, 142.

palaces to sack. For more than a thousand years neither art nor commerce in the Aegean had ever been at so low an ebb ; and not for another two hundred years was there to be any sign of recovery. Scarcely before the seventh century do we find promise of anything better ; then, late and at length, begin the Hellenic colonizing movement and, as a result of it, the stimulus of contact with the latest Egyptian and the bastard Phœnician art—the sorry scaffolding by means of which the great fabric of Greek art was in the first instance built.

The late Dr. Hogarth maintained in a brilliant pamphlet[1] that to speak of a collapse of Aegean civilization was unsound. "The whole history of humanity", he argued, "shows the index of civilization not to be art. The acme of art production has always been attained during political stages of autocracy or limited aristocracy, which precede the acme of general well-being. . . . In Italy, France, China, Japan, India, and our own land the greatest art periods now lie removed in the past ; and in each the breaking down of aristocracy was followed by a decline in the quality and quantity of art production, but with concomitant advance in the quality and the quantity of artisan work. Yet is the Italian or French civilization of the twentieth century not higher than in the seventeenth ? How does British civilization to-day stand to that of the time of Elizabeth ? Art declines in quality when it ceases to be the main concern of a dominant class ; but civilization will still broaden and grow because society enfranchised on a wider basis substitutes for art-interest a concern for the conquest of mechanical force." Accordingly he holds that it was a good thing that the imperialism first of Knôssos and then of Mykênai should be destroyed, since the separate towns and villages which they had dominated were thereby set free to develop their own " popular civilization ".

In itself this argument is obviously sound. Hogarth has no difficulty in showing that the breaking up, even by violence, of an advanced and cultured society may be a good thing, if it means freeing a people from the dominion of a ruling class or dynasty, and compelling them to develop for themselves those qualities of self-reliance and clear thinking which they were not encouraged to possess when looked after by their " betters ". But it is rather a different matter to deny that in the present

[1] *The Twilight of History* : Oxford, 1926.

PLATE XVI

(a)

(b)

(c)

(d)

(e)

DECLINE OF AEGEAN ART: II

(a) from Mykênai, L.M. III. a, c. 1300; remainder L.M. III. b, "Sub-Mycenæan," twelfth century
or later; (b) from Cyprus, (c) (d) from Philistia; (e) from Rhodes

case any decline of civilization has taken place. It can be argued that a very real " decline and fall " did take place in the Aegean during our period—a decline not only of art, but of security, of material wealth, and of knowledge of geography, perhaps of history, too—with all that this last point implies in the narrowing and cramping of men's outlook on the world and its life.

The decline of art is so obvious as scarcely to need mention ; to pass from the lithe and accurate figures of a Minoan vase or fresco to the geometric abstractions that represent the human form in the art of the earliest Iron Age at Athens is an experience that needs no comment. The great painted vases that did duty for tombstones in this early Athenian cemetery are of good craftsmanship enough, but as original or creative art they simply do not exist.

But the decline has affected those other matters, too, of which Hogarth makes no mention. To see evidence of it in the matter of general security of life and goods, one need only compare Homer's world with the age when Knôssos and the wealthy cities of Crete could afford to be unfortified. In material wealth a deplorable wastage must have occurred in the course of the age of wars and plundering raids whose melancholy chronicle we have just been studying. And evidence of the cessation of oversea trade and travel and knowledge of other lands is likewise conclusive. We have already mentioned the way in which the poet of the Odyssey, while he mentions the Kimmĕrioi of the Crimea (which is evidence of considerable geographical knowledge on the part of his forerunners) proceeds to betray the depths of his own ignorance by locating them in the West ; but even more striking is the oft-quoted evidence of the Geometric pottery itself. " Mycenæan " pottery of the fourteenth century is much the same wherever it is found, from Sicily to Egypt ; clearly it is the work of a cosmopolitan and much-travelled age. Geometric differs in style from district to district, almost from valley to valley ; clearly it is the work of a stagnant age in which men know little of the world beyond their immediate neighbourhood.

But such a decay of art, wealth, personal security, and human knowledge of the world is surely best summed up in precisely the phrase " collapse of civilization ".

The four separate local dialects which Herodotos distinguished
in the Ionia of his day are presumably likewise relics of this
same home-keeping age ; and indeed the same may be true of
the great Ionic dialect itself, the mother of all these four and
of the Athenian dialect too. Some of the dialects of historic
Hellas were, clearly, spoken in the shape in which we know
them in the Late-Minoan Age itself ; this is most obviously
true of the Arkado-Cypriote dialect, as we have seen ; and we
have seen, too, that there is reason to connect the division of
all the Greek dialects into a " Western " and an " Eastern ",
a Conquest and a pre-Conquest group, with an original double
migration of the Greek-speaking peoples, at various periods
into the land.[1] All this is largely inference from the distribution of the dialects in historic times ; and a rather different
inference is suggested by the distribution of the Ionic states.
Leaving out of count the great cities founded by colonizing
swarms after 800 B.C., we find the Ionian states to be a very
compact group. It does look as if Ionic were simply that local
dialect of the " pre-Conquest " type of Greek which was
developed by the cities whose religious centres were the shrine
of Poseidon Helikônios at Mỹkăle and, more especially, the
holy island of the Delian Apollo.

Of the Dorian dialect the same may be said. It, too, was
spoken, in the Dark Age, throughout and not outside of a
definite and continuous area, though a less compact area than
the Ionic—from Argos and Sparta, by way of Crete and the
southern Sporades, to Knidos and Rhodes. When we find
attention drawn to the fact that the Doric dialects, and the
kindred Boiotian, are characteristic of exactly those regions
where Minoan civilization flourished[2] it is tempting to hazard
the guess that these dialects represent the " Conquest " type
of Greek as modified by contact with the pre-Hellenic Aegean-
speaking " Minoans " who learned their Greek from the Hellenic
invaders.

By 950 B.C., then, Minoan civilization in the Aegean had
been transformed into proto-Hellenic barbarism. Little later,
if at all, the struggle of the Philistine colonists against the
overwhelming numbers of the Semites ended in disaster. In
Sicily the native Bronze Age civilization, cut off from the

[1] p. 36.   [2] Cf. Wace, in *C.A.H.*, II, p. 467.

Aegean imports that had influenced it so deeply and for so long, proceeded to stagnate. In one quarter only did the old Aegean culture survive into Hellenic times.

This district was Cyprus. Here the vase-painting of the early Iron Age was never quite so jejune as in most parts of the Aegean, and it preserved a distinct likeness—though, perhaps, rather that of a caricature—to Mycenæan art. Here, too, a variety of the Aegean linear script was used far into the Hellenic period, and used to write Greek, for which language it is not really very well suited. The Greeks of the Aegean might adopt the letters of the Phœnician alphabet, with their Semitic names ; but such was the tenacious conservatism with which the Cypriotes clung to their ancient culture that they firmly resisted the adoption from the hated Semites even of what any unbiassed observer must have recognized to be an obvious improvement. Cyprus had its own separate school of epic poetry in the Dark Age, too, if we may trust the modern suggestion that the " Cyprian Verses ", that curiously named poem that filled such an important place in the heroic cycle, was so-called from the land of its origin ; and it seems highly probable that the Thalassocracy-List is right in its statement that the Cypriotes possessed the strongest sea-power in the Levant for the space of a generation, immediately before the rise of the Tyrian and Sidonian power.

Cypriote society and government, too, like Cypriote art, were recognizably "Minoan" even in Hellenic times. When the Greeks of Cyprus, as of Ionia, revolted against Persia about 500 B.C. they were led to war by their patriarchal kings ; and chariotry, long obsolete in Greece, still formed an important part of a Cypriote force.[1] And of the houses in which these princes dwelt we have learnt something of late from the excavations of the Swedish expedition under Dr. Gjerstad. At Vouni, the ancient Sŏloi where the friend of Solon, king Philokypros, reigned, a sixth-century Cypriote prince's palace was laid bare. It was a well-built masonry building of imposing size—over 100 metres square ; and many of its details—its light-wells, staircases, magnificent rooms, above all its capacious magazines—are as thoroughly Minoan in style as if it had been built six centuries earlier.[2]

[1] Hdt., V, 113.
[2] Gjerstad, in *Illus. London News*, Sept. 22, 1928, p. 500 ; *Antiquity*, Vol. II (1928), pp. 189-191.

At last even in Cyprus the heirs of all the ages of Minoan culture forgot their seamanship, and we have reached the beginning of the two centuries during which such maritime trade as existed in the Mediterranean was in the hands of the Phœnicians sailors of Arvad Tyre and Sidon. The Tyrian Chronicles, that Flavius Josephus read and praised,[1] claimed even for colonies so far west as Utica in Africa and Gaddir, (Gadeira, Gades, the modern Cadiz) in Spain, a very high antiquity indeed.[2] One hesitates to accept these statements as fact ; but archæological evidence for or against them is lacking. In Cyprus, too, the Canaanites won a footing at the " New Town " which the Greeks called Kition. In the Aegean they became well-known enough to be credited by Greek antiquaries with half the blessings of Greek material civilization, really the legacy of Minoan Crete. A score of passages in Herodotos and Homer show how large a place these carriers of " Assyrian cargoes "[3] filled in the mind of the naïve and untravelled Dark Age of Hellas.

In all this it was Sidon that took the lead ; the fact that Homer speaks of Sidonians repeatedly, but never mentions Tyre, finds interesting comment in what was till lately the oldest Phœnician inscription known.[4] In it an eighth century governor in Cyprus speaks of Hiram, King of Tyre, as " King of the Sidonians ", which term was evidently in a fair way to become the national name of the populations of all the group of seaboard towns.

And in the ninth century also—not earlier, as, according to Dr. Randall MacIver, the archæological evidence shows—took place another event most pregnant for the future : the arrival of the first Etruscan bands from the eastern Mediterranean on the west coast of Italy.

The theory of the Lydian origin of the Etruscans may, in a cursory treatment of the question such as the present, be taken as proved, and the literary evidence for it has been summarized on an earlier page.[5] It seems likely that they came to the

[1] See above, p. 63.
[2] 1100 and 1087 B.C. respectively, according to Velleius Paterculus, I, 2 ; cf. pseudo-Aristotle, "Wonders", chap. 134, quoting a Phœnician source.
[3] Hdt., I, 1.
[4] C.I.S., I, 5 ; cf. 1 Kings XVI, 31, where Ethbaal of Tyre is given the same title.
[5] pp. 60 ff.

west, more immediately, not from Lydia, where the native
historian Xanthos did not mention their departure and where
the Greeks had recently annexed the whole of the coast, but
from either or both of two not far distant regions. One of
these is the south-east corner of Asia Minor, where the god
Tarkhun was worshipped. His name, which in Asia is
repeatedly found, from Hittite to Roman times, as part of a
human name, seems to reappear in that of the Etruscan
culture-hero Tarchon,[1] that of the town Tarquinii, and that
of the famous Etruscan dynasty of early Rome. The other
region is the north Aegean, where, as we have seen, there were
still surviving pockets of Tyrrhenian and Pelasgian " barbaroi "
even in Hellenic times ; where, on Lemnos, there was found
some time ago a tombstone of very Etruscan-seeming type,
both in the appearance and armament of the warrior sculptured
thereon, and in the alphabet and language of his epitaph ;
and where, on the same island, della Seta has recently
discovered their necropolis. One hundred and thirty cremated
burials were found. With the women was buried a certain
amount of jewellery, and with both sexes pottery, that shows
the influence of the Mycenæan and Greek geometric styles ;
but there was also a grey and black ware resembling the well-
known black Etruscan *bucchero ;* and with the men were
buried not the sword and spear of the Greek warrior but the
axe and dagger of Etruria and the east.

Many of the similarities between Etruscan and Anatolian
culture have been mentioned above : the matriarchal system
in tracing genealogies, divination by entrails, many proper
names, and certain other linguistic points,[2] and even a distinct
resemblance to the heavy-featured Hittite physical type.
But the resemblance is nowhere better marked than in this
matter of the equipment of warriors. Larthi Atharnies, the
early Etruscan Lucumo, whose tombstone is extant, wears in

---

[1] In the east, Tarkondimotos or Tarkondêmos of Kilikia (Dio Cassius,
I, 14 ; Plut., *Antony*, 61) and Tarcundarius of the Gallogræci (Cæsar, *Civil
War*, III, 4) bear the same names as Tarkhundarawas of Arzawa in the Tell-
el-Amarna letters and Tarkudimme of the only known bilingual Hittite and
cuneiform inscription. In the west the name of the early hero known from
Vergil and other sources, and of the Roman tyrants, reappears as an Etruscan
family name (Tarchnas, Tercenna, etc.) in several inscriptions.

[2] Frazer, in *Anatolian Studies presented to Sir W. M. Ramsay*, p. 140,
quoting Vilh. Thomsen, " *Remarques sur la parenté de la langue étrusque*",
draws attention to some remarkable resemblances to certain Caucasian dialects.

the sculptured relief " a dress and buskins of quite Asiatic style ",[1] and carries a curved sword which is none other than the δρέπανον, the " reaping-hook " as Greek military humour called it, of the Lykians, Solymoi, and other Asian tribes.[2] So with the other of the two most famous early Etruscan stelæ, that of Aules Feluskes[3] (Aulus the Faliscan, Aulus of Falerii ?). He carries the round shield and wears the horse-hair-crested helmet of the north-Syrian Hittites and of certain Taurus mountaineers[4] ; the same which were later adopted by Assyrians and Greeks. And he brandishes in his hand no other weapon than the Double Axe of Asia and Crete. One is reminded of the double-axe found along with the pre-Roman " fascis " of the Etruscan Lictor's Tomb[5] ; of the single-bladed axes carried by one of those " types of the Etruscan Army " depicted on a famous engraved situla[6] ; of the axe-armed warriors of Lêmnos ; and of the axe wielded by the Trojan Peisandros in his fight with Menelaos in the Iliad.[7]

The Etruscans, it is interesting to find, were almost certainly a literate folk at the time of their arrival in Italy. It used to be believed that they derived their script—that rather clumsy variety of the Greek alphabet which we ourselves have inherited from Rome—from the Greek colonists of Cumae. Further scrutiny, however, discloses the fact that the Etruscan alphabet contains some letters found in the Lydian, but not in that of Cumae (that which renders the " F " sound in " Feluskes " is an example) ; while several consonants are closer to Semitic than to any known Greek forms. It seems that the Tyrrhenes, at the time of their migration, were probably already in possession of a form of the new Phœnician alphabet which, as we have seen, was in this age gaining wide currency in the Eastern Mediterranean world.

[1] MacIver, The Etruscans, p. 18.
[2] For the drĕpănŏn in Italy, cf., in addition to this stele, a terra-cotta akroterion from Falerii figured by della Seta (Italia Antica, Plate 220). For its use in Asia Minor, cf. Hdt., VII, 92-3 (on the Lykians in Xerxes' army), Lindos Temple-Chronicle, entry xxiv (trophies captured from the Solymoi by the Rhodian colonists of Phasêlis) and also the painted bas-relief from Konia figured in Texier's Asie Mineure, Plate 103 (=Schreiber's Atlas of Classical Antiquities, XXXVIII, fig. 3.).
[3] Plate II, a.
[4] The men of Urartu, well depicted on the bronze gates of Shalmaneser in the British Museum.
[5] MacIver, Villanovans and Early Etruscans, fig. 56.
[6] MacIver, The Etruscans, Plate I.
[7] Il., XIII, 601 ff.

"Mare Milkers"?
(Il. XIII. l. 5)

TYRRHENOI
(c. 9th Cent B.C)

THRA

PAIONES

THRAKES

Iôlkos

Lariss

THERMESSA

(Lipari Is)

Cape Krimissa

Eryx

SIKANOI

A Krimisos   Minoa   Late Minoan
              Pottery finds

Thebes

MYKENAI

I

A

Knôssos

Phaistos

Sea
allia
13

THE EASTERN MEDITERRANEAN
in the Early Iron Age; about
1400 — 900 B.C.

Mountains over 6000ft. shaded

L   I

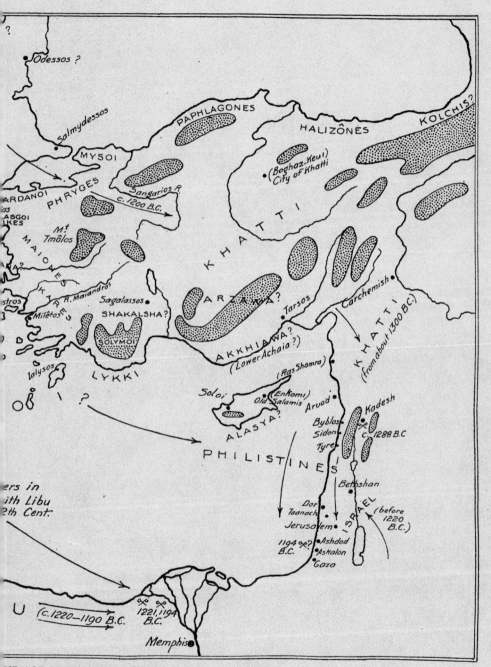

THE AGE OF THE SEA-RAIDERS

[face p. 242

THE AGE OF THE SEA-RAIDERS

In this connection additional interest attaches to the legends of Aeneas—Homer's Aineias—at the site of Rome. As we have it, the legend is a late compilation, and contradicts Homer, who, as we have seen, tells us that Aineias re-founded the Dardanian kingdom after the departure of the Achaians. Still it would be a mistake to think of it as lacking any substratum of truth at all. The Story of Aeneas, though beautified by Vergil, was not invented by him; nor is it an isolated phenomenon. Widely spread in Greek times on the coasts of Italy and Sicily were legends of the foundation of this town or that, long ago by "fugitive Trojans" or "Greeks who lost their way when returning from the war". It is unlikely that they are all entirely fictitious, though no doubt the desire to glorify the origins of one's own city influenced other poets besides Vergil. The fact probably is that the earliest explorers of Hellenic times found widely current in the west stories of earlier settlers who had likewise come from the east oversea, or even the descendants of such settlers still living there. In their usual manner, the Greeks attached all these scattered migration-legends to the Tale of Troy; and the obvious way of doing it was to call them "Achaians who got lost" (like Odysseus and Menelaos, only worse) in cases where their language was recognizably Greek, and fugitive Trojans when it was not. A well-known example of the latter alternative is furnished by the civilized Elymians of Eryx and Egesta or Segesta in north-west Sicily.[1]

It is perfectly possible, therefore, that a body of sea-raiders from the east, but not belonging to the Etruscan horde, did indeed land somewhere south of the Tiber in the early Iron Age, and that their help did save the Aryan-speaking Latins of the plain-country from being overwhelmed by their kinsmen and enemies of the hills, the later Sabellian wave of the same Aryan Italic stock. The help was timely; for at that time, as we know from some old local traditions of the upper Tiber region, the Sabellian advance was pressing the "Aborigines" hard.[2]

So perhaps it is for this reason that, apart from Etruscan influence, there are some points in which the civilization of Latium is curiously reminiscent of that of the Aegean of old.

[1] Thk., VI, 2.
[2] D.H., I, 14.

While the Hellenes, with their swift love of beauty and strange carelessness of material comfort, inherited the artistic genius of Crete, in these material things, prosaic but useful, such as roads, aqueducts, and drains, the mantle of Daedalus seems to have fallen upon the engineers of Rome. The art of building, like that of divination, and like the cruel practice of gladiatorial fights, might have been learnt by the Latins from the east by way of Etruria ; but in one matter—that is to say, in several details of defensive armour—the Latins curiously reproduce old Aegean practice while Etruria does not. This statement applies not only to the old ceremonial shields, the figure-of-eight shaped *ancilia*, but to the equipment of the soldier for war. With his lobster-like jointed body armour, like that of the Shardana, with the circlet of feathers on his head,[1] like that of the Philistines, with the semi-cylindrical shield that appears on the " Siege-Vase ", and with the helmet with cheek-pieces seen on an older vase from Crete, the legionary of the Punic Wars must have borne an astonishing resemblance to the Aegean sea-raider of a thousand years before.

[1] Polybios, VI, 23. 12.

CHAPTER XII

Darkness and Dawn : the Genius of Homer

οὐ μὲν γάρ τί πού ἐστιν ὀϊζυρώτερον ἀνδρὸς
πάντων, ὅσσα τε γαῖαν ἔπι πνείει τε καὶ ἕρπει.
— *Iliad*, XVII, 445-6 ; Zeus *loquitur*.

μὴ μὰν ἀσπουδί γε καὶ ἀκλειῶς ἀπολοίμην,
ἀλλὰ μέγα ῥέξας τι.
— Hektor, in *Il.*, XXII, 304-5.

THESE centuries, which witnessed the decline and fall of the first European civilization, form an even more than usually discreditable chapter of the history of mankind. It has been a story of violence, plunder, and murder, of ineffectiveness on the part of the guardians of civilization, and of only too successful opportunism on the part of the forces of disorder. It ends, as we have seen, in chaos and social collapse.

Nevertheless, the travail of the Aegean world was not wholly fruitless. Much has been written of the " Greek miracle "— the portent, that is, of the almost sudden appearance at a particular time and place of a nation so amazingly gifted and including so great a proportion of men of genius as has never been seen either before or since. And in the last analysis, no doubt, a miracle it must remain. Just so, biology and physics in the last resort bring us no nearer an answer to the questions, " What is the world ? " and " What is life ? " But research can push the limits of mystery much further back ; and this is true of human questions like the mystery of the Greek genius, as well as of those investigated by the great inhuman sciences. Clearly we can say at least this much ; that the Hellenic race was in a very real sense produced by the age of confusion in the Aegean. In the crucible of this age were blended the artistic instincts and sense of form of Mediterranean man, the stubborn love of independence of the people of the mountain zone, the lucidity of thought of the wanderers who invented

Aryan speech, and the irreverent daring of the north ; and the combination of these elements took place under conditions which made it certain that none but the fittest should survive. In the age of the migrations, the individuals who produced children and grandchildren, can in no generation have out-numbered those whose lineage failed.

It is an entirely different spectacle to that presented by modern America. There, too, are to be found many of the most energetic individuals of every European type ; but owing to the comparatively orderly conditions obtaining there, the promiscuous cross-breeding and severe natural selection, from which alone a satisfactory blend of national character-istics would be likely to result, have so far not taken place. The Greeks, at the end of the Dark Age, emerge not as a mere mixture of races but as a genuine mixed race.

Probably in the ninth century appears Homer,[1] who marks an epoch ; he is both the writer to whom we owe much of our knowledge of the latest Minoan or transitional civilization, and also, above all, the first of the great Hellenes. With some observations on his genius and his enormous influence, this treatise may appropriately close.

The nineteenth century used to emphasize the virile " Aryan " barbarism of Homer's work ; the civilized traits in Homeric society were supposed to be the result of the poet's ascribing an idealized version of the manners of his own day to the age of which he wrote. The discovery of the Minoan world has shown us the truth, that Homer depicts not in any way a primitive society but on the contrary the latest, even the declining years of a civilization already very old. Homer's own art, indeed, tells the same tale. The plot of the Odyssey, with its swift plunge " in medias res " and explanation of the position by one character to another, is as highly developed as that of any modern novel ; nor is Homer's hexameter in any way a primitive literary instrument. The Homeric poems can have only been the product of a long period of literary evolution. They must have come not at the beginning of an epoch in civilization, but at the end.

And yet there is much that is indeed barbaric in the tone of Homer's work ; much that is indeed even primitive in its attractive freshness. His delight in describing the pleasant

[1] Cf. p. 6, above.

things of life—horses, baths, food, armchairs, the beautiful manners of his chiefs—is, it has been well said, the delight of a child describing its first party.   With all the refinement and even sophistication of his art, he keeps a freshness and sureness of touch like that of the stone-age artists who painted the boar and bison in the Altamira caves.   Minoan art of the great Palace Period had something of that spirit, but it was not strong enough at all points, for instance in its treatment of the human figure in profile, to break through the convention of an age.   It has not quite Homer's unerring truth, the truth of an artist to whom it never seems to have occurred that the thing could be done in any other way.

Homer's delight in fighting is not only genuine but inexhaustible.   He can be as gruesomely descriptive as any war-novelist of our own day—and he enjoys it !   Clearly, there is more in Homer than can be found in late Minoan civilization. A naïve joy in battle and conquest has come back into the world as civilization fails—just as in western Europe, after the decay of Latin civilization, the same joy reappears once more in the Lay of Maldon or in Beowulf.   Homer is in short a true Greek in that he unites in himself the refinement of the civilized Mediterranean and the vigour of the uncultured vandals from without.   The latter appears in each Homeric battle, but most of all in the culmination of the Iliad, in the irresistible onrush of Achilles before which every hope of resistance is shattered as man after man goes down.   The former appears in the poet's feeling for the defeated enemy—recognition of their courage and pity for their fate—and in the brilliant similes by which, time and again, he opens a way of escape from a scene of weariness and bloodshed to a scene of peace : children building castles on a sandy shore, or sundering mists round a rocky shoulder of the hills, or a field white for the harvest, and men working in the corn.

The Iliad is full of passages that exemplify this breadth of sympathy in the poet whose favourite subject, on the whole, is always simply victory in battle.   For instance, when Hektor drives against Patroklos, with Kebriones, his charioteer :

" . . .   And Patroklos over against him from his chariot, sprang to the ground with his spear in his left hand ; and in the other hand he held a stone, bright and jagged, and his hand covered it.   Firm planting his feet he hurled it, nor long delayed ; nor was the cast in vain, but he struck the charioteer of Hektor, Kebriones, Priam's bastard son, as he held the reins, on the forehead with the sharp rock ; and the stone brought both brows together, as the bone gave way, and the eyeballs slipped to the ground in the dust there before his feet, and like a diver he fell from the well-wrought chariot, and the life left his frame ; and knightly Patroklos mocked at him, and said : ' Ha, truly this is a nimble man ! How neatly he dives ! Surely, if he were in the fish-haunted sea, this man would win food for many, diving for oysters, plunging from a ship, even if it were stormy weather, since now on land he dives so neatly from his chariot. So there are divers among the Trojans, too ? ' "

Thus the barbarian, with his grim and somewhat laborious humour. The poet is still in his element in describing the furious fight that ensues over the fallen hero, working up, as is his manner in a climax, to one of his lion- or storm-similes, and then suddenly the passage closes, quite quietly, in the peace of death.

(Hektor and Patroklos fight over the body like two hungry lions over a slaughtered deer) :

" . . . And as an east wind and a west battle together, to bow before them a deep wood in a mountain glen, of oak and ash and the thin-barked cornel tree—and the trees lash one another with their slender twigs, with wondrous noise and crashing as they are broken—so the Trojans and Achaians sprang upon one another and slew, and none took thought of ruinous flight. And many a sharp spear stuck there in the ground about Kebriones, and many a feathered arrow, leaping from the bowstring ; and many a great stone made men's shields to quiver, as they strove about him ; but he lay in the eddying dust, mighty and mightily fallen, forgetful of his knightly valour ".[1]

So, when Agamemnon has slain Iphidamas : " . . . there he fell, and slept an iron sleep, poor soul, far from his wedded wife, bringing help to his countrymen ; far from his bride, and he gat no joy of her, for all the price he paid ".

So again : " Diomedes the valiant in battle slew Axylos, Teuthras' son, who dwelt in well-builded Arisbe ; a rich man, who was the friend of all, for he dwelt by the wayside, and

[1] *Il.*, XVI, 733-50, 765-76.

welcomed all who passed by.   But none of them stood before him then, nor protected him from piteous death   .   .   .   ".[1]

But it is the similes that best show the almost Shakespearean breadth of Homer's interest in the world and in humanity. At every salient point in the story they appear ; most usually as the culmination of a great descriptive passage, where as a mere matter of technique they form a convenient means of bringing a paragraph to an end.   They go far towards making the Iliad what it is, above all others the epic of human life— not merely the epic of Achilles, nor even, as the Greeks called it, the epic of the Tale of Troy.

Take the passage in Book II describing the advance of the armoured sea-raiders at Troy, with its impression of steady, menacing movement, flashing bronze and tramp of innumerable feet :

" Even as ravening fire devours a boundless wood, amid mountain peaks, whence the blaze shines afar, so, as they moved, from the armour of countless men went forth the gleam everywhere beneath the broad heaven.

" And as the many races of the feathered birds—wild geese, and cranes, and long-necked swans—in an Asian water-meadow, among the channels of Kaÿstros, fly this way and that exulting in their wings, and settle down clamorously, that all the meadow rings with their cries ; so those many tribes of men poured forth from ships and huts into the plain of Skamandros ; and the earth resounded terribly beneath the feet of the horses and men.   And they took their stand in the flower-bright meadows of Skamandros, like to the leaves and blossoms in spring for multitude.

" Even as the thronging hordes of flies flit about the byre on a farm, in springtime, when the pails are full of milk ; even so many were the long-haired Achaians who over against the Trojans took their stand in the plain, purposed to smite them asunder ".[2]

More than once in the middle of a battle-piece Homer obtains an extraordinary effect by turning for a comparison to a scene not only of peace, but of the life of children.   It is thus that, with one of his rare flashes of humour, he compares the stubborn retreat of Aias, son of Telamon, to the stubbornness of a donkey :

[1] VI, 12-17.   [2] II, 455-73.

" As when a donkey on his way past a cornfield has defied little boys, a stubborn donkey, over whom many sticks have been broken, and he goes into the rich field and crops it ; and the children beat him with sticks, but their strength is the strength of babes ; and with might and main they drive him out—when he has eaten as much as he wants ;—even so, tall Aias . . . " etc.[1] Or again, when Phoibos Apollôn himself sweeps down at the head of the Trojan charge, and casts flat down to the earth the entrenchment of the Achaian camp, the poet compares him to a child making and overthrowing sandcastles at its play by the sea.[2]

But perhaps the finest of them all is the simile to which the poet compares the gleam of hope that arises for the weary defenders of the ships, when Patroklos brings down the ordered lines of the Myrmidons against the Trojan flank :

" Now Patroklos first let fly with his shining spear, straight into the midst where the press was thickest, by the stern of valiant Prôtesilaos' ship ; and he smote Pyraichmes, who led his Paĭonian horsemen from Amydôn, by Axios' noble stream. Him he smote, on the right shoulder ; and on his back in the dust he fell with a groan, and around him the Paĭones were afraid, for Patroklos struck terror into them all, by slaying their leader, who was their best in fight. And he drove them back from the ships, and quenched the burning fire ; and the ship, half-burnt, was left there ; and the Trojans fled, and the Danaans poured after them between the hollow ships, and endless was the din. And as when from the top of a high mountain Zeus the thunderer drives thick clouds away, and all the peaks are seen, and the high crags and ravines, and the infinite air splits open unto the sky ; —even so the Danaans, having thrust back the devouring fire from the ships, drew breath for a moment ; but there was no rest from war ; for not yet did the Trojans flee in rout before the warlike Achaians, but still stood their ground, and gave back from the ships only perforce ".[3]

Not even translation can ruin passages like these ; but how much is lost in the process, with the ring of the Greek language and the swift movement of the verse, every reader of Homer's own version knows.

[1] XI, 557-62.   [3] XVI, 284-305.
[2] XV, 362-4.

Homer's genius as a poet and story-teller won for him enormous influence over the whole of Greek literature ; it also led to his being accepted, illogically but naturally, as an authority on every kind of subject from statecraft to theology. His verses really were, as the modern phrase has it, " the Bible of the Greeks ". In Plato, any unintelligent conservative of whom Sokrates may ask one of his leading questions, usually starts by offering him a quotation from Homer—a " text from Scripture ", in fact—in answer. The consequences of this treatment of Homer as almost inspired were far-reaching ; farther reaching, in fact, than is often realized.

For the Bible of the Greeks was not the product of a religious or reverent society or age.[1] The age of the sea-raids must certainly have been an age in which men had often cried unto the gods in their trouble, and the gods had neither harkened nor delivered them out of their distress. The result is that Homer's chieftains, though spasmodically pious in their own way, stand in no such awe of their gods as might be expected. " Lord Zeus, you are the greatest rascal of all the gods," cries that favourite of heaven, Menelaos, as his sword-blade falls, shattered, upon the helmet of his foe.[2] " The best omen is to fight for your country", snaps Hektor—though he adds some pious remarks about trusting in Zeus—when the timid Polydamas draws his attention to some portent of ill.[3] And like hero, like poet. Homer's gods, it has been truly said, are invariably either stage-machinery or comic relief. The earliest dirty story in European literature is the one in the Odyssey, sung by a court-minstrel to an appreciative audience of those god-fearing and god-favoured people, the councillors of King Alkinöos. And it concerns a god and a goddess, Ares and Aphrodite, trapped in adultery by Hêphaistos, the injured husband, who summons the other gods to come and laugh at his victims ; which they do. This is by no means the only Homeric passage which depicts the gods in undignified positions and their morality as below the best Homeric human standard ; but it is the most noticeable, and it makes further citations scarcely necessary. It is true that when Homer introduces the gods as " machinery " they are dignified enough ; but in all the poet's surviving work there is scarcely a trace of anything that we should call genuine religious feeling.

[1] Cf. p. 200.　　　[2] *Il.*, III, 365.　　　[3] XII, 243.

On an earlier page we compared the irreligious tendencies of Homer's world to those of the Viking Age. It is by considering the difference between the sequels of the two ages that we can best see Homer's profound though indirect influence on the history of thought. In mediæval Europe, as society grew stable again and as the stream of raiders from without ceased to flow, religion regained its hold ; the pious Norman, whose religion strengthens him in the course which he desires to adopt, replaces the godless Norseman who had little if any religious feeling at all. To a certain extent the same development takes place in Greek history. The old Aegean civilization had been deeply religious, perhaps even dominated by religion ; and the Greek city-state, too, lavished labour and skill upon its temples, and built them high on the citadel where all might see ; it, too, made its holy-days its chief times of festivity and recreation. And yet, with all this, the humanized gods and goddesses, with their adventures, beautiful or puerile or scandalous, who were part of the legacy of the Homeric epic, could never recover their hold over the hearts of individual men. The worship of the Olympic gods, like mediæval Catholicism, served well enough as a medium for the artistic self-expression of an age ; but it could not supply the religiously inclined with a personal experience that satisfied them, nor could it, as even in its most perverted forms Christianity always could, provide intelligent men with authority on which to criticize and advance beyond the limited morality of their own age.

The reason is not far to seek. To the Greek, when things grew normal again after the migrations, the " great days of old " lay in the time of the heroes, and the chief surviving relic of that great age was the Epic, in which he found the gods usually unmoral and often immoral ; usually, though not always, beautiful and majestic ; fit inspiration for an athletic contest, a statue, or an ode, but of little use to the philosopher, and entirely unsympathetic to the simple everyday sorrows of mankind. To the mediæval Frenchman, the great culture of the past was that of Rome, and the great surviving representative of Rome was the Roman Church. It, like the state-religion of the Greeks, was prepared to use and bless his artistic impulses, identify itself with his civic or racial patriotism, and provide pageantry for his days of festival ; but it could also provide an account of itself and of the universe that satisfied the best minds of Europe for some centuries, and a personal religion that satisfies millions at the present day ; while, in the matter of ethics, it had always at its heart the record of the teaching of Christ, overlaid to some extent by " the tradition of the elders ", but too great ever to be wholly smothered by the attempts of the average man to explain its more uncompromising and revolutionary passages away.

The extraordinary difference between classical and mediæval civilization seems to result, very largely, simply from this difference in their intellectual heritage ; for Greek literature gives us no grounds whatever for supposing, as many appear to do, that the Hellenes of the sixth or fifth century B.C. were on the average any less religiously inclined than the western Europeans of the thirteenth A.D., or than any other race of men at any age. They may have been more intelligent, but that is not necessarily the same thing. Many characters in Euripides speak disrespectfully of religion, but so does the hero of *Aucassin and Nicolette*. The soldiers who fought their way through Kurdistan with Xenophon show just as much rough piety as a mediæval *routier* ; and Xenophon himself, an educated Athenian of the time of the great sceptical sophists, and an admirer of the free-thinker Sokrates, shows himself repeatedly a devoutly religious man, and moreover clearly expects all his readers to take his religion for granted. In Thucydides we read how the most splendid armament that ever sailed from Athens failed of its object largely through a panic at home, caused by a religious outrage, and of how the same armament failed to escape from a bad position and met with dreadful and irretrievable disaster, entirely through the superstition of the state's most trusted citizen and general. Thucydides himself was probably an atheist who " conformed " outwardly ; but so brilliant a Hellene as Plato is as religious in tone as a Schoolman ; so religious indeed that he invented all the paraphernalia of a Catholic state, including the Inquisition, for himself without assistance.

But the gods who inspired the deepest religious feeling of an ancient Greek were seldom the cold bright humanized Olympians of Homer's pantheon. Nearly always it was, in the case of one influenced by philosophy, a single Godhead conceived of by some thinker's brain, like the God of Plato ; in the case of simpler natures, some local god or " maiden "—

it mattered little that under Epic influence she might have been identified with Athene or Artemis—worshipped with barbarous and cruel rites, such as Homer's confident chiefs ignore, and not infrequently retaining, in ritual or title, some trace of the fact that she had once been worshipped in animal or monstrous form.[1] Most widely worshipped and most deeply revered of all were the gods of the mystery-cults ; vegetation-spirits like Dionysos or Persephone, daughter of the Earth-Mother Dêmêtêr ; gods whose worship presently, under the influence of the " Orphic " religious revival became, by a natural association of ideas, connected with thoughts of salvation and a life beyond the grave ; spirits of the seed-time and harvest, givers of bread and wine, gods who wandered on earth poor and unknown, who were persecuted and ill-treated until the time came for them to be glorified, or who descended into the House of Hades, and who rose again.[2]

The Greeks then were anything but an irreligious people. Nor was mediæval Christendom lacking in acute critical minds. Yet the fact remains that the swiftly-developing civilization of our own day derives its inspiration from ancient Greece through the Italy of the Renaissance, and that the Middle Ages are to most of us merely an interesting historical backwater. Hellenism produced free thought, much brilliant philosophy, and more than the germ of many of our sciences. Mediæval thought originated nothing, unless its version of Christianity can be called a new religion ; it produced nothing even at second hand except the arid and sterile subtleties of the scholastic Aristotelians ; it kept man's intellect in chains for a thousand years, and all but succeeded in prolonging the bondage further yet. The Greeks—even fifth-century Athens—could persecute heresy on occasion ; but they did it only after much graver provocation and never with half the zeal that the Dominicans or after them the Jesuits showed.

Now it is probable that we owe it to Homer that the great pioneers of science and free thought in Greece were not forced

---

[1] Cf., e.g., Paus., VIII, 42. 3 on the horse-headed Dêmêtêr of Phigaleia ; ibid., 41. 4, on the fish-tailed Artemis Eurynome, in the same backward region ; id., VII, 18. 8, on the horribly cruel rites of Artemis Laphria at Patrai.

[2] All of which beliefs are at least as old as the sixth century, being embodied in the myths related—in the usual cheerful humanizing epic manner—in the " Homeric " Hymns to Dêmêtêr and Dionysos.

to recant, or terrorized, as thousands in mediæval Christendom must have been, into keeping their doubts and questionings a secret all their lives. Nothing could have involved men like St. Dominic or Innocent III in the fearful tragedy of their war against the light except their firm conviction that heresy struck at the very foundation of all order, moral and political, divine and human. To the good Catholic, his religion united in one synthesis every possible interest of his life ; his personal desire to feel that he was not forgotten and hope of everlasting happiness, his private ethics, his loyalty to the state, his beliefs about the origin of the world and the purpose and destiny of man. Innovating criticism of his beliefs on any of these points was a direct threat to all. Let him go astray on any of them, and hell with all its imagined nightmare of eternal torments yawned under his feet. The self-interest of kings and governing classes, the religious fervour of saintly men, the prejudice of the eternal plain man against anything that makes him change his ideas, the panic cruelty of a whole population who firmly believed in hell for all but true believers, all were united against the critic of any essential part of the social and religious order of the time. The good is the worst enemy of the better, and mediæval Catholicism was good enough to be a very terrible foe to the free spirit of man.

The " Bible of the Greeks " on the other hand presented enough glaring weaknesses, as a handbook of religion, to form no obstacle to criticism at all ; on the contrary, it invited criticism of no very reverent kind. It was not merely that Greek religion possessed no body of established dogma which it was death to question. The quotations from Homer in Plato show that Greeks were quite ready to treat Homer as just such an " inspired " authority. It was Homer's own flippant and irreligious attitude that made things difficult for the would-be faithful, and fairly demanded criticism from the thinker. " Homer and Hesiod have ascribed to the gods all the deeds that are shameful among men " complains Xenophanes, before the sixth century was at an end ; and his words became a commonplace of thought. Men like Xenophanes and Plato, genuinely religious at heart, were forced to reject out of hand the vile tales of the mythology, and to assert, relying simply on the " inner light ", the goodness and unity of God. But once this step was taken, religious criticism had been set on foot ; and it is of the nature of religious criticism to end no man knows where. No one could feel that the critic who rejected the story of Ares and Aphrodite taken in adultery was undermining morality or the family or social life. Again, owing to the fact that Homer's Achaians took no interest in the mystery-cults, the folk-religion of the Mediterranean world, it was possible to contradict the theology of the epic without coming into conflict or even contact with the one type of personal religion in which ordinary men fervently believed.

In short, the Bible of the Greeks not only did not provide the groundwork of a system of dogmatic theology that could be taken seriously by anybody ; it made it practically impossible that any such system should ever be produced. Accordingly that many-sided genius, Plato, who, surfeited with the freedom of his day, saw clearly the advantages of a paternal and intolerant dogmatism, proposes to exclude Homer from his ideal state, lest he provoke, by his scandalous tales, irreverent speculations about the nature of the divine.

Homer thus facilitated the rise of Greek speculation, which is the parent of all modern science and philosophy, because his genius as an epic poet secured the survival of his irreligious tales, to provoke doubt and questionings in an otherwise religious age. Without him, the path of the heresy-hunter would have been easier, that of the heretic far more difficult. It is impossible to calculate how much we owe to the fact that one of the supreme poets of all time perpetuated, in some of his weaker moments, the flippant irreligion of the Achaian chieftains in the latest days of the old Aegean world.

But the same poet did mankind a nobler service in the passages in which he, through his characters, sets forth his own outlook on life. No one has ever better expressed in words the point of view of the man who fights on without expectation of victory and without hope that a future life will redress the balance of this. And this is to a greater or less extent the position of all Homer's heroes, for, as might be expected, the poet's outlook is profoundly sad.

He does not believe, it is true, that the personality ceases to exist at death. That belief is only found in Greece in a more advanced and intellectually self-conscious age. He does share the belief in some kind of " survival ", common to most primitive religions and traceable in Neanderthal man. But his beliefs are not of such a kind as to be comforting. Some few favourites of the gods—Menelaos, because he wedded the daughter of Father Zeus, and Rhadamanthys the Just—never die, but are carried away to eternal bliss, in the Elysian Plain, where neither snow nor rain nor storm-wind ever comes[1] ; but for most men there is one fate, the survival of a pale ghost (not the man's " self ", as a terrible line in the Iliad makes plain[2]) in a sunless Sheol at the end of the world, where only the asphodel grows, and where the " strengthless dead " have no pleasure but the remembrance of their lives, and talk together in thin voices like the twittering of bats.

"No man ever was happier than you, Achilles," says Odysseus, in the Eleventh Book of the Odyssey, where the land of ghosts is described ; " for in life we Argives honoured you like to the gods, and now again you are mighty among the dead, now that you are here. So grieve not at your death, Achilles."

But Achilles replies :

"Speak not good to me of death, glorious Odysseus. I would rather be on earth as the servant of another, in the house of a poor man where there was but little sustenance, than be lord over all the dead whose lives are done ".

The only thing that gives him pleasure is to hear of the prowess and good fortune of Neoptolemos his son :

"Thus I spoke ; and the ghost of Aiakides, the swift of foot, strode away with long strides over the meadow of asphodel, glad, because I said that his son was a man of mark ".

The same impression is given in the words used to describe the passing of Patroklos, wounded to the death by Hektor ; words which the poet cunningly uses again in describing Hektor's death :

"Thus as he spoke, the end of death covered him ; and the spirit fled from his limbs and was gone to the land of Hades, lamenting its fate and leaving his manhood and youth ".[3] It is little wonder that the Epicureans, with their assurance that after death there was no life at all, nor desire of life, gave thanks

[1] *Od.*, IV, 561-9.
[2] *Il.*, I, 4.
[3] *Il.*, XVI, 855-7 ; XXII, 361-3.

to their master as having delivered mankind from an over-mastering fear.

Even as regards men's life on earth, the violence and insecurity of the Heroic Age have made of Homer a pessimist "There stand two vessels beside the door of Zeus, of gifts such as he gives, even evil gifts ; and another there is of good "— and if a man gets some good fortune as well as the inevitable bad, then he may consider himself very reasonably lucky.[1] The speaker of these lines is Achilles himself, young, gallant, successful, but saddened by the loss of his friend, the companion of so many achievements and labours, and by the shadow of an early death that hangs over himself.

The question is an obvious one, " How is a man to live his life, whose beliefs are so gloomy as these ? " And to this, Homer has a clear and definite answer, but not an easy one.

The passage in which Homer most definitely faces the riddle of life is in the Sixth Book of the Iliad, that supreme achievement of the greatest poet of all ages, and incidentally a book which, like many of the finest passages in the poem, has remarkably little to do with the poet's ostensible subject, the Wrath of Achilles. Homer's only and sufficient justification for putting it in is the book itself.

Out of the still raging battle goes Hektor, back into Ilios, to bid the women pray to the gods for help in holding back the onslaught of Diomedes, Tydeus' son. This done, and refusing his mother's offer of wine, " lest it unstring my limbs ", he goes on to rout out his brother Paris, who, having precipitated the war, is now skulking at home, after a narrow escape from death at the hands of the injured Menelaos. Him he finds dallying with Helen and fondling his armour, and rebukes him sternly though with restraint. Paris, having no excuse to make, admits his fault, and tries to get a word of approval out of Hektor, by expressing his readiness to go and get into his armour and come out to the battle now without delay.

" ' But Hektor of the glancing helm answered him not a word. Then Helen with gentle words addressed him :

" Brother of mine, evil bitch that I am, I wish that on the day I was born a whirlwind had carried me away, to the mountains or the swell of the resounding sea, and there the waves had drowned me, before these deeds were done. But

_Il._, XXIV, 525-6 and ff.

since the gods had this grievous plan for me, then I wish at least I were the wife of a better man, who cared for his honour[1] and for the reproaches of men. This creature has no sound heart, nor ever will ; one day he will regret it. But come in and sit down on this chair, my brother ; for it is upon you that the most trouble has come, for the sake of shameless me and for the madness of Paris. Upon us has Zeus laid an evil fate, that even in after time we may be matter of song among men yet to be '.

" Then tall Hector of the glancing helm replied :

" ' Do not bid me sit down, Helen, though in kindness you speak. Already my heart bids me hasten to help the men of Troy, who sorely feel the lack of me. But hurry him on, and let him be swift of his own accord, that he may overtake me before I leave the city. For I, too, will go home, that I may see my nearest—my wife and little son ; for I do not know whether I shall come back to them again or whether even now the gods will lay me low by the hands of the Achaians '."

Even Helen, as she compares Paris and Hektor, seems to feel, with one of her swift revulsions of feeling, that there are things better worth having than a handsome face and form. But Hektor, thinking of his own wife, feels the same, and has better things to do with his few minutes' leisure than to carry on a flirtation with fair Helen, or even act as her father confessor.

He finds Andromache on the city wall, looking out towards the fighting. A maidservant carries the baby at her side. They talk together with perfect candour ; from his wife Hektor has no secrets—not even his bitter forebodings of what the issue of the war must be.

" And Hektor smiled when he saw the babe, without speaking ; and Andromache came and stood at his side, in tears, and placed her hand in his, and spoke and addressed him :

" ' My lord, your courage will be your death ; you have no pity for your little child, nor for me, who shall soon be left your widow, for the Achaians will kill you, rushing upon you all together ; and for me it would be better to be dead if I lose you, for I shall have no other comfort if you should fall, but sorrows only. I have no father or mother ; for him the noble

---

[1] ὃς ἤδη νέμεσιν.

18*

Achilles slew when he sacked the happy city of the Kilikes,
Thebe of the high gates. He slew Eëtion ; but he did not
spoil him ; of respect to him, he refrained from doing that ;
he burnt him with all his splendid armour, and piled a barrow
over him, and round it the mountain-fairies planted elm-trees,
the daughters of mighty Zeus. And I had seven brothers at
home, and all of them on the self-same day went down to
the house of Hades, for all of them the swift-footed noble
Achilles slew, fighting for our shambling cattle and white
sheep. And my mother who was queen in the wooded vale of
Plakos, Achilles brought hither with the rest of the spoil,
and set her free in exchange for a heavy ransom ; but in her
father's house the Archer Artemis slew her. Hektor, you are
my father and mother too, and brother and strong husband.
Have pity, and stay here on the walls, and do not leave your
child an orphan and your wife a widow. Bid the host take
up their position beside the fig-tree where the city is easiest
to approach and the wall is weakest ; for thrice the enemy's
champions tried to storm it there '.   .   .   .

" But to her tall Hektor of the glancing helm replied :

" ' Surely I take thought for all these things, my wife ; but
I should feel sore shame before the Trojans and their long-robed
dames if I were to skulk from the battle like a coward. Nor
does my own heart bid me do so, for I have learned to be valiant
always and to fight in the foremost ranks of Troy, winning
renown for my father and myself. For well I know this in my
inmost heart—that the day shall come when holy Troy shall
fall, and Priam and the folk of Priam the warrior. But I do
not grieve so much for all the pain of Troy hereafter, nor even
for my mother and the king my father, nor for all the gallant
brothers of mine who will fall in the dust before the enemy,
as for you, when one of the armoured Achaians leads you
weeping, taking away your day of freedom ; and in Argos you
shall weave at another's loom, and draw water from the spring
Messêis or Hypereia ;   .   .   .   but over me in death may the
mounded earth be piled, before ever I hear your crying and see
you carried away '.

" With these words glorious Hektor held out his hands for
the baby ; but the child drew back with a shriek into the bosom
of his fair-girdled nurse, terrified at the shining bronze and
the horsehair plume that nodded threateningly from the

helmet's crest. Then his loving father and the lady his mother laughed aloud, and Hektor took off his shining helmet and laid it on the ground. Then he kissed his son and dandled him in his arms and prayed to Zeus and the other gods :

" ' Zeus, and ye other gods, grant that he, too, may be famous among the Trojans, as I am, and an excellent man of might, and a strong lord in Ilios ; and may men say " He is far better than his father ", when he comes back from war ; and may he bear the bloody spoils of an enemy he has killed, and gladden his mother's heart '.

" With that he gave back the child to his dear wife, and she received it in her fragrant bosom, smiling through her tears ; and her husband pitied her when he saw, and laid his hand on her shoulder, and said, ' My lady, do not be too deeply grieved for me. No man shall send me to Hades before my appointed time ; but his fate I vow no man has ever escaped, craven or hero, from the moment of his birth. Now go home and look after your own work at the loom and distaff, and bid your handmaids do their tasks ; and the war shall be a care to us men, and most of all to me, of all that are in Ilios '."

Then, with consummate art, the poet turns back to Paris :

" Now Paris did not linger in his lofty house, but put on his splendid armour, gay with bronze, and sped through the streets on nimble feet. As when a stall-fed horse, full-fed at the manger, breaking his tether, gallops across the plain, one that is accustomed to bathe in some fair-flowing river, speeding exultantly ; and high is his head and his mane streams on his shoulders, and confident and gay he gallops toward the herds and pasturage of horses : so Paris, Priam's son, came down from the citadel, gleaming in his armour like the sun, laughing aloud ; and quickly he came up with Hektor, when he was about to turn away from the place where he talked with his wife. Then godlike Alexandros was the first to speak "—and, being Paris, proceeded to make up to his brother and fish for a compliment :

" ' Brother, I must be hindering you in your eagerness ; I was too long and did not come true to time as you bade '."

But Hektor does not rise :

" ' My friend, no right-minded man could despise your prowess in battle ; you fight well. But of your own accord you are slack and unwilling ; and I am ashamed because of you when I hear the bitter things said of you by the Trojans, who are hard pressed for your sake. But let us be going ; and the rest we will make good afterwards, if ever Zeus may grant to us to set up in our halls a cup of freedom to the eternal gods in heaven, when we have driven the goodly-greaved Achaians from the land of Troy '."

A few minutes later the two brothers are again dealing death in the forefront of the battle.

In this and other passages Homer without help from god or man, religion or philosophy, but with only his own barbarian soul to rely on, faces all the ill that there is in the world : its harshness and violence, its pointless and indiscriminate suffering, including the suffering of the innocent for the crime or folly of others. And to the question " How can we bear this ? " his only answer—no answer for " tender minds "— is " By courage ". Hektor's advice to his wife is simply to carry on with the work in hand. In the meantime, as the poet's whole work points out, the world is full of beautiful and delightful things, on which the wise man will let his mind dwell as much as possible—not on the sorrows of humanity. Homer's similes show what sort of things it was that he loved ; all simple and elemental delights : the sun and stars ; mountain, woodland and river ; the sea in all its moods ; the life of wild creatures, birds, and children ; the farm and its work ; as well as more sensational and awe-inspiring spectacles, such as storm and flood and the blazing war-beacon, flashing ill news from isle to isle by night. (And yet a certain type of criticism is still fond of saying that " the Greeks " had little feeling for nature, apparently because they were free from the fanciful romanticism of the last hundred years.) Again, what a splendid animal healthfulness breathes in some of the " stock " phrases : " And they stretched forth their hands upon the dainties that lay ready " ; " They took the gift of sleep " ; or " They washed off in the sea the great sweat that was on them ".[1] Homer is a pessimist, but he does not wallow in his pessimism. " The world has still much good, but much less good than ill " is a sentiment that expresses his point of view ; but it is likely that Homer would have shifted

---

[1] Il., X, 572.

the emphasis by putting it the other way round : the world is mostly bad, but there is much good in it for all to see and to enjoy.

His princes have not even the comfort of ambition ; for they already possess all the material comfort that their world has to offer, and the modern idea of service to the state is of course quite alien to them. " The state " can hardly be said to exist, and so far from sharing the modern belief in progress, Homer is firmly convinced (not without reason, living when he did) that the world is getting worse. The only ambition that the chiefs do manifest is that " infirmity of noble mind ", the desire to be well remembered ; that manifestation of the human craving for survival which reappears so prominently under the Roman Empire. They do—such is man—voluntarily undergo discomfort, weariness and danger, even though the only reason for so doing which they can invent for themselves is the desire for fame. Achilles, Homer's favourite among all his valiant company, had a choice of fates ; a long life of quiet prosperity as king of the Myrmidons in their valley in Thessaly, or lasting fame and death in the war at Troy. He chooses the latter, with full realization of all that it implies ; in spite of his love of life, in spite of pity for his father and mother, in spite of the irrevocableness of his decision : " I hold no ransom sufficient for my life, not in all the wealth that they say Troy held of old, that noble city, in time of peace, before the Achaians came. . . . Cattle and sheep may be lifted in the foray, and bronze-ware may be bought, and horses of chestnut mane ; but to bring back a man's soul none may avail by price nor prowess, when once it has passed the barrier of his teeth ".[1]

For the rest, they derive some consolation from the reflection that this is the common lot of man. Achilles comforts Priam, father of his enemy, come to plead for the body of Hektor, by showing him that his own father also will be bereaved in his old age, even as Priam is. In the same strain, in battle, he grimly comforts the young Trojan who begs in vain for quarter : " You, too, my friend, must die ; why this lamentation ? Patroklos died, who was a far better man than you. And do you see how fair and tall I am ? Yet over me too stands death, and powerful fate. The morning shall come, or

---

[1] Il., IX, 401-3, 406-9 ; and for the two Fates, cf. following lines.

evening, or mid-day," when he also must fall.[1]   It is a reflection
which has somehow consoled many ages.   So, Horace :

> Omnes eodem cogimur, omnibus
> Versatur urna serius ocius
> Sors exitura.

So, C. H. Sorley wrote home from France, not very long before
he himself was killed in action : " ——'s death was a shock.
Still, since Achilles' κάτθανε καὶ Πάτροκλος, ὅ περ σέο πολλὸν
ἀμείνων . . . no saner and splendider comment on death
has been made, especially when, as here, it seems a cruel
waste".   Mr. Housman echoes the same thought :

> As I gird on for fighting
>   My sword upon my thigh,
> I think on old ill-fortunes
>   Of better men than I.
>
> .   .   .   .   .   .
>
> What evil luck soever
>   For me remains in store
> 'Tis sure much finer fellows
>   Have fared much worse before.
>
> So here are thoughts for battle
>   That ought to make me brave,
> As I gird on for fighting
>   My sword that will not save.

Courage, the love of honour, and the realization that reverses
are the common lot ; it must have been of inestimable value
to those Greek pioneers of clear thought, sanity, and freedom,
whose fight against the barbarian in man was always so hard,
that their own greatest poet in days of old had enshrined for
ever in verse the figure of the man who with every detail of
circumstance against him, "carries on."   The character of
Hektor makes the " Bible of the Greeks " not, after all, wholly
unworthy of the name.   It also makes nearly unbearable the
long episode in which the gods betray him to his death.[2]
Hektor the gentle knight, who, as Helen says over his body,
had never a cruel word even for her,[3] while the ruins of the
Trojan army pour through the gates into the town, stays

[1] *Il.*, XXI, 106-11.
[2] Whole of Book XXII.
[3] XXIV, 762 ff.

outside, in spite of all remonstrance, leaning his shield against a tower. " Thus his parents with tears addressed their dear son, with many entreaties ; but Hektor would not obey, but awaited the terrible Achilles as he drew near." The same pride that forbade him to withdraw his army under cover of night, when Achilles reappeared in the field—" and that " as now in despair he reflects to himself, " would have been far the better plan "—forbids him to escape so easily, " now, when I have ruined my people by my own infatuate folly ". He runs over in his mind every possible course, even to that of trying to make terms with the conqueror, but realizes how hopeless that attempt would be. " It is no time now, around some oak or rock, to hold sweet converse with him like a boy with a maid. Better to fight."

Most painful of all, his courage momentarily fails. " Thus he thought, as he stood there ; and Achilles drew near, like to the war-god, that warrior gleaming-helmed . . . and on Hektor came terror, as he gazed ; and he dared no longer stand there, but left the gates behind him and fled in fear." He runs so swiftly that even Achilles cannot run him down.

Zeus dooms him to death, and Athene in the likeness of his brother Dêiphobos lures him into facing Achilles again ; Hektor, in a glow of gratitude, thanks this one comrade who has dared to stand by his side. Achilles throws his spear, and misses—but Athene wafts it back into his hand unseen. Hektor throws, and hits—but the spear falls back from the magic armour of the other. " And Hektor was angered . . . but he had no second spear ; and he called aloud to Dêiphobos of the white shield, and asked of him a long spear ; but he was nowhere nigh. Then Hektor understood. . . ." But there is no second panic ; he is cool and steady again. Perhaps the finest lines that Homer puts into his mouth are those which he utters as he draws his sword for his last hopeless charge. ". . . And now my fate is upon me. Still, not without effort and not without honour may I fall, but having first done some great deed for men unborn to hear of."

It is the same spirit as that of the old English epic, voiced by the veteran retainer at Maldon, as the East Saxons close up their thinned ranks against Olaf's Vikings for a last stand : " Heart the higher, thought the bolder, courage the more, as our strength fails ". Perhaps the whole matter is best summed up in the words of the Lykian chieftain in Book Twelve ; words which Housman has closely and effectively paraphrased :

> Comrade, if to turn and fly
> Made a soldier never die,
> Fly I would ; for who would not ?
> It is no pleasure to be shot.
>
> But since the man who runs away
> Lives to die another day,
>
> .   .   .   .   .
>
> Therefore, since the best is bad,
> Stand, and do the best, my lad.

" Friend, if, once we had escaped this war, we were to be ageless ever and immortal, then neither would I fight myself among the foremost ranks, nor yet urge you on to the battle, the glory of men. But now, since surely the fates of death stand over us, in myriad ways, that no man may escape nor avoid—let us go on."

THE END

INDEX

Abantes, 232
Abdi-Khiba, 118
Abimelech of Tyre, 120
Abishai, 170
Abner, 168
Absalom, 170
Abydos, 54, 218
Achaians, 35 and n.; origin, 38;
  manners, 39; in Thessaly, 69-70;
  in Pamphylia (?), 119, 137; attack
  Hittites (?), 137, and Egypt (?), 138;
  society and civilization, in Heroic
  Age, 198-211; Trojan War, 211-222;
  Dialect, 204-5; and Dorians, 210,
  225
Achilles, Achillens, at Troy, 213ff.; in
  Homer, 257; character, 13, 263
Achish of Gath, 167; name = Anchises,
  162
Adrastos, 207
Aeneas at site of Rome, legend of, 243
  See also Aineias
Agamemnon of Kyme, 231 n.
Agamemnon of Mykênai, 213ff.
Agias of Troizên, 15
Ahiram of Byblos, sarcophagus of, 172
Aia, Aiaian Isle, 190, 193
Aias of Lokris, 15n., 213
Aias son of Telamon, 213ff.; in Homer,
  249-50
Aidôs, 203
Aiêtes, 190-1, 195
Aigina, 117 n.; Dorians at, 229
Aigisthos, 223-4
Aineias, 109; in Trojan War, 214, 218;
  restores Troy, 222; legends of, in
  Italy, 243
Aiolidai, 70-1
Aiolians, dialect of, 36; in Asia, 231,
  233
Aithiopis, 15
Akaiwasha, 138
Akhhiawa, 119-21, 137
Akhnaton, 108, 117-8
Akiamos, 151; and similar names, ib.,
  n.
Alaksandus of Uilusa, 121
Alasya (= Cyprus ?) raided by Lykki,
  108; devastated by sea-raiders,
  146; Wen-Amen in, 181
Alêtes, 229
Alkathöos, 22-3 and n.
Alkmaion, 207
Alphabet, see Writing
Althaimenes, story of, 90
Amazons, 53, 127, 131

Amber, 72, 105, 188
Amenhotep III, 69, 99, 108
Amenhotep IV = Akhnaton, q.v.
Amorgos, 88
Amphiaraos, 207
Amphion, 107
Amphitryon, 107
Anchises, pedigree of, 109; name =
  Achish (?), 162
Andreus, 120n.
Androklos, 233
Andromache, 257-9
Andromeda, 138, 153
Antarawas of Akhhiyawa, 119
Apatouria, 232 and n.
Apollo Smintheus, 89; Sarpêdŏnios, ib.
  n.; Alasiôtes, 146-7; Dêlios, 238
Archandros, 124
Archilochos, date of, 54
Architeles, 124
Argo, see Argonauts
Argolis, colonized by Cretans (?), 75ff.;
  under Achaians, 200, 206; Dorians
  in, 228-9, 230
Argonauts, legend of, 15, 189-197; in
  Homer, 16n.
Argos, meaning of name, 132 n.; under
  Achaians, 207, 213; Dorians at,
  228-9, 230
Argos, the dog, 108
Ariadne, 100
Arkadian dialect, 36-7; in Cyprus, 40,
  104
Arkadians, 213, 229
Arktînos, 5-15
Armour and Weapons: Homeric, 10,
  11, 39, cf. Plate 13, d, e; Minoan,
  Plate 13, a, b; Etruscan, 61, 241-2,
  Plate 2, a; Hittite, 61, Plate 2, b, c;
  of Shardana, 111-12, cf, 214, Plates
  11, 12; of Philistines, 143, Plates
  11, 12; of Lykians, and Solymoi,
  143, 242; of Goliath, 163; Aga-
  memnon's corselet, 214; Roman,
  243-4. Cf. also Sword
Arne, 208
Artemis Orthia, 230; Laphria, 78,
  254 n.; Sarpêdŏnia, 89 n.
Arthur, legends of, 22, 204
Aryans, 33-8, 69-70
Ashdod, late survival of Philistine
  language at, 162
Ashkenaz, 215
Asia, origin of name, 156
Askalon, foundation-legends of, 151,
  153; war with Sidon, 158

INDEX

269

Double Axe, in Crete, 30, 85, 89 ; in Asia Minor, 72 ; Etruria, 242, Plate 2 ; Levant, Plate 12
Dragons, 138, 153, 209
Dragon's Teeth, legend of, 196
Dryopes, 229 n., 232
Dudkhaliyas III, K. of Hittites, 137
Dudkhaliyas IV, K. of Hittites, 141
Dymânes, 205

Echemos, 228
Egyptian Hittite Wars, 118, 132ff.
Elis, 228
Elymians, 243
Enkomi, 120
Ephesos, 232-3
Epidauros, 117 n. ; Dorians at, 229, 230 n., 232 ; colonies from, 230 n., 232
Epigonoi, epic of the, 16 and n.
Eratosthenes, chronology of, 52ff.
Erechtheus, 149
Erythrai, 87-8
Eryx, 98 n., 243
Etruscans, origin of, 60ff., 240-2 ; on Lêmnos, 241 ; personal names, 234 n., 241 and n.
Euboia, 48, 148, 229 n., 232
Eugammon, 5, 15
Eumaios, story of, 185-8
Eumêlos, 15
Eumolpos, 148-9
Eunêos of Lêmnos, 194
Euripides, 253
Eurypylos (Urpalla ?), Kêteian chief, 216, 221
Eurypylos of Kôs, 205
Eurystheus, 204, 206
Euxine, *see* Black Sea

Fibulæ, 34 ; in Cyprus and Philistia, 146 ; in Crete, 210 ; " Spectacle "-fibula at Sparta, in Balkans, in Hungary, 227
Flood, Deukalion's, 123

Gaza, called Minoa, 154, 169
Geometric style in vase-painting, origin of, 225
Gergithes, 134 n., 155
Girgashites, 156
Glaukos of Lykia, 126-8, 215
Golden Fleece, 190-1 ; origin of legend, 193, 194
Gournia, Plate 3 ; destruction of, 95
Gyges of Lydia, date of, 56
Halikarnassos, 230
Halizônes, 215
Hatiba, queen of Alasya, 181
Hebrews, *see* Khabiru

Hekataios of Milêtos, pedigree of, 49
Hektor, 220 n., 221 ; character, in Homer, 247ff.
Helen, 213ff., character, in Homer, 258-9
Hellanikos, on Homer, 17 ; on Pelasgoi and Tyrrhênoi, 60, 61
Hellas, 123 n.
Hellenes, origin of, 36, 123, *cf.* 214
Hellŏpia, 123 n.
Herakles, labours of, 15, 16 n. ; as culture-hero, 78 ; " Lydian " H.= Atys (?), 114 n. ; and Hêsione, 153 ; as sea-raider, 203-5. Children of, 228
Hermione, daughter of Menelaos, 224
Hermione, city, 117 n., 229 n.
Herodotos, on Homer, 6, 17 ; and local tradition, 25 ; on Minôs, 31 ; on Dorians, 35, 50 ; chronology of, 50, 54, 55 ; on Pelasgoi, 59ff. ; on Etruscan origins, 60, 61 ; on fall of Minôs, 96 ; on Ionians, 232-3.
Hesiod, date of, 5-6 ; quoted, 223
Hêsione, 153
Hiram, K. of Tyre, 240
Hittites, and Etruscans, 61 and n., Plate 2 ; and Mykenai, 115, Plate 7 ; wars with Egypt, 118, 133ff. ; attacked by sea-raiders, 137 ; famine, 138 ; fall of their empire, 141. *Cf. also* 215-6
Hivites, 156, 159
Homer : name, 3 ; date of, 6 ; originality of, 8 ; geography in H., 13 ; his genius and influence, 246ff.
Homeric Question, 3-17
Horemheb, Pharaoh, 118
Hylleis, 205
Hypachaioi, 121, 153

Ialysos, 104, 137
Iapetos (=Japhet ?), 156
Ida, Mount, 84, 89
Idomeneus, 213
Iliad, structure of, 8-9
Ilios, 109, 205, 222 ; *see* Troy
Iôlkos, 76, 189, 192
Ionia, colonization of, 232ff.
Ionians, 232ff. ; tribes of, 235 n. ; dialect, 36, 238
Iphigeneia or Isaac story, 162
Iron, among Hittites and Philistines, 160, 163 ; Chalybes, 188 ; rare among Homer's Achaians, 200, but *cf.* 211 ; weapons of, in Crete, 210 ; in Balkans and Central Europe, 226-7
Isaac story, *see* Iphigeneia
Ish-baal (=Ish-bosheth), son of Saul, 168

Over fifty volumes are now available

THE HISTORY OF CIVILIZATION

A COMPLETE HISTORY OF MANKIND FROM
PREHISTORIC TIMES TO THE PRESENT DAY
IN NUMEROUS VOLUMES DESIGNED
TO FORM A COMPLETE
LIBRARY OF SOCIAL
EVOLUTION

Edited by

C. K. OGDEN

of Magdalene College, Cambridge

Published by

KEGAN PAUL, TRENCH, TRUBNER & CO. LTD.

BROADWAY HOUSE: 68-74 CARTER LANE, LONDON

1932

THE HISTORY OF CIVILIZATION

THIS series marks one of the most ambitious adventures in the annals of book publishing. Its aim is to present in accessible form the results of modern research throughout the whole range of the Social Sciences—to summarize in one comprehensive synthesis the most recent findings of historians, anthropologists, archæologists, sociologists, and all conscientious students of civilization.

To achieve success in this stupendous undertaking, the new French series, *L'Evolution de l'Humanité*, in which the leading savants of France are collaborating with the Director of the Bibliothèque de Synthèse Historique, M. Henri Berr, is being incorporated. Distinguished historians, both European and American, are contributing volumes in their several departments.

The field has been carefully mapped out, as regards both subjects and periods ; and, though the instalments will be published as they are ready, the necessary chronological sequence will be secured by the fact that the volumes of the French collection will be used as a nucleus. Each work will be entirely independent and complete in itself, but the volumes in a given group will be found to supplement one another when considered in relation to a particular subject or period.

The volumes are uniformly bound in a fine art-cambric cloth, with specially designed gold lettering and emblem, royal octavo in size.

THE TIMES LITERARY SUPPLEMENT devoted a leading article to the first four volumes, in which the series was described as being " composed by all the talents ".

THE MANCHESTER GUARDIAN wrote that " it is a heroic attempt, which will be sympathetically watched, to bring some light into the vast mass of ill-organized knowledge which we owe to modern research and so make it available in the end for the guidance of the world."

NATURE, the leading scientific journal, in a six-column review, provides a striking summary of the aims and objects of the series : " The History of Civilization promises to be perhaps the most important contribution so far undertaken towards the task of organization and systematization of the social studies. A glance at the prospectus makes us anticipate a library of masterpieces, for the best workers of France, Great Britain, and some other countries are contributing from their own speciality and are attempting to bring it into line with the con-tributions from neighbouring fields and with the results of general sociology. Including all the volumes of the important French collection, *L'Evolution de l'Humanité*, the English library contains additions and improvements which will place it above its continental counterpart. The volumes already issued bear out our best hopes."

*The following plan, comprising just under one hundred titles, though not definitive, will serve to convey a general notion of the nature and scope of the enterprise :**

A. PRE-HISTORY AND ANTIQUITY

I INTRODUCTION AND PRE-HISTORY

*Social Organization	W. H. R. Rivers
The Earth Before History	Edmond Perrier
Prehistoric Man	Jacques de Morgan
*Life and Work in Prehistoric Times	G. Renard
*The Dawn of European Civilization	V. Gordon Childe
Language: a Linguistic Introduction to History	J. Vendryes
A Geographical Introduction to History	L. Febvre
Race and History	E. Pittard
*The Aryans	V. Gordon Childe
From Tribe to Empire	A. Moret and G. Davy
*Money and Monetary Policy in Early Times	A. R. Burns
*The Diffusion of Culture	G. Elliot Smith

II THE EARLY EMPIRES

The Nile and Egyptian Civilization	A. Moret
The Mesopotamian Civilization	L. Delaporte
The Ægean Civilization	G. Glotz
*Minoans, Philistines and Greeks	Andrew Robert Burn

III GREECE

The Formation of the Greek People	A. Jardé
*Ancient Greece at Work	G. Glotz
Religious Thought of Greece	L. Gernet and A. Boulanger
Art in Greece	W. Deonna and A. de Ridder
Greek Thought and the Scientific Spirit	L. Robin
The Greek City and its Institutions	G. Glotz
Macedonian Imperialism	P. Jouguet

IV ROME

Primitive Italy and Roman Imperialism	Léon Homo
The Roman Spirit in Religion, Thought, and Art	A. Grenier
Roman Political Institutions	Léon Homo
Rome the Law-Giver	J. Declareuil
Economic Life of the Ancient World	J. Toutain

* An asterisk denotes that the volume does *not* form part of the French collection *L'Evolution de l'Humanité*.

The Roman World	*Victor Chapot*
*Ancient Rome at Work	*Paul Louis*
The Celts and Celtic Expansion	*H. Hubert*
The Later Civilization of the Celts	*H. Hubert*

V BEYOND THE ROMAN EMPIRE

Germany and the Roman Empire	*H. Hubert*
Ancient Persia and Iranian Civilization	*Clement Huart*
Chinese Civilization	*M. Granet*
Chinese Thought	*M. Granet*
*Feudal Japan	*G. F. Hudson*
*A Thousand Years of the Tartars	*E. H. Parker*
*Nomads of the European Steppe	*G. F. Hudson*
India	*(Ed.) S. Lévi*
*The Heroic Age of India	*N. K. Sidhanta*
*Caste and Race in India	*G. S. Ghurye*
*The Life of Buddha as Legend and History	*E. H. Thomas*
*The History of Buddhist Thought	*E. H. Thomas*

B. CHRISTIANITY AND THE MIDDLE AGES

I THE ORIGINS OF CHRISTIANITY

Israel, from its Beginnings	*Adolphe Lods*
Jesus and the Birth of Christianity	*C. Guignebert*
The Formation of the Church	*C. Guignebert*
The Advance of Christianity	*C. Guignebert*
*History and Literature of Christianity	*P. de Labriolle*

II THE BREAK-UP OF THE EMPIRE

The End of the Ancient World	*Ferdinand Lot*
The Eastern Empire	*C. Diehl*
Charlemagne	*L. Halphen*
The Collapse of the Carlovingian Empire	*Ferdinand Lot*
The Origins of the Slavs	*(Ed.) P. Boyer*
*Popular Life in the East Roman Empire	*Norman Baynes*
*The Northern Invaders	*B. S. Phillpotts*

III RELIGIOUS IMPERIALISM

Islam and Mahomet	*E. Doutté*
The Advance of Islam	*L. Barrau-Dihigo*
Christendom and the Crusades	*P. Alphandéry*
The Organization of the Church	*R. Genestal*

IV THE ART OF THE MIDDLE AGES

The Art of the Middle Ages	*P. Lorquet*
*The Papacy and the Arts	*E. Strong*

V RECONSTITUTION OF MONARCHIC POWER

The Foundation of Modern Monarchies	*C. Petit-Dutaillis*
The Growth of Public Administration	*E. Meynial*
The Organization of Law	*E. Meynial*

VI SOCIAL AND ECONOMIC EVOLUTION

The Development of Rural and Town Life   G. Bourgin
Maritime Trade and the Merchant Gilds   P. Boissonnade
*The Court of Burgundy   Otto Cartellieri
*Life and Work in Medieval Europe   P. Boissonnade
*The Life of Women in Medieval Times   Eileen Power
*Travel and Travellers of the Middle Ages (Ed.) A. P. Newton
*Chivalry and its Historical Significance   (Ed.) Edgar Prestage

VII INTELLECTUAL EVOLUTION

Education in the Middle Ages   G. Huisman
Philosophy in the Middle Ages   E. Bréhier
Science in the Middle Ages   Abel Rey and P. Boutroux

VIII FROM THE MIDDLE AGES TO MODERN TIMES

Nations of Western and Central Europe   P. Lorquet
Russians, Byzantines, and Mongols   (Ed.) P. Boyer
The Birth of the Book   G. Renaudet
*The Grandeur and Decline of Spain   C Hughes Hartmann
*The Influence of Scandinavia on England   M. E. Seaton
*The Philosophy of Capitalism   T. E. Gregory
*The Prelude to the Machine Age   Mrs. Bertrand Russell
*Life and Work in Modern Europe   G. Renard and G. Weulersse
*London Life in the Eighteenth Century   M. Dorothy George
*China and Europe in the Eighteenth Century   A. Reichwein

A special group of volumes will be devoted to

(1) SUBJECT HISTORIES
*The History of Medicine   C. G. Cumston
*The History of Witchcraft   Montague Summers
*The Geography of Witchcraft   Montague Summers
*The History of Money   T. E. Gregory
*The History of Taste   J. Isaac
*The History of Oriental Literature   E. Powys Mathers
*The History of Music   Cecil Gray

(2) HISTORICAL ETHNOLOGY
*The Ethnology of Africa   L. H. Dudley Buxton
*The Peoples of Asia   L. H. Dudley Buxton
*The Threshold of the Pacific   C. E. Fox
*The South American Indians   Rafael Karsten
*The American Indian Frontier   J. G. Macleod
*The Ethnology of India   T. C. Hodson
*Death Customs   E. Bendann

*In the Sections devoted to MODERN HISTORY the majority of titles
will be announced later.*

6

VOLUMES PUBLISHED

The following volumes have already been issued. They are arranged roughly in the order in which they were published. But their place in the scheme of the whole series may be discovered from the list above :

THE EARTH BEFORE HISTORY : *Man's Origin and the Origin of Life*

By EDMOND PERRIER, *late Hon. Director of the Natural History Museum of France.*

With 4 maps, 15s. net.

" It goes back to the birth of the world and the transformations of land and water, and takes us through the growth of life on the planet, the primitive animal forms, the peopling of the seas, and the forms of life in the primary, secondary, and tertiary periods, to the growth of the human form. Thus, starting from the origin of matter, it leads us in easy stages to *homo sapiens* himself."

Daily News,

" A remarkable volume."—*Yorkshire Post.*

PREHISTORIC MAN : *A General Outline of Prehistory*

By JACQUES DE MORGAN, *late Director of Antiquities in Egypt.*

With 190 illustrations and maps, 12s. 6d. net.

" A notable and eminently readable study in the early history of civilization, and one well worth its place in the great series now being issued by the publishers. It bears on every page the impress of the personality of its author, who strives to give the reader a clear, composite picture of early civilization taking one topic after another."—*Nation.*

" A masterly summary of our present knowledge at a low price. As a full survey the book has no rival, and its value is enhanced by the lavish illustrations."

New Leader.

SOCIAL ORGANIZATION

By W. H. R. RIVERS, LL.D., F.R.S. *Preface by* PROFESSOR G. ELLIOT SMITH.

Second edition, 10s. 6d net.

" *Social Organization* is the first volume of the series of historical works on the whole range of human activity. May the present book be of good augury for the rest ! To maintain so high a standard of originality and thoroughness will be no easy task."—JANE HARRISON, in *Nation.*

The book is a great contribution to the sum of human knowledge in the region of pure sociology."—*Daily News.*

7

THE THRESHOLD OF THE PACIFIC: *an Account of the Social Organization, Magic, and Religion of the People of San Cristoval in the Solomon Islands*

By C. E. FOX, LITT.D. *Preface by* PROFESSOR G. ELLIOT SMITH.

With 14 plates and 40 text illustrations, 18s. net.

" A masterpiece. One of the very best contributions to ethnology we possess. It has, besides its intrinsic value as a masterly record of savage life, also an indirect one ; it is a remarkable testimony to the indispensable need of scientific method for the observer. His account of magical ritual and spells will become a classical source for students. The account of the life-history of the individual is depicted with a clearness and fulness unrivalled in ethnographic literature . . . "—*Times Literary Supplement.*

LANGUAGE : *a Linguistic Introduction to History*

By J. VENDRYES, *Professor in the University of Paris.*

16s. net.

" A book remarkable for its erudition and equally remarkable for originality and independence of thought."—*Sunday Times.*

" As an introduction to philology this volume is a splendid piece of *haute vulgarisation,* for which anyone who at all loves words or who is at all curious about language, must be grateful. It covers nearly all the ground from every useful angle. A wide, level-headed and erudite study."—*Nation.*

A GEOGRAPHICAL INTRODUCTION TO HISTORY

By LUCIEN FEBVRE, *Professor in the University of Strasburg.*

With 7 maps, 16s. net.

" A masterpiece of criticism, as witty as it is well-informed, and teeming with nice observations and delicate turns of argument and phrase."

Times Literary Supplement.

" A broad, clear-headed introduction to the fascinating study of human geography. It is much more than a text-book for the student : it is a work that anyone with no knowledge of geography can read with avidity, for it is the greatest of pleasures to watch the clear logical thought of the writer rapidly treating with masterly power these great and important topics."—*Nation.*

THE HISTORY AND LITERATURE OF CHRISTIANITY : *from Tertullian to Boethius*

By PIERRE DE LABRIOLLE, *Professor of Literature at the University of Poitiers. Foreword by* CARDINAL GASQUET.

25s. net.

" A masterly volume. A scholar of the finest accomplishment, an enthusiast for his subject, and himself an artist in letters, he has produced a book comprehensive and authoritative, and also a joy to read from the first page to the last."

Universe.

" This interesting and valuable book."—W. L. COURTNEY, in *Daily Telegraph.*

8

LONDON LIFE IN THE EIGHTEENTH CENTURY
By M. DOROTHY GEORGE.
Second impression. With 8 plates, 21s. net.

" Mrs. George, by her cumulative method, imparts a shuddering impression of the brutalised life led by the masses under the first two Georges. Her work is full of eloquent detail. All who like to get at close quarters with history will feel immensely debtors to her industrious research and faculty of clear statement. And she will have the satisfaction of restoring faith to many minds in the reality of progress."—*Observer*.

" One of the best pieces of research in social and economic history which have appeared for many years."—*Nation*.

A THOUSAND YEARS OF THE TARTARS
By E. H. PARKER, *Professor of Chinese in the Victoria University of Manchester.*
With 5 illustrations and maps, 12s. 6d. net.

" Professor Parker takes us back to a period roughly contemporaneous with that of the foundation of the Roman empire, and shows their history to be, like that of the Northern barbarians and Rome, a constant struggle with China. With an unfamiliar subject the book is not an easy one to read, but the author has done all that was possible to enliven his subject and has certainly succeeded in giving us a most valuable text-book."—*Saturday Review*.

CHINA AND EUROPE: *their Intellectual and Artistic Relations in the Eighteenth Century*
By ADOLPH REICHWEIN.
With 24 plates, 12s. 6d. net.

" Among the volumes of the monumental History of Civilization, this study of the influence of Chinese art and thought on the European art and thought of the eighteenth century will find not the least popular and distinguished place. The chapter headed ' Rococo ' will be of especial interest to connoisseurs. . . The illustrations are numerous and beautiful."—*Sunday Times*.

" A fascinating subject. The references to literature are admirably full and complete."—*Times Literary Supplement*.

THE DAWN OF EUROPEAN CIVILIZATION
By V. GORDON CHILDE, B.Litt.
Second Impression. With 198 illustrations and 4 maps, 16s. net.

" Higher praise of Mr. Childe's book, which forms a volume of the monumental History of Civilization, could scarcely be given than to say that it is in all respects worthy of the volumes which preceded it."—*Sunday Times*.

" He has done a very great service to learning, and given a clear and reliable outline of the earliest civilization of Europe. His book ' fills a gap ' indeed."—*Nation*.

" A very fine piece of work."—*Manchester Guardian*.

MESOPOTAMIA : *the Babylonian and Assyrian Civilization*

By L. DELAPORTE, *Professor in the Catholic Institute of Paris.*

With 60 illustrations and maps, 16s. net.

"This book is for the most part very good. The author has handled his difficult material cleverly. Where he succeeds is in his admirably written description of the social life, of which he makes a fascinating story. Here is presented an entertaining picture of the inhabitants in 2000 B.C. Then from the earlier Babylonians he passes to the Assyrians, dealing with them in a similar excellent way. This is one of the best books of its kind which we have seen for some time."—*Times Literary Supplement.*

THE AEGEAN CIVILIZATION

By G. GLOTZ, *Professor of Greek History in the University of Paris*

With 4 plates, 87 text illustrations, and 3 maps, 16s. net.

"This is a marvellous summary, divided into four books, describing in detail the material, social, religious, artistic and intellectual life of the people. Every one of these sections is full of interesting and new knowledge. A wonderful book, thoroughly scholarly and attractive in presentation."—*Birmingham Post.*

"Reads like a romance . . . presents a very vivid picture of this marvellous civilization."—*Times Literary Supplement.*

THE PEOPLES OF ASIA

By L. H. DUDLEY BUXTON, M.A., F.S.A., *Lecturer in Physical Anthropology in the University of Oxford*

With 8 plates, 12s. 6d. net.

"Although the physical characters of the principal racial strains are described in some detail, the author keeps before his readers the bearing of these data upon the broader problems of racial distribution, as well as the intensely interesting question of the interaction of race, environment, and modification by contact due to migration. The exposition of anthropological method given in an introductory chapter is admirably lucid."—*Manchester Guardian.*

RACE AND HISTORY : *an Ethnological Introduction to History*

By E. PITTARD, *Professor of Anthropology in the University of Geneva.*

Second Impression. With 9 illustrations and maps, 21s. net.

A companion to Febvre's *Geographical Introduction to History*, which estimated the value of "environment" as a factor in history, while the present volume considers the "racial" factor. "No one is better qualified to compose a thoroughly level-headed treatise on the subject of race. For the peoples who occupy a conspicuous place in history, and especially the peoples of Europe, no better guide could be found."—*Times Literary Supplement.*

LIFE AND WORK IN MEDIEVAL EUROPE, *from the Fifth to the Fifteenth Century*

By P. BOISSONNADE, *Professor in the University of Poitiers.*
Translated with an Introduction by EILEEN POWER, *D.Litt.*

With 8 plates, 16s. net.

" His work is so interesting that it is to be hoped he will follow Sir James Frazer's admirable example and take each chapter in turn for the purpose of converting its highly concentrated essence of history into a more ample dish for scholars. His subject is attractive and his pages are eminently readable by laymen."—*Times Literary Supplement.*

" There is no book in English which gives so clear and comprehensive a view of the labour question all through the Middle Ages. Readers will find no single volume so useful and so readable as this."—G. G. COULTON, in *Observer.*

LIFE AND WORK IN MODERN EUROPE, *from the Fifteenth to the Eighteenth Century*

By G. RENARD, *Professor at the College of France, and* G. WEULERSSE, *Professor at the Lycée Carnot. Introduction by* EILEEN POWER, *D. Litt., Reader in Economic History in the University of London.*

With 8 plates, 16s. net.

" This can certainly be pronounced a most useful book. There is nothing that covers anything like the same ground; indeed, there is actually no book in English which even pretends to give an outline of European economic history as a whole. It is interestingly written, and is a storehouse of valuable information."—*New Statesman.*

TRAVEL AND TRAVELLERS OF THE MIDDLE AGES

Edited by A. P. NEWTON, *Rhodes Professor of Imperial History in the University of London.*

With 8 plates and maps, 12s. 6d. net.

" This work is no mere collection of stray essays, but in some respects the most important contribution to the history of medieval travel since Professor Beazley's *Dawn of Modern Geography* and the new edition of Yule's *Cathay.* . . . We have said enough to indicate that this work is one which should appeal both to the general reader and to the scholar. The illustrations are good."—*Times Literary Supplement.*

CHIVALRY : *Its Historical Significance and Civilizing Influence*

Edited by EDGAR PRESTAGE, *Camõens Professor in the University of London.*

With 24 full-page plates, 15s. net.

" This is an excellent book, at once learned and entertaining, a valuable addition to our painfully limited library of medieval studies. The book is worth having, and there is an abundance of beautiful illustrations."—*Daily News.*

" An equally interesting and beautiful volume, a piece of work which appeals alike to the general reader and to the specialist in history."—*Journal of Education.*

11

ANCIENT GREECE AT WORK : *an Economic History of Greece from the Homeric Period to the Roman Conquest*

By G. GLOTZ, *Professor of Greek History in the University of Paris.*
With 49 illustrations, 16s. net.

" This is a learned but thoroughly interesting description of farming, industry, and business in general in ancient Greece, and should interest the student of economics as well as the classical scholar, since it shows practices developing from their simplest form. Besides giving hard economic facts the author makes interesting remarks on the Greek attitude to slaves, to foreigners, and to labour. This is a very readable and unusual book."—*Spectator.*

" A really fascinating economic history of the Greek people."—*New Leader.*

THE FORMATION OF THE GREEK PEOPLE

By A. JARDÉ, *Professor of History at the Lycée Lakanal.*
With 7 maps, 16s. net.

" One reader at least will tell the world he has enjoyed the book, has profited by it, and is not yet done with it ; he means to use it again, and meanwhile ventures to tell others interested that this is a book for them."—*Nation.*

" He has given his readers an analysis of the course of events in the various City states in their external relations *inter se* and with other peoples, of their political, social, and intellectual development, of Hellenic expansion and of Hellenic unity, which is little short of brilliant."—*Nature.*

THE ARYANS : *a Study of Indo-European Origins*

By V. GORDON CHILDE, *B.Litt.*
With 8 plates, 28 text illustrations, and a map, 10s. 6d. net.

" Mr. Childe has followed up his interesting book, *The Dawn of European Civilization*, with another archæological study not less scholarly and sound. By a joint use of philological deduction and archæological induction, he contrives a thoroughly scientific handling of the problem."—*Times Literary Supplement.*

" Here is a book that must be of perennial interest, for it covers the whole field to the time of writing, and is precisely what a work dealing with problems of enormous intricacy should be."—*New Statesman.*

FROM TRIBE TO EMPIRE : *Social Organization among the Primitives and in the Ancient East*

By A. MORET, *Professor in the University of Paris, and* G. DAVY, *of the University of Dijon.*
With 47 illustrations and 7 maps, 16s. net.

" The object of the authors of this valuable addition to the series is to demonstrate how Empires grew from the primitive totemistic clan. Leaving M. Davy's excited, learned, and highly controversial dissertation on primitive society for M. Moret's calm review of the history of the Ancient East is like passing from storm into quiet. M. Moret's story remains the most lucid and satisfactory general survey of the Ancient East that has yet appeared. It is the very romance of history, and he would be dull indeed who did not find recreation and delight in these stirring pages."—*New Statesman.*

12

THE HISTORY OF MEDICINE, *from the time of the Pharaohs to the end of the Eighteenth Century*

By C. G. CUMSTON, M.D.

With 24 plates, 16s. net.

"Will be an invaluable source of reference to those who wisely remain students all their days. Beginning with the first dynasty of the Pharaohs, the ideas and the personalities of medicine are described in a manner which compels wonder for the amount of literary research, thought, and time which must have been devoted to its construction."—*British Medical Journal*.

"The book should be as interesting to the general public as to the doctors."—*Sunday Times*.

THE HISTORY OF WITCHCRAFT AND DEMONOLOGY

By MONTAGUE SUMMERS, *editor of Congreve, Wycherley, etc*.

With 8 full-page plates, 12s. 6d. net.

"Mr. Summers has just the literary style to do justice to the stewing of witches' broth or the licentious dancing of the Sabbat. This book is one of the most masterly products of psychological-historical literature; and one feels that the editor of this learned series was perfectly justified in including in it such a storehouse of facts. Mr. Summers has our hearty thanks. His book is enthralling."—*Outlook*.

"No more learned, no more copiously documented work on the subject has seen the light for a long while."—*Birmingham Post*.

THE GEOGRAPHY OF WITCHCRAFT

By MONTAGUE SUMMERS.

With 8 full-page plates, 21s. net.

"The *History* described the general characteristics of European witchcraft in the middle ages; the present volume gives particulars of actual witches in the various countries of Western Europe. Mr. Summers includes within the scope of his exceedingly painstaking work all the varieties of the black art, from cattle laming to the concoction of love philtres, to demoniac possession and unnatural vice. The book is beautifully produced and contains some excellent illustrations."—*Spectator*.

THE CIVILIZATION OF THE SOUTH AMERICAN INDIANS, *with special reference to Magic and Religion*

By RAFAEL KARSTEN, Ph.D., *Professor at the University of Finland, Helsingfors. Preface by* PROFESSOR E. WESTERMARCK.

25s. net.

"A very solid piece of work. . . Whether Professor Karsten be right or wrong in his contentions, his book can be read with the utmost profit, because he cites the evidence fully and fairly."—*Times Literary Supplement*.

"Dr. Karsten can congratulate himself on having written a work that will form not merely a contribution to the ethnology of South America, but also a valuable addition to the small number of really useful works on the ideas of the less cultured peoples."—*Saturday Review*.

PRIMITIVE ITALY, *and the Beginnings of Roman Imperialism*

By LEON HOMO, *Professor in the University of Lyons.*

With 13 maps and plans, 16s. net.

" This able and scholarly work, which has summoned to its aid all the resources of anthropology, archæology, epigraphy and philology. Here is laid bare the real history of Rome's origins, and especially of her Etruscan origins. A volume characterized alike by scientific caution and a marked power of lucid reconstruction."—*Spectator.*

" He gives us a spirited account of the development of Rome from her obscure origins to her establishment as the dominant power of the Mediterranean world. It would be hard to find a clearer or better proportioned account of the stages by which Rome achieved the miracle . . ."—*Times Literary Supplement.*

ANCIENT ROME AT WORK : *an Economic History of Rome from the Origins to the Empire*

By PAUL LOUIS.

With 4 illustrations and 6 maps, 16s. net.

" The main stages in Rome's imperial progress are indicated, and the economic causes of her decline are adequately analysed. Agriculture and commerce, industry and finance, roads and communications, slavery and its developments, the rise of the colonate, and the influence of guilds are dealt with in turn, and their bearing on society and the social structure are discussed. . . . The volume presents a vivid, rapidly-moving picture of the economics of the Roman State."—*Times Literary Supplement.*

THE ROMAN SPIRIT *in Religion, Thought, and Art*

By A. GRENIER, *Professor in the University of Strasburg.*

With 16 plates and 16 text illustrations, 16s. net.

" I have not space to set out all the things in the book that have interested me and given me pleasure. The sections on religion and literature are fresh and stimulating. The classical scholar and the general reader can be recommended alike to read every page of this admirable book."—*Nation.*

" A brilliant interpretation of Latin literature and religion."—*New Leader.*

ROME THE LAW-GIVER

By J. DECLAREUIL, *Professor in the University of Toulouse.*

16s. net.

" The level of scholarship is extremely high, and the treatment hardly more technical than the subject-matter demands. The author traces the development of Roman law from its origin to its codification, and on to the later refinements which in their range, subtlety, and realistic logic have given it such unrivalled universality and completeness. While recommending this valuable synopsis as a whole, we may note as specially significant the chapter on the organization of credit."—*Saturday Review.*

THE LIFE OF BUDDHA, *as Legend and History*

By E. J. THOMAS, D.Litt., *Under Librarian in the University Library, Cambridge.*

With 4 plates and a map, 12s. 6d. net.

" He has produced an authoritative account of all that is known of the life of the great teacher. We would recommend this important work to all interested in Eastern philosophy."—*Spectator*.

" The treatment of his subject is as thorough as one could wish. His knowledge of the sources, his historical sense, and the soundness of his judgment make him a safe guide in a field in which there are many pitfalls. The book is a worthy addition to a notable series."—*Manchester Guardian*.

ANCIENT PERSIA, *and Iranian Civilization*

By CLEMENT HUART, *Member of the Institute of France.*

With 4 plates, 35 text illustrations, and a map, 12s. 6d. net.

" A very good account of the cultural history of old Iran. A vivid picture of the country and an account of the scripts is followed by a history of the Achæmenids, Arsacids, and Sassanids. The real value of the book consists in the excellent analyses of the cultural data referring to each epoch : the social organization, the religious cults and beliefs, and the artistic productions. The powerful character sketches of the monarchs and heroes receive new life from the background in which they are set."—*Nature*.

" An admirable epitome of the known facts."—*New Statesman*.

ART IN GREECE

By A. DE RIDDER, *Curator at the Louvre Museum, and* W. DEONNA, *Director of the Geneva Museum of Art and History.*

With 24 plates and 66 text illustrations, 21s. net.

" A fascinating addition to the series. The authors have written attractively not only of Greek art from its beginnings to the Hellenistic period and its final decline, but of everyday Greek life and its relation to art and the artists of the time."—*Daily News*.

" Even on the most familiar ground it is remarkably fresh and penetrating."
New Statesman.

MONEY AND MONETARY POLICY IN EARLY TIMES

By A. R. BURNS, B.Sc. Econ.

With 16 plates, 25s. net.

" He has treated the subject with care and caution and shown clearly what the puzzles are. He deals mainly with Greece and Rome, slightly with Assyria, and gives a paragraph at the end of each chapter to the wholly independent and interesting coinage of China."—*Times Literary Supplement*.

" He is to be congratulated. The book is a striking contrast to the previous superficial treatments of the subject. Documents have been searched and the material obtained, digested, and presented in a most readable form."
Economist.

15

THE NILE AND EGYPTIAN CIVILIZATION

By A. MORET, *Professor at the College of France.*

With 24 plates, 79 text illustrations and 3 maps, 25s. net.

" This brilliant story of Egyptian society.   M. Moret's peculiar contribution to Egyptology is that he has taken the *disjecta membra* of Egyptian history and of them has built anew the living body of that amazing culture. What was it that secured to Egypt a civilization more stable than that of any other of the great kingdoms of antiquity ? M. Moret tells us. It was the Nile, coupled with the establishment of a religious system imposing its sanctions on every social duty.   As seen in his sympathetic retrospect, this great religion is curiously attractive. It was the real moral and spiritual force permeating the whole of Egyptian life. Art and science and literature ministered to it, and it sustained for milleniums the most massive, coherent, and amiable civilization the world has known."—*Times Literary Supplement.*

THE HISTORY OF MUSIC

By CECIL GRAY.

12s. 6d. net.

" Here is just the book readers have been looking for, and looking for too long in vain. No music-lover would find it other than arresting from cover to cover.   Its distinction of style . . its meticulous accuracy . . its fresh and original standpoint.   It is not too much to say that it is one of the most illuminating books of this decade."—SIR RICHARD TERRY, in *Queen.*

" A book which is quite one of the best of its kind."—*Observer.*

THE ROMAN WORLD

By VICTOR CHAPOT, *Professor at the Ecole des Beaux-Arts.*

With 2 plates and 12 maps, 16s. net.

" This survey of the Roman Empire presents in a compendious form an account of the expansion of Rome, the machinery of provincial government, and finally a survey of the Empire and its fortunes province by province. This is the fullest account of the Empire which has appeared in English since the translation of Mommsen's two volumes nearly fifty years ago.   It is enriched by the discoveries that have been made in the meantime, and its excellent bibliography brings the sources up to date. The volume has some useful maps."

Times Literary Supplement.

MACEDONIAN IMPERIALISM, *and the Hellenization of the East*

By P. JOUGUET, *Professor in the University of Paris.*

With 7 plates and 5 maps, 21s. net.

" He has told a most fascinating story and told it so well that it forms an excellent sequel to the ordinary histories of Greece. Particularly valuable is his account of the Hellenization of Asia and of Egypt, of the public and private life of the latter, and of the establishment of the Greek and Macedonian military and other colonies. To read his book shows that no one can afford to neglect the study of the Hellenistic period, which was responsible for many fundamental elements of modern civilization."—*Times Literary Supplement.*

THE AMERICAN INDIAN FRONTIER

By WILLIAM CHRISTIE MACLEOD, *Assistant Professor in the University of Pennsylvania.*

With 13 maps, 25s. net.

" It is a tale, alike for its romantic and its historical values, well worth the telling ; and it is not likely to find many tellers so competent and so vivid as Professor Macleod. His book is an important contribution to historical ethnology. The picture of American Indian culture drawn, with a wealth of colour and atmosphere, by this leading authority is in many ways attractive. The erudition is enlivened by innumerable human touches."—*New Statesman.*

GREEK THOUGHT, *and the Origins of the Scientific Spirit*

By L. ROBIN, *Professor in the University of Paris.*

With a map, 21s. net.

" His contribution will probably rank as one of the finest in the series. For immense erudition combined with perfect clarity of expression the book can have few equals."—*Nature.*

" Apart from his account of the three outstanding figures of Greek philosophy [Plato, Aristotle and Pythagoras], a special meed of thanks is due to him for his full treatment of Plotinus and of the Stoics. Professor Robin's work is characterized throughout by an exceptional sense of proportion."—*Times Literary Supplement.*

LIFE AND WORK IN PREHISTORIC TIMES

By G. RENARD, *Professor at the College of France.*

With 9 plates, 12s. 6d. net.

" In a text which is always informing and never dull, it is hard to know where to begin or when to stop [quoting]. Throughout there is a pithiness of diction resulting in memorable epigram. In short, the conjunction of style and matter is so fortunate that it gives the whole volume the individuality that marks a contribution to literature as contrasted with a mere textbook. The student who wishes to use it in the latter capacity will get from it just the right stimulus to send him forward. He will be made to realize the importance of the evolution of the useful and decorative arts. He will be conducted through a veritable museum of curious and telling facts. In short, there is inspiration in everything that Professor Renard has written."—*Times Literary Supplement.*

THE COURT OF BURGUNDY

By OTTO CARTELLIERI.

With 25 plates, 21s. net.

" Professor Cartellieri chose a period steeped in romantic colour. When he began to work he was fascinated by the rich and splendid culture of the brilliant court. But there were bigger matters, as he found the more he explored, and his attention turned to spiritual and social questions. The result is the work of a specialist, who has the gift of attractively presenting pictures of a strange period, its life and manners, its art, literature, and music, its ruler and Court, how the knight and the lady lived, the feasts, jousts, and tourneys."—*Times.*

" His richly-illustrated volume is a learned and engaging guide to the culture of late medieval society at its most brilliant."—*Saturday Review.*

17

THE HEROIC AGE OF INDIA
By N. K. SIDHANTA, *Professor of English at Lucknow University.*
12s. 6d. net.

"A valuable contribution. The Heroic Age is an epoch in practically all races and cultures. They all show characteristics which the Indian age also displays. The *Mahabharata* is his principal quarry; the heroes of that epic seem near to us. With their drinking and love-making, their chivalry and brutality, they are of the schoolboy age of humanity. It is a delightful world to which Professor Sidhanta transports us. Not only scholars but all who would recapture the illusions of boyhood owe him a debt."
Times Literary Supplement.

THE GREEK CITY, *and its Institutions*
By G. GLOTZ, *Professor of Greek History in the University of Paris.*
16s. net.

"The theme of this admirable book is the autonomous Greek city as it appeared in time from its first dim beginnings in the Homeric age down to its overthrow by Philip of Macedon. It combines great learning with philosophical power, and with a pure and lively style. It, of course, contains the facts, but it contains much more. His remarks on ostracism and the selection of magistrates by lot are good examples of his knowledge and his reasoning power."
Sunday Times.

"He is eminently qualified to write of Greek institutions, and his account of the evolution of man as a 'political animal' in Greece is enriched with the results of discovery since the days of Fustel de Coulanges, whom he rivals in logic and lucidity."—*Times Literary Supplement.*

ROMAN POLITICAL INSTITUTIONS, *from City to State*
By LEON HOMO, *Professor in the University of Lyons.*
16s. net.

"No other English book presents in so convenient a form the story of the stages through which the Roman Constitution arrived at its ultimate form of absolute monarchy and bureaucratic organization. From a description of the rise of the oligarchy, he proceeds to give a lively account of the period of transition in which the ideals of Pompey and Cæsar, Principate and Monarchy, struggle for the victory, and goes on to show how the Principate of Augustus passes by inevitable development into the military monarchy of the later Emperors."
Times Literary Supplement.

THE ECONOMIC LIFE OF THE ANCIENT WORLD
By J. TOUTAIN, *Sometime Member of the French School at Rome.*
With 6 maps, 16s. net.

"He has written a lucid and attractive volume, mainly concerned with Greece and Rome. But he sketches the beginnings of trade in primitive society, the history of Carthage, and the dawn of commerce in prehistoric Italy as well as the development of Etruria. Those who imagine that capital is a modern phenomenon may be commended to the chapter on capitalism in Republican Rome from the Punic Wars onwards."—*Spectator.*

MINOANS, PHILISTINES AND GREEKS : B.C. 1400-900
By A. R. BURN, *sometime Scholar of Christ Church, Oxford.*
With 16 plates, 15s. net.

" A comprehensive study of the Late Bronze and Early Iron Ages in the Eastern Mediterranean for which there is now ample evidence. The author's reconstruction becomes an enthralling, sometimes a thrilling, reanimation, in which a continuous narrative is evolved, and the Hebrew legends of the Judges and of Saul and David and the Greek epic traditions of Minos and Theseus and of the wars of Thebes and Troy are set in historical perspective. A remarkable book."—*Morning Post.*

DEATH CUSTOMS : *an Analytical Study of Burial Rites*
By E. BENDANN, *Ph.D., A.M.*
12s. 6d. net.

" The beliefs and customs associated among primitive peoples with death and the disposal of the body make up a complex manifold, the analysis and explanation of which is a rich field for the ethnologist ; they give us too some insight into savage philosophy. The author makes an intensive investigation in this field, over Melanesia, Australia, North-East Siberia and India. Her criticisms on the Diffusionist school are shrewd and her study is to be commended."
Times Literary Supplement.

CHINESE CIVILIZATION
By M. GRANET, *Professor at L'Ecole des Langues Orientales.*
With 12 plates and 5 maps, 25s. net.

" The imposing story of China's past achievements becomes a clear account of the emergence of an obscure tribe from the unknown lands of central Asia to the proud position of leader of Asiatic civilization. The second part of the book is devoted to a careful analysis of Chinese society, life, customs, cities, feudalism, and the numerous social changes wrought by the change of Court and the growth of moral ideals. The author displays a rare combination of restrained imagination and careful scholarship. The book should be read widely, and will be a necessary part of the equipment of students of Asiatic history for some time to come."—*The Spectator.*

THE END OF THE ANCIENT WORLD, *and the Beginning of the Middle Ages*
By FERDINAND LOT, *Professor in the University of Paris.*
With 3 plates and 3 maps, 21s. net.

" The author strikes a new note in the theory he puts forward that the influx of the barbarian hordes was not the regenerating element which produced the new ideas of the Middle Ages. The author holds that the real regeneration of mankind only appeared when Islam challenged the superstition and idolatry of the Dark Ages, when the reformed Papacy became at last conscious of its mission and when feudalism was able to establish, however imperfectly, something which could give rise to the modern state. The book has an excellent bibliography and index and can be heartily recommended."—*Listener.*

" This masterly book."—*The Spectator.*

ISRAEL, *from its Beginnings to the Middle of the Eighth Century*

By A. LODS, *Professor at the Sorbonne.*

With 12 plates and 41 maps and text illustrations, 25s. net.

This book fills a distinct gap in the long list of modern books on the Old Testament. Its peculiar value lies in the careful and lucid way in which Professor Lods, from his exhaustive knowledge of the results of recent excavation in Palestine, has given us a convincing picture of the early cultural background of the Hebrew people, enabling us to see the religious, social, and political life of Canaan when Abraham and his descendants were settling down in the land. The effect of the culture of the great empires of Egypt and Babylon upon Canaan is drawn in bold outlines, giving us the clue to the unique development of Hebrew religion, at once influenced by and protesting against the religious and social patterns of its environment.

CASTE AND RACE IN INDIA

By G. S. GHURYE, *Reader in Sociology, Bombay University.*

10s. 6d. net.

One of the most remarkable developments in the history of sociology is the institution of caste. To grasp its significance is one of the first requirements for understanding some of the problems of modern India, the history of its social structure, its complex religious development, and its future destiny. This volume has been written by an Indian author who knows the actual facts from within, and who has combined a mastery of the principles of anthropological science with a knowledge of the modern theories of caste.

Volumes which are nearing publication include:

NOMADS OF THE EUROPEAN STEPPE
By G. F. HUDSON.

About 12s. 6d. net.

THE HISTORY OF BUDDHIST THOUGHT
By E. J. THOMAS, D.LITT.

About 12s. 6d. net.

THE CELTS AND CELTIC EXPANSION
By H. HUBERT.

With 4 plates and 55 maps and text illustrations, about 21s. net.

THE RELIGIOUS THOUGHT OF GREECE
By L. GERNET and A. BOULANGER.

CHINESE THOUGHT
By PROFESSOR M. GRANET.

INDIA: *a Survey*
Edited by SYLVAIN LÉVI.